HISTORIES OF SEXUALITY

HISTORIES OF SEXUALITY

STEPHEN GARTON

ROUTLEDGE
NEW YORK

First Published 2004
by Equinox Publishing Ltd.
Unit 6, The Village, 101 Amies St., London, SW11 2JW

www.equinoxpub.com

Simultaneously published in the USA and Canada
by Routledge
270 Madison Avenue, New York, NY 10016

Routledge is an imprint of the Taylor & Francis Group

© Stephen Garton 2004

Typeset by CA Typesetting, Sheffield
Printed and bound in Great Britain by Antony Rowe, Chippenham, Wiltshire

British Library Cataloguing in Publication Data
A catalogue record for this book is available from the British Library

Library of Congress Cataloging in Publication Data
A catalogue record for this book is available on request from the Library of
Congress

ISBN 0-415972-29-9 (hbk)
ISBN 0-415972-30-2 (pbk)

For Iain Cameron

(1948–2002)

CONTENTS

PREFACE

A history of sexuality runs the risk of confirming popular fears that academics are capable of ruining even the most simple of pleasures. This book, however, is written in the hope that histories of sexuality (although not necessarily this one) can enlighten and, occasionally, even delight. At their best such histories offer a means of investigating the clash of instinct and culture – how seemingly timeless and natural behaviours shape and are in turn shaped by history. Sexual practices may persist through time but history also illuminates how sex and sexuality are surprisingly mutable. This capacity of history to unsettle and surprise is evident in many of the works discussed here. In less than 40 years the history of sexuality, as a definable area of scholarly enterprise, has grown from a few works describing past attitudes and behaviours into an enormously rich field that sustains its own journal, a number of monograph series and countless seminars, conferences, articles and books. Moreover, this field has moved well beyond accounts of exotic ideas and strange obsessions to embrace sophisticated analyses of such issues as subjectivity, identity, power, desire, gender and embodiment. Through these studies we now have a much more detailed account of past sexual ideas, beliefs, practices, fantasies and struggles.

This picture has been pieced together through numerous invaluable inquiries. Historians are always conversing with the past, asking questions of the surviving evidence, listening for the answers and then reformulating their questions. They also argue with each other. Like any vibrant field of inquiry the history of sexuality is full of the cut and thrust of debate. There are important issues at stake here in the development of plausible explanations of the past. Historical accounts can only flourish if they take the time to savour the sustenance provided by others who have gone before, even if they end up finding what has been served disagreeable. This book looks at this process – how historians have made histories of sexuality through the 'double helix' of researching the past and arguing with each other. It explores how historians have understood sex and sexuality across different times and places and how the assumptions, debates, theories and politics of the present have shaped our perceptions and understandings of this past.

This book is a critical survey of some key debates within this emerging area of scholarship. It is certainly not an effort to write a comprehensive history of sexuality, although it will touch on the key findings of many historians. Nor does it attempt to provide an adequate coverage of all the relevant historians or debates in the field. The historiography on sexuality is now so vast as to be beyond the reach of any single text and, while the pursuit of comprehensiveness might result in a very large and more or less adequate compendium, it would probably miss the vital process of 'making history'. This book has a different trajectory, offering both a study of specific debates and a history of the history of sexuality. It traces the emergence of this field of inquiry: the early efforts to theorize sexuality as subject to historical change, the stark differences over whether sexuality was an essential, timeless force or the product of social and historical conditions, and more recently the attempts to move beyond this constraining dichotomy.

In pursuing these aims this account shifts between the terms sex and sexuality. At times the focus is on sex, defined here as intertwined practices of pleasure, desire and power. These practices include, but are not confined to, intercourse or other acts of penetration. Sexuality, on the other hand, refers to the ways sexual practices are turned into signifiers of a particular type of social identity. Conventionally, sexuality is seen as a personal orientation of desire, something we all have and something that manifests itself in different forms in each individual. In this framework sexuality also tends to cluster into types – heterosexuality, homosexuality, sadomasochism and the like. But such commonplace wisdom blurs the differences between practice and identity. Recently historians have focused on distinguishing these things. Same-sex practices may occur across a wide range of times and places, but is a homosexual identity found with equal frequency? As we shall see, this is a matter of debate. But in this context it is important to state that I am not drawing a rigid distinction, common amongst some historians of sexuality, between acts and identity. Sex can play a part in the formation of a range of identities. Equally, sex alone does not always determine identity. In the following chapters it is clear that gender, concepts of masculinity and femininity, as well as race, class and status intersect with sex in different times and places to determine a range of identities. These complex interplays between sex, culture and identity are the source of much debate amongst historians and one of the key themes of this study.

The first chapter provides a conspectus of the historiography and many of the debates explored in later chapters build upon this initial discussion, adding flesh to its bare bones. In part this survey indicates the shallow foundations for the history of sexuality and affirms the efforts of those seeking a more sophisticated grounding for the enterprise. Equally, the analysis attempts to situate the evolution of this field of historical inquiry in its own historical and political context. The emergence of the field, some of its early proponents and many of its central concerns were embroiled in the history of the last half-century. The politics of gender, race and sexual identity, the effort to legitimate gay, lesbian, feminist and anti-colonial struggles, and the dominance of key terms such as repression, liberation, patriarchy and masculinism resonate throughout many of the studies under scrutiny here. And while many historians have sought to move beyond the constraints of these original concerns, these ideas, concepts and founding debates have shaped the history of sexuality in profound ways.

A book such as this is by its very nature selective. My aim is not so much to tell the history of sexuality, but rather to examine the ways in which it has been told. To do this requires case studies, particular debates and arguments that reveal how history comes into being. This study confines its focus largely to the West, mainly because so much of the historiography has been concerned with developments in Britain, Europe and America. There is, of course, a growing and rich literature on the history of sexuality in Asia, Africa and Latin America, but on the whole these sit outside my effort to mark some tentative signposts in an already extensive field. That they do so is no reflection on their importance, only on the limitations of a manageable study.

Most historians, by force of the difficulty of recovering the past, naturally confine their studies to specific times, places and themes – be it the late Roman Empire, Renaissance Venice or early-twentieth-century New York. Similarly, most choose a specific theme within these cultural and historical contexts, such as homosexuality, cross-dressing, prostitution, courtship, marriage or myriad other aspects of sex and sexuality. Exceptionalism is an abiding tension within most historiographies. By trying to take a longer view (from antiquity to the late-twentieth century) and a broader canvas (Britain, Europe and America) this book attempts to highlight some general themes – such as the pervasiveness of the sexual oppression of women, the persistence of tropes of active/passive in the understanding of sex – and develop some comparative perspectives on different sexual regimes. While this book does not offer a systematic comparative analysis of the type developed for racism by scholars such as George Fredrickson, it works from the premise that the historiography of sexuality will gain immeasurably from greater attention to historical and cultural comparisons.

Few could be more conscious than I am that space constraints have resulted in neglect of major historians and vital works. In part that is a measure of the scope of the field. It also reflects the origins of this study as a course offered to undergraduates. Much of what is chosen for closer examination here first ran the gamut of classroom trial and error. I found some of the key debates explored here worked very well for students. Other debates dropped by the wayside (both in the course and in this book), not because they were unimportant, but because they did not engage the interest of students as much as I had hoped. A few topics, however, have survived student apathy. Try as I might, sexual renunciation remained something that failed to catch the imagination of most 20-year olds.

As I have tried to suggest this study is not an effort to 'cover' the area, but instead offers a series of inquiries into how it works. Inevitably people will, quite rightly, question my choices as well as my interpretations. Nonetheless, the exploration of debates in this book does uncover a wealth of fascinating detail about past ideas and practices. By focusing on historical debates about sex and sexuality the book does seek to bring to light a number of important insights from a wide range of historians into general transformations in sex and sexuality over the *longue durée*.

This study is structured through a mix of thematic and chronological approaches. After the initial survey of the emergence of the field, the next four chapters take particular debates about the history of sexuality in specific historical periods – Greek and Roman antiquity, the early Christian epoch, medieval and Renaissance Europe, and early-modern Europe and America. The key themes here are homoeroticism, gay and lesbian subcultures, asceticism and the valorization of marriage. The next three chapters, however, concentrate on the Victorian era, largely in England and America, a key area of debate in the field and the focus of an enormous body of historical enquiry. These chapters (6, 7 and 8) develop different aspects of nineteenth-century sexuality – debates about Victorianism itself, problems of race, class, nation and Empire and the feminist critique of Victorian sexual culture. The final three chapters move through the twentieth century. Chapter 9 examines debates about the emergence of sexology and discourses of perversion in the late-nineteenth and early-twentieth centuries. The next chapter focuses on twentieth-century challenges to concepts of sexual abnormality by investigators such as Alfred Kinsey. The final chapter examines debates about the nature of the 1960s and 1970s 'sexual revolution'.

The history of how this book came to be explains something about the shape it has taken. In 1989 I decided that I needed to know more about the history of sexuality. By then the work of Michel Foucault, Jeffrey Weeks, David Halperin and a host of others was becoming well-known

and of significance for my research interests in areas such as incarceration, lunacy, poverty and crime. The best way I know of coming to grips
with a field is to offer a course in the subject. Thus, in 1990, I embarked
upon the perilous task of teaching a course about which I knew very little.
Most weeks I was just a step or two ahead of the students (and some weeks
I found myself some way behind). Fortunately they were tolerant, and I
hope stimulated by these preliminary forays into a vast field of scholarship. But that did not mean they left me in peace. On the contrary, they
challenged me to explain my ideas every step of the way, and those challenges have given this book the shape it has. Even more important, my
students did some extraordinary research of their own, uncovering all
manner of references which I knew nothing about, and putting forward
arguments that punctured my own early speculations. I can confidently
say that I learned a lot from them.

In the course of this project I incurred other significant debts. There
are four very important ones. Glenda Sluga not only helped with European references, she asked me again and again what I was doing and how
was I proposing to do it. Barbara Caine was a very early influence shaping this work. Her studies of British feminists raised important questions
about sexuality, gender and power that have been an inspiration ever
since. We occasionally need cheering words from our colleagues to keep
the spirits high, and Barbara and Glenda never failed to encourage.
They read and criticized the manuscript with great thoroughness and
insight, forcing me to undertake a lot of necessary rethinking. Stephen
Robertson, a relative newcomer to Sydney, has enlivened the intellectual culture of our department. He also read the entire manuscript
making astute criticisms and giving me the benefit of his own extensive
knowledge of the history of American sexuality. Judith Allen has been
a longstanding friend and colleague, and one whose own research into
sexuality, which began more than 20 years ago, and continues apace
today, probably started this whole ball rolling. Judith took time out from
her own busy writing schedule to give the manuscript a very searching
critique. The final version has greatly benefited from these readings.
The errors, misunderstandings, mistakes and misinterpretations are my
responsibility alone – the product of lack of imagination and evidence
of the folly of an overly active administrative life.

Other colleagues have helped in more ways than they probably imagine. Shane White took on the burden of introducing me to American
history and over the years lent me many books and articles from his
extensive library to ensure that I kept abreast as best I could of current scholarship. More importantly he, with more good grace than I
deserved, kept his frustration at my absences from Moore Park in check
while I tried to put finger to keyboard. Others, such as Nick Eckstein,
Paul Knobel, Peter Brennan and Kathryn Welch, gave me the benefit

of their own expertise for which I am very grateful. Regrettably, the untimely passing of close friend and colleague Iain Cameron robbed this book of his critical input. Iain had often acted as second marker for the essays in the course and encouraged both the students and myself to continue our efforts. His own teaching in the areas of 'crime and deviance' and 'film and history' were models of how good courses should be run and were deservedly some of the most popular in the department. We all miss his enthusiasm, warmth, wit and good cheer.

Foolishly (at least in terms of finishing this book), half way through the first draft I took on a new position which required even more meetings than usual. The task of completing the manuscript seemed beyond my capacity. It would not have been finished without the support and encouragement of Ros Pesman and Elizabeth Webby. Ros, who twisted my arm to take the position in the first place, agreed to me taking time off, and more generously provided the money for a replacement so that I could be free to write. Elizabeth Webby agreed to take on this onerous task, even though she had much better things to do. I am grateful to both of them for their support and help.

Sometime later the first draft required extensive revision and this meant ducking out of the office at all times of the day (and not turning up on other days), so that I could complete the manuscript. Such dereliction of duty requires a loyal and skilled staff to cover for you when demands for immediate action from above hit the table. Maree Williams and Anne Campbell did a very good job hiding my delinquencies. Anne also helped by getting the bibliography in order and Maree with some of the final formatting. Terry Heath, Mark Leary, Naomi Ramanathan and Mark Molloy kept the ship afloat while the captain was away (actually they kept it afloat when he was there as well).

Books require publishers and editors. I'm very grateful that Janet Joyce, Val Hall and Audrey Mann have worked so hard to bring this project to completion. Roderick Campbell laboured long and hard over the proofs and index. My sincere thanks also go to Catherine Johnson, Curator of Art, Artifacts and Photographs at the Kinsey Institute, who searched the wonderful collections of the Institute to find some suitable cover images.

Finally, Julia and Anna exhibited remarkable tolerance of my selfish efforts to bring this project to fruition. Julia read and criticized the manuscript with her customary insight and eye for detail. Equally important, both of them, with grace and good cheer, let me shirk my familial duties to troop up to the attic to do some more work. Nothing would have been possible without their loving support.

Sydney
March 2003

Chapter 1

WRITING SEXUAL HISTORY

Sex is one of the few things about which historians can be certain. Without heterosexual penetration we would not be here to ruminate on the past. Of course, there is much more to sex, even heterosexual sex, than reproduction. But for many historians, sex is a constant – outside history. For a discipline committed to charting social, political and economic change, sex was something biological, natural and beyond historical inquiry. What is the point of writing about something that happened in all times and places? Instead sexual practices found their way into history through other means. For some social reformers, such as Margaret Sanger and Howard Brown Woolston, reflections on the history of birth control or prostitution served to underpin claims for legislative change. These histories, written by reform-minded amateurs rather than professional historians, served to illustrate the errors of the past.[1] More common amongst University-based historians was the tradition of subsuming sex within a wider concern with morality. Pioneering nineteenth-century historians, such as William Edward Hartpole Lecky, made the history of European morals a legitimate area of inquiry, one properly subject to observable patterns of change over time.[2] Such an approach, however, made moral codes historical, leaving sexual behaviour timeless and unchanging.

While many historians, until the 1970s, accepted the force of biological and psychological theories of sexuality, other disciplines were very interested in the cultural webs that entangled the sex drive – courtship rituals, sexual initiation rights, marriage customs, religious sanctions, superstitions, beliefs, childbirth practices, and child-rearing traditions. Pioneering anthropologists, such as Margaret Mead, charted rich cultural differences in the organization of sexual life.[3] Sexologists, such as Norman Haire, took up anthropological insights to highlight the historical and cultural diversity of sexual practices and customs.[4] More importantly, for both anthropologists and sexologists, the sexual life of 'exotic cultures' was a way of pointing to the limitations of Western sexual practices. In both disciplines sex and sexuality was a fixed domain of human experience, which was then subjected to different forms of cultural organization. These forms of organization then could be compared on the basis of how much they repressed 'natural' sexual instincts. Importantly, these studies suggested that some sexual practices were culturally and historically specific.

A few adventurous historians took up these ideas and attempted to write histories of sex that stressed difference and change. One of the earliest and most important is Hans Licht's *Sexual Life in Ancient Greece* (1932).[5] Licht argued that masturbation, perversion, tribadism, prostitution and sexual licence were widespread and compatible with civilization. Erotic literature was at the heart of classical culture. More importantly, Licht asserted that homosexuality was widely practised, acceptable and the source of much of the cultural richness of the classical era. Such a conclusion was implicitly a plea for tolerance of modern homosexuality. Others attempted to bring sex to the forefront of the history of morals tradition, giving it a more radical edge. Gordon Rattray Taylor's *Sex in History* (1953)[6] covered an enormous historical sweep from early Christian Europe to the twentieth century. Although he stressed the variety of sexual customs in the history of Europe he concluded that, despite apparent diversity, there was a 'remarkable continuity in the sex attitudes that form part of Western culture'.

The novelty of his focus on the history of customs, however, was subsumed into a more conventional stress on the history of attitudes. For Taylor, if sex was constant and morality historical, then 'excessive' regulation of sex lives was arbitrary and contestable. Thus the past and 'exotic cultures' both served to suggest that modern sexual life had failed to foster healthy outlets for natural sexual drives. History became a critique of modern Western sexual culture and a weapon in a variety of reform struggles rather than an area of historical enquiry marked by a diversity of viewpoints and approaches. More importantly, what was missing from these works was any plausible theory of how sex might be made part of history. For such historians the past was a reservoir of illustrative examples of exotic practices and strange views, but they did not ask how or why sexual practices and sexual identities might change. Morality changed; sex did not.

This relative neglect of sex as a subject of historical inquiry was overcome in the 1960s and 1970s. In the context of sexual revolution and new movements, such as gay liberation and feminism which put sexuality at the centre of contemporary politics, the history of sexuality became a concern for both activists and historians (and historians who were also activists).[7] Within a decade the trickle of works on the history of sexuality had become a flood. And since the 1970s the history of sexuality has become an area of significant growth – a definable sub-discipline not merely the hobby of a few – spawning numerous theses, conferences, books, articles and even specialist journals, such as the *Journal of the History of Sexuality* (1991). More importantly, it is a field that now encompasses a variety of approaches and viewpoints in creative tension with each other. The field became an arena for major theoretical debates, often crudely characterized as the struggle between 'essentialists' and 'social constructionists', over the nature of sexuality and how it operated over time.[8] More recently, historians have sought to move beyond this dichotomy to theorize how sexual identities and practices can be both historical and transhistorical – a concern with questions of difference and continuity in the organization of sex throughout history. How and why historians sought to make sexuality a central concern of history are themes that weave themselves throughout many of the forthcoming chapters in this book.

The Emergence of Sexual History

The roots of the expansion in historical fascination with sexuality are diverse. One avenue was through the history of ideas. This was an outgrowth of the older Lecky tradition of the history of morals. In 1959 Keith Thomas's seminal essay on 'the double standard' made sexual attitudes a legitimate object for intellectual history. Thomas diagnosed what he saw as a pervasive historical difference in the ways sexual behaviour in men and women were viewed. Thomas argued that 'unchastity is for a man…mild and pardonable, but for a woman is a matter of utmost gravity'. For men the role of the rake or seducer was acceptable and even embedded in English institutions of marriage and the law. Although the 'rake' ideal was contested by the Christian ideas of reciprocal fidelity and the growth of middle-class respectability in the Victorian era, the acceptance of the sexual rights of men and antipathy to women who 'betrayed' their calling as wife and mother was deeply rooted in English culture.

The key to this pervasive ethic was 'the desire of men for absolute property in women'. Although Thomas highlighted the need to examine gender in the history of ideas and how 'the double standard' shaped moral conduct and its regulation, 'unchastity in men' appeared to be a timeless ethic but one open to contest in specific times and places. For Thomas, like Lecky before him, morality not sexuality was historical. Nonetheless, arising out of this renewed interest in ideas came a number of studies of attitudes towards such social problems as prostitution, the age of consent, social purity and 'white slavery'.[9]

More ambitious was the effort of American literary scholar Steven Marcus to provide a theory of historical change for sexuality.[10] *The Other*

Victorians (1964) contrasts an 'official' nineteenth-century British view of sexuality as contained and controllable with the abundant evidence for an extensive network of pornographers in England since the seventeenth century. For Marcus, Dr William Acton, a prominent physician who wrote extensively on prostitution and venereal diseases, exemplified the official view. Acton believed that children and respectable women did not suffer from sexual feelings. Desire, however, was a potent natural force that surged through the bodies of men (and fallen women), and if left unchecked could lead to ruin. Acton turned sexuality into a problem – the source of disease and the social evil of prostitution. In his view sexuality was something that threatened the body and had to be channelled into the safer waters of marital sexual congress. The body itself was a fixed reservoir of sexual energies that if drained could never be replenished. Masturbation or sexual excess wasted these finite energies, depleted the body, leading to nervous debility and physical decline. In Victorian sexual culture, through the eyes of Acton, sex was something to be feared.

At the very time that Acton was writing, however, there was a thriving market in Victorian pornography. Marcus provides a detailed analysis of the extensive pornography collections of bibliographer-scholar, Henry Spence Ashbee, the 11-volume anonymous autobiography *My Secret Life* and a plethora of nineteenth-century pornographic novels. The key feature of Victorianism for Marcus is the extraordinary gap between the dominant moralistic culture of restraint and the thriving subculture of pornography. The two are mirror opposites – one repressed, troubled, limited, focused and moral and the other characterized by inexhaustible excess, repetition, plenitude, insatiability, in Marcus's terms a 'pornotopia'.

The 'excessive repression' of Victorianism, Marcus suggests, drove sex underground, fuelling the pornography industry. Thus repression and pornography were integrally linked. This connection was reinforced by Marcus' argument that the pornography industry only began to take off in the late-seventeenth century. Thus the gradual shift towards Victorian 'moralism' through the eighteenth and early-nineteenth centuries paralleled the rise in pornography. It also paralleled the development of the novel as a new form within English literature, detailing the inner lives and social values of thrift, individual initiative, endeavour, self-control, self-consciousness and respectability promoted by the emerging middle class. Marcus, as a literary critic, was at pains to distinguish between pornography and the novel as being very different forms of literature. But for Marcus their historical connection was no accident. Drawing on Weber, Marcus linked Victorianism, the novel and pornography, to the rise of capitalism, puritanism and individualism.

The question for Marcus becomes that of why bourgeois sensibilities produced the proliferation of pornography. The answer, he believed, lay in the work of Sigmund Freud. For Freud, sexuality was an irresistible natural instinct that had to be tamed or channelled into other activities in order for civilization to progress. This process of sublimation was a necessary engine for the rise of capitalism, but it came at great emotional and physical cost. Instincts could never be completely overcome and thus sublimation involved a constant struggle between sexuality and civilization. Sublimation and repression were imperfect tools in the war against unconscious desires. For Marcus, the more society repressed sexual expression, the more Victorians had to find other outlets for their instincts, so they turned to the underground world of pornography and prostitution for sexual fantasy and satisfaction.

Paralleling this argument about the interconnection between moralism and licentiousness was Marcus' claim that this peculiar Victorian world was itself now past, strange and alien to modern readers. By placing Victorianism in the past Marcus suggests that this sexual culture was historical – the product of specific conditions and now a world we have lost. Thus Victorianism was bounded by other sexual regimes. Prior to the seventeenth century, according to Marcus, sexuality was relatively open and accepted in both art and life, and thus there was no need for an extensive pornography industry. On the other side, Freud represented for Marcus the crucial break with Victorian sexual culture. Psychoanalysis was a science that revealed the psychological mechanisms that structured sexuality. Freud demonstrated that sexuality was itself a consequence of necessary repression, but that excessive repression fostered neurosis. By implication Marcus saw Victorianism as a 'neurotic' culture, while modern society had learned from Freud that sexual liberalism was a healthy and culturally enriching social attitude.

Freud is the key to understanding Marcus' text. On the one hand, Marcus was committed to the idea that sexuality was a natural drive present in all people and all cultures. Civilization, however, required a measure of repression to promote human progress. On the other hand, too much repression could harm both individuals and cultures. The implication of Marcus' conception of Victorianism is that the role of the historian is to chart the historical fluctuations between periods of excessive repression and relative liberalism. This conclusion rests on his theorization of a link between two related yet opposite sexual cultures. But Marcus' argument about sexual cultures, or more properly culture/subculture, is crude and poorly substantiated. Many historians have questioned the significance of William Acton as the major exemplar of Victorianism, arguing that even in the mid-nineteenth century many medical specialists rejected his views.[11]

Moreover, the idea that pornography was little in evidence before the seventeenth century and, by implication, in decline after Freud, is not borne out by the abundant evidence for a flourishing pornography industry in modern culture. Equally problematic is Marcus' use of the concept 'Victorian sexuality'. Marcus sees Victorianism as an undifferentiated phenomenon. In doing so he focuses almost entirely on heterosexuality, largely ignoring homosexuality, transvestism, and other forms of sexuality. Hence he fails to see the variety of subcultures and practices that disrupt any simple notion of 'Victorianism'. Nonetheless, Marcus's idea of the history of sexuality as a circular process of alternating periods of light and excessive repression was one of the first attempts at a systematic historical account of sexuality, one that influenced later historians.

Another important contribution to the history of sexuality in the 1960s, was social interactionist sociology. Prominent sociologists such as Peter Berger and Thomas Luckman argued that society constructed social roles, which people came to adopt as 'scripts' for forms of interaction with other members of the community. This was a powerful assertion of the primary importance of social context in the construction of social behaviour. Out of this school of thought came an intense interest in sex roles and how ideas of ideal male and female behaviour powerfully constrained the actions of individuals of either sex. From 1970 the journal *Sex Roles* (a 'journal of sex research') provided an important forum for the investigation of how sex roles shaped sexual behaviour. Labelling and deviancy theory, pioneered by sociologists such as Howard Becker, also provided a framework for seeing sexual deviancy as a social phenomenon rather than a natural or biological anomaly. Labelling theory explored how in specific social contexts behaviours that were different from dominant social norms were stigmatized. For Becker group identity was forged through the defining of 'outsiders' as deviant. Thus societies provided a range of 'scripts' for normality and abnormality and these roles varied considerably across different cultures, indicating their social character.[12]

In 1968, leading British social interactionist Mary McIntosh formulated a provocative theory of homosexuality that proved to be very influential for English historians of sexuality.[13] McIntosh questioned the self-evidence of homosexuality, arguing that it was not a 'condition' or 'social problem', biological or environmental in origin, but a social role. The scientific work that argued that homosexuality was a disease was a means of social control not an objective analysis of behaviour. In contrast, focusing on homosexuality as a social role allowed social scientists to step outside apparatuses of social control, to explore how roles create expectations, and investigate the extent to which individuals fulfilled these expectations. More importantly, McIntosh claimed that the way homosexuality was made into a social problem, rather than homosexuality itself, should instead become the object of study. To cement this argument McIntosh pointed to Australian Aboriginal, African, Middle Eastern and Native American cultures, where homosexual behaviour was an accepted social role. Further, she resorted to historical evidence, arguing that a definable homosexual subculture did not develop in England until the seventeenth century. By arguing that the homosexual role did not exist in all societies, McIntosh hoped to prove that while homosexuality was timeless, the stigmatized role of homosexual was the result of specific social and cultural processes.

McIntosh anticipated a number of subsequent developments in the history of sexuality.[14] The view that the homosexual role was a social fact, rather than a biological, medical or psychological condition, was an important shift of emphasis that underpinned much later sociological and historical analysis. Similarly McIntosh's argument that the homosexual only became a distinct 'figure' at a particular historical time has become commonplace, although, as we shall see, there is much dispute over when this moment of emergence actually occurred. But the social interactionist and deviancy theory insistence on homosexuality as a label imposed on the marginal by dominant social groups, ignores the extent to which homosexuals themselves created styles of dress, speech and behaviour that distinguished them from mainstream culture.

In drawing on ideas of social control and labelling, social interactionists, like McIntosh, locate the emergence of the homosexual as a process of social repression. Homosexual behaviours may have existed in all societies, but in specific cultures and times something happened to make people classify those behaviours as deviant. But why some behaviours and not others are classified as deviant in particular times and places is not well explained in this framework. Nonetheless, McIntosh was one of the first to make a crucial distinction between social acts and distinct social types, thus making homosexuality (and by implication other forms of sexuality) an historical question. It was an approach that British social historians and gay activists such as Jeffrey Weeks and Kenneth Plummer found enormously influential.[15] Through their work the distinction between homosexuality and 'the homosexual role' became a vital question for the history of sexuality.

Another potent influence on the growth of interest in the history of sexuality was social history. Although social history had a respectable lineage back to the 1890s, by the late 1960s it took on a more radical edge. A newer generation of social historians, inspired by civil rights and other liberation movements championed 'history from below' against an historical establishment wedded to the history of elites. The *Journal of Social History* was established in 1967 and similar journals on both sides of the Atlantic, such as *History Workshop* (1974), *Radical History Review*

(1975) and *Social History* (1976) soon followed.[16] Social historians sought
to recover the experience of ordinary people and much of this research
focused on such themes as work, crime, slavery, peonage, prostitution,
street life and forms of struggle by the working classes, racial minorities and the poor. Social history also fostered an interest in the private sphere – the world of home, family, child-rearing, domestic violence
and love. Sexuality became one dimension of a private world now worth
exploring.[17]

The social history of sexuality was given added impetus by radical
movements of the 1960s and 1970s. Civil rights, the sexual revolution,
anti-psychiatry, student and prison activism, and most importantly for
sexuality the feminist and gay liberation movements were crucial to the
growing interest in the history of sexuality. These movements spawned
their own journals, notably the *Journal of Homosexuality* (1974), *Feminist
Studies* (1972), *Women's Studies* (1974) and *Signs* (1975), which published
important early articles on the history of sex roles, sexual attitudes and
sexual practices.[18] Early 'second wave' feminists such as Betty Freidan,
Shulamith Firestone, Germaine Greer, Kate Millett and Robin Morgan made sex an important aspect of the pervasive patriarchal oppression of women. Women were denied sexual autonomy, chained to men's
demands for sexual access, driven into prostitution and assaulted, raped
and humiliated if they refused. A key struggle was to create opportunities for women's sexual autonomy.[19]

Similarly gay activists pointed to the endemic homophobia of Western culture. Throughout history gays and lesbians had been persecuted,
subject to criminal prosecution and punishment or seen as the victims
of a pathological disease requiring medical treatment. Feminists, gays
and lesbians turned to history to provide the substance for their claims
of oppression and to recover those women and gays who had struggled
against the social and cultural structures that inhibited their freedoms.
Feminist, gay and lesbian historians (many of whom will appear later in
this book) set out to document how repression was a central dynamic in
sexual oppression and liberation, a means for overcoming enslavement
within a patriarchal and homophobic culture.

Despite the importance of the 'sexual revolution' and new movements for women's and gay liberation in exciting interest in sexuality,
the early efforts to bring sex into history were problematical. For feminist and gay historians of the 1960s and 1970s the history of social regulation, policing, imprisonment, motherhood, the family, prostitution,
sexism and homophobia were key areas for uncovering the endemic
oppression of women and gays across time. Although by the early 1980s
some feminists such as Carol Vance, Linda Gordon and Ellen DuBois
were seeking to expand feminist horizons beyond oppression to such
issues as pleasure, much of this interest focused on the present rather

than the past.[20] The problem for historians became how to link theories of pervasive and structural oppression into a narrative of women, gays and lesbians who had fought for sexual freedom. The challenge was to make women, gays and lesbians the subjects as well as the objects of history.

Despite their common cause, with hindsight what is most notable is the difference between early feminist and gay historians over the significance of sexuality. In many of the pioneering works of women's history, such as those by Patricia Branca, Renate Bridenthal and Claudia Koonz, sexuality was merely one sphere of oppression amongst many. In these works sexuality actually rated only passing mention. Of more importance for women's history was work, wages, childcare, motherhood and the family.[21] Even in areas more directly related to sexuality such as birth control and prostitution, the important pioneering contributions of historians, such as Linda Gordon, Judith Walkowitz and Ruth Rosen, focused more on issues such as misogyny and social repression than on sexuality.[22] Histories of prostitution, for instance, sought to reconceptualize the trade in women's bodies as a form of work, thus pushing sexuality off the stage. The women's history focus averted attention from the question of prostitution as sexuality – men's sexuality.[23]

In contrast, for gay historians sexuality was at the heart of oppression. The thrust of gay history was to uncover evidence of homosexuality in the past, the prominent gays and lesbians, the thriving subcultures and the struggles for sexual expression in the context of considerable heterosexual and religious antagonism to the 'love that dared not speak its name'. Here was a project of recovery, to make visible what had been hidden. Prominent gay histories, such as Jonathan Katz's *Gay American History* (1976), sought to reveal the rich documentation that existed for gay and lesbian history.[24] Lesbian history also sought to uncover a past previously 'hidden from history', focusing on female eroticism, the nature of women's friendships, the emergence of a lesbian community and the intersections between lesbianism and feminist politics.[25] These studies revealed that for centuries gays and lesbians had resisted oppression and forged a rich underground sexual culture. Thus tropes of oppression and resistance became central in writing gay and lesbian history. Such interpretative frameworks also shaped some of the pathbreaking general histories of sexuality on both sides of the Atlantic. Jeffrey Weeks' *Sex, Politics and Society* (1980) and Estelle Freedman and John D'Emilio's *Intimate Matters* (1988) put social repression and struggles for sexual freedom at the centre of the history of sexuality.[26]

Nonetheless, these early feminist and gay histories left sexuality largely untheorized. Sexuality may have been the source of oppression for women, gays and lesbians but the concept was itself not subjected to any serious scrutiny. Indeed many activists saw sexuality in psychoanalytic terms. Sexuality was a biological instinct subsequently shaped by culture. Thus for feminists, gays and lesbians sexuality seemed to be part of nature and oppression arose out of culture and history. While historians such as Jeffrey Weeks and Ken Plummer, following McIntosh, saw a difference between homosexuality and the homosexual role, for them homosexual desire was part of human sexuality and beyond history. The homosexual was a role created by homophobic cultures. Thus sexual identities were the product of repression and control. This framework was radically challenged by the work of French philosopher Michel Foucault, who argued that sexuality itself was a recent historical phenomenon.

Foucault's *History of Sexuality*

Foucault's *History of Sexuality Volume 1* (first published in 1976 and in English translation in 1978) now stands out as the key text in the historiography of sexuality. It is a work that has elicited extraordinary levels of both praise and condemnation. As the title of the original French edition, *La Volonté de savoir* (literally 'the will to know') suggests, this was far from a conventional historical account of sex practices and sexuality. It was a short prolegomenon for a new approach.[27] Foucault envisaged that it would be followed by a series of substantive studies of specific themes in nineteenth-century sexuality – 'the hysterisation of women's bodies', 'the pedagogisation of children's sex', 'the socialisation of procreative behaviour' and 'the psychiatrisation of perverse pleasure'. None of these volumes eventuated, although two further volumes on the history of sexuality in antiquity were published. Nonetheless, the first volume captured the imagination of many historians. Although this introductory volume focused on a similar question to that of McIntosh – how a 'condition' was made – Foucault's analysis marks a distinct departure from social role and deviancy theory. Rather than accepting sexuality as natural and roles as social, Foucault argues that both sexuality and sexual identity were historical.

In this preliminary volume Foucault sets out to contest the dominant ways of seeing sexuality and its history. Overall it represents a sustained critique of psychoanalysis. Foucault's point of entry into this engagement with Freud is Steven Marcus' distinction between Victorianism and modernity. Instead of seeing Victorianism as a distant past left behind by the insights of Freud, Foucault argues that modernity is still in the grip of a Victorian fascination with developing a science of sex. Rather than Freud being a break with moralism and superstition, ushering in new enlightened and scientific theories of sexuality, Foucault places Freud as part of a continuum of scientific efforts to decipher the 'truth of sex', going back to the seventeenth century.[28] Freud, then, was not the key to our liberation from Victorianism, but rather another instance in a longer genealogy of sexual discourse that claimed the mantle of science. Equally, instead of psychoanalysis ushering in new methods for uncovering the truth of sexuality (in the unconscious), Foucault argues that many psychoanalytic techniques (association, dream analysis, the talking cure) drew on a longer history of Christian confessional designed to elicit the truth from those under scrutiny. Psychoanalysis was thus part of Victorianism, not a way of escaping it.

For Foucault, an important feature of previous studies of the history of sexuality was the 'repressive hypothesis'. As we have seen, Marcus was firmly of the view that 'official' Victorian culture was characterized by excessive repression of sexuality. Sex was seen as a troubling condition best contained within the domain of marriage. But outside of this relationship it became shrouded in mystery, spoken of in metaphor or in abstract scientific terms. It was consequently subject to severe prohibitions, and had to find illicit outlets in prostitution, hysteria and 'deviancy'. In this context Freud offered liberation from repression. But Foucault turned this characterization on its head, arguing that instead of silence Victorianism sanctioned a proliferation of discourses about sexuality. Victorianism spoke endlessly about sexuality in a variety of precise contexts – the family, school, work, the doctor's surgery, the clinic, the asylum, and the prison. Sexuality became the subject of numerous sciences – medicine, pedagogy, psychiatry, demography, epidemiology, criminology, psychoanalysis – each with its own specific elaboration on the nature of sexuality.

Moreover, within these diverse discourses sexuality operated on different levels. It was an individual problem requiring correction and treatment, such as the masturbating child or the hysterical woman. Sexuality could also be incorporated into disciplines investigating the habits of whole populations such as demography, epidemiology and pedagogy. These sciences constituted a realm of 'bio-politics', concerned with the investigation and regulation of such problems as the reproduction of the species, marriage and divorce rates, the prevention of the propagation of the mentally defective or the spread of epidemic diseases (notably venereal diseases). But whether at the individual or the global level, Foucault argued that the discourses and practices did not repress sexuality but instead provided the repertoire of ideas that made sexuality explicable. More radically, he suggested that the idea of sexuality was itself constituted by particular discourses on sex. Similarly various sexual identities, such as the homosexual, the sadist, the voyeur or the transsexual, were not transhistorical but in fact the outgrowth of new ways of classifying sexual behaviours. Thus in a striking and controversial formulation Foucault argued that Victorianism did not repress sexuality but instead produced it.

The idea that scientific knowledge and moral codes produce rather than repress goes to the heart of Foucault's historical project, most evident in *Discipline and Punish* (1975) and the first volume of his *History of Sexuality*. In these works Foucault explores the nature of power since the eighteenth century through an examination of specific human sciences such as economics, psychiatry, biology, sexology, penology and criminology. Discourses, he argues, are regulated frameworks of statements, born out of precise practices, such as diagnosis, confinement, isolation, consultation, practices that develop in specific social spaces such as hospitals, clinics, factories, army barracks, schools, prisons and asylums. Foucault concludes that modernity is characterized by a new modality of power. Until the late-eighteenth century power was largely juridical – the force of the 'monarch's will' and the 'law', framed around ideas of crime, obedience and punishment. Infractions of the law required retributive justice and harsh punishments designed to deter others from offending. But capitalism, individualism, the collapse of absolutism and the rise of democracy worked to forge new modes of power; specifically disciplinary powers that sought to regulate behaviour, movement and thoughts.

This notion of a shift from juridical to disciplinary modes of power highlights one of the weaknesses in Foucault's penchant for dramatic juxtaposition (most evident in the opening section of *Discipline and Punish*). It is all too obvious that while disciplinary power has flourished, juridical forms of power have similarly continued and even strengthened their hold. Nonetheless, Foucault's analysis of disciplinary power has been enormously influential. His studies of the ways discourses such as criminology, medicine, pedagogy, psychiatry and psychoanalysis shape human actions and how these discourses worked through specific practices to govern the actions and conduct of individuals have transformed theoretical debates about the nature of power.

Instead of seeing power as an instrument to be used by contesting bodies such as political parties, social elites or classes, as in much liberal and Marxist political theory, Foucault sees power as relational, embedded in all social relationships. Disciplinary power focuses on minds and bodies, encouraging individuals to perform particular actions, move to certain rhythms and act in particular ways. These disciplinary modes of power were pervasive, entangling the body in complex webs and networks of surveillance, assessment and regulation. More importantly, the scientific discourses that sustained disciplinary powers created new subjects and identities, such as the hysterical woman, criminal, masturbating child, mental defective, sadist, homosexual, degenerate and a host of other types and categories.

One of Foucault's best known formulations of the differences between juridical and disciplinary power is his discussion of the sodomite and the homosexual. Before the nineteenth century, he argues, the sodomite was someone who committed unnatural acts, most commonly anal sex, and as a consequence was arrested and punished. But the sodomite was not a particular type of person, with recognizable traits, merely a law-breaker (albeit in some jurisdictions a serious offender). In fact he could be a husband, a priest, a farmer or any other type of person, but what singled him out was the commission of an illegal act. In contrast, the homosexual was a distinct species of person, marked by peculiar habits of speech and thought, specific styles of clothing and walking. These external attributes signified the type as much as the nature of the sexual act. But the sexual act also came to connote a particular 'species', in their essence different from those whose desire was organized around other types of sexual orientation.

For Foucault, the homosexual was the product of new disciplinary powers, mainly medical, whereas the sodomite was the product of juridical regulation. Disciplinary powers produced subjects like the homosexual, and specific discourses provided the frameworks in which people came to recognize themselves. This process of recognition made people into subjects. They came to see themselves as a certain category of person and sought identification with persons of similar disposition or sought guidance and therapy if they found their state disagreeable.

Medical, criminological and psychiatric discourses in particular specified the symptoms that allowed for the diagnosis of pathological subjects. Criminology offers another example of this process. By the late-nineteenth century crime was no longer simply an act of law breaking. The 'birth of the prison' in the early- to mid-nineteenth century gathered criminals together in large penitentiaries. In these places of confinement criminals became the objects of scientific investigation. Criminologists sought to uncover the attributes inmates had in common with a view to defining what it was that differentiated criminals from law-abiding people. Criminology thus produced 'the criminal', recognizable, depending on the particular school of criminology one used, by the shape of the ears or the forehead, the presence of tattoos, poor mental test results, the place where one lived or types of speech and dress. The designation of the criminal as a particular type meant that criminologists favoured incarceration and treatment of criminals before they even committed a crime. If criminals could be diagnosed by observing their physiognomy or through detailed investigation of their social and family circumstances, then criminal acts were irrelevant in defining criminals and an unnecessary guide for dealing with criminality.

More fundamentally for our concerns here, Foucault argued that sexuality itself was a product of disciplinary power, only emerging as a concept in the late-nineteenth century. Such a statement runs against the grain of conventional wisdom, so we need to be careful here to spell out the precise framework in which such a statement makes sense.[29] Foucault is not suggesting that before the nineteenth century there were no same-sex relationships, sadists, masochists or other practices arising out of sexual desire. What he analyses are the historical shifts in the ways sexual desire has been understood, made explicable and hence governed. The emergence of a concept of sexuality in the late-nineteenth century marked a new way of understanding desire and these concepts produced new ways of governing sex acts. The shift from sodomite to homosexual was one instance of this broader change.

Even in relation to heterosexuality, however, there were important changes. Before the nineteenth century, according to Foucault, the law and the Church (he was writing in the context of Catholic France) were the instruments for interrogating and governing sex. The law determined what constituted natural and unnatural sex acts and punished perpetrators of the latter. The Church, however, was primarily concerned with the conduct of marital sexual relations, not what would later be called deviant sexuality. Until the nineteenth century religious authorities largely concentrated on prescribing appropriate and inappropriate sexual acts between husbands and wives (favouring those things that lead to procreation). Sexual desire in these contexts did not constitute subjectivity – one was a citizen, a serf, a farmer, a wife and a host of other things, and desire only worked to differentiate the sinner and law-breaker. But in the Victorian era new discourses, such as medicine, sexology, pedagogy and psychiatry, made sex and sexual desire a problem requiring investigation.

These discourses constructed elaborate typologies of distinct desires, a 'perverse implantation' to use Foucault's term. Underpinning this fascination with sex and desire was the idea that sexuality was at the core of one's being. What most marked a person was the form and object of their desire. In this context it became imperative to define heterosexuality and its discontents, or more accurately normality and abnormality. It is no coincidence that heterosexuality and homosexuality were concepts developed in the late-nineteenth century as they mutually defined and reinforced each other. These concepts marked the boundaries of a field of practices and discourses that worked to construct modern sexual identities marked by the object of one's desire.

Foucault represents a significant departure from previous understandings of the history of sexuality. Instead of seeing sexuality as a biological and psychological drive that was then organized by social forces, he argues that sexuality itself was a distinct and recent development. For Foucault, sexuality was not a thing to discover, but a framework of inquiry. The idea that desire was characterized by fundamentally different orientations, that everyone had a particular type of desire and that deciphering the nature of this type represented a fundamental insight into individual being was for Foucault something new to the nineteenth century. Neither the Church nor science had attempted to investigate the problem of desire in quite this way before. And to give focus to these investigations scientists invented the concept of sexuality. Within this general field of inquiry they then sought to uncover diverse types of sexual orientation, the manifestations of sexuality.

At first glance there would appear to be strong common ground between Foucault and the arguments of Mary McIntosh, both seeing the homosexual as an invention of a particular time and place. But this resemblance masks a significant difference in approach. Foucault does not see the relationship between desire and society as one of repression, where larger forces of social control shape desire for their own ends. Instead, for Foucault, power works from the ground up. Sexuality did not spring forth from the minds of significant scientists to then frame the work of social institutions. Foucault instead sees sexuality as the product of numerous experiments in the organization of health, instruction and criminal justice. These late-eighteenth- and early-nineteenth-century developments produced new ways of viewing and ordering human behaviour. Local institutions became laboratories for the investigation of specific populations, sites for novel practices of social organization and engine rooms for the production of knowledge about the human subject. From these diverse sources emerged more systematic efforts to develop scientific accounts of social behaviour. Social practices produced ideas, ideas were systematized into discourses, which in turn shaped practices. For Foucault, knowledge and power were intimately linked, rather than one merely being the product of the other.

Foucault's critique of theories of repression, however, was not a celebration of disciplinary powers. It was a forensic analysis of their operation and an invitation to work towards overcoming their effects. The production of categories of sexuality served to fix and limit desires and bodily pleasures to specific practices – if one was a sadist, one had to act in certain prescribed ways. For Foucault, disciplinary powers tamed the body and desire, failing to allow for multiplicity, diversity and a plurality of pleasures. Sexual identities tied people back into the spaces and discourses that produced these new subjectivities: one could be arrested and punished for illicit desires, subject to abuse from strangers who objected to your type or one might seek treatment for one's affliction. In other words, discourses on sexuality were forms of domination that rendered bodies docile and compliant, subject to the understandings of specific knowledges and the practices that produced them.

There is something refreshing about Foucault's formulation of the problem of sexuality. It refuses to answer conventional 'what' questions about sexuality (is it biological, psychological or social?) and 'why' questions (was it a consequence of repression, the economy, puritanism?). Most importantly it does not seek to make sense of sexuality by seeing it as merely the reflection of something more real such as instinct, class relations, capitalism, modernity or gender domination. Instead it asks seemingly innocuous, but ultimately subversive 'how' questions – how do discourses work? What objects do they specify? What effects do they produce? How might they be subverted? Foucault seeks to make disciplinary power sensible in its own terms, with its own specific and historical logics, operations and effects. In his intensely descriptive analysis, Foucault seeks to undermine pervasive frameworks for understanding sexuality (psychoanalytic, biological, Marxist, sociological) by stressing its profound historicity. Moreover, by exploring the ways in which forms of supposed liberation from sexual repression (mainly psychoanalysis) were in fact forms of domination, Foucault critically challenges radical liberation politics and offers a new framework for developing a politics of resistance.

Foucault argues that forms of domination are inextricably linked with their subversion. If discourses produce identities and disciplined bodies then forms of resistance need to refuse these ways of understanding the self. Here we can see that Foucault's work is a complex response to particular social and political events, primarily sexual liberation, gay liberation and the crisis in Marxism in the 1960s and 1970s. Marxism was the key ideology of the European left in the immediate postwar years. By the 1960s, however, the hegemony of Marxism on the left was under threat from a variety of new social movements – students, patients, prisoners, women, gays, lesbians – which did not see the anticipated class revolution as necessarily a source of liberation. These groups sought to contest power where it operated, in their own lives – the classroom, the hospital, the prison and the bed.

New liberationist movements did not want to defer confronting power until communism had 'solved' oppression, but instead worked in diverse ways to undermine the operation of power at its point of most direct operation. Radical movements confronted power by refusing to accept that sexual 'deviancy' was pathological, contesting the authority of teachers to impose truth, opposing the power of psychiatrists to incarcerate the 'mad' and pointing to the complicity of penology, which claimed to reform but instead sanctioned brutality. Although many Marxist theorists sought to draw links between Marxism and radical liberation movements, the differences between a theory of class oppression and movements concerned with sexuality, gender and incarceration strained the legitimacy of traditional left politics.

Foucault was a theorist who drew inspiration from these new liberation struggles. He sought to reconceptualize the nature of power, domination and resistance in terms that made sense of the strategies

deployed by these movements. But his relationship to these movements was ambivalent. He remained profoundly sceptical of liberationist claims. If sexuality was a product of specific discourses and practices
of recent origin, it made no sense to strive for sexual liberation. Liberation implied that sexuality could be freed from repression. But Foucault
had argued that sexuality was produced, not repressed, by power. For
Foucault, there was no domain of pure freedom untainted by power
(freedom was itself a product of particular historical discourses and practices) and sexuality could not be liberated as it was inextricably linked
to power. Moreover, although Foucault has come to be a key theorist for
what came to be known in the 1980s and 1990s as 'identity politics', his
work also questioned identities as points for political mobilization. For
instance, gay liberation contested medical arguments that homosexuality was a disease, arguing that homosexuality was an acceptable and
normal form of sexuality. Gay liberation promoted pride in one's sexuality and encouraged the development of a mutually supportive and
open community of gays and lesbians. But, for Foucault, embracing a
gay identity also fixed subjectivity as either gay or not gay, prescribing
certain types of relationships and bodily pleasures. Such identities did
not allow for a multiplicity or diversity of desires and pleasures except
in the narrow context of a same-sex partner. Thus identity politics could
liberate bodies from some forms of power, but also inscribed them in
new relationships of power and knowledge.

The two subsequent volumes of Foucault's projected six-volume
series, however, represented a significant shift of interest away from the
program outlined in the first volume. In these later volumes Foucault
focuses on technologies of the self – how people came to recognize
themselves as a particular type of subject and govern their own conduct.
Instead of focusing on questions of knowledge, disciplinary power and
the production of identities he explored concepts such as truth, freedom and the subject. The projected studies of the hysterical woman,
the masturbating child, the perverse adult and the fecund heterosexual
couple that were to be the basis of an extensive history of the formation of sexuality in the nineteenth century were abandoned. Instead, his
new theoretical concerns were elaborated through an examination of
the uses of pleasure and the maintenance of the self in classical Greece
and Rome.

The shift from knowledge and power to subject, truth and freedom
in part emerged as a response to criticisms of his earlier formulations.[30]
Although Foucault had always insisted that domination was met by opposition, his analysis of resistance was at best perfunctory, more an assertion
than an object of serious inquiry. In the framework of knowledge, power
and domination, how power was exercised and worked was uppermost
and, despite assurances that resistance was evident, more often than

not in Foucault's formulations pervasive disciplinary powers seemed to work relentlessly on bodies and minds. Although Foucault asserted that these identities also provided the point for political resistance, there is a pervasive and oppressive quality to the disciplinary powers of the 'carceral archipelago' and the sexual sciences that are the subjects of his most important texts. Power was both individualizing and totalizing. It produced specific identities and cemented subjection to the dictates of such discourses as criminology and psychoanalysis. But how people recognized themselves as subjects within these disciplines and practices was assumed rather than investigated. Equally important, Foucault left opaque the ways subjects could transform, resist or subvert the power that had produced them. Was power merely about domination? What was freedom? How did one recognize the truth of one's self? In what ways were certain forms of conduct required to realize one's self?

These are some of the questions underpinning Foucault's final two volumes of the *History of Sexuality*. Both volumes are much more concerned with examining the formation of the self within discursive regimes, a question alluded to in the first volume but poorly developed. Foucault's focus becomes the various technologies by which people work on and make themselves subjects – how they find the truth of themselves within specific cultural frameworks. This represents a more positive conception of discourse, as a field of possibility for becoming. Moreover, in related writings Foucault is also concerned to counter some of the prevailing representations of his work as a nihilist philosophy, where individuals are inscribed forever in regimes of knowledge and power. While Foucault retained his critique of liberationist politics, he turns to a new concern with ethics as a way of negotiating freedom within specific power relationships. Freedom was not absolute. Nor was it the absence of power. Rather, for Foucault, freedom was an ethical agreement to create specific spaces relatively free of discipline. Thus power was not only the site for the production of subjectivity, but also for freedom itself – a contingent and historically specific freedom, undergoing constant renegotiation. Ethics was the sphere in which people could work to secure a limited but meaningful domain in which to make their own lives.[31]

Despite their new theoretical and political concerns, the later volumes reinforce Foucault's argument about sexuality. By examining technologies of the self in ancient Greece and Rome, Foucault attempts to show that the body and bodily pleasures were only one aspect of concerns about the self. Equally important were such things as diet, daily regimen, one's relationship to the polis or the state, and styles of interaction with wives, youths and slaves. All of these forms of conduct were ways of making oneself a citizen. Far from sexuality being the totality of the self, as in contemporary Western culture, in antiquity bodily pleasures were part of a much broader problem of proper conduct. In demonstrating how other identities and forms of conduct were prevalent in the West, Foucault reinforces his claim for the historicity of sexuality and the identities it has produced. In effect it is a plea for a politics to escape the tyranny of sexuality and an entreaty to explore bodily pleasures outside of the frameworks imposed by sexuality.

Essentialism and Social Constructionism

During the 1980s and early 1990s the historiography on sexuality was characterized by many historians as a debate between essentialism and social constructionism. Social constructionists argued that essentialism was an assertion of immutable and transhistorical manifestations of sexuality. Essentialists believed that there were individuals in all cultures and times primarily driven by same-sex desire, thus establishing homosexuality as a legitimate, natural and normal aspect of human sexuality. They sought to trace the continuities in sexuality across time and culture. Social constructionists, on the other hand, drawing on Foucault's radical historicizing of sexuality, stressed discontinuity, focusing on the specificity of sexual practices and the diverse ways such practices were understood. Major advocates of social constructionism, notably David Halperin, John Winkler, Edward Stein and Robert Padgug, took up Foucault's argument about sexuality as a recent ideological development as a way of undermining the claims that sexuality, and more particularly homosexuality, was a central feature of human culture.

Despite claims that social constructionism was beyond question (most notably at the 1987 'Homosexuality, Which Homosexuality' Conference in Amsterdam), there are problems in this way of conceptualizing the historiography of sexuality.[32] First, the debate itself was largely the work of those who identified themselves as constructionists. They defined 'essentialism' as a theoretical position, in order to assert the distinctive nature of their own approach. It was not a term that supposed essentialists usually accepted, although a few, such as Rictor Norton, have come to embrace it.[33] Secondly, there were a number of important historians of sexuality, such as Jeffrey Weeks, Judith Walkowitz and Carroll Smith-Rosenberg, who were active in the field before Foucault's work had made a substantial impact. Although many of these historians would later see themselves as constructionists, and acknowledge the contribution of Foucault, the roots of their historical enterprise lay elsewhere. They drew their inspiration from the new social history, deviancy, social role and labelling theory, and the broader struggles of gay liberation and feminism. Finally, the social constructionist group was hardly a unified movement. Despite this, the belief that the history of sexuality was a war between essentialism and social constructionism was widespread, and this shaped much of the cut and thrust of debate in the 1980s and 1990s.

Essentialism largely emerged out of the movement for 'gay history'. In the 1950s and 1960s homosexual activists, through such organizations as ONE Institute and the Mattachine Society, challenged the prevailing idea that homosexuality was deviant behaviour and an illness requiring therapy. Part of their campaign to recognize the 'normality' of homosexuality was an interest in history, particularly Greek and Roman history, which was taken as evidence that homosexuality was both accepted in the past and responsible for some of the highest achievements of Western culture.[34] In the late 1960s and 1970s a more radical 'gay liberation' movement emerged, demanding the removal of forms of discrimination against homosexuals, and proclaiming the virtues of gay community. This gay liberation movement also exhibited an interest in uncovering the history of 'queer communities', establishing a long lineage of homosexual lifestyles, subcultures and practices.[35] The thrust of this enterprise was to uncover homosexuality in the past, documenting a lineage of gay culture.

One of the most influential 'essentialists' was the Yale University medievalist John Boswell. Although Boswell stoutly rejected the essentialist label, his work certainly stood out from the dominant constructionist paradigm. His histories of homosexuality in Europe, from Rome in the early Christian period till the late medieval period, are works of extraordinary depth and insight, although on balance his general approach to the history of sexuality leads down a dead end. Nonetheless, his early work on 'social tolerance' of homosexuality since early Christian times was in the forefront of the new 'gay history'.[36] It was also a sustained and critical commentary on Catholic doctrine. By charting the history of tolerance within Western Christianity before the Reformation, Boswell explored the ways in which same-sex relationships had been accepted within the early Church. He sought to establish that leading medieval clerics had been 'gay', and that homosexuality had been both visible and culturally enriching. Thus, he suggested, the homophobia of the contemporary Catholic hierarchy was based on ignorance of Church history.

In charting the history of social tolerance Boswell focused on evidence for the existence of self-conscious homosexual subcultures in early Christian and medieval Europe. A number of assumptions underpinned this work. First, he believed that same-sex relationships had occurred throughout history in all cultures and periods. Secondly, he argued that only in times of social tolerance were forms of same-sex community able to flourish. Periods of tolerance fostered the growth of subcultures able to express and communicate forms of same-sex desire, or more properly a 'gay sensibility'. Thus, for Boswell, the key concept for 'gay history' was the emergence of such sensibilities, and his work sought to uncover historical evidence for the existence of such a subculture within the Church in the twelfth century. But the definitive factor for the existence of subcultures was tolerance. Repression of these subcultures prevented the publication, communication and proliferation of texts that testified to a gay sensibility thus preventing the historical recovery of same-sex history. But this involved more than a lack of evidence. Boswell suggests that repression actually destroyed gay subcultures, reducing homosexuals to isolated individuals pursuing secretive sexual acts.

In contrast, periods of tolerance fostered same-sex communities, cemented by writing, art, a 'patois' known only to those in the community, cultural codes and forms of address that constituted a gay sensibility. Here we can see important dimensions of Boswell's approach. This was not a history of homosexuality, but rather a history of gay subcultures. Moreover, taking a long perspective, the history of gay subcultures was largely one of recurrent periods of toleration and intolerance. Despite the striking differences in subject matter between Boswell's history of medieval homosexuality and Steven Marcus' account of Victorian heterosexuality, there are some marked similarities in approach. Both make subculture the key concept for uncovering the history of sexuality. More importantly, both see the history of sexuality as largely one of recurrent periods of tolerance and repression.

Despite favourable comment from Foucault, social constructionists such as David Halperin savaged Boswell's approach. Boswell was accused of failing to appreciate the fact that the sexual cultures of late antiquity and early Christianity were organized around the ideal of men as the active partners, and women, slaves and youths as passive partners. In such a context terms such as homosexuality and heterosexuality could not and did not exist. Thus the effort to uncover a gay past was to impose the present on the past. Halperin, in particular, stressed the inherent anachronism in Boswell's search for a 'gay history'.[37]

The idea of essentialism itself was largely worked out in response to Boswell's work. Boswell, however, rejected the characterization of his work as 'essentialist', and instead sought to recast the debate as one between nominalists (social constructionists) and realists (essentialists).[38] This strategy was unsuccessful. Very few historians bothered to engage with this new terminology (except to reject it), but Boswell saw himself as belonging to neither category. On the one hand, he accepted the social constructionist argument that terms such as homosexuality did not exist until the nineteenth century, and that past sexual cultures were organized in vastly different ways to the contemporary West. Nonetheless, he continued to assert that there were general tendencies towards same-sex desire and sexual preference in all sexual cultures. Thus it was valid to use concepts such as homosexuality as heuristic devices to understand these processes. Without such a concept, he argued, there was no possibility of gay history.

More importantly, Boswell engaged in new research on 'same-sex unions' to undermine the social constructionist claim that the sexual cultures of Greek and Roman antiquity were organized around the ideal of active/passive, where same-sex desire was largely pederastic. He uncovered a rich tradition of same-sex 'marriages' in ancient Rome and the early Christian and medieval eras: sexual relationships between adult men sanctioned by Roman tradition and later the Church.[39] Such a finding opened up important new perspectives on the diversity of same-sex desires and practices in the past. But in seeking to draw parallels between the past and the present, Boswell added fuel to the constructionist critique that he was more interested in finding similarity than establishing historical difference. This criticism is too harsh. Both similarity and differences are important ways of engaging with the past, but the focus on difference, historical specificity and the foreignness of the past has come to dominate historical scholarship in recent years, pushing the work of historians like Boswell, somewhat unfairly, to the margins.

Social constructionists may have been united in their opposition to essentialism but in other ways they were a very diverse group. While all were committed to the idea that sexuality was open to historical investigation, theoretically and methodologically there were clear differences in approach. A significant group of social constructionists, such as Jeffrey Weeks, Kenneth Plummer, John D'Emilio and Estelle Freedman, drew their main inspiration from the new social history of the 1960s and 1970s.[40] Committed to the recovery of the lives of ordinary people they saw history as a field to explore how people made their own history.[41] As Jeffrey Weeks argued, paraphrasing Marx, 'we are the makers of sexual history...we may not make it in circumstances entirely of our own choosing, but we have more choice than we often believe'.[42] This 'new left' faith in social action clearly implied that sexuality and struggles over sexuality were forged within larger economic, class, gender and race contexts. Similarly in the 1990s a newer generation of social historians, notably George Chauncey, argued forcefully for seeing sexuality and new ideas of sexual identity as embedded in wider social structures such as the economy, urban life, and forms of social order. Chauncey combined a sophisticated sense of the diverse contexts shaping sexual life with a precise and detailed ethnographic recreation of urban sexual subcultures.[43]

Most of these social historians are circumspect about the contribution of Foucault to the history of sexuality. While they acknowledge his influence in theorizing sexuality as historical, they have been less enamoured of his broader emphasis on sexuality and sexual identities as products of scientific discourses. For social historians it is essential to place the construction of sexual identities within specific social and political structures of power and inequality. They take issue with the poststructuralist emphasis on language as an independent and autonomous realm that constructs social life. Social historians see this relationship the other way round. For them language and identity are reflections of deeper social structures.

Weeks, in particular, has an ambivalent relationship to Foucauldian theory, despite being an important intellectual mediator between French poststructuralism and English social history.[44] For instance, Weeks insists that both he and Mary McIntosh anticipated Foucault's key insight that the homosexual was an identity of recent origin. More importantly, although Weeks sees Foucault as central to the critique of essentialism and an important theorist of sexuality, he argues that Foucault failed to adequately explain why forms of knowledge change. Where Foucault interrogates forms of knowledge, how they work and their complex intersections with social practices, Weeks, and others such as D'Emilio and Freedman, are more interested in movements for sexual reform, mechanisms of historical change and how sexuality is embedded in wider structures of class, gender and race. In other words, social historians assert that Foucault has failed to situate discourses within their causal context. Moreover, these social historians are interested in the ways the state regulates sexuality, seeing the state as a site of social repression. In contrast, Foucault sees the state as an effect of mechanisms of disciplinary power and governance, a product of discourses and practices, not an independent tool in the hands of particular ruling groups and interests.[45]

These critiques undervalue the contribution of Foucault to the field. While interactionists, and historians like Weeks, may have seen the homosexual as a social role, they still left sexuality as natural and beyond history. Other historians have more fully appreciated the radical historical project of Foucault. These historians have stressed the importance of discourse in the construction of sexual identity. It is in the larger realm of language and discourse that forms of sexuality are inscribed within culture. And it is in the contest of ideas that new identities emerge. A notable advocate of this position is David Halperin, who has made a substantial contribution to the history of sexuality in ancient Greece and to theoretical debates about the historical nature of sexuality. Halperin, along with others such as Arnold Davidson, John Winkler, Robert Padgug and Froma Zeitlin, has been in the forefront of the movement seeing homosexuality, and sexuality more generally, as a recent phenomenon.[46]

These historians have used the work of Foucault to theorize the problem of a time 'before sexuality'. In Padgug's notable phrase 'before sexuality there were sexual acts not sexual identities'. For Padgug, Foucault's distinction between juridical and disciplinary power is best understood in the domain of sexual practices as a shift from the regulation of sexual acts to the policing of sexual identity. In other words, 'before sexuality' the law punished those who committed offences such as sodomy after the commission of the offence. But from the late-nineteenth century doctors, sexologists and a variety of other authorities sought to define the homosexual as a distinct species with a view to correcting their conduct. In doing so they created the corpus of behaviours that have come to characterize 'the homosexual'. Notions of the homosexual only made sense in relationship to concepts of heterosexuality. Thus at the end of the nineteenth century doctors, psychiatrists and sexologists, like Richard von Krafft-Ebing, set out to document the rich variety of sexual variations in the form of sexuality or, like Freud, went further to uncover the psychological causes of these differences. In doing so these scientists constructed a discourse of sexuality.[47]

Nonetheless, there are shades of difference within this broadly Foucauldian school. For example, in more recent work Halperin has attempted to qualify Padgug's distinction between acts and identities. For Halperin, this distinction between law and discipline is useful for explicating different modalities of power but this does not mean that forms of sexual identity and subjectivity did not exist before the invention of sexuality. The nature of these earlier identities was undoubtedly different to that of the late-nineteenth century but, for Halperin, Padgug's distinction is too rigid. Instead, Halperin has argued that the idea of a before and after sexuality fails to pay sufficient attention to the historically specific forms of identity constructed within particular cultures and historical periods. The ways in which sexual practices made particular identities needs to be grounded in specific historical accounts.[48] In a series of provocative books and articles Halperin has been at the forefront of social constructionist debates about the historicity of sexuality itself.[49]

Despite the importance of Foucault to the field of sexual history, there have been significant critiques of his approach. We have already seen that social historians have criticized Foucault for failing to link sexuality to social and economic forces. Other theorists have pointed to forms of oppression that Foucault ignored. For example, many have identified race as an important absence in Foucault's theory, although Ann Laura Stoler has indicated ways in which Foucault did grapple with this problem.[50] Such critics have attempted to move beyond Foucault to explore the intersections between colonialism, race and sexuality.[51] We will examine some of these issues in greater detail in a later chapter. Another important critique, however, has come from feminists. They have pinpointed Foucault's neglect of gender as an important flaw in his history of sexuality. This is certainly a glaring absence. Foucault's analysis of the emergence of sexual discourses and new sexual identities in the late-nineteenth century sees sexuality as a general discursive formation. For Foucault, discourse itself is the key issue rather than how discourses structured crucial differences between male and female sexuality. In describing his project as the history of the 'desiring man' Foucault obscures the way desire was gendered.[52]

Some prominent feminists, such as Catharine MacKinnon, have questioned the utility of histories of sexuality for feminism because they potentially undermine the necessity to theorize universal patterns of gender and sexual oppression. Foucault's insistence on the specificity of sexuality undermines the feminist campaign to diagnose forms of gender oppression that exist in all times and places. MacKinnon argues that Foucault and other historians of sexuality have turned the field into the study of masculine pleasure, exploring what 'turns them on' and ignoring persistent problems such as rape, sexual abuse, prostitution and pornography that undermine the idea of sexuality as 'good'. These social constructionists have been able to do so because they refuse to theorize gender.[53] Other feminists, however, such as Gayle Rubin, have sought to define a theoretical ground that could simultaneously combine an awareness of pervasive transhistorical structures of oppression with sensitivity to women's agency and change over time. What Rubin sought was an approach that was at once historical, and alive to the persistence of female oppression in all times and cultures.[54]

MacKinnon's insistence on the gender blindness of the historiography of sexuality ignores the extent to which male and gay historians such as Weeks have taken gender as a central dynamic of their studies. Nonetheless, her identification of gender as a striking absence in poststructuralist theories of sexuality and discourse is forceful. Other feminist theorists, however, have been less dismissive of Foucault, but no less critical. Scholars such Carolyn Dean, Eloise Buker, Lynn Hunt and Teresa de Lauretis, have been instrumental in arguing that the absence of the category of gender in Foucault's work renders it unable to adequately theorize the historical processes through which sexuality is produced. In other words gender blindness is not just an unfortunate missing piece that can be simply added; it undermines the very terms of the project.

Thus Foucault fails to really examine how the homosexual-heterosexual divide or the constitution of separate male and female subjects are historically constructed. As Teresa de Lauretis argues, by failing to 'take into account the different solicitation of male and female subjects, and by ignoring the conflicting investments of men and women in the discourses and practices of sexuality, Foucault's theory...excludes, though it does not preclude, the consideration of gender'.[55] These feminists have argued that the history of sexuality requires gender theory.[56]

This call to gender theory has been taken forward by a number of feminist historians. In contrast to the early women's history focus on female oppression, which relegated sexuality to the margins of the discipline, sexuality became a major theme in feminist history of the 1980s and 1990s. A new generation of feminist historians sought to take Foucault's idea of the radical historicity of sexuality and place it within a framework of feminist gender analysis. This has produced some path-breaking work in the history of sexuality, which will be the focus of discussion in later chapters.[57]

Judith Butler, however, has argued that a worrying bifurcation remains within contemporary theory between sexuality and gender.[58] Despite the efforts of feminist historians to absorb sexuality into the history of gender, Butler diagnoses a separation between the feminist interest in gender and the gay and lesbian interest in sexuality. Within queer studies there has been an attempt to distinguish theories of sexuality from theories of gender, allocating the investigation of sexuality to queer studies and that of gender to feminism. Butler identifies founding essays in queer studies, such as those by Gayle Rubin, as an attempt to restrict the scope of feminism to gender and open up sexuality, not just to gay and lesbian studies, but to sexual minorities more generally. While lesbian and gay studies focus on sex and sexuality as the key theoretical point of departure, feminism, especially evident in the work of Joan Scott, has given priority to gender.[59]

For Butler, and others such as Biddy Martin, neither gender nor sexuality can be reduced to the other; it remains vital 'to insist on their interrelationship'. The separation of questions of sexuality from questions of sexual difference impoverishes theorizations of sexuality. Without reference to masculine and feminine, histories of sexuality make the masculine 'the sex which is one' and gay and lesbian liberation 'dovetail with mainstream conservatism'. Butler insists that 'both feminist and queer studies need to move beyond and against those methodological demands which force separation'.[60]

One of the key issues highlighted by Butler's analysis of the necessary intersections of sexuality and gender is the problem of sexual difference. This puts the sexed body at the centre of analysis. Foucault highlighted the body as a key theoretical problem in the analysis of power, knowledge and sexuality.[61] For Foucault the body is an unsexed and neutral surface, something that is inscribed and formed by disciplinary powers. Feminists have also seen the sexed body as biological and natural, acted upon by social forces that create gender difference. Pervasive ideologies create a hierarchy of bodies, masculine and feminine where gender becomes the imposition of cultural systems of power on the body.

Judith Butler and others such as Teresa de Lauretis, however, have attempted to develop more complex accounts of embodiment. For them the concept of the sexed body, the body as the site for the representation of sexual difference, is an attempt to bring culture and biology together.

Sexual difference 'can be reduced neither to a biological difference nor a sociological notion of gender'. In this framework the body is not neutral and then made social, it is constructed as sexed within biology. In other words biology is itself a discourse, and the division between culture and nature an artificial one. For Butler, the body becomes semiotic and symbolic; neither fully formed by nature nor fully inscribed by culture. Nor is the body merely a surface on which culture writes specific scripts. Instead the body is an active biological, psychological and cultural agent intersecting in complex ways with disciplinary powers to create cultural and political domains of gender and sexuality. The concept of the sexed body attempts to bring together gender and sexuality.[62]

Others, such as Caroline Walker Bynum and James Farr, however, have argued that Butler's radical social constructionism is inadequate to grapple with complex problems of embodiment; the ways in which bodies can be seen as both sites of cultural production, but also forms of somatic resistance to cultural inscription.[63] Nonetheless, these scholars have shifted their focus to such questions as the body in an effort to escape the political problems of identity politics. More recently, feminist theorists have taken up Foucault's critique of subjectivity arguing that sexual identities are forms of cultural, historical and political production, which serve to regulate the body and its pleasures. Fixing identities around such frameworks as woman, swinger, gay, lesbian, paedophile and fetishist serve to constrain and regulate bodies. These theoretical debates about sexuality, gender, sexual difference and the body have eroded the old dichotomy of essentialism and social constructionism in the history of sexuality.[64]

Another influential challenge to social constructionism has come from within queer studies. Eve Kosofsky Sedgwick's insightful analysis of homo/heterosexual discourses in *The Epistemology of the Closet* (1990) sought to undermine arguments about the construction of the homosexual identity at the end of the nineteenth century. Focusing mainly on the work of Foucault and Halperin, Sedgwick questioned their historical narrative of the emergence of the homosexual, replacing older notions of the sodomite and the invert. She argued that social constructionists created falsely homogenous categories such as the homosexual and the heterosexual. For Sedgwick, sexual identities are unstable, contradictory and overlapping, and the notion of a sharp break between premodern and modern sexual identities ignored the ways earlier sexual categories, identities and practices persisted within newly emerging identities. In other words, the social constructionist effort to make the modern homosexual an historical figure perpetuated an obsolete identity politics. Social constructionism, she argues, imposed a problematical unified identity on a shifting field of discursive contest and signification.[65]

Sedgwick's critique of constructionism, in turn, raises questions about the body. In the early elaborations of the social constructionist approach, such as those by Foucault, Padgug and others, the body is seen largely as a neutral, undifferentiated entity which discourses then construct into an historically specific identity. But feminist and queer theorists have argued that the body, desire and sexual difference have a material basis as well as a social one and that discourses work to transform biology into culture. In other words, the body is not a thing freely available for cultural invention. Social forces and language construct something by transforming material entities not merely by inventing them. Thus bodies and desires can resist efforts to construct them. These theorists of corporeality point to a more dynamic interaction between matter and culture than social constructionist accounts.[66]

Such arguments have begun to influence the ways historians write about sexuality. For example, Robert Nye has adopted the stance of 'moderate social constructionism'. For Nye, also paraphrasing Marx, 'history makes sexuality…but not exactly as it chooses'. In other words, the material body creates the physical and anatomical horizons for bodies and pleasures, which puts limits on the array of expressions available for what we call sexuality. History might create an 'extraordinary diversity' of expressions of sexuality, but there are material and physiological limits to this diversity.[67]

The response of social constructionists to these feminist and queer theory critiques has been instructive. David Halperin, in particular, has revised some of his earlier theorizing of the history of sexuality. While now accepting that social constructionism is obsolete, he has forcefully argued for the continuing relevance of Foucault's genealogical approach to sexuality. For Halperin the evolution of the modern homosexual does not disappear despite the force of Sedgwick's critique. Instead it is vital to acknowledge that the 'coexistence of different models of homosexual difference in the discourses of sexuality today is the cumulative effect of a long process of historical overlay and accretion'.[68] For Halperin 'historicism' is central to any properly historical account of sexuality. Historicism becomes a strategy that accommodates 'aspects of sexual life that seem to persist through time as well as the dramatic differences between historically documented forms of sexual experience'.[69] The key issue for Halperin, however, remains the need to uncover historical difference, to insist, like Foucault, on the radical historicity of sexuality and sexual identity.

Conclusion

In the second half of the twentieth century the history of sexuality has emerged as a major field of historical inquiry. Sexuality, instead of being something natural, came to be seen by historians as subject to historical change. But how sexuality was made historical, and what might be the motors of historical change, became the object of intense scholarly and theoretical dispute. Where some saw sexuality as relatively constant but affected by cycles of repression and tolerance, others came to see major sexual identities, such as heterosexuality and homosexuality, as relatively recent in origin. The driving force for the emergence of this field of sexual history has been gay liberation. Questions about the history of homosexuality and gay identity have dominated the historiography of sexuality. Where feminists sought to see sexuality as part of gender, gay theorists made sexuality itself the focus of analysis. By the 1990s, however, these divisions, between essentialists and social constructionists, and between sexuality and gender, came under greater critical scrutiny. What has emerged is greater feminist interest in sexuality itself, and an insistence from feminists, queer theorists and historicists, on the importance of exploring both continuities and differences in the history of sexuality.

These theoretical disputes have had a marked affect on interpretations of the sexual past. In subsequent chapters we will explore in more concrete detail the way historians have constructed the history of sexuality in particular times and places. Throughout the following chapters the emphasis is not just on the history of past sexual practices, but on how history as a discipline is actively engaged in the recovery of the past. Historians are not just presenters of the past, locked in the archives revealing historical truth. Nor do historians naively impose the present on the past, distorting the past for political ends. Rather they work at the intersection of a range of scholarly practices that require dynamic interactions between the past and the present. In exploring these processes in relation to particular historical debates about past sexual cultures we will return to many of the ideas and historians raised in this chapter.

Chapter 2

RULE OF THE PHALLUS

Ancient Greece and Rome have shaped Western culture in profound ways, and remain a source of intense cultural, philosophical and historical interest. As the supposed cradle of modern civilization, Athens and Rome have functioned for centuries as the source for numerous reflections on such fundamental questions as freedom and democracy. Classical antiquity also laid the foundation for such disciplines as ethics, geometry, metaphysics and aesthetics.[1] The one exception to this scholarly interest has been sexuality. Many of the classic accounts of the ancient world, such as those by Jacob Burckhardt, Wilhelm Kroll or H.I. Marrow, ignored, or only mentioned in passing, the importance of 'male love' in Athens and Rome. A few adventurous scholars, such as Fredrich-Karl Forberg in the 1820s and Hans Licht (Paul Brandt) and Theodore Hopfner in the 1930s, highlighted the prevalence of 'male homosexuality' in antiquity but their work lay outside the mainstream of classical studies.[2] In the early 1960s homophile social reformers, such as J.Z. Eglinton, turned to a history of 'Greek love' in an effort to preach the virtues of 'pederasty'.[3]

The scholarly silence on ancient homosexuality was not really broken until the early 1970s when scholars such as Jeffrey Henderson and John Boardman opened up the field. In 1978 Kenneth Dover published his authoritative study *Greek Homosexuality*, which put homosexuality, or more correctly pederasty, at the centre of Greek culture.[4] Pedagogic and erotic relationships between male citizens and youths were, for Dover, the cornerstone of Greek culture, evident in philosophy, art, and literature. The existence of such relationships was hardly a revelation, but Dover succeeded in highlighting how important and widespread pederasty was in classical civilization.

In the context of the profound and longstanding antagonism to homosexuality in the West, it is not surprising that ancient sexuality was relegated to the margins of scholarly inquiry. A crucial factor generat-

ing greater interest in ancient homosexuality was the 1970s gay liberation movement and the project for a 'gay history' that uncovered the
rich tapestry of homosexual life and culture in past times. The Greco-
Roman world provided an abundant source of evidence to demonstrate
that homosexuality was natural, not 'deviant'. In a world that valued the
classical past, this presented an opportunity for gay activists to claim a
legitimate place within contemporary culture and make a case for new
laws and attitudes to 'liberate' homosexuals. This gay veneration of classical antiquity, however, was questioned by feminists like Eva Keuls, who
argued that ancient Athens was an intensely misogynist culture, where
the symbolic and literal use of the phallus signified social dominance.[5]

More recently, however, the focus of current debate has been on the
differences between antiquity and the modern West. Even more importantly debates in this field have been used to question the very concept
of sexuality itself. Although Dover defined homosexuality as a preference for 'sensory pleasure...with persons of one's own sex', the nature
of Greek homosexuality raised real doubts for him about the utility of
this concept. He thought sexual and quasi-sexual were preferable terms
because of the readiness of ancient Greeks to recognize the 'alternation
of homosexual and heterosexual preferences'.[6] Michel Foucault heightened this ambivalence about the relevance of concepts of homosexuality to antiquity. Foucault and others, such as David Halperin, John
Winkler, Paul Veyne, Froma Zeitlin and Maud Gleason, have argued
that the ancient world was 'before sexuality'. In other words, they saw a
fundamental break between the ancient and the modern world, stressing profound differences which undermine the supposed similarities
between 'Greek love' and contemporary homosexuality. This was a key
issue in the Foucauldian effort to argue that sexuality was a definably
modern discourse and not a transhistorical presence in all cultures.

This argument has been contested. John Boswell, Amy Richlin,
Eva Cantarella, Rabun Taylor and others have sought to draw parallels
between ancient and modern homosexuality, attempting to stress continuities against the rising tide of efforts to promote difference. The ground
of contest between these historians is often highly technical, based on
disputes over the translation of specific ancient Greek and Latin words.
Another complicating factor, one often overlooked by the participants, is
the problematical assumption that Athens and Rome are similar enough
to constitute a single classical culture. While they share much in common, there are marked differences. For instance, Romans viewed sodomy
with much greater ambivalence than Athenians did. Similarly, women in
Rome had a higher civic status than their counterparts in Athens. Some
of the historiographical debates examined here arise, in part, because
historians use Roman cases to refute arguments based on evidence from
Athens and vice versa. At the same time, historians have sought to move

beyond a narrow focus on pederasty to explore the nature of female sexuality in antiquity, providing other areas of debate about sex in antiquity.
Many of the disputes are also theoretical and conceptual. They take us
into some of the key questions in the historiography of sexuality: What is
sexuality? What is the relationship between sexual acts and sexual identities? How do sexual regimes regulate conduct?

Dominance and Submission

There is now substantial agreement about key features of Greco-Roman
sexual life. It seems clear that same-sex unions between older men and
youths were common, tolerated and, in many instances, praised as the
highest form of 'love' in both Athens and Rome. Despite disputes over
the applicability of homosexuality to the understanding of sexuality
in antiquity, most commentators accept that there were profound differences between male sexual practices in antiquity and those in the
Christian West. These differences were clearly specified by early-twentieth-century commentators, such as Sigmund Freud, who argued that for
the ancients the primary focus of sexuality was aim not sexual object.[7]
By this he meant that men were not concerned with the gender of their
sexual partners, but the type of act they would perform. This was a
crude formulation, but it highlighted a fundamental rupture between
the sexual cultures of the ancient and the modern worlds, a distinction
that has become the focus of much commentary and analysis.

The central trope of Greco-Roman sexual culture was activity/passiv-
ity not homosexuality/heterosexuality.[8] In other words, what constituted
one's status and identity was whether one was the active, penetrating
partner or the passive, receiving partner. The gender of the sexual partner was a relatively minor consideration. This active/passive trope was
embedded in a larger structure of social relations overwhelmingly focused
on gender, power and authority, or more specifically maleness and citizenship. The defining features of ancient sexual regimes can be sketched
more fully, but with some important qualifications. Certainly the hierarchies were more rigid and the cult of pederasty far stronger in Athens
than Rome. While free boys were permissible sexual objects for Greek
citizens, sodomizing youths was forbidden in Roman culture. Nonetheless, as John Winkler has argued, sexual activity was symbolic of a larger
relentless competition for dominance. Men had to assert their authority
over others in order to establish their claim to citizenship. Sex, like war,
was a domain for the representation of social status.[9]

Only male citizens were fully sexual subjects. Women were relegated
to the margins in ancient sexual culture, with the major deliberations
about sexual conduct in antiquity overwhelmingly concerned with the
male citizen. In this regard, however, we should not see ancient sexual

culture as unitary, homogenous and uncontested. There were many disputes in ancient literatures over the most appropriate behaviours, dispositions, regimens and ethics for governing sexual life. Moreover, some historians have suggested that Athenian women were not as 'repressed' as many historians have assumed.[10] Others have seen erotic sensibilities embedded in all aspects of classical culture.[11] These revisionist efforts have not overturned the view that classical Athenian sexual culture was highly ordered, hierarchal and prescriptive. But prescriptions for appropriate conduct do not necessarily mean that they reflected or described actual sexual behaviour. They are, as we shall see, also points for the mobilization of resistance, subversion and the formation of alternative identities.

The fundamental requirement for sexual conduct was that the male citizen be the active partner in any sexual encounter. It was perfectly acceptable (to a greater or lesser extent, according to different authorities) for men (meaning male citizens) to have sexual relations with wives, concubines, male or female slaves and prostitutes, as long as the citizen was the active, penetrating partner. In Greece freeborn youths were also available as sexual objects, provided the youth was the receiver rather than the giver of passion. To be penetrated was to submit symbolically to the authority of another, something that shaped the whole fabric of citizenship and dominance in the ancient world. Thus it was often the case that soldiers taunted opponents with charges of effeminacy and their fondness for sodomy.[12] Warriors defeated in battle, and less commonly those guilty of serious crimes, could be raped by male citizens or subject to similar punishments, such as penetration by radishes (although historians have speculated that 'radish' in this context means a vegetable somewhat larger than a modern radish).[13]

Enforcing sexual submission or humiliation was a means of asserting dominance. At the same time, most men married – an arrangement between families chiefly concerning property and social networks – and had children with wives to perpetuate their lineage. Although many men demonstrated a great love and affection for wives, they were able to conduct a variety of other sexual relations, mainly with slaves, prostitutes and concubines. While individual men may have had a preference for either men or women, it was perfectly acceptable for these partners to be of either sex, as long as the man remained the active partner. To be the passive partner compromised one's claim to citizenship and authority. Thus there were very specific sanctions against sex between male citizens of the same status because these threatened codes of masculine dominance.

This concern with being active, penetrating, masculine citizens made 'boy love' a major issue in ancient texts. Youths destined to become male citizens were the object of considerable sexual attention and anxiety.

Citizenship was not conferred until one was 'fully a man', able to go into battle and participate in the life of the polis or the state. This usually occurred around the age of 15 for Romans and 18 for Greeks. Again there appears to be marked differences between Athens and Rome in the attitude to 'boy love'. In Roman culture there were specific sanctions against loving the sons of other citizens. The earlier age for battle in part signalled a desire for Roman boys of good families to shift to the status of man more quickly, leaving little time for the development of pederastic relationships. Although 'boy love' was still idealized in Roman texts, this was more an abstract and aesthetic ethic, and one generally focused on the sexual use of boyish slaves and prostitutes. At the same time there were sharp injunctions on freeborn youths to avoid sodomy.[14]

The elaborate deliberations on 'boy love' are far more characteristic of Athenian culture. From the age of about 14, when 'down' appeared on their cheeks, freeborn youths were in a liminal state, between childhood and manhood, undergoing the physical and mental training in the gymnasia and forums that would equip them to take their place as citizens. These youths were the focus of an extensive 'erotics' built around the pedagogic relationship of teacher and pupil. Numerous texts extolled the virtues of the 'love of boys' and advised on the forms this should take and the ethics, procedures, responsibilities and requirements for this experience. The atmosphere of the gymnasia and forums was highly charged; youths were typically naked in the gymnasia, and more generally the dynamics of male citizens interacting with 'flowering youths' was one that fostered erotic interest. For historians, such as Eva Cantarella, pederasty was a form of initiation rite into manhood, one that provided a safe outlet for homosexual desire.[15] But others have contested this claim. For Halperin, these initiations were not rituals for the expression of desire, but performances embedding a fantasy of male reproduction in Greek culture. They were about the politics of masculine authority rather than sexuality.[16]

The volume of prescriptive literature and philosophical reflection on 'boy love', however, suggests that it was also a troubling relationship, one that entailed risks and possibilities that threatened the social order. As David Cohen has argued, codes of male honour generated profound ambivalence about male same-sex unions, particularly pederasty. Far from being a form of initiation there were elaborate injunctions for youths to resist courtship.[17] On the one hand, the intense atmosphere of 'boy love' could exacerbate rivalry, jealousy and competition amongst male citizens and youths, which could undermine current and future social bonds. On the other hand, the ambiguities in the transition of youths from objects of affection to male citizens raised serious issues for the proper conduct of such relationships. When was it appropriate to

initiate a boy into this pedagogic and erotic circle? Even more importantly, when should such relationships end and the youth shift from
being the passive to the active partner? Would the pleasures learned as
a youth be so overwhelming that the youth would fail to make the shift
to full manhood? Would submission as a youth forever compromise and
dishonour the adult citizen?

These unsettling questions were central preoccupations in much of
the ancient philosophical and prescriptive literature. The possibility
of troubled transitions to manhood was evident in satire, mockery and
gossip. For instance, Julius Caesar was ridiculed by his critics as 'wife to
all men and husband to all women', after rumours that he prostituted
himself while a young soldier of 19 to King Nicomedes of Bithynia.
There was always the fear that youths might exploit their appeal for
commercial gain. Aeschines charged Timarchus with having prostituted
himself in his youth, the penalty for which was the loss of social status and important rights of citizenship. Even in Athenian literature the
pederastic ideal was open to ridicule. Aristophanes, in *The Wasps*, refers
to the citizens who preyed on youths as 'poofta aristocrats' (a term that
translates well into contemporary Australian vernacular).[18] The pedagogic practices guiding the transition from youth to manhood were
meant to ensure the formation of male citizens, but in the interstices of
desire, authority, social conflict, life and actual relationships, there was
potential for contest, rumour and antipathy, undermining the status of
citizens.[19]

Although male citizens had few restrictions on the number and variety of sexual partners they could enjoy, this was far from being a 'libertarian' paradise. First, this was not a culture that recognized a multiplicity
of desires. Although some scholars, such as Eva Cantarella, have sought
to get around the problem of widespread heterosexual and homosexual sex by characterizing the sexual cultures of antiquity as bisexual,[20]
Foucault, Halperin and others insist they were not 'bisexual' in the way
we understand this term today. Male desire was not differentiated by
sexual object, but was singular and focused on assuming a position of
dominance in all sexual encounters.[21] Secondly, this was not a culture
of sexual freedom. In fact Greco-Roman sexual culture was a highly
regulated regime, replete with numerous rules of conduct, deportment
and practices for the refinement of the self. These rules and practices
regarding sexual conduct were intimately tied to the formation of the
identity of the male citizen. Rules of conduct governing sexual practices
were part of a wider advice literature on matters such as diet, exercise,
daily regimen, moderation, excess, relations with wives and moral disposition more generally.

Foucault investigated these complex ethics, dietetics and therapeu-
tics in the final two volumes of his 'history of sexuality'. He demonstrated

that there were intricate ways in which all of these domains of practice
– diet, exercise, deportment, conduct, sex – were interrelated, governing
the 'uses of pleasure'. Care needed to be exercised in all these spheres
to ensure continued mastery of the self, a state threatened by excess,
indulgence, impurity and passivity. By the Roman period these concerns
underpinned a gradual shift of interest from the problem of pleasure and
'boy love' towards a more intense focus on bodily discipline and 'the care
of the self '. By late antiquity there was growing interest in such practices
as male sexual continence, as a measure of self-mastery and a means of
preserving the body from the ravages of indulgence.[22]

Women in Antiquity

The intense historical interest in pederasty is understandable given
the androcentric nature of these cultures. More recently, however, historians have sought to recover the sexual history of others in ancient
Greece and Rome. The lives of wives, daughters, slaves, freed slaves,
concubines and prostitutes are particularly elusive. Although the documentation on elite women in Imperial Rome is certainly comparatively voluminous, in the main the experiences of women and slaves are
largely refracted through the texts produced by male citizens. We have
to read between the lines and concentrate on occasional references and
comments to speculate on the sexual life of those who were not male citizens. In particular, the evidence on the sexuality of women and slaves
is usually found in prescriptive and medical literature, which is useful
for male representations of female sexuality, but less useful for actual
practices. Male and female sexuality in the classical world was marked
by contest and diversity.[23]

There has been important work on the lives of these other Greeks
and Romans, particularly the wives of citizens. On the one hand, wives
and female slaves were seen as property and women more generally
considered both property and sexual objects, always passive in contrast to the man's dominance. In a number of texts wives were also seen
as authorities within the home, a role valued by their husbands. And
while men participated in a wholly male public culture, women were
left alone to shape their own private social networks. In Athens, in particular, women were confined to the domestic sphere. The names of
women could not be uttered in public until after their death. In Rome
women were accorded higher social and legal status but their sphere
was still the home. They were the mothers of future citizens and the
guardians of culture.[24] There is even some evidence that Jewish legal
teachings on the rights of women to sexual intercourse within marriage
may have influenced the greater valorization of marriage in Imperial
Rome.[25] More conventionally, women were seen as fecund, invested with

a definably 'female power over life and sexuality'. This involved them in a female world of midwives and wet nurses, where women's knowledge of biology and reproduction could circulate. Lesley Dean-Jones has argued that in some contexts women saw their bodies as superior life-giving entities to that of the expendable bodies of male warriors.[26]

In myth and literature, however, women could also be threatening, licentious and powerful. In ancient Greece there were powerful goddesses, and some festivals worshipping Aphrodite and Demeter were restricted to women. In these festivals, argues Winkler, women could humorously subvert both male pride in sexual prowess and assert the importance of women's networks.[27] Linguistic evidence, however, suggests that images of threatening female sexuality were more common in Latin culture. For example, there is no equivalent in Greek for the Roman word *virago* (literally man-woman), suggesting a threatening, voracious female sexuality. Common words such as *moecha/moicha* meant adulteress in Greek, but sexually dominating woman in Latin.[28] On the other hand, *tribades*, women who penetrated both women and men (with dildos or a large clitoris), were the source of fascination and fear in both ancient Greece and Rome.[29]

Other literature, however, attested to the pleasures of the marital bed. In Greek literature women were generally represented as either heavily susceptible to animal lust (thus requiring strict control) or ignorant and uninitiated in sexual matters. By the late Hellenistic and early Roman times a literature emerged celebrating sexual symmetry and mutual love between husband and wife. Ideas of pleasure and fidelity until death appear in Latin drama and poetry. Even in Greek dramas male authors 'painted a many sided picture' of female sexuality, which suggested that in normal life marital sex was an important factor for Athenian husbands and wives.[30]

There were opportunities for women, within the structure of ancient social life, to pursue their own desires (albeit within very constrained contexts defined by the dominant male culture). Studies of legal texts provide important insights into women's options and the regulation of their choices. Trials for sexual assault, rape and adultery, for example, have left evidence of married women being involved in long-term relationships with men other than their husband. There is a considerable body of literature on the problem of adultery, including legal discourses on the rights of wronged husbands (it was one of the few contexts in which male citizens had the right to kill another citizen). Cases of adultery point to the existence of men and women prepared to flout the law in the pursuit of their desires. Such evidence suggests important ways in which women asserted some agency within the patriarchal structures of antiquity.[31]

In the same vein there is both literary and non-literary evidence of women taking female lovers. The literature on female homoeroticism is sparse but in the work of the seventh-century BCE Greek poet Sappho, and the Roman poet Sulpicia, we can see the ways in which classical literatures celebrated female sensibilities and the opportunities for erotic association among women.[32] John Boswell and Lin Foxall have also uncovered legal references in ancient Greek and Roman texts to 'women lying with each other' and to forms of permanent or semi-permanent relationships amongst women.[33] In the next chapter we will explore in greater detail the profound cultural anxieties generated by female homoeroticism.

Another useful, although partial, way into the sexual world of women comes through the rich corpus of medical and prescriptive literature. This literature again is overwhelmingly concerned with men, suggesting that masculine ideals were remarkably fragile and unstable. But such literature also provides evidence of broader understandings of the nature of gender. There were two major frameworks in which the biological nature of gender was understood in antiquity – Hippocratic and Aristotelian. The rich corpus of Hippocratic writings on nature and biology represented women and men as fundamentally different animals. Women were characterized by an excess of blood, which left them 'teetering on the brink of ill health', requiring regular periodic discharge to prevent serious illness. Aristotle, on the other hand, argued that women were undeveloped men. In other words, they had a similar physiology, with menstrual blood seen as similar to male semen. Women, however, were inferior because of their failure to develop. Although these two systems of biology jostled for dominance gradually the Aristotelian system emerged as the most influential.[34]

Galen, the Greek physician of the second century CE, provided the most systematic and influential account of ancient biology and medicine, crystallizing widespread understandings in the ancient world. Although Galen claimed a lineage from Hippocrates, his conclusions were largely Aristotelian. For Galen, men and women shared one body type, women were in fact men who had not developed (the uterus being represented as a penis that had not dropped outside the body). What distinguished male and female was the amount of heat and energy generated in the body; maleness being full development arising from adequate body heat, while femaleness was a consequence of relative coldness. Women were moist, damp and imperfect. This idea of the 'one-sex body' dominated European concepts of biology and gender until the late-eighteenth century.[35]

In this schema it was possible for gender to shift emphasis and even change altogether. Men could become feminized if they were passive rather than active, or if they were excessively active they could dissipate their energies. Women if active could generate sufficient heat to become more masculine. Thus gender, or more properly masculinity and femininity, were fluid states that required rigid regulation to ensure relative stability. While men were represented as bold, courageous, innovative, reasoning and active, women were often seen as polluting, formless, putrefying, wet, potentially insatiable (robbing men of their heat) and threatening. Masculinity was constantly confronted by the enervating potential of femininity and this necessitated a complex sexual and social regime to produce and perpetuate masculinity.

The ancient literature on the body also provides important insights into sexuality, and is one of the spaces where men reflected on the 'nature' of women and their sexual appetites and capacities. It provides the framework in which sex acts with either gender were 'normalized'; for all bodies, despite their differences, were really the same body in different stages of development. Equally, for Galen and a number of ancient authorities, orgasm was essential for procreation. Orgasm more generally was seen as the consequence of the heating of bodily fluids, arising from friction on the skin and other bodily movements. And in this moment of 'heat' lay the conditions in which life could be generated (life itself being the possession of heat). A few, notably Aristotle, disputed the necessity of orgasm for procreation, but prevailing opinion supported this view. In this context we can venture some conclusions about the nature of marital sexuality. It placed a primacy on orgasm for both partners to ensure reproduction and supporting this was literature on the arts of arousal and stimulation. Considerable attention was focused on the problem of passion and how passion could be heightened and regulated to ensure orgasm and reproduction.

Male Love

Despite the growth of interest in the sexual lives of non-citizens, male love has dominated historical scholarship. Does this mean these were homosexual cultures? The emphasis of scholars, such as Halperin, Winkler and Foucault, on the primacy of the active/passive dichotomy in the organization of male desire, is an effort to counter the idea of 'Greek homosexuality'. But not all historians have accepted their conclusions. For instance, David Cohen and John Thorp have argued that there were competing discourses on sex and citizenship that highlight more complex dimensions to the construction of masculine subjectivity. They provide close readings of some key philosophical tracts, such as Plato's *Symposium*, arguing that embedded in these texts were notions of homosexuality and heterosexuality. Thorp, in particular, argues that some of these texts recognized three distinct categories of desire 'gay, lesbian and straight', which are remarkably 'close to our own category in fundamental ways'.[36]

Others have pointed to adult male sexual relationships as evidence for the existence of ancient homosexuality. Eva Cantarella, for example, insists that sexual preferences existed in antiquity, ones that lead to ridicule, ostracism, punishment and even death. She argues that the Foucauldian obsession with discourses of self-mastery overlooks the problem of sexual desire, which cuts across social convention.[37] John Boswell, in particular, has argued that some citizens flouted the pederastic ideal of male love. Even more importantly, these transgressions were tolerated and condoned. He points to the vast Latin literature that reflected on the relationship of Patroclus and Achilles in Homer's *Iliad*. Much of this literature explored the erotic nature of this relationship between two male warriors. There might have been an age difference but both were old enough to fight. Boswell also cites Zeno's advice that 'boy' lovers should be kept until they were in their late 20s, well after the age of manhood. More pointedly, he argues that Plato 'characterised same-sex unions very pointedly as permanent, exclusive unions of coevals'.[38]

Literary evidence is of course vulnerable to the implication that it is representation rather than practice. Boswell moves to safer ground when he cites actual examples of adult male relationships. For example, there was a rich Spartan literature on the advantages of having armies composed of lovers (all having achieved manhood), as this promoted loyalty, bravery and a willingness to avoid shaming loved ones. Although some historians now dispute the reality of the 'Sacred Band' of Thebes, a famous military troop of lovers who fought side by side, the rapid spread of the story, points to a utopian fantasy of erotic male bonding.[39] Boswell cites other famous relationships such as that between the Roman Emperor Hadrian and Antinous, which began as a pederastic encounter and lasted past the age of manhood for the Emperor's lover. Boswell's most original contribution, however, is his analysis of ceremonies to solemnize formal unions between adult same-sex couples (that is both men in full beard) in late antiquity. Male same-sex relationships, Boswell concludes, were both possible and acceptable.

Boswell's conclusions are controversial. In seeking to find close parallels in the Greco-Roman world to modern categories of sexual preference – heterosexual, homosexual and lesbian – he asserts the transhistorical nature of same-sex desire. His emphasis on adult male lovers (and to a lesser extent female lovers) certainly does indicate that ancient homosexuality was 'far more varied and flexible' than the focus on pederasty would suggest. But the attempt by scholars such as Boswell, Cohen and Thorp, to find ancient homosexuality has been contested by David Halperin, who argues that these historians have confused homosexuality with 'inversion'. For Halperin, the effeminate man, who cross-dressed or exhibited other signs of 'femaleness', was not a marker of homosexuality, but one of either passivity or heterosexual excess. For instance, the adulterer was often represented as effeminate. Thus Halperin argues that equating effeminacy with homosexuality is a mistake. While male inversion (men adopting feminine traits) was known in antiquity and the source of ridicule and legal sanction, modern homosexuality – the exclusive desire for men irrespective of whether one was active or passive – was unknown.[40] Similarly Craig Williams argues that masculinity in antiquity involved both the avoidance of effeminacy and the performance of the insertive role in the sex act. While there were certainly citizens who almost exclusively had sex with other men, the key division in antiquity was not homosexual and heterosexual but men and non-men.[41]

This debate over whether the male sexual cultures of antiquity contained a homosexual element has become a major source of contention within sexual history. In recent years much of the contest over the characterization of sexuality in antiquity has focused on subcultures of passive adult males in ancient Athens and Rome. For some historians, these groups parallel gay subcultures in early-modern and modern Europe and America. Moreover, the *kinaidoi* of Athens and *cinaedi* of Rome were the object of great opprobrium, amounting for some historians to homophobia. For Halperin, however, this search for modern parallels fails to see the profound differences between male passivity and contemporary homosexuality.

Passive Men

Passive, effeminate men offended the sexual and social codes of the Greco-Roman world. As we have seen, to be the recipient of male desire was a form of submission to male dominance, and thus required of wives, slaves, concubines, prostitutes and boys. Male citizens who submitted to the sexual will of another, even that of a male citizen, flouted the fundamental social and moral codes that sustained ancient masculinity, citizenship and social order. Similarly, in the literature on the body, effeminate men (those with insufficient heat to sustain masculinity) denoted a problem of 'lack', a deficiency in life force. They were inadequate and ill-equipped to take on the role of citizen. Within the cult of pederasty 'overly feminine boys were disdained'. A boy was beautiful because he 'manifested the acme of masculinity'.[42] Effeminacy challenged the fabric of the ancient social order and it is not surprising that there is a rich literature on its origins, dangers and consequences. Nonetheless, if Boswell's work on same-sex unions is taken seriously, there was clearly scope for men to blur the boundaries of masculine identity. But within the ancient texts there is a category of effeminate men singled out for their preference for being passive partners in erotic relationships – the *kinaidoi* in ancient Greece, and the *cinaedi* in the Roman world.

We must be careful, however, not to see all 'passive' men as belonging to the class of *kinaidoi* or *cinaedi*. Maud Gleason has shown that not all men who 'submitted' to the desire of another man fell into this class, including, for instance, warriors forced to submit after defeat. In a fascinating reading of ancient texts on physiognomy, Gleason has argued that some men who lived as full citizens, enjoying all the rights of citizenship, were thought to be feminine in disposition.[43] Their public deportment, attitudes and behaviour were sufficiently ambiguous for them to remain accepted within the boundaries of the citizen class. These texts, however, devoted considerable space to uncovering and specifying the signs of a particular group of passive men, the *androgynoi*. These men were characterized by softness, slack limbs, mincing steps, a shifting gaze, tilted heads, upturned palms and thin, shrill voices. They were seen to be a group whose gender was especially indeterminate, and easily distinguished from ordinary citizens. Although *cinaedi* literally meant sexual deviants rather than effeminate men, it became a synonym for *androgynoi*, and the typical signs of the *androgynoi* were those by which the *kinaidoi* and the *cinaedi* were recognized. In many contexts *cinaedus* was also used to mean loathsome, licentious and reprehensible. Male prostitutes were known as the *publici cinaedi*, but others were thought to be generally recognizable by their mannerisms and appearance. In particular they were said to suffer a disease or infirmity, something that could be caught either by contact with another *cinaedus*, touching certain magical statues or excessive indulgence.

Some historians have questioned whether the *cinaedi* or *kinaidoi* really existed, or were in fact rhetorical devices used to enforce codes of manly behaviour. Amy Richlin, however, has made an excellent case for seeing the *cinaedus* as a real figure, subject to ridicule, ostracism and legal sanction.[44] Through an engaging reading of a wide range of difficult legal, medical and literary sources, Richlin has mounted a strong case for the existence of a clearly defined and distinct subculture of effeminate men in the Roman world. They were widely recognized by their mannerisms, appearance and behaviour and were the subject of gossip, ridicule, abuse, rape and other harsh punishments. Richlin uses the concept of subculture to explore the sign systems through which people could be identified and punished. These sign systems also allowed effeminate men to bond together and forge a separate identity. By wearing women's clothes, talking and walking in particular ways, inhabiting particular spaces, through ceremonies and festive occasions, the *cinaedi* were able to come together as a community. In other words, Greco-Roman culture with its distinctive sexual regime aiming to produce masculine identity could also become the point for travesty, transgression and the making of other identities.

Richlin's case for the existence of a subculture of *cinaedi* is strong, but she draws some controversial conclusions on the basis of the evidence. Her aim is to draw parallels with modern homosexuality. For Richlin, the *cinaedi* form a distinct subculture or community based on a preference for passive homosexuality and were subject, as a consequence, to considerable persecution. By implication, the existence of a subculture of 'passive' men also meant a group of male citizens willing to engage as the active partner with the *cinaedi*, but this group escapes her attention. Although arguing that the term homosexuality cannot be applied to Greco-Roman culture without qualification, Richlin asserts that male same-sex relations were condemned (at least between two citizens) and those who chose passive sexuality can be termed homosexuals. This is largely because they were identified as a group and subject to a type of persecution similar to 'homophobia'.

Richlin rejects the Foucauldian claim that sexuality and homosexuality are modern terms that cannot be deployed to understand past societies, particularly Greco-Roman culture. In particular, she argues against the efforts of Halperin and Winkler to claim that there were no distinct sexual species or identities in antiquity. She uses the *cinaedi* to argue that, on the contrary, there were sexual subcultures with very specific identities and social codes, concluding that the qualified use of the concept of homosexuality for understanding Greco-Roman culture is relevant and illuminating. Richlin's interpretation stresses continuities rather than differences, allowing for a focus on social practices rather than discourse. She emphasizes this oppression and homophobia provides a direct homology for modern homosexuality. Implicitly Richlin suggests that desire transcended social construction. It was an essential force, with deep psychological or biological roots, which drove men to create an urban culture in defiance of the social forces shaping sexual practices.

David Halperin has vigorously contested Richlin's arguments.[45] First, he argues that Richlin has caricatured Foucault's theories, in an effort to make him an easy target. Halperin goes to some lengths to explain Foucault's distinctions between the sodomite and the homosexual and acts and sexuality, suggesting that Foucault used these distinctions to analyse modalities of power – the shift from law to normalization. He was not making 'an empirical claim about the historical existence or non-existence of sexually deviant individuals'. More importantly, Halperin argues forcefully for the necessity of distinguishing between the *cinaedi* and homosexuality. The *cinaedi* may have been repugnant and the object of punishment, but this was because they disturbed gender identities not because of the gender of their sexual partner. He points to the work of Gleason and Craig Williams, who contest the too easy association of *cinaedi* with passive homosexuality,[46] and concludes that

Richlin has largely resorted to 'superficial resemblances' to advance her case for continuity.

Halperin's argument has merit. His delineation of the specific context of Foucault's argument and the way that it has been 'misread' by many historians is well made. He might have gone even further. If we examine the second and third volumes of Foucault's *History of Sexuality*, there is a shift from power and knowledge to the formation of the subject. Foucault, in his last works, was very much alive to the problem of subjectivity, and how people made themselves subjects within distinct discursive formations.[47] So Foucault, contrary to Richlin's claims, did not make an artificial distinction between acts and subjectivities, or juridical subjects and the subjects of normalization. He was concerned very much with questions about the formation of the subject and identity (although he never uses the concept identity as such) across a broad span of time.

Moreover, Richlin's use of the term homophobia is troubling. Without qualification she equates the persecution of the *cinaedi* with antipathy to homosexuality in modern cultures. But many social groups throughout history have suffered persecution and we would not call these the result of homophobia. Richlin implies that it is homophobia in this instance, because the *cinaedi* are being punished because of their homosexuality. In effect, she has made her case by sleight of hand – the *cinaedi* are homosexuals because they suffer homophobia and it is homophobia because they are really homosexual. Despite the importance of the work she has done in recovering the history of this social group, Richlin's conclusions about homosexuality are rather forced and her critique of Foucault weak.

Rabun Taylor has attempted to redress some of these weaknesses. His interesting work on 'pathic subcultures' in ancient Rome insists, like Richlin, that homosexuality is an adequate term for understanding sexuality in antiquity. But Taylor moves beyond Richlin's focus on homophobia to make other analogies between modern and ancient homosexuality. He explores two 'pathic worlds'. The first is the fertility/mother Goddess religious cult of Galli, a small group of cross-dressing men who engaged in castration and devoted themselves to a cult of chastity. The second is the urban subculture of bathhouses, brothels and private houses, similar, Taylor suggests, to the 'molly houses' of the seventeenth century. In these places 'foppish' men, perfumed, brilliantly dressed and elaborately coiffed, formed their own urban subculture. These men, the *cinaedi*, enjoyed being penetrated.

Taylor develops the analysis of the *cinaedi* in two important ways. First, he demonstrates that these men were not exclusive in their sexual tastes. They were expected to, and did engage in penetration of women and men. Secondly, the existence of this world meant that men participated in it as both active and passive partners. Sometimes it was the older partner who took the passive role, at other times the younger. Thus, Taylor concludes, there was a world of reciprocal male relationships in ancient Rome, similar to the urban 'molly' subculture of early modern Europe.[48]

Halperin remains unconvinced. Although he has qualified his earlier antipathy to the idea of sexual subcultures in antiquity, he insists that what is at stake here is not sexuality, but gender inversion. His renewed interest in the nineteenth-century idea of 'inversion' is a way of analysing subcultures while insisting on historical difference. While homosexuality is recent, inversion has a longer history. What makes these ancient subcultures 'pathic' is not male love but the flouting of masculine codes of conduct. Halperin makes the vital point that within these subcultures the active partner is never the object of ridicule. What is most important in antiquity is the challenge to gender stereotypes. Thus seeing these subcultures as homosexual is not only anachronistic, it also distorts the real nature of the social pathology that concerned the ancients.[49]

Halperin's argument seems plausible when we look more closely at the sexual practices that were the subject of special sanction. We have already seen how passive male sex acts were the object of widespread anxiety and subject to harsh punishments in particular contexts (although in other contexts they were accepted). Two sexual practices in particular signified passivity – anal penetration and oral sex. Both acts were the subject of particular abhorrence in ancient Greece and Rome.[50] On the face of it there is no intrinsic reason why anal or oral sex should constitute passivity. And, of course, ancient authorities were not concerned with these acts in themselves, but the role of the man who was anally penetrated and the one who took the penis in his mouth. But even here the ascription of 'passivity' is far from clear cut – the man penetrated or the one performing fellatio might be as 'active', if not more so, than the partner in these acts. Passivity was a cultural not a natural fact.

What these cultural anxieties reveal is the centrality of the phallus to the framework of Greco-Roman sexual culture. Of course the phallus is a potent signifier in many (if not all) cultures. But the way the phallus functioned, the ways it structured sign systems and language, and regulated sexual customs and rules of conduct, has varied significantly. In ancient Greece and Rome what constituted activity was the use of the phallus. Not using the phallus in the sex act (putting aside, as ancient commentators did, arousal arising from being penetrated or performing fellatio) constituted passivity. This helps to explain that what concerned male citizens in Athens and Rome was not merely activity and passivity, because such concepts are inherently ambiguous, but the 'proper' use of the phallus.[51]

There is nothing unique in the cultural abhorrence of anal and oral sex. This is found in many times and places, and even heterosexual oral sex is still illegal in some American States. But to dwell on this longer history of sanctions against these two acts fails to do justice to the cultural specificity of the ways ancient Greek and Roman authorities understood these practices, and how they framed a larger Greco-Roman sexual culture. In the Christian West, even in the early part of the twenty-first century, anal and oral sex acts are seen by many church authorities to be 'against nature'. These are not acts for the purposes of procreation, and are thus the subject of religious, and in some cases, legal sanction. But for ancient Greeks and Romans civilization was an advance upon nature, and therefore what was best about ancient culture was the triumph over nature.[52] In this context sex acts which could not lead to conception were normal and acceptable. But sex acts in which men did not use their phallus in a direct and purposeful way, where the phallus was not penetrating some orifice, did transgress codes of sexual conduct. Such acts undermined the symbolic purpose of the sex act as an assertion of dominance and a signifier of citizenship.

In the context of these ancient phallic cultures, Richlin and Taylor's arguments about homosexuality gloss over key differences between antiquity and modernity. For Richlin, the effeminate *cinaedus* is similar to the modern homosexual, both the victim of homophobia. But here she puts terms together (passive and homosexual) from two very different sexual regimes and fails to see the significance of Gleason's distinction between the passive and the effeminate citizen. In modern Western cultures what is most troubling about homosexuality is the gender of the participants in the sex act, not what acts they perform (oral, anal, fetish, masochistic, sadistic and so on). Similarly it is irrelevant in modern culture whether one penetrates or is penetrated in the homosexual act. But these distinctions are crucial in ancient Athens and Rome. There the gender of the sexual partner is of less concern and the type of act of paramount importance. The differences, as Halperin argues, are important if we are to fully understand the sexual cultures of antiquity.

Conclusion

The debates about sex in ancient Greece and Rome raise vital questions about the history of sexuality. Should we focus on the evidence for the existence of such practices as same-sex unions in many times and cultures? Or should we be more concerned to place particular sex acts within their specific historical context, seeking out the particularities of meaning that informed and shaped sex acts in the past? Can we distinguish a time 'before sexuality' when Western culture was more concerned with sexual acts than identities? The debate about the *cinaedi*, effeminacy and pathic subcultures disrupts this simple dichotomy. What distinguishes the sexual regimes of classical antiquity from modernity is not an opposition between acts and sexualities, but the specific identities they produce. Modern sexual culture produces sexualities structured around the gender of the sexual partner one chooses as well as the acts one prefers. Greco-Roman sexual cultures, however, were intimately tied to a larger socio-political apparatus producing male citizens. The identity, power and dominance of citizens resided in the political, dynastic, social and economic order of ancient society. Sexual practices, however, were a key representational domain that functioned to signify dominance. Sex was an arena where citizens were required to perform their mastery. To perform something different risked opprobrium, ridicule and punishment.

The question for historians is whether analogies between past and present illuminate or distort the past. On balance the use of concepts of homosexuality to describe sexuality in antiquity obscure more than they reveal. The identities produced and the practices that were of most importance for the formation of the subject are fundamentally different in the ancient and modern worlds. We will return to a number of these themes and questions in later chapters. But if our concern is with the way sex acts functioned within particular sexual cultures and how those sexual cultures were tied to larger questions of identity, subjectivity and the self, it is important to spell out the distinctive features of Greco-Roman sexual life.

Chapter 3

SEXUAL AUSTERITY

According to the first-century BCE Roman geographer Strabo, the annual religious festival at Canopus in Roman Egypt was marked by singing, dancing, devotional duties and sexual licentiousness. There may have been many Greek and Roman philosophers, religious authorities and doctors who warned of the perils of sexual excess, counselling the virtues of moderation, but, as 'Canoptic life' suggested, religion and sexual licence were not entirely incompatible.[1] Four hundred years later Christianity had wrought a dramatic shift in the relationship between sex and religion. In the Eastern Church influential founders such as John Chrysostom preached an ideal of Heaven 'uninflamed by any lustfulness...[in which] there was no desire for sexual intercourse'. In the Western Church, St Augustine, one of Christianity's most important Fathers, preached the doctrine of 'original sin', clearly linking sex to 'man's' fall from grace. While St Augustine was prepared to sanction marriage as an acceptable relationship, sex within marriage was only permissible for the purposes of procreation.

St Augustine and other early Church Fathers struggled to overcome the clash between their belief in the necessity to transcend bodily desires and the need for sex to perpetuate the Christian flock. While affirming marriage they at the same time espoused chastity as the highest spiritual ideal. For St Augustine, a good Christian loved the 'woman that God created...while he hates the corruptible and mortal relationship and marital intercourse'. Early Church Fathers were troubled by the 'corruptions of the flesh' even within marriage, and promoted ideals of 'spiritual marriage' and transcendence of carnal cravings through sexual continence.[2]

Did the coming of the Christian era two thousand years ago usher in a new period of sexual austerity? Did the Christian emphasis on celibacy and sex within marriage represent a clear break with the pagan ethics of the 'uses of pleasure'? Common sense might suggest that

Christianity was a decisive rupture with the past, but scholars disagree over the differences between the pagan and Christian sexual cultures of late antiquity. While most accept that an emphasis on sexual fidelity and monogamy within marriage, and an idealization of chastity and sexual renunciation, marked the early centuries of the Christian era there is little agreement over the importance of Christianity in these shifts. Instead there has been a growing emphasis on the pagan origins of these new sexual ethics. Although many scholars argue that Christianity made a decisive contribution to reshaping the way sexual relations were understood, there is widespread agreement that the shift towards an ethics of austerity and fidelity began within pagan Rome. By the first century CE, the terms of what Foucault calls the 'moral problematisation of pleasures' had moved away from an interest in the regulation of pederasty and the 'proper' uses of slaves and concubines towards a concern with women, marriage and the self.[3]

Christianity and Sexuality

What effect did Christianity have on sexual practices? Historians of early Christianity have pointed to a heightened emphasis on monogamy, sexual fidelity within marriage and an idealization of chastity. Some have also charted deeper currents of profound distaste for sexuality, evident in widespread condemnations of women as the source of 'man's spiritual corruption'. St Paul crystallized many of these Christian sentiments regarding sex. For him 'it is good for a man not to touch a woman', but if men and women could not 'contain themselves, let them marry'.[4] Early Church Fathers forged a persistent opposition between a chaste elite whose chances of salvation were enhanced by renunciation, and the unruly laity whose desires could only be tamed by marriage.

Running through early Christian texts was a profound hostility towards sex, bodies and women, particularly sexually active and menstruating women. There was a long lineage of ambivalence about menstruating women in Western culture. In Hippocratic and Aristotelian texts menstrual blood was the origin of women's inferiority and difference to men, but there were no classical taboos against intercourse with a menstruating woman.[5] In contrast, some early Christians regarded intercourse with a menstruating wife as a mortal sin. Origen, a third-century CE Greek Church theologian, saw the body more generally as a 'fetter' or 'prison', a punishment for the fall from grace. More pointedly, he saw women as 'slaves to lust...worse than beasts', constantly threatening the continence of men.[6]

Christian perfection required the transcendence of the body, the will to move beyond material and earthly needs to higher spiritual aspirations. In its most extreme form, the desire to overcome the body could lead to extraordinary efforts of asceticism, and in a few instances self-mutilation and castration. In the third and fourth centuries CE a number of young Christians, notably St Anthony and John Climacus, retreated to the deserts of Egypt to wrestle with the temptations of the devil. Living on their own in caves for many years (St Anthony lived to be over 100 years old), fasting, sustained by food supplied by disciples, and preaching the virtues of a continent life, the Desert Fathers embodied a deeper struggle with the mysteries of the relationship between the body and the soul. For these men sexuality, as Peter Brown argues, was a privileged site for ascetic practice because it 'lurked with such baffling tenacity' within the body.[7]

Despite the ambivalence about female bodies, one of the attractions of early Christianity was that it provided 'new careers and avenues of patronage for women'. This may have contributed to the eventual conversion of the Roman aristocracy to Christianity.[8] As Elizabeth Clark has argued, alongside the Desert Fathers was a rigorous female tradition of ascetic renunciation. Melania the Elder and the Younger, Olympias, Paula and Demetrias, embraced asceticism just as vigorously as the Desert Fathers. Within Christianity women could be both the 'devil's gateway' and the 'bride of Christ'. The emergence of female monasteries where aristocratic women could retreat into a life of spiritual devotion and charity, freed women from the demands of domestic and familial roles and invested them with considerable political and spiritual power.

The growing religious influence of women in early Christianity disturbed Church leaders. Some viewed asceticism more generally with suspicion. More importantly, Church Fathers, such as St Augustine and John Chrysostom, struggled to reconcile female authority with their view that the role of woman was servitude. By the end of the fourth century CE Christian authorities were united in the view that women could not be teachers or priests and had to accept a subsidiary role within the Church. While religious life still held attractions for women their formal power was subsumed under the authority of a male hierarchy.[9]

Early Christians were not the only religious group profoundly ambivalent about sexuality. As pagan Roman culture and society unravelled, a number of sects and religious cults emerged incorporating elements of early Christianity, promising spiritual salvation, and seeking followers. Gnosticism, Manichaeanism, Encratites and numerous smaller sects challenged the evolving Christian church. Many early Christians, notably St Augustine, flirted with some of these other cults before finally committing to Christianity. Some historians have also argued that the pervasive Christian condemnations of sexuality and the body were founded less on the teachings of Christ than on efforts to compete with these rival religious sects.

The connections between Christian, Gnostic and Manichaean attitudes to the body and sex are obvious. For instance, many Gnostics,
such as Marcion and his followers, believed that nature was evil, and
so practised celibacy. Tatian, an Encratite teacher, thought that sexual
intercourse had been invented by the devil.[10] Even Judaic cults, such as
the Essenes, exerted a profound influence on both pagan and Christian
thinking. They rejected pleasure as evil and advocated continence.[11]
Like early Christianity, such cults accepted reluctantly the institution of
marriage but stressed that the highest form of marriage was 'spiritual',
freed from the necessity for intercourse.[12] Indeed there was considerable overlap between their attitudes to sex, marriage and the body and
those of Christians.

Numerous scholars have argued that similar attitudes were prevalent in classical and late antiquity amongst pagan philosophers. The
Stoic philosopher Seneca urged husbands to 'resist the onset of passion
and not be rashly impelled to the conjugal act'. Seneca also referred to
desire as 'the noxious breath of sensual pleasure'. Similarly, Pliny the
Elder 'commended the example of the elephant which mates only once
every two years'. Others, such as Cato and Laelius, paraded as virtues
the fact that they were virgins at marriage and remained faithful to
their wives. Such sentiments might be seen as part of a longer classical
tradition of moderation in sexual conduct. Other Roman philosophers,
however, strike a stronger chord with early Christianity. Apollonius of
Tyana (first century CE) 'took a vow of celibacy and kept it throughout
his life'.

Moreover, a number of early Christian theologians drew on pagan
ideas of late antiquity in order to develop Christian sexual ethics. Pliny
the Elder's praise of the chaste pachyderm was still cited as an authority by Christian theologians as late as the thirteenth century. Justin the
Martyr (c. 150 CE) drew on Stoics, such as Seneca, to argue for the virtue of continence and the need for marital fidelity. In the same vein
Clement of Alexandria, in his effort to outdo Gnostic denigration of
marriage, cited Stoic condemnation of indulgence 'in the pleasures of
love'.[13]

What then did mark out early Christian teachings on sex, marriage and the body from prevailing views in late antiquity? There is a
strong tradition of seeing Christian ideas as 'a revolution in sexual attitudes and practices'. Historians such as Elaine Pagels have stressed the
radical differences between Christians and pagans over sexuality. For
Pagels, the Christian emphasis on freedom and moral choice made sex
a sin and renunciation the means for freeing oneself from the world.
Christian authorities increasingly interpreted Genesis as a story about
disobedience and moral responsibility. While there were sharp theological disputes over the 'naturalness' of desire, the propagation of ideas

of original sin represented a means of freeing Christians from Roman culture.[14]

Although the deep differences between pagan and Christian teachings are widely acknowledged, some historians have sought to stress the continuities between Christianity and non-Christian teachings and their impact.[15] Medievalist John Boswell argues forcefully that Christianity 'had a less dramatic impact on modes of coupling than its leaders wished and its apologists (and critics) have pretended'. He concludes that many changes in regard to sexual and romantic relationships 'antedated or bore only incidental relationship to Christian teaching', suggesting that by the fourth century CE 'European society (whether pagan, Jewish or Christian) came to expect monogamy and sexual fidelity in marriage'. Moreover, Boswell argues that two of the most important influences on Christian antagonism to eroticism were Roman law and Rabbinic teaching.[16]

Although Boswell questions the extent of fundamental change in the character of marital unions and the singular importance of Christianity in refashioning social and sexual behaviour, he does highlight some important transformations in attitudes and legal procedures for the regulation of sex. The most significant was the profound devaluation of marriage. Although early Church Fathers supported the institution of marriage, urging monogamy and fidelity, it was also apparent that marriage represented a flawed compromise with the material world of the flesh. A fervent embrace of Christian principles required a renunciation of human pleasures and material needs for the greater goal of spiritual transformation and salvation after death. Hand in hand with the denigration of marriage was a growing suspicion of eroticism, evident in the disappearance of passionate, sexual love from Latin *belles lettres* after the fourth century CE.[17]

Boswell is clearly wrestling with the familiar problems of continuity and discontinuity in historical explanation. What persisted in European culture in the early Christian era? What changed? And what were the causes and consequences of shifts in attitudes to marriage and eroticism? His resolution of some of these problems has to be seen in the context of his wider project on same-sex unions. In his two major works, *Christianity, Social Tolerance and Homosexuality* (1980) and *Same-Sex Unions in Pre-Modern Europe* (1994), Boswell uncovers evidence of the acceptance of 'gay' subcultures in Europe since antiquity. As we saw in the previous chapter, one of Boswell's targets was the prevailing view that pederasty was accepted in antiquity, while relationships between adult men were condemned. His more important target, however, was the idea that Christianity ushered in an age of intolerance towards emotional and erotic relationships between men. For Boswell there was a profound transformation in sexual ethics in antiquity, but this rupture was apparent long before Christianity had a significant impact on Roman culture.

In charting tolerance of homosexuality Boswell seeks to problematize modern accounts of homosexuality as unnatural and deviant, especially those based on religious authority. In his second major work in particular, Boswell argues that the Christian Church accepted same-sex relationships and even had ceremonies paralleling and largely replicating marriage services solemnizing unions of adult men. Moreover, some of these male unions, notably that between the late-third and early-fourth century Christian martyrs Serge and Bacchus found a secure place within Christianity. These two martyrs were Roman soldiers of high standing who shared a household. They were executed for their religious beliefs and subsequently recognized in Christian iconography as the classic paired saints. Traditionally these saints have been seen as part of a larger group of soldier martyrs, men who turned to Christ after a life of war. Boswell, however, teases out ambiguities in the masculine representations of these men, hinting at sexual undertones overlooked by earlier commentators. More importantly, he argues that the story of Serge and Bacchus was frequently invoked in religious ceremonies celebrating male unions. Thus Boswell attempts to demonstrate that there was a recognizable group of adult male homosexuals whose presence was acknowledged and accepted in the early Christian era.

Despite his awareness of the elements of change in theological and philosophical teachings on ethics, sex, and institutions such as marriage, Boswell's central focus is on continuity in the structure of emotional relationships during the first millennium. In the previous chapter we explored some criticisms of his interpretation of male relationships in classical and late antiquity and in the next chapter we will examine more closely some of the conceptual problems of his analysis of subcultures and tolerance. Nonetheless, Boswell's rigorous exegesis of difficult and obscure sources has opened up important dimensions into the history of same-sex relationships. His analysis of male same-sex unions is central to his wider argument about continuities in Western sexual mores across the first millennium. Like other scholars he has mounted a convincing case for tracing many aspects of early Christian ethics and theology to their roots in pagan culture.

Boswell argues that an ethic of sexual austerity first began to emerge within pagan culture. Its immediate cause was the declining birth rate amongst the Roman elite. Thus there was an increasing emphasis on marital unions and procreation within Roman law and a tightening of regulations governing divorce. These principles governed early Christian understandings of marriage, creating a sharp tension in Christian theology. On the one hand, the prevailing readings of the teaching of Christ, reinforced by the persistent strand of asceticism in Greek and

Roman elite culture, situated celibacy, virginity and renunciation as the highest ideals. On the other hand, Church Fathers sought to work within existing Roman cultures adopting their growing emphasis on key institutions such as marriage. Paradoxically Christian theology came to both promote marriage and denigrate it, seeing marriage as the desirable option for the laity, but celibacy as the course for those with a higher spiritual calling within the Church.

Another historian who has focused on continuities between pagan and Christian culture is Bernadette Brooten. Her path-breaking study of female homoeroticism has some striking parallels with the work of Boswell.[18] Both seek to recover a history of same-sex relationships and see Christian ethics as an extension of pagan attitudes. But Brooten takes issue with Boswell for his gender blindness. Although Boswell purports to be analysing same-sex relationships more generally, his focus is almost exclusively male homoeroticism. For Brooten, female homoeroticism cannot be collapsed into a history of male same-sex relationships because attitudes to love between women were decidedly different to that between men. Where Boswell charts an acceptance of male same-sex unions within pagan and early Christian culture, Brooten highlights the persistent antipathy to love between women. Contrary to the view that the popularity in late antiquity of the writings of Greek poet Sappho (seventh century BCE) signalled a tolerance of female homoeroticism, Brooten demonstrates that Roman commentators used this literature to define female deviancy. In the hands of such commentators it confirmed prejudices against love between women.

Brooten draws on an extraordinarily wide range of obscure texts often overlooked by other scholars – a rich literature on magic, astrology, dreams, physiognomy and medicine. She documents a long history of fear and anxiety about sexual relations between women and demonstrates that female homoeroticism was widely known and discussed. There was no acceptance or toleration of this practice, suggesting that the history of lesbianism might move to a very different chronology than that of male homoeroticism. For Brooten, there were fewer turning points in the history of female homoeroticism because of the persistent structures of male domination. Love between women challenged the phallocentric cultures of pagan and Christian antiquity, and the response to this challenge has shaped the historical experience of lesbians ever since. In the hands of influential Church Fathers, such as St Paul, longstanding antagonism and fear of female homoeroticism found a very secure and continuing place within Christian doctrine.

Despite Brooten's critique of Boswell they share some common ground. Brooten situates her work within the tradition of lesbian history just as Boswell identifies as a gay historian. But the affinities are deeper than this. Brooten uncovers a rich terminology condemning female homoeroticism. Words such as *tribas*, *virago*, *frictrix* and *lesbia*, served to represent the mannish, sexually aggressive, active woman as an object to be feared. Indeed some evidence suggests that clitoridectomies were performed on such women. Like Boswell, and other scholars such as Amy Richlin, Brooten argues that a lively subculture of homoerotically inclined people existed in antiquity. The members of this subculture were identified by habits of speech, clothing and behaviour that marked them out and made them subject to ridicule and punishment. In other words, there were specific social identities based on sexual orientation in antiquity – *cinaedus* for men and *frictrix* or *tribas* for women. Moreover, she explores how these identities were medicalized within ancient discourses. Thus Brooten takes issue with the Foucauldian tradition that sees sexual identities as a recent phenomenon.[19]

Foucauldian historicists, such as David Halperin, have contested these claims. In a searching critique of Brooten, reminiscent of many of his commentaries on Boswell and Richlin, Halperin has challenged the idea that these subcultures constituted a sexual identity in the modern sense.[20] Although Halperin warmly endorses Brooten's argument that lesbian history moves to a very different rhythm to that of homosexuality, he characterizes her project as an attempt to uncover the 'real' lesbian identity behind the distinctive cultural forms of antiquity. So, although Brooten points to the differences between the sexual identities of antiquity and modernity, these differences are the superficial overlay of history and culture on the continuous culture of female homoeroticism. In other words, Halperin condemns Brooten for using an ahistorical concept of lesbianism. This is too harsh. Elsewhere Brooten clearly indicates that she is using this concept in a very specific sense, relevant to the context of antiquity, defining lesbian in the medieval sense to mean a woman who 'behaves like a man' not in the modern sense of women who love each other.[21]

Brooten's definition, however, highlights an important slippage in her argument. In some contexts she implies a continuous link between the *tribas* of antiquity and the lesbians of the late-twentieth century. They are all part of a lesbian continuum. At other times Brooten seeks to identify the differences between the discourse on female homoeroticism in antiquity from that of the present day. This is where Halperin's argument carries some weight. What most concerned the ancients was not the sexuality of the *tribades* but their challenge to gender stereotypes. Although there was some ambiguity, as Brooten shows, about whether tribadism encompassed both the active and the passive partner, in the vast majority of texts it is the 'mannish' *virago* that is the source of concern. Thus what is at stake in antiquity for Halperin is not sexuality but gender.[22]

Both Boswell and Brooten, however, provide illuminating accounts of the continuities in sexual morality and practice in classical and late antiq-

uity. In opening up important questions about male same-sex unions and
the ways in which such unions found a place in early Christian theology
Boswell represents a fundamental challenge to contemporary Christian
condemnations of homosexuality. Similarly, Brooten's documentation of
a persistent Christian condemnation of female homoeroticism provides
important insights into how Church teachings have been fundamental in suppressing love between women across two millennia. Nonetheless, the stress of both Boswell and Brooten on continuities in attitudes
blinds them to some of the deeper shifts in the way sex was understood
and practised. In contrast, other historians, notably Michel Foucault and
Peter Brown, have stressed the profound transformations in sexual ethics in antiquity and the early Christian era. They have concentrated on
the 'tectonic' shifts from classical antiquity to the early Christian era in
sexual culture, society, ethics and the cultivation of the self.

A New Sexual Ethics

In his two final volumes of his *History of Sexuality* project, Michel
Foucault focused on the problem of pleasure and the self in classical
antiquity. In developing the problem of how modern individuals came
to recognize themselves as subjects of sexuality, Foucault argued that he
felt obliged to first chart the longer genealogy of the desiring subject
and its relationship to the truth of being.[23] This led him to a concern
with key moments in the formation of these problems for Western culture: classical Greece from the fourth century BCE and pagan Rome in
the first centuries after Christ. A further volume on developments after
the third century CE in the early Christian era, the focus of this chapter,
remains unpublished but there are sufficient clues in his other books
and essays for us to glimpse the direction of his history of the desiring
subject.[24]

Some of Foucault's critics have dismissed him as an historian of discontinuity, implying that the concentration on the specificity of past
cultures is more political than scholarly. In their view, the focus on discontinuity raises questions about the accuracy of his account.[25] This
is an overly simplistic reading. One of Foucault's central concerns was
certainly to disrupt Whiggish historical narratives of progress. In his
early studies of madness, the clinic, economics, grammar, biology and
the prison, Foucault concentrated on a few decades at the end of the
eighteenth and beginning of the nineteenth centuries as moments of
profound rupture in the organization of knowledge and power. In contrast Foucault's analysis of the desiring subject in antiquity moves away
from the notion of rupture. Like many historians of this period Foucault
sees deep affinities between the ideas of early Christian theologians and
pagan philosophers, doctors and political thinkers.

Indeed he goes further than many. Where Boswell traces connections between Roman and Christian thought in antiquity, Foucault points to a longer tradition of concern with asceticism, sexual austerity and moderation stretching back to classical Greece. Throughout antiquity, he argues, 'the sexual act was seen as difficult to master'. This appears to be a disavowal of his early concern with discontinuity, but appearances can be deceiving. While the questions of austerity and the enjoyment of pleasures were ones of long duration, the problems around which they clustered shifted slowly but significantly over the 600 years from the fourth century BCE to the second century CE. In classical Greece the 'moral problematization of pleasures' was most intensely focused on the relationship with boys. By the early centuries after Christ the point of greatest moral reflection was on sexual relations between men and women. What emerged was a 'profoundly altered ethics and a different form of constituting oneself as an ethical subject of one's sexual behaviour'.[26]

Foucault accepts that the ideal of austerity has a long history but resists the temptation to see the origins of Roman ethics in the teachings of classical philosophers such as Plato and Aristotle. In part this is because Foucault shifts our attention away from the exemplary philosophical texts of antiquity, focusing instead on obscure medical, dietetic and health tracts, studies of dreams and guides for daily conduct. Through these sources he charts a profound shift in emphasis. The ideal of austerity was highly prized, particularly in relation to the love of boys. A key signifier of the integrity and spiritual nature of the male citizen's desire and his mastery over the body was the capacity to exercise restraint. The domain where these strictures were most forcefully debated in classical Greece was in relation to boys. But in the century before the birth of Christ, Foucault argues that there was a growing apprehension about the bodily effects of sexual desire. Increasingly, sex was associated not just with the problem of mastering desire or justly asserting one's status over others, but with pervasive problems of evil and disease. Sex itself came to be seen as a potentially dangerous imperfection and the individual a frail object subject to ills associated with sexual activity.

In this context there was an increasing focus on renunciation and the need to ground gratification in the 'laws of nature' rather than the dictates of civilization. The heightened fears and concerns about the potential evil effects of sex went hand in hand with a greater valorization of marriage as an institution that fostered moderation. Foucault charts a growing emphasis on the ideal of 'reciprocal marriage'. This is an argument that has been developed by a number of historians of the Roman family. Richard Saller and Susan Treggiari, in particular, argue that companionate marriage was the norm amongst the Roman elite by the last

century of the republic.[27] Historians, such as Cantarella, who maintain
that the Roman family remained a 'unit under the strong, authoritarian power of a paterfamilias', have challenged this conclusion.[28] Others
have questioned the 'valorization of the conjugal bond', pointing to the
coexistence of traditional views of marriage as a hierarchal relationship
of authority, with the new emphasis on marriage as a partnership.[29]

This is an important area of debate. Whether the family by the end
of the republic was less authoritarian than formerly is an important
issue in understanding conjugal sexuality in late antiquity. But even if
the family remained largely under the domination of the paterfamilias,
there was clearly a growing interest in marriage as the most appropriate institution for the governance of male desire. As we have seen there
was a strong antipathy in Roman culture to pederasty, and relations
with the sons of citizens was strictly forbidden. But sexual licence with
boyish slaves and prostitutes was acceptable. Ideologies of Roman manhood encouraged citizens to take on many lovers of either sex as long as
they were the dominant, masculine instigators.[30] Moreover, Cantarella
argues that in the first centuries CE there was an increase in citizens
openly flaunting their preference for being penetrated.[31]

In the context of a declining birth rate amongst the elite and increasing social mobility of those outside the elite, the growth of licentiousness
and unmanly effeminacy was a social threat. One response was a growing insistence from the beginning of the Roman Empire on the importance of the marriage bond and the desirability of privileging marital
sex. For example, the Emperor Augustus, in a wide-ranging series of
marriage laws, sought to encourage marriage amongst members of the
elite and he conferred greater legal standing on those women who produced more than three children.[32]

These shifts in the significance and meaning of sex, according to
Foucault, constituted a broader reorganization of the relationship of the
citizen to the self. In classical antiquity, as we have seen, sex was a means
by which citizens signified their dominant social status, and this dominance had to be tempered by moderation, justice and higher moral values. Gradually, however, alongside an ethics of deportment in matters
of sex, there was a growth in the literature on the ill-effects of sexual
indulgence. This required the development of what Foucault calls an
'art of existence dominated by self-preoccupation'. This meant a growing emphasis on self-control, a greater concentration on the self and
the relationship of one's self to others, a closer scrutiny of the body and
the effects of sex on its functioning and more active attention to sexual practice itself. Inquiry and vigilance became the hallmarks of new
forms of scrutiny of the self.

Foucault also alludes to a further, profound shift in moral systems
associated with Christianity, which instituted a new 'modality' in the

relationship of the self. The precise nature of this further shift remains unclear, as the proposed fourth volume of Foucault's history remains unpublished. But we can glimpse some of its dimensions in his comments on the new forms of self-scrutiny available through techniques such as confession. Confession was a new technology that served to formalize a relationship to the self (speaking about one's failings and offering to atone for them), but it also invested authority over the self to a particular force, the confessor. Instead of merely monitoring one's own spiritual and ethical progress the Church became the arbiter of each individual's success and failure. For the Church, the issue of most intense concern was the functioning of the marital relationship: the extent to which it was 'spiritual', how it operated within specified limits of tolerance and how one might transcend the temptations of the flesh.[33]

Another historian who also sees a significant shift in ethics, and understandings of sex and the body is Peter Brown. His focus is more firmly on the nature of early Christianity. Brown, in his path-breaking study of sexual renunciation accepts that many of the essential elements of early Christian ethics, notably sexual austerity and renunciation, had their origins in classical Greek philosophies of the dualism of mind and body. But equally, like his friend and colleague Foucault, he is insistent that there were marked shifts in the understanding of sex and its relationship to the body and society in the early Christian era. Where Foucault saw a slow but profound shift in the evolution of a particular style of relationship to the self, Brown highlights the confusion and conflict over the role of sexual renunciation in early Christianity. For Brown, sexual renunciation as an ideal of Christian life only came into being in 'fits and starts'. It was an object of dispute between different Christian sects.

Brown traces these conflicts across the early Christian world, from Ireland to the Euphrates, in the Western and Eastern Churches, in ascetic sects and those who opposed asceticism, and in the myriad movements such as Gnosticism and Manichaeanism that competed with Christianity. He recovers marked divergences over the value of asceticism, virginity, the extent of pollution due to menstruation, and the relationship between a celibate hierarchy and the laity condemned to the sins of the flesh.[34] The dynamic nature of this account highlights some of the strengths and weaknesses of Foucault's genealogical methodology. In seeking to trace the lineage of the present in the past, Foucault charts the evolution of modalities of power and ruptures which transform them in fundamental ways. His focus is on the ways particular modes of power come into being, and the forms of domination and subjection that they institute. But those movements and ideas outside of lines of descent fall by the wayside. Brown, however, finds a place for a huge variety of ideas and practices, reconstituting a more complex and contingent past.

Early Christianity, argues Brown, was rooted in a profound unease about 'the present age'. Although Christians shared many of the prevailing pagan social codes of continence and austerity, they also developed a radical critique of classical culture. In imagining a world beyond the material one of the present, where final absolution, forgiveness and fulfilment would be achieved, Christians were able to alter in profound ways the cultural baggage they inherited from the world of classical and late antiquity. Thus Brown points to fundamental shifts in the meaning and significance of sexuality in the early Christian era. He identifies three major pressures which shaped the landscape of early Christianity: the tendency to treat 'sexuality as a privileged ideogram of all that was most reducible in the human will'; the tendency to 'herald sexual renunciation as a privileged emblem of human freedom'; and the tendency to 'regard the body itself, by reason of its sexual components, as a highly charged locus of choice, of admiration in its virgin state and of avoidance in its sexually active state'.[35]

Although early Christians drew on the writings of pagan philosophers, doctors and political thinkers, they transformed these ideas in fundamental ways. In the pagan world the body and sex had been natural things that had to be mastered. Sexual urges were accepted as ever present, things that needed to be controlled, regulated and subjected to techniques for their appropriate use. Thus the body and desire were incorporated into a wider domain of moral reflection. Christianity, however, prised the self from the physical world, making the body and sexuality something to overcome. The ways in which the body could subvert the will, and the intractability of sexual urges manifest in the body, were signs of evil, of man's fall from grace. Sexuality became the site of human bondage; renunciation was the key to liberation.

Although asceticism and renunciation were highly valued practices in the ancient world, Christianity gave them new meaning. Where renunciation had once been a means to exemplify one's mastery, one's superior status as a citizen and hence one's claim to be a citizen of the city, it now came to be a means of breaking away from the solidarities of the old city. Christians imagined new forms of freedom and association that transcended the material city, creating more abstract and complex entities such as the Church, the Christian community and the City of God. Christians may have developed an uneasy accommodation to the civic spaces of pagan cities, adapting, defending and transforming them, but at the same time they envisaged something beyond the present and the material world.[36]

Christians were now at war with the body and sexuality; these were aspects of the self to defeat in order to return to God's grace. Thus Christian theologians devoted considerable energy and enterprise to deciphering the signs of desire, rooting out its symptoms in order to engage with the enemy and overcome it. In very interesting readings of the writings of St Augustine, historians such as Erin Sawyer and Kim Power have mapped how the Church Fathers developed an ascetic vision of Christian manhood in which women were seen as corrupting, fleshy and polluting. In contrast, men embodied the will to transcend feminizing desire. St Augustine evoked 'powerful sexual images, metaphors, and memories in order to test the strength of the will's power to overcome and subdue errant desires'. But by intertwining pleasure and renunciation St Augustine intensified the desires and fragmentations he sought to overcome. His efforts to defeat sexuality were caught in a narrative that in fact produced desire. Christian writers like St Augustine, argues Sawyer, helped to place desire, sex and the body at the centre of the moral universe, evoking desire in the process of attempting to overcome it.[37]

Conclusion

Christian ideals of virginity, chastity and austerity seeped slowly into the wider culture of late antiquity. Such ideas fell on fertile soil. The theme of austerity, in particular, had wider resonance and a considerable lineage in the pagan cultures of classical and late antiquity. On balance, the historians of rupture between pagan and Christian sexual ethics, such as Foucault, Pagels and Brown, seem to be on firmer ground than historians of continuity in the early Christian era, such as Boswell and Brooten. Early Christianity was divided by a momentous fissure: between an acceptance of prevailing non-Christian sexual and marriage customs and a new desire to entirely abandon the world of the flesh. Many early Christian Fathers accepted that renunciation could only be the choice of the few who devoted themselves to God. The majority of Christians would continue to live in this world, embroiled in relationships that hindered their hopes of salvation in the next life.

Thus the early Christian Church was remarkably tolerant of the social and sexual arrangements of the laity. Although the Church valued marriages based on fidelity, it accepted other common arrangements such as concubinage. When Augustine sought to marry into the Milanese Catholic elite his concubine returned to Africa and could claim the protection of the Christian community there as a 'voluntary widow'.[38] To climb up the Church hierarchy, however, Augustine had to pledge himself to a life of sexual continence. Thus the Church accepted many pagan cultural and sexual practices, while at the same time preaching the virtues of a radically austere alternative.

This simultaneous working within and working against prevailing practices opened up the Church to ridicule. In the fifth century, for example, the fertility cult festivities of the Lupercalia 'were enlivened by ditties on the adulteries of the Roman clergy'.[39] One question that has engaged some historians is whether Christianity succeeded in transforming the sexual habits and practices of social groups outside the Church hierarchy. Although Christianity was built on pagan foundations, the Church preached the virtues of fidelity, continence and renunciation with greater intensity than most pagan philosophers. How effective were such teachings in changing the sexual and social customs of the wider population?

John Boswell was sceptical of the impact of Church teachings on people outside the hierarchy. He carefully distinguishes between ideas and practices. Although he is alive to the significant changes in laws and ideas, for Boswell key features of pagan and Christian ethics did not affect the conduct of sex amongst the majority of people in the pagan world. Despite Christian asceticism and the Roman emphasis on sexual fidelity, 'divorce and remarriage, concubinage, and even prostitution remained common in Christian Europe throughout the Middle Ages'.[40] In a striking allusion he argues that Christian attitudes and practices 'resembled the rain in Mediterranean cities that fell on the population, ran off, and was redistributed to most through the artefacts of civilization', most importantly through the law courts.[41] Thus there was a slow evolution towards Christian morality, but it took nearly a millennium to embed itself in European culture.

The Church could, through the pulpit, the confessional and canon law, exert some influence on the habits and practices of the Christian laity. While concubinage and prostitution persisted, the Church insisted that marriage was the only acceptable relationship for sexual conduct. Open flouting of Christian morality was really only an option for the social elite of Christian Europe. Even the elite, however, had to acknowledge Christian teaching and submit to the ministrations of the Church. Priests devoted considerable attention to monitoring and regulating sexual practices within marriage, frowning on all those that did not lead to procreation. Sexual practices purely for personal satisfaction, and the delight in pleasure for pleasure's sake, were seen as abuses of marriage.[42]

The exact spread and impact of these teachings is difficult to determine. Some historians, however, have sought to gauge the spread of Christian practices. Of course there is a paucity of sources on the sexual lives and customs of the vast bulk of people in late antiquity and the Middle Ages. Although some scholars have asserted that the early Church was able to 'assert its own control over family, faith and morals', through an educational campaign based on teachings and fear, the evidence for such a claim is by no means clear.[43] Birth rate evidence provides another avenue for investigation. Detailed demographic modelling by Jean-Louis

Flandrin suggests that there was a marked decline in the European population from 500 to 1050. As James Brundage has argued, it 'might be reasonable to infer' that Church regulations and penitential prescriptions against sex within and outside marriage 'may have been in part responsible' for this decline in population. Such a conclusion, however, is based on the coincidence of the spread of Christianity and the decline in population. The inference is perhaps further strengthened by the rise in population after 1050, at a time when the Church's rulings on marital sexual practices became more liberal. Nonetheless, 'since we cannot say with any certainty what proportion of the population is likely to have followed' Church law and teachings the 'relationship, if any, between the penitential rules on marital abstinence and population changes remains uncertain'.[44]

Nonetheless, it is clear that after a millennium the Church had emerged as a major social and cultural institution, framing and shaping the lives of most Christians and thus the culture of most of Europe. The extent to which Church teachings transformed the sexual practices of Christians, however, is more ambiguous, as we shall see in later chapters. But, in placing sex at the centre of the struggle for God's grace, Christian theologians made sexual conduct more than something to utilize for pleasure and something to master to assert one's social status. For the citizens of classical antiquity, sex was just one arena for self-mastery. For the Church, however, sex became something at the very core of being, to be overcome in the search for a higher existence. Ironically, by seeking to overcome the earthly pleasures of the flesh, early Christians placed sex at the very heart of their reflection on the nature of humanity.

Chapter 4

CHRISTIAN FRIENDSHIPS

By the end of the first millennium the Christian Church was firmly established as the dominant religious institution in the West. No longer vying with paganism for the affections of the majority, the Roman Church, until the Reformation, provided the framework in which European peoples understood their place in the cosmos, their relationship to God, their chances for salvation, and the modes of conduct for a Christian life. The Church was not only a vehicle for the elaboration and propagation of Christian theology; it was also a powerful and extensive network of institutions that was a central force in European society and politics. Although an essentially hierarchical institutional system, with the Pope at its apex, the Roman Church through its monasteries, bishops, local churches, nuns and priests worked its way into the fabric of everyday life. The Council of Trent (1545–63) gave an even stronger hand to the Church to more closely regulate marriage and the family. The Church may have had unrivalled religious authority but it was anxious to maintain its supremacy by suppressing heresy and witchcraft, even to the point of burning the eccentric sixteenth-century Italian miller Menocchio, whose radical cosmology involved a metaphor of cheese and worms to explain the chaos of existence.[1]

Although in many areas pre-Christian ideas, customs and rituals survived, through its teachings, canon law, confession and penitentials, the Church exerted enormous influence over marriage, the body and sexual practices. The linking of sex, flesh and the body with sin, cemented in the early Christian era, became the dominant framework in which sex was understood. Sex was something to be renounced, a manifestation of sin, and a hindrance to be overcome in the search for spiritual salvation. Monastic and ascetic practices served to demarcate a religious elect whose path to salvation was smoothed, from a laity condemned to the temptations of the flesh. But even for those unable to escape the bonds of the flesh, there were powerful strictures governing marital sexual relations that helped to demarcate 'unnatural' and 'natural' sex acts. This distinction became an important point of contest in the government of sexuality for the next millennium.[2] Increasingly Church teachings came 'to reify binaries such as clerical/lay, celibate/married, male/female' in its campaigns to eradicate sin.[3] In this context women were idolized as the 'Virgin Mary' or condemned as the vehicle through which the devil corrupted men.[4] In the place of marriage and family Church Fathers from the fourth century came to prize an ideal of Christian friendship to cement bonds between men.[5]

Historians like John Boswell have argued that it took nearly a millennium for Christian teaching to penetrate all levels of European society and culture, but once Christianity was firmly established two key questions confront historians of sexuality.[6] First, did Christianity provide new discourses and practices that went beyond denial to shape forms of erotic experience? Historical work on medieval spirituality highlights a strong tradition of ecstatic experience amongst men and women in enclosed orders. Secondly, we have to ask whether Christianity had a marked effect on sexual practices outside of religious institutions.

Although there were powerful religious strictures on certain sexual practices there were also vibrant popular, medical and scientific literatures that offered an alternative framework for understanding sex. This literature advised on sexual techniques, identified common sexual diseases and provided a wider framework for understanding the body and gender. There was also a rich romance literature on pleasure, courtship, unrequited love and desire in medieval and Renaissance Europe. The Church was not the only authority that Europeans turned to for their knowledge of sex. Finally, a range of evidence points to continuing practices of licentiousness, especially in aristocratic and court circles. More surprisingly, legal evidence suggests that an older culture of pederasty, shaped by ideals of active and passive masculinity, was still prevalent in Renaissance Europe. In other words, sexual discourses and customs from classical antiquity may have persisted despite Church teachings. Far from Christianity destroying older sexual traditions, a range of sexual practices and cultures continued to thrive.

The Fear of Bodies

The Christian fear that bodily pleasures were the means by which the devil corrupted the soul impelled the early Church Fathers to advocate sexual renunciation. Women were a source of pollution. A rigorous policing of the self was needed to diagnose the signs and symptoms of sin. And practices of penance, prayer and asceticism were developed to purge the body and the soul of temptation. There was a rich theological tradition spelling out the dangers of the flesh and the importance of renunciation. But, as we have seen, renunciation was the path for an elect few, the Church believing most Christians faced a future enmeshed in the temptations of the flesh. These attitudes hardened in the Middle Ages. The Gregorian reforms of the eleventh century finally outlawed married clergy and dissolved double monasteries. At the same time women's monasteries were enclosed. New inquisitorial procedures were developed to root out heresy and occult practices. These reforms aimed to create a distinct difference between the Church and the laity, cementing Church authority. The elect were there to guide and punish. The laity were advised to channel their carnal desires into marriages, which ideally calmed and tamed lust. Despite this, the pollution of sexual bodies was something to be feared even in lay marriages. Spiritual or celibate marriages were highly praised.[7]

Christian friendship, celibacy and spiritual marriages were not easy choices. Priests, nuns and the Church had to be vigilant to maintain these ideals in practice. What developed was a rich theological literature on sex, bodies, the devil and sin. Largely inspired by St Augustine and St Jerome, Church texts also elaborated on the diversity of 'unnatural' practices that good Christians should avoid. Major medieval theologians, such as St Thomas Aquinas, went to great lengths to spell out the nature of vice. For Aquinas, women were more prone to sexual lust and less subject to reason. Their role was procreation within marriage. Men had to overcome the temptations of sex – it was sinful, irrational and dangerous to both the spirit and body. Worse were unnatural practices. In his *Summa Theologiae* (1273) he identified four classes of unnatural vice: masturbation, bestiality, coitus in an unnatural position and copulation with the same sex.[8]

Unlike pagan texts of classical antiquity which favoured sexual practices which were not found 'in nature' as evidence that civilization was higher than nature, by the end of the Roman republic Latin medical and ethical texts were turning to nature as the test for what was appropriate. Of course, what constituted 'natural' and which behaviours amongst animals were considered a model for human conduct was the source of intense debate. For example, the first-century CE philosopher Plutarch claimed that there was no same-sex mating among animals, while his contemporary Pliny the Elder described such practices amongst doves, hens, partridges, geese and ducks.[9] Despite the potential for confusion and dispute, Christian theology relied heavily on the trope of 'nature' to ground its concern with sexual practices. Those that could not be found in the natural world (amongst animals) were deemed unnatural and particularly sinful. Ideas of sins 'against nature' were important instruments for enforcing Church doctrines. But there was a tension in the deployment of this discourse on nature. On the one hand, nature was the measure of what was an acceptable practice. On the other hand, the aim of Christian practice was to transcend nature in order to purify the soul.[10]

The transmission of theology and church doctrine to the laity was a complex process. Distinctive practices, most notably the confession, evolved to assist the Church in the government of sin. From the sixth century penitentials, or confessional handbooks, originating in Ireland but then spreading to the rest of Europe, advised priests on how to uncover and decipher the signs of sin in the statements of those who came to confession. Penitential books proliferated in medieval and Renaissance Europe, spelling out an elaborate array of 'unnatural' acts, drawn largely from theological *Summae*. These penitentials dealt with many things other than sex, such as theft, perjury and homicide. But there was a rich sexual vocabulary in the penitentials dealing with problems such as fornication, adultery, use of aphrodisiacs, masturbation, incest, rape, nocturnal pollution and sodomy. The language of the penitentials was saturated in morally and emotionally loaded terms, even for sexual relations between husbands and wives. These texts, according to Pierre Payer, represented a 'strenuous combat against urges and forces in human nature'.[11]

The ideal of renunciation found its home in retreat from the world of the flesh. Asceticism flourished in the monasteries and nunneries for those who chose life in a religious order. These were places for devotion and the pursuit of spiritual salvation free from the mundane world of family and marriage. The Gregorian reforms of the eleventh century and the decree of Pope Boniface VIII (1298) enforcing the perpetual cloistering of nuns heightened the distance between religious institutions and society. Despite the idealization of religious retreat and asceticism, priests and nuns were subject to a rich literature of ridicule, satire and sexual innuendo that continued down to the Enlightenment. These texts often depicted monasteries and nunneries as places of sexual licence, debauchery and sin. The Lollard tracts in fourteenth-century England, for example, associated sodomy with the clerisy.[12] The reality was often far from the world of imagination, but nonetheless the enclosed world of religious orders did offer opportunities for sexual contacts. The intense and intimate nature of religious life held perils for those seeking salvation, and religious orders had to police the relationships of inmates within these walls and beyond. Strict regulation forbade 'lewd kissing and caresses'.[13]

Moreover, the power of the Church failed to prevent some priests from pursuing a life of 'the flesh'. Historians have uncovered evidence which suggests that, despite the strictures on celibacy, by the sixteenth century as many as 45 percent of rural clergy in parts of Germany had, or were suspected of having concubines. The laity and young men and

women in training for taking orders were vulnerable to sexual overtures. Solicitation during confession was common and in response,
from the 1560s, the Church introduced the closed and divided confessional box.[14] Historians have certainly uncovered cases of sexual licence
within the Church. Guido Ruggiero has noted instances of priests seduc-
ing young boys in Renaissance Venice.[15] Similarly in sixteenth-century
Seville a number of priests were convicted and burned at the stake for
sodomizing young men.[16] Relationships between nuns are much more
difficult to uncover, not least because medieval and Renaissance authorities understood sex very much in terms of penetration, and found
it difficult to even conceive that female homoeroticism was possible.
Nonetheless, Judith Brown has uncovered a case of a sexual relationship between two nuns in sixteenth-century Pescia, resulting in the vir-
tual imprisonment of one for over 30 years.[17]

Restricting our vision of religious sexuality to instances of 'mis-
conduct' fails to grapple with the complexity of spiritual experience.
There is a rich feminist historiography on nunneries as places of female
empowerment. Here women, although subject to a male hierarchy and
severe restrictions over their movements and behaviour, could escape
the burdens of child-rearing and household management, freeing them
to pursue spiritual devotion and artistic endeavour.[18] There were many
notable female clerics who made an extraordinary contribution to European religious and cultural life. For example the Benedictine abbess
Hildegard von Bingen (1098–1179) exerted tremendous influence over
the life of her nuns. She used her power to influence wider Church politics, experienced intense spiritual visions, wrote extensively on theology,
medicine and the physical sciences, and composed poetry and numerous musical works of great power and distinction. Within this medieval
and Renaissance female spiritual world there was considerable devotion
to religious ecstasy.[19]

Some women who embraced religious life were afforded opportunities to explore the limits of spiritual and bodily pleasure. This raises
intriguing questions about what constitutes sexuality. Should it be confined to specific acts, either alone or between people, with some aim
of sexual release or can it embrace a wide range of bodily sensations
without some specifically sexual outlet? On the other hand, do we distort the spiritual dimensions of religious ecstasy if we understand it
as a form of sexuality? There is no easy answer to such questions. But
there is no reason to see this as an either/or dilemma; religious ecstasy
can (and perhaps should) be seen in both a specifically religious framework, and as a way of expanding our understanding of sensual bodily
pleasures.

Caroline Walker Bynum has argued that there was an intimate relationship between the female body and religious practices in medieval

Europe.[20] For Bynum medieval spirituality, especially female spirituality, was 'peculiarly bodily'. Female religious figures had vivid visions, suffered trances, levitations, or catatonic seizures, many talked of tasting and kissing God, and many also engaged in intense forms of self-torture, such as whipping, hanging, cutting the flesh, or jumping into icy ponds or hot ovens. Through these practices of religious ecstasy, women reported transcendent experiences arising from their efforts to imitate Christ and contact him through direct physical sensation. There were clear erotic overtones to many of these acts, but more importantly women saw and experienced spirituality as an intensely bodily experience. This was in part because medieval theologians saw no marked distinction between the body and the soul. The body was a means of access to the divine: resurrection it was believed would involve both the body and the soul.

Women were generally seen to be closer to the world of the flesh and the body. This was the source of male fear and the persistent Church antipathy to a female priesthood. But bodily sensation and ecstasy were ways in which women could most acutely express their devotion and exhibit signs of grace. Nor was there a rigid differentiation of gender based on the body. Although the male body was paradigmatic, biological sex was labile. Women's bodies were seen as undeveloped men's bodies, and Christ was thus often depicted in medieval iconography as a woman. Women were considered inferior to men, but gender was a fluid category for medieval theologians and scientists, allowing women to claim a connection to the experience of Christ through bodily sensations. If Christ could bleed, feed, die and give life, women mystics could also. Bodies, then, were a means for women to represent their connection to Christ.[21]

Through bodily sensations and visions women could secure a place of significance in medieval Christianity. Many of these practices seem bizarre to modern eyes, but the strength of Bynum's account is its capacity to illuminate the peculiar world of medieval Christianity. Its understanding of the body, the soul, gender and sex is very different to our own. If we are to make some sense of widespread practices of self-mutilation, mortification and punishment, and obtain some insight into strange forms of bodily sensation such as stigmata, catatonia or mystical visions, it is crucial to reconstruct the world in which such things were seen as possible and explicable. Through these means women experienced intense ecstasy and physical pleasures difficult for some of us to comprehend. And although there is a sexual component to many of these sensations they are much more than merely erotic. Bodies, Bynum suggests, are constructed in diverse ways, and need to be placed in precise cultural and historical contexts in order to be made historically meaningful.

Passionate Bodies

Religion was not the only framework in which Europeans understood sex. Alongside the rich theological traditions advocating renunciation, chastity and spiritual marriage were literary, medical, philosophical, scientific, astrological and myriad popular understandings and precepts that offered more frank advice on sex and procreation. While much of this information was shaped by broader Christian principles, some of it, by interrogating the problems of love, health and procreation, lets us glimpse secular influences on the sexual culture of medieval and Renaissance Europe. But these secular literatures do not necessarily bring us any closer to the experiences and ideas that shaped the lives of ordinary people. Medicine, natural philosophy and the romance literature of courtly love were largely the preserve of social elites proficient in Latin. The mechanisms by which these knowledges shaped vernacular advice and how popular traditions influenced Latin-based culture are opaque.

Certainly we know that from the twelfth century some Latin texts were translated into vernacular languages. Other writers took ideas from the Latin tradition and transposed them into popular advice manuals. Equally interesting is the spread of ideas on sex, health and the body from Arabic scholarship into the Christian world after crusaders opened up the West to influences from the East. Some of the abstract ideas of medicine and philosophy also find their way into both high and more popular literary forms, such as the tales of Chaucer and the poetry of 'courtly love'.[22] Thomas Laqueur has argued that the crucial agents of transmission of scientific and medical ideas to the wider populace were midwives, surgeons, merchants and artisans who eagerly read the vernacular translations of Latin texts.[23] Whatever the means of transmission, historians have increasingly turned to the largely Latin literary and scientific sources to explore European sexual cultures in the first half of the second millennium.[24]

The Latin and vernacular literature on marriage and love offers important insights into the sexual *mentalité* of medieval and Renaissance Europe. There is a deep division in this literature, between the writings on marriage which see this union as one of property, alliance, procreation and fidelity, and those on romance which conjure up a world of passion and desire. These worlds, however, were not entirely separate. Although marriage was largely arranged, historians such as Georges Duby have uncovered instances of rebellious girls who flouted ideals of marital restraint and men who expressed intense erotic desire for their wives. Some husbands railed against Church teachings that encouraged wives to be chaste.[25] Running against the grain of marital fidelity, however, was an extensive literature on male sexual licence. Courtship and the higher ideal of love for its own sake cut across prescriptions that marriage should be contracted for familial and social alliances. This literature offered rich fantasies of rape, seduction, abduction and love that transgressed social conventions. Often such love could be tragic, true passion running counter to social convention, marriage and alliance. The tales of Tristan and Isolde, Abelard and Heloise, Guinevere and Lancelot, popular in the Renaissance, idealized a transcendent love. Equally such tales warned of the consequences of passions that infringed ties of blood, loyalty and social convention.[26]

Love was also a rich source for satire. Mikhail Bakhtin and others have explored the elements of carnival in medieval culture, where the world was 'turned upside down'. Instead of a culture of constraint, these comic genres created the opposite – a world of endless desire. Sixteenth-century French author François Rabelais' tales of the ribald and indulgent giants, Gargantua and Pantagruel, satirize religious and secular authority and represent a world of inexhaustible bodily appetites.[27] In other texts, notably those of fourteenth-century English author Geoffrey Chaucer and Italian satirist Giovanni Boccaccio, romance, marriage and fidelity are revealed to be a sham. In these tales men lose all sense, such as the old bachelor in Chaucer's 'The Merchant's Tale', and become abject and ridiculous. Similarly Boccaccio's *The Decameron* explores a world of cuckoldry, betrayal, desire and passion.[28]

Although much of the literature that has survived was for the educated classes, some of it was written or translated into vernacular languages. The oral and folk traditions of medieval and Renaissance Europe, however, are more difficult to uncover. The illiterate obviously did not read much of this Latin and vernacular literature. This requires historians to read between the lines in conventional historical texts for the echoes of popular beliefs. Some literary traditions picked up themes and stories from popular oral and folk traditions, appropriating and transforming them for a larger audience. Others often depicted (and satirized) popular notions and prejudices through characters from the lower orders. Medical and scientific texts often went to the trouble to refute folk notions of disease to push the claims for their own insights.[29] Although the evidence is partial, there were pervasive cultural and literary currents across all levels of European society that played with desires beyond those found in 'spiritual marriage'. This was not a world of renunciation, although it offered many a cautionary tale of the follies and tragedies of love and passion.

The themes of passion, love, seduction and betrayal were echoed in medical and philosophical literatures. Medical texts offered advice on the cures for 'lovesickness'. There was also an extensive advice literature on such problems as impotence and the measures required for birth control. Moreover, there was concern about the consequences of celibacy.

Medical and health tracts argued that bodies produced superfluities, such as semen, blood and bile, which needed to be expunged to maintain balance and good health. In such texts celibacy was injurious to health.[30]

Medical and philosophical literatures were not always divorced from theological ideals. There were many popular warnings against the consequences of excessive sexual indulgence, notably the widespread belief that prostitutes would become infertile. On the whole, however, secular culture put an emphasis on sex as a normal activity for both men and women. Impotence, for example, was grounds for the dissolution of marriage and thus a disease to be cured.[31] The popular notion of the 'marriage debt', where both husband and wife could demand sexual favours from each other when they so desired, reinforced the idea of marriage as a union for procreation. It also defined marriage as a relationship for the mutual satisfaction of desires.[32] In the same vein, ideas about the process of conception itself, where women and men both produced seed that combined in sexual intercourse to conceive children, placed a high premium on the necessity for female orgasm.

Thomas Laqueur has argued that the one-sex model of the body dominated European understandings of sex and gender, from antiquity until the early-eighteenth century.[33] As we have seen, there was a pervasive neo-Aristotelian belief, systematized by Galen in the second century CE, that there was only one human body, the male body. Women were undeveloped men, and female organs such as the uterus and the ovaries were visually represented as penises and testes that remained within the body. These ancient prescriptions withstood the challenge of new medical techniques. In the sixteenth century writers, such as Vesalius, saw anatomy and dissection as a means of overthrowing the largely philosophical speculations of Galen. Nonetheless, when doctors opened the body they saw organs in very culturally specific ways – the uterus was an inverted penis.[34] Science tended to confirm the one-sex body.

We need to explore the implications of this understanding of the body further because it provides an important framework for commonplace ideas about sex. The body may have been singular in structure, but it manifested itself in different forms – male, female, hermaphrodite and numerous gradations along a continuum. What distinguished these forms were not fundamental biological differences, but relative dispositions of heat and cold, dry and moist characteristics. Men were seen as hotter, women as cold and moist (hence the failure of their organs to form outside the body). Hermaphrodites were somewhere in-between these extremes. Within this cultural framework, sex was organized around the coming together of an active, hot partner with a passive cold partner. The sex act was a means of heating bodies to an extent that produced 'seed' in both partners, necessary for conception to take place. In antiquity such ideas framed the antagonism towards sex between adult men, while at the same time providing a space for pederastic relationships based on an active/passive model. In Christian Europe these ideas reinforced Church antipathy to sex, because intercourse and unnatural vices robbed men of their vitality.[35]

Although these were widely shared views (both popular and elite) they did not go uncontested. For instance, some writers in the late Middle Ages revived Aristotle's belief that female orgasm was not necessary for conception. But the one-sex model largely survived such challenges. Moreover, it accommodated contradictory evidence. In 1559 Renaldus Columbas claimed to have 'discovered' the clitoris, a finding which might have suggested that female bodies were not undeveloped male bodies but also had external signifiers of resemblance. The one-sex body, by using metaphors, analogies and vague descriptive terms, blurred distinctions between bodies. As Laqueur argues, the lack of precise anatomical terms for female genitals reflected the propensity to see the female body as a version of the male.[36] The one-sex body remained the framework in which sex was understood, pointing to the powerful ways in which culture shaped knowledge. What was required for the emergence of two-sexed bodies, argues Laqueur, was not the discovery of the truth of sexual difference, but a new cultural framework in which to read the body (as we shall see in the next chapter).[37]

If there was one body there were certainly two genders. Laqueur argues that gender was a crucial framework for organizing social difference. Bodies may have been singular in structure but gender, organized around the tropes of active/passive and hot/cold, prescribed sharply differentiated roles for men and women. These roles were not based on a sexed body, but on the differences in the manifestation of a single body. Gender, then, became a system for assigning social roles and behaviours, most evident in the debates about the 'gender' of the hermaphrodite. Rather than seeing the latter as something in-between (as science and medicine envisioned this figure), legal and social decisions (ones often arising out of sodomy trials) were made to allocate hermaphrodites to one gender or the other, with the expectation that they would adopt the behaviour of the gender to which they were assigned. Laqueur cites the case of one 'female' hermaphrodite permitted to remain a woman until the age of 25 and then required to assume a male gender role.[38] Similarly, there were rich literary fantasies and folkloric tales of girls changing into men. In some stories young women engaged in heated exercise suddenly turned into youths.[39] For Laqueur, the one-sex body meant that bodies were fluid in their presentation, while gender was a rigid system which prescribed distinct spheres of gendered behaviour.

People did not always conduct themselves by the dictates of science, religion, literature and folklore. Despite clear religious sanctions against sex outside marriage there is abundant evidence that premarital sex was widely practised and accepted – people often married after having children or where the bride was pregnant. Some regions even allowed trial marriages, while prohibitions against adultery seem to have been widely disregarded.[40] Moreover polygamy, concubinage and rape were common, while the culture of courtly love praised the virtues of seduction and paraded a virile ethic in eroticized clothing, such as elaborate codpieces.[41] Studies of medieval and Renaissance marriage also indicate that many unions fell far short of the ideals of theological teaching. Despite the constraints imposed on women by Church and society, many resisted the demand to be obedient and silent. They turned to poetry and prose to voice their concerns. Others turned to the law to prosecute rapists, demand property and seek annulments of unsatisfactory unions.[42]

Local studies provide some of the most important insights into medieval and Renaissance marriage and sexuality. Joanne Ferraro's study of marriage in Renaissance Venice is an excellent example. Ferraro explores the Church court records on marital litigation uncovering a world of intense conflict, violence and betrayal. Upper-class Venetians prized honour, class and wealth over affection and compatibility. Bribery and corruption were devices to influence the courts. Individual cases reveal numerous instances of wives leaving violent and abusive husbands, contests over dowries and husbands who put their wives into prostitution to increase the family income. On the other side, there is also a rich archive of female adultery, marital fraud, male impotence and courtesans who sought to become virtuous wives. While these legal struggles were shrouded in a language of complaint, emerging out of these contests was a prevailing expectation that wives be treated well, economically supported and have satisfying sex lives. These expectations sit within a wider Venetian culture where priests, neighbours, friends and midwives sought to advise and regulate the conduct of the married couple. Midwives often instructed brides in their sexual duties. Others counselled forbearance for the sake of honour and respectability. This litigation arose because wives and husbands refused such advice.[43]

Most of the literary, medical and legal evidence also suggests that concubinage and prostitution were widespread, especially amongst the patrician classes. The existence of prostitution tells us much about male sexuality. Men seeking sexual services outside marriage was widely tolerated. Some medieval and Renaissance towns legalized brothels, others turned a blind eye to their existence, and only a few attempted to stamp out commercial forms of sex. The main historical debates about prostitution, however, have been about the prostitute rather than the client. One of these debates returns us to the question of 'sexual identity', and whether such identities existed before the nineteenth century.

Ruth Mazo Karras argues that the term 'prostitute' or *meretrix* signified any woman who engaged in sex outside marriage. For Karras, the *meretrix* became a 'sexual identity', a sinful, transgressive, disreputable character. Prostitute became a permanent social identity. Other historians, such as Carla Freccero and David Halperin, however, argue that Karras confuses social identity with psychosexual orientation. The term *meretrix* more closely approximated whore than prostitute and did not signal inherent deviant identity but social transgression. It was the public nature of her transgression, not the fact of multiple sexual partners, that constituted the identity of the prostitute.[44]

What is more difficult to uncover is the extent of practices such as prostitution and concubinage. The significant insights of demographic historians, such as Peter Laslett and Jean-Louis Flandrin, into birth, marriage and the family are based on evidence from the seventeenth century. They have generally concentrated on reconstructing marriage and birth practices in a few specific cities that have good records. Detailed demographic work for earlier periods, however, is more speculative and historians have had to rely on literary and theological records. For example, Philippe Aries, on the basis of such sources, argues that there was a long tradition of marriage as an indissoluble union in Europe. He suggests that for much of Europe marriage was the chief social bond, and it governed the sexual life of the majority of people. While adultery, seduction, prostitution and concubinage were well known, they were largely the preserves of the upper classes.[45]

The persistence of marriage has to be placed in the context of other demographic facts, most importantly the late age of marriage for many young men in Europe. The evidence for this is also partial, largely studies of some important towns in Italy. By the early Renaissance young apprentices, aristocrats and members of the emerging mercantile classes were delaying marriage until their late twenties. Thus there was a growing bachelor class in cities such as Venice and Florence. This bred a virile, masculine culture which demanded sexual services from prostitutes and 'common women', and promoted the widespread practice of rape and seduction.[46] Late marriage was a means of keeping a check on population growth, although it raises intriguing questions about why such customs did not lead to a significant incidence of illegitimate births. It also raises interesting but unanswerable questions about the extent of 'unnatural' sex between men and women and the prevalence of homoerotic and same-sex practices.

The Persistence of Tradition

Same-sex eroticism was prevalent in medieval and Renaissance Europe, just as it had been in classical and late antiquity. This is hardly surprising. Writing the history of 'homosexuality' in this period, however, involves more than documenting same-sex unions. As we have seen in relation to antiquity, the history of homosexuality involves questions of culture, subculture and identity that have been the point of significant dispute. Medieval and Renaissance anxieties about 'unnatural' acts created a context in which same-sex unions were widely condemned. Christianity afforded little tolerance of such relationships. Although Christian theology, and practices such as confession, aimed to stamp out unnatural sex, which included all those acts, even between husbands and wives, which could not lead to procreation, the very existence of these forms of regulation suggest that such practices were prevalent.

This was not just a problem of 'homosexuality'. During the medieval and Renaissance periods sodomy took on a very broad meaning, encompassing all unnatural sex acts, largely oral and anal, whether they occurred between men and women or people of the same sex. The 'sodomite', the person who sodomized someone else, became a source of great concern. Laws were enacted prescribing severe penalties for sodomites. Nevertheless, such practices persisted. More importantly, same-sex relationships, despite the sanctions against them, continued to flourish. In some instances they even flourished within the Church. Theology and institutional religion was never a monolithic culture. There were, as we have seen in the discussion of ecstasy and the body, ways in which men and women could turn ideas to their own ends, exploiting the fissures, contradictions and possibilities in religious and secular ideas and prescriptions. Although there is some illuminating work on lesbianism in this period, the bulk of the historiography, reflecting both the bias of the surviving evidence and the interests of gay historians, focuses on men.[47]

A number of historians have argued that a distinct 'homosexual' identity emerged in medieval and Renaissance Europe. Joseph Cady, for example, argues that the idea of 'distinct sexual orientations, heterosexual and homosexual', was established in sixteenth-century Europe. Others, such as Giovanni Dall'Orto, try to sidestep the issue of identity by analysing Renaissance homoeroticism, but in doing so he largely accepts the idea of a homosexual identity.[48] One of the most important scholars in this field is again John Boswell. As we have seen, Boswell was an important contributor to the debate about same-sex unions in late antiquity. He has also made a substantial contribution to the history of medieval homosexuality. The themes of sexual subculture, tolerance and intolerance, as in his work on antiquity, feature prominently in his pioneering study *Christianity, Social Tolerance and Homosexuality* (1980).

In this work Boswell distinguishes between homosexual and gay. Drawing on the research of modern sexologists like Kinsey, Boswell assumes that same-sex desire is universal, but that only under special conditions does this fact create social networks, or an identifiable gay subculture in which such desire can be acknowledged and flourish.[49]

The context for the emergence of a gay subculture, argues Boswell, is social tolerance. This is the framework in which he develops a narrative of gay history in medieval Europe. For Boswell, there was a well-established gay culture in Rome during late antiquity, fostered by diverse social contacts afforded by large urban centres and Latin *belles lettres*, which provided the means for the expression and cultivation of same-sex love. The rise of asceticism, increased government regulation of morality and the breakdown of urban subcultures as Roman culture began to crumble, led to a growing hostility to 'gay people'. Hostility to eroticism more generally within Christianity, and the rural, family ethos of the early Middle Ages meant that gay people had few opportunities to bear witness to their desires. While medieval Christians were largely indifferent to homosexual behaviour (making it part of a wider concern with 'unnatural acts'), the climate of antagonism to the body and desire, undermined gay subcultures (except in Spain), making gay people largely invisible in the early Middle Ages. There were 'individual expressions of homosexual love', but few social networks in which such expressions could find a larger audience.

The revival of city life expanded urban social networks in the eleventh century, however, and again created the conditions for the emergence of a gay subculture. These networks allowed for closer association and social contacts. Moreover, they supported the reappearance of 'gay literature'. Through religious and secular poetry, painting and sculpture, 'gay people' were able to foster a distinct sensibility and forms of expression and communication that cemented social bonds based on sexual preference. Gay people became prominent and influential at many levels of society, and 'homosexual passions' were celebrated and the subject of public discussion. In the latter half of the twelfth century, however, there was a growing popular and theological antagonism towards minority groups. Crusades against non-Christians, efforts to stamp out heresy, the expulsion of Jews from Europe, and by the thirteenth century, the Inquisition, 'all testify to an increasing intolerance' of those who fell outside the mainstream of Christian morality.[50]

Boswell's 'gay history' is one of cycles of tolerance and intolerance. This is less a history of homosexual desire than a study of the triumphs and trials of gay literary expression. Moreover, Boswell admits that the mechanisms for changes in levels of tolerance are difficult to trace. Nonetheless, given the difficulties of the evidence, Boswell's account is a significant achievement. His idea of 'gay history', however, is relatively

static, imposing contemporary notions of gay identity on the past and
then mapping the contexts in which it flourishes or is repressed. In this
framework the concept 'gay' is a blunt instrument, largely signifying a
minority subculture, which is either present or absent in history. Thus
Boswell does not investigate the meanings attached to actual sexual practices, the formation of specific sexual identities, how these varied over
time, or their place within a wider economy of desires and practices.
Even within its own terms this focus on literary expression has pitfalls.
Boswell devotes considerable effort to reading medieval poetry 'against
the grain' to decipher the literary codes which gave expression to gay
desire. He explores how within the tradition of 'courtly love' tropes, such
as 'unyielding youth', classical references to Ganymede or biblical ones
to David and Jonathan, signified passionate attachment between men.
These literary tropes were a means of communicating a 'gay sensibility'
to other members of the subculture.[51]

Other historians have contested his methods and conclusions. Boswell's
reliance on literary sources has put him at odds with social historians.
Drawing on legal and medical sources, social historians have uncovered
evidence for a continuing tradition of sexual subcultures throughout
medieval and Renaissance Europe. Rather than cycles of tolerance, where
subcultures thrived or withered, depending on the wider social context,
social historians such as Guido Ruggiero and Alan Bray have found thriving subcultures of sodomites in places as diverse as fourteenth-century
Venice and late-sixteenth-century London. Such subcultures undermine
Boswell's notion of cycles of tolerance. Instead the evidence suggests a
longer and continuous history of cultures of 'male vice'.[52] In some social
contexts, such as the seventeenth-century Caribbean buccaneer community, sodomy was commonplace.[53] Even within the field of theological
and literary history historians have contested some of Boswell's claims.
Pierre Payer and James Brundage have pointed to severe condemnation of male sodomy in the penitentials of the eleventh and early-twelfth
centuries, just the time when Boswell sees a growing tolerance of male
love.[54]

One of the most important contributions to this revisionist historiography of homosexuality is Michael Rocke's study of male culture in
Renaissance Florence, *Forbidden Friendships* (1996).[55] Rocke, like many
Renaissance commentators and subsequent historians, notes the reputa-
tion of Florence as a haven for 'unmentionable vice', a city where sodomy
flourished. There are numerous references to this practice, although, as
we have seen, before the eighteenth century sodomy encompassed a range
of 'unnatural' practices, not just sex between men. In Renaissance Florence there was clearly great anxiety about the extent of sodomy. Despite
a revival of interest in classical culture in this period, this fascination with
antiquity did not extend to tolerance of male love. The Church continued

to assert that sodomy was a sin and there were strong legal sanctions making sodomy 'a crime punishable by severe penalties, including death by burning'. In 1432 the city government established the Office of the Night, a magistracy solely for pursuing and prosecuting sodomy.

All of this might suggest support for Boswell's contention that intolerance reigned after the twelfth century, but Rocke's forensic analysis of the records of the Office of the Night reveals that over 70 years (until 1502), in a city of 40,000 inhabitants, as many as 17,000 men were incriminated at least once for sodomy. Despite widespread condemnation of sodomy, and rigorous policing of this crime, the majority of Florentine males in the fifteenth century were charged for engaging in homosexual relations. Far from intolerance suppressing homosexuality, a significant culture of male homosexual relations flourished.

This sodomite culture was vastly different to Boswell's 'gay subculture'. Far from being a small but thriving enclave of male passion, the legal evidence suggests that sodomy was widely practised by the majority of male Florentines. Moreover, these acts of sodomy were distinctive. Most of the cases prosecuted by the Office of the Night involved an active, penetrating adult man and a passive, penetrated youth. The defining trope of sexual relations in this act was not the gender of the participants, but active or passive sexual roles. Adult men, in considerable numbers, engaged in such acts taking the active role and thereby affirming, not undermining, their status as virile, manly, normal men. Thus men who were the active participants in relations with boys shared many manly characteristics with those who were active with women. In fact, most of the men brought before the Office of the Night were also husbands and fathers. While the Office policed both the men and the youths in these relationships, punishments for the adult men were comparatively light.[56]

The policing of 'sodomites' raises important questions about the relationship between religious and legal doctrines and popular sexual culture. The evolution of Christian doctrine led to severe condemnation of sodomy and most European and later American jurisdictions made sodomy an offence incurring severe punishment, even death. There is a striking difference between the official culture of antiquity and that of the Christian West. In antiquity 'unnatural' acts were not the source of formal legal sanction, although anal penetration of youths from good families was forbidden in classical Rome. What concerned citizens in antiquity was the passive male. In contrast, both participants in unnatural acts could be subject to punishment in the Christian West. Moreover, often it was the active penetrating 'sodomite' who was the object of greatest concern. Thus Christianity transformed the perception of unnatural acts in profound ways and this translated into legal regulations governing the conduct of sexual acts.

Nevertheless, in Rocke's account male culture in Renaissance Florence bears a striking similarity with that of ancient Greece and Rome.[57] The practice of adult males having relationships with youths appears to have been prevalent in both antiquity and the Renaissance world. More importantly, the key distinction governing these sexual cultures was active/passive, not homosexual/heterosexual. The active penetrating partner was manly and the passive adult man became the object of derision. Despite Christian doctrine and prevailing laws, popular attitudes were shaped more by codes of active/passive and injunctions against gender transgression than by a simple revulsion against unnatural acts. Of course, it is impossible to tell the extent of this particular Renaissance sexual culture. It may have been confined to a few towns in Italy or certain classes. More historical work needs to be done to determine whether similar cultures operated in other parts of medieval and Renaissance Europe.

Conclusion

Michael Rocke's study raises the intriguing possibility that, despite a thousand years of Christian theological condemnation of sodomy, a subculture of same-sex unions between men and youths persisted in Europe. While secular authorities policed both partners in these relationships, and punishments could be harsh for both the penetrator and the youth penetrated, codes of masculinity affirmed the manliness of the active sexual partner. In both antiquity and the Renaissance the passive adult man was the source of greatest cultural anxiety. These were the men who infringed popular codes of appropriate masculine behaviour. A key question confronting historians is whether these pederastic practices were part of a sexual underworld of great longevity, or something that had emerged relatively recently in Renaissance Italy. We cannot conclude definitively one way or the other at this point. But the answers to such a question have important implications for the way that we write the history of sexuality and sexual cultures. At the very least the evidence of pederasty in both antiquity and medieval and Renaissance Europe points to a fundamental rupture between pre-modern and modern sexual cultures: between those organized around active/passive and those organized around homosexual/heterosexual. If such a distinction is useful we might then ask when does sexual modernity emerge?

Chapter 5

MAKING HETEROSEXUALITY

The eighteenth century carries large burdens. Phrases such as age of revolutions, Enlightenment, industrial revolution, end of the Ancien Régime, birth of the asylum and rise of Romanticism have been widely used to capture the momentous social and cultural changes taking place in eighteenth-century Europe and America. More recently, historians such as Richard Godbeer, Edward Shorter and Randolph Trumbach have added sexual revolution and gender revolution to the panoply of transformations that marked the transition from early- to late-modern Europe and America. The eighteenth century, however, was in many respects the culmination of transformations stretching back much further. How far is in dispute. English historians often talk of the 'long eighteenth century', to signify the years from the 1680s to the 1810s. But for some historians the changes associated with the gender revolution are found from the sixteenth century, when the emergence of subversive urban subcultures, rising literacy and cheap books created the context for a dramatic increase in the production and distribution of pornography, satire and radical political tracts.[1] Other historians, such as Guido Ruggerio and Alan MacFarlane, trace significant elements of the revolution back to the thirteenth century and even earlier.[2]

One of the defining events of the early-modern period is the Protestant Reformation of the sixteenth and seventeenth centuries. Protestants rejected many of the key doctrines of the medieval Church, such as the importance of good works, the authority of the papacy and the significance of tradition. As Merry Wiesner-Hanks has argued, sex was also an integral part of the Reformation. Protestants attacked the vow of celibacy and proclaimed sex within marriage as the key to affection and domestic harmony. Sexual desire was natural and part of God's plan. For Luther, 'refusal to have sexual relations within marriage constituted grounds for divorce'.[3] Accompanying the praise of sexual relations within marriage went a fierce condemnation of sodomy, prostitution, contraception, abortion and adultery. Protestantism did not challenge the traditional Catholic stress on the need to scrutinize marriage and sexuality. Protestant sermons, courts, consistories and congregations were institutions for closely regulating sexuality and maintaining social discipline.[4] For some historians there are continuities between Catholic and Protestant attitudes towards sex.[5]

Did the intense Protestant scrutiny of sex and marriage fundamentally alter the lives of ordinary people? This is a question we have broached before in relation to Catholic teachings. Some historians, such as Eamon Duffy, have stressed the profound transformations in village life wrought by the Protestant Reformation. It destroyed a socially undifferentiated and harmonious village community life and created a more oligarchic and individualist society.[6] In the realm of sex, however, the evidence is more ambiguous. Certainly there is abundant evidence that prostitution, concubinage and sexual licence flourished in early-modern Europe and America, just as it had in the West before the Reformation. A number of works have focused on the emergence of a significant 'libertine' culture in early-modern Europe, while others have highlighted the 'sexual freedom' of the American frontier.[7] The larger question of changes in marriage and sexuality, however, has become the focus of considerable debate within historical demography. The survival of good runs of birth, baptismal and marriage records for many counties and villages in England and North America affords some useful speculations about continuity and discontinuity in early modern sexuality.

These demographic changes underpin wider debates about the sexual revolution in eighteenth-century Europe and America. For historians such as Edward Shorter, the eighteenth century is characterized by a 'release of the libido', escaping the strictures of Christian and social morality.[8] Others see it as an age of domesticity and romantic love in Europe and America, when the 'middling sort' emerged as a significant social and moral force.[9] But a few historians have sensed deeper transformations within Western sexual cultures. For Thomas Laqueur, this was the moment when biological differentiation between the sexes first emerged, allowing for the embodiment of gender, with profound consequences for the understanding of both sex and gender.[10] Randolph Trumbach argues that early-modern Europe witnessed the end of the long tradition of understanding sex as an act between active and passive partners. In its place came the idea that sex should be between those of different sex – male and female. Thus Trumbach sees the eighteenth century as most notable for the making of heterosexuality.[11]

Marriage and Procreation

Historians of early-modern Europe, particularly England and France, have been able to chart with some precision important dimensions of the sexual behaviour of ordinary people. As we have seen, sources for the history of sexuality are partial, often excellent for an account of attitudes, but more opaque for a history of practices. They mainly consist of literary, artistic, theological, philosophical and scientific accounts of sex, treatises on morality and guides for the proper conduct of sexual life. Often these are admonishments to change one's behaviour, not necessarily descriptions of how people actually conducted sexual relations. Thus much of the history of sexuality is a study of attitudes and the clash of different sexual cultures. To get around these limitations social historians of sexuality have turned to court and police records to uncover the history of sex acts. This approach has opened up important new insights into the nature of sex and sexuality in the West. These legal sources have enabled historians to explore areas such as domestic violence, sodomy, impotence, divorce and sexual underworlds. Nonetheless, legal sources have their own limitations. They offer important insights into undercurrents of sexual behaviour and the lives of those who came before the courts. Although social and cultural historians of sexuality have been able to read between the lines to explore more general conclusions about sex in the West, legal records leave largely untouched the lives of people who escape the purview of the law (Church and secular).

The abundance of early-modern British, European and American parish and local records on births, deaths and marriages, however, has created significant opportunities for historians to map larger patterns of sexual behaviour amongst the general population. Demographic historians have been able to use these records to reconstruct the formation of families, average age at marriage, birth rates and the incidence of illegitimacy, providing some fruitful propositions about how the majority of people conducted their sexual lives. For the early-modern period historians have been able to move beyond the partial evidence of court records, the impressionistic evidence of advice literature and the abstract formulations of science, to tell us something about the sexual practices of many people from different social groups.

Marriages and births in Western Europe since the late-sixteenth century and America since the mid-seventeenth century demonstrate clear patterns. The age of marriage was usually high, in the late twenties for men and early twenties for women, until the mid-eighteenth century when it began to fall. Moreover, the fertility rate was low, keeping the European population relatively stable, with minor upswings and downturns generally in response to economic conditions. But from the early- to mid-eighteenth century there was a remarkable exponential increase in the population, nearly doubling within a century in England. This was largely due to an increase in the number of births rather than a decline in the mortality rate. Although fertility rates were higher in colonial America, they demonstrate a similar exponential increase during the eighteenth century.[12] But the birth rate thereafter begins to fall significantly, although the timing of this fall varies considerably, beginning in France from the 1780s, America around 1800, England around 1850 and the 1880s in Australia. The decline in the birth rate will be examined more fully in the next chapter. The key demographic trend of eighteenth-century Europe and America, however, was the dramatic rise in fertility.

An important dimension of these fertility patterns was that legitimate and illegitimate births, as well as the rate of women who gave birth soon after marriage (prenuptial pregnancy), moved to a similar rhythm. These rates were traditionally low in the sixteenth and seventeenth centuries and all rise sharply in the late-eighteenth century. This suggests that illegitimacy and prenuptial pregnancy, far from being 'deviant' acts or reactions against prevailing cultural values, were instead part of larger social patterns of fertility. While conception before marriage was common, 'bastardy' was not, despite the existence of Foundling Hospitals in Europe to deal with this social problem. Certainly 'bastardy' existed but it only accounted for a small proportion of all births.[13] A similar pattern is evident in colonial America. In parts of New England a third of all first-born children were conceived out of wedlock, while three-quarters of these mothers had married by the time they gave birth.[14] In other words, many couples who engaged in premarital sex either agreed or were forced to marry before the birth of the child.

Putting marriage alongside birth patterns also highlights some important issues. The numbers of marriages rose significantly during the eighteenth century. This was a result of more people deciding to marry (and hence a significant decline in the number of adults who never married) and a fall in the average age of marriage (from the late to the early twenties for men). Although these decisions created the opportunity for more births, the rate of illegitimacy also rose exponentially at this time. Thus there appear to have been broader social influences on conception. Both married and unmarried women, after centuries of keeping the birth rate relatively steady, decided either to engage in sexual intercourse more frequently or let their children come to term more often (or both).[15] In a suggestive argument Mary Fissell has noted a renewed assertion of male control over female fertility in English child-bearing guides of the late-seventeenth and early-eighteenth century. In a reaction against women's increasing political activism in the social and political upheavals of the mid-seventeenth century, men asserted that woman's most important role was in the home as mothers. In other words, fertility rates reflected a larger crisis in gender relations.[16]

The rise in the fertility rate, however, has more usually been tied to rising real incomes, industrialization and urbanization. As marriage was traditionally seen as the basis for creating an independent economic unit, sufficient resources were required before a couple could be relatively secure about their future. Historians have seen this as the basis for the late age of marriage and stable fertility rate in pre-industrial Europe. Before the eighteenth century couples generally waited until they had the means to support children before they embarked upon marriage. Fertility control was a means of managing economic circumstances. Better times usually meant a rise in fertility. Tight community bonds in villages sustained these patterns across the centuries. But industrialization, migration, enclosures and urbanization undermined these entrenched social traditions, freeing people to pursue their desires, while rising incomes allowed many to enter marriage at an earlier age.[17]

Despite general agreement about these patterns of births and marriages, demographic historians have rightly urged caution in their interpretation. Reconstructing the history of population from local records, particularly in North America, overlooks the role of migration in population change. On the colonial frontiers many inhabitants of towns and communities married and bore children before settling down, leaving no marriage or birth records. Similarly, although the general trends are illuminating, they do tend to obscure distinct local peculiarities and differences. For instance, it is clear that illegitimacy rates were traditionally lower in western and northern Europe than in southern or Eastern Europe.[18]

Equally important, historians such as Peter Laslett and E.A. Wrigley have noted variations in the patterns between different parishes in England. In addition, some particular communities, such as the Quakers and other dissenting sects, had marriage and birth patterns that were different to the norm.[19] In the American colonies overcrowding and land shortages were not as severe as Europe and birth rates were consistently higher. Finally, class was also a factor. The rise in the birth rate began in the European aristocracy of the late-seventeenth century. Rising fertility in the eighteenth century, however, was most apparent amongst the emerging working classes.[20] Increasing working-class fertility has been tied to the economic and cultural effects of wage labour. For David Levine, industrialization created a demand for child labour, an incentive for working-class couples to reproduce to increase household income.[21] Similarly, Henry Abelove has argued that the issue is not so much fertility, but a new acceptability of intercourse as a sexual

practice. Foreplay declined as factory discipline increased. For Abelove, the pervasive ideology of industrialism gave couples a new faith
in their capacity to support offspring and inspired an ethic of sexual
production.[22]

Moreover, it is clear that what constituted a legal marriage was by
no means uniform across Europe and America. Some local areas only
accepted unions sanctioned by church ceremony as marriages, while
others counted as legitimate customary unions based on an exchange of
vows before witnesses. In other parishes a statement of intention could
allow 'legitimate' sexual intercourse. In colonial America informal marriages, especially amongst the poorer classes, were common. Some of
these unions were celebrated through simple ceremonies and pledges,
but they remained outside the purview of secular and church authorities. Despite the occasional efforts of legal authorities to prosecute couples living in informal marriages for adultery, many colonial Americans
remained remarkably oblivious of the requirement to have the church
sanction their union.[23]

Local variations and gaps in the sources aside, in general the significant rise in fertility for married and unmarried women in the eighteenth century represents a dramatic change in family formation in
Western Europe and America. Since the sixteenth century in Europe
and the seventeenth century in America, fertility rates had been relatively steady. The evidence suggests that the European population
had probably been relatively stable for at least three centuries. Why
did marriage and fertility patterns undergo such rapid change during the eighteenth century? The dramatic increase in marriages, and
in legitimate and illegitimate births, has been seen as a 'sexual revolution', but the nature of these changes, revolutionary or not, has been
contested.[24]

Controlling Fertility

Much of the work on the period of relative stability in early-modern
European and colonial American populations has attempted to tie
patterns of marriage and birth to the economic and social contexts of
pre-industrial societies. If resources were scarce, then it was essential
that communities develop customs, traditions and practices that managed those resources, to avoid starvation and rising rates of mortality.
A late age of marriage and intervals between births were means for
managing scarcity. Elaborate courtship rituals were another means by
which communities sought to impose restraints on marriage and sexual
experimentation.[25] Couples engaging in sex before marriage could, of
course undermine such strategies, although as we have seen many of
these couples subsequently married.

Some historians, such as Peter Laslett and Edward Shorter, have stressed the importance of religious ideas promoting continence before marriage. They cite evidence for a small decline in marriages and births in early- to mid-sixteenth-century England, when Puritans held significant social and political influence. Moreover, they have argued that the close social ties of pre-industrial village life afforded fewer opportunities for sexual contact outside marriage.[26] Studies of seventeenth- and eighteenth-century New England, however, have shown that despite Puritan moralism church authorities were concerned about the extent of licentiousness in the community and local courts were kept busy prosecuting 'fornicators, adulterers, lewdness, bigamists, incest and sodomites'.[27]

Despite the religious, legal and community controls over sex, fertility rates remained more responsive to economic circumstances than religious doctrine. The question is how did Europeans and Americans ensure that fertility rates remained steady for so long. Abstinence is one answer, although as we have seen Protestants unlike Catholics celebrated marital sexual relations. Another answer is the availability of sexual 'outlets' that did not turn up in the records on births. While recourse to prostitutes could carry the risk of conception, in was hardly in the financial interests of working women to interrupt their livelihood. Prostitution, however, by offering a sexual outlet for men may have provided a means of ensuring that both single and married men had access to sexual services without the attendant consequences for them of conception. This may have helped keep both married fertility and illegitimacy low.[28] There were other sexual opportunities that left few records of births. On the American frontier, for example, sexual relations between white men and native American women and between masters and slaves were widespread, largely outside the purview of authorities and any consequences were absent from parish birth records.[29] Same-sex relations, appear to have been common and likewise left no mark in the birth and baptismal records.[30]

Contraception would seem to be another important contributor to stable fertility rates. The Catholic Church had certainly warned against the evil of birth control since medieval times, suggesting that such practices were well known. A wealth of anthropological and historical research points to the widespread use of birth control in many cultures. Barrier methods and withdrawal would appear to have been common in early-modern Europe and colonial America. Evidence does indicate that prostitutes had a range of effective contraceptive methods, such as vaginal tampons. But barrier methods were unreliable, particularly before the widespread use of sheep intestines for condoms from the late-seventeenth century.[31] Withdrawal and mutual masturbation were common forms of 'birth control', within and outside marriage, although withdrawal was unreliable. Another factor may have been the resort to long periods of suckling infants (up to three or four years) as a form of contraception, although such practices had to withstand the insistence by some husbands that breast-feeding interfered with sex, and the desire by women of the 'better off' classes to engage wet-nurses to free them from the burdens of feeding infants.[32]

Breast-feeding, however, cannot explain the low rate of prenuptial conceptions and illegitimacy amongst women giving birth for the first time. Angus McLaren argues that the condom, which became available in the early 1600s, seems to have played little part in either the rise or decline of fertility in the eighteenth century. It was mainly used to guard against catching syphilis from prostitutes. The evidence suggests that infanticide and abortions or induced miscarriages using potions, instruments or heavy exercise were common resorts for unwanted pregnancies.[33]

While we know that most early-modern Europeans and American colonists married late, on average ten years after puberty, and that the proportion of births before couples married was low, how people organized their sexual lives in the years before marriage, let alone during marriage, is difficult to fathom. Historians cannot rely on statistics to answer such questions, but have to turn to more impressionistic sources of evidence, such as letters, diaries and daily journals, all of which are more common amongst the 'better off' classes than the 'common people'. Advice manuals indicate which issues were thought important by authors hoping to capture a wide readership. For the poorer classes, court records are useful, but again they only open up a world of practices that infringed the law.

The evidence is partial, but illuminating. For example, Edward Shorter argues that masturbation was uncommon in pre-industrial Europe, largely because there was little medical or theological literature condemning it. More commonly, forms of erotic play between youths and girls in local villages offered opportunities for sexual experimentation. He cites evidence from Scandinavia and Germany of 'nightcourting', where youths visited local girls and slept the night with them, usually fully clothed. In France the custom of 'French kissing' in public between courting couples was common, some of which, through the wearing of special clothing, allowed for mutual masturbation. Thus there were a variety of avenues for erotic contact that did not involve penetration.[34] Richard Godbeer has documented the widespread practice of 'bundling' in Puritan New England. Parents invited young men to spend the night with their daughters. This commonly lead to sexual contact, but Godbeer argues that it was a means by which parents controlled the choice of husband, and prenuptial pregnancy was a small price to pay for such control.[35]

One of the most interesting attempts to explore premarital sexuality in early-modern Europe is Tim Hitchcock's analysis of the writings of an eighteenth-century English excise officer and charity school master.[36] John Cannon's memoirs, over 700 pages of manuscript written in the 1740s, offer a rare opportunity to explore courtship, marriage and sexuality before the population explosion of the mid-eighteenth century. These frank writings recount Cannon's initiation into sexual life during his adolescent years. At the age of 12 he learned to masturbate from an older school friend, a practice that he continued, with some frequency, throughout adolescence. Such evidence points to the flaws in Shorter's reliance on medical and theological writings to chart the history of masturbation.

More interesting, however, is Hitchcock's study of Cannon's sexual life in his early twenties when he began to associate with women. Cannon certainly had erotic contacts with a number of women, one of whom he courted for nearly ten years but did not marry. Although he lost his virginity to one woman, much of his erotic life involved no penetrative sex. There was a great deal of fondling, caressing and probably mutual masturbation, but actual penetration was rare. Indeed Cannon seemed to associate penetration with either marriage or prostitution. He only had sexual intercourse in one relationship before marriage, with a servant girl. This suggests that people took the marriage relationship seriously, organizing their sexual lives around an association between marriage and procreation, and exploring other ways of achieving satisfaction before marriage. Such evidence reinforces Shorter's arguments, and the work of others, notably John Gillis, on early-modern European adolescence as a time of sexual play and deferral of marriage.[37]

Population stability in early-modern Europe and America was built around practices that controlled fertility. Delaying marriage, prostitution, masturbation, fondling, and sexual contacts on the frontier were all ways of preventing too many recorded conceptions. Birth control assisted, as did abortion and infanticide, when these measures failed. The close scrutiny of social life in small communities restricted efforts to live outside these norms. Sexual life for many men or women from a wide range of classes, however, was organized around the primacy of marriage, fostering forms of erotic contact that did not lead to conception before marriage. These practices were relatively successful as bastardy and prenuptial pregnancy rates were low. Nonetheless there was widespread tolerance of premarital sexual intercourse between couples who intended to marry. Within marriage, withdrawal, suckling, abstinence and sexual play helped to keep the birth rate relatively stable.

Libertine Cultures

Why did these early-modern attitudes and sexual practices change? The demographic revolution of the eighteenth century was largely as a consequence of higher levels of fertility. From the 1690s in America and the 1740s in England and Europe people began to marry earlier and have more children. Many historians have established a strong correlation between fertility and the impact of rising incomes, the increased demand for labour, industrialization and urbanization. People had more economic resources and did not need to delay marriage for as long to save sufficient resources to support children. Higher incomes could support more children within marriage. The shift to large urban centres in search of work weakened community surveillance and the close regulation of sexual habits. Wage labour gave young men and women independent means, and independence encouraged individualism creating a *mentalité* of satisfaction of wants based on sentiment and romantic attraction rather than the requirements of family alliance.[38]

Edward Shorter has argued that working-class youths and women drove this 'sexual revolution'.[39] Young working-class men and women freed from the constraints of pre-industrial society by the 'liberating' effects of capitalism flocked to the cities in search of work. There they could pursue romance on their own terms. The working class was most affected by the dramatic social upheavals of the industrial revolution and were integral to rising rates of marriage and fertility. But the evidence for this conclusion is rather thin. There are few sources supporting the idea of a conscious working-class effort to transform traditional sexual customs, although it is clear that rising rates of illegitimacy amongst the plebeian classes of eighteenth-century Britain in part reflected the rising incidence of informal marriages.[40] Moreover, the evidence of widespread poverty, disease and malnutrition associated with rapid urbanization and industrialization (evident in a parallel rise in the mortality rate) suggests that Shorter's formula of capitalism and the cult of individualist consumption as the driving force for sexual change is overly simple. Moreover, he ignores the ways in which working-class women remained within a wider masculinist culture, which governed their sexual behaviour through new codes of respectability. The city did not free women from moral scrutiny, but instead allowed men to develop new forms of regulation, reducing the opportunity for women's sexual freedom.[41]

In contrast Lawrence Stone sees the aristocracy, the middling ranks and country gentry as the driving forces for new sexual freedoms.[42] Sixteenth- and seventeenth-century patrician and middling sexual culture was sharply divided. On the one hand, marriage was primarily a relationship to produce children, particularly male heirs, and largely used to cement social bonds between families. It was not considered a relationship based primarily on sentiment or sexual companionship. On the other hand, patrician men sought 'love, companionship and sexual pleasure' from mistresses and extramarital affairs. During the eighteenth century, however, people in upper social strata increasingly saw marriage as a union for the satisfaction of sexual desires. Companionate marriages based on personal choice increased, and people began to criticize the habit of delaying marriage, promoting instead the ideals of romantic love and happy passionate unions of loving couples. For Stone, the ethic of companionate marriage required the collapse of moral Puritanism and the emergence of ideas that people should marry for love rather than property.

In Puritan New England there was also an increase in fertility rates in the eighteenth century. Richard Godbeer, however, sees the American 'sexual revolution' as a complex contest between parents and children. In the eighteenth century Puritan moral codes began to loosen their hold over young men and women. Again the rise of towns and cities assisted the decline of the local community bonds that had sustained New England society. As Puritan moral codes relaxed their hold, people asserted traditional sexual mores such as tolerance of premarital sex amongst betrothed couples. Informal unions, adultery and illegitimacy became more common. The spirit of revolt fostered by the impact of the American Revolution further encouraged a less restrictive sexual climate. Young people experimented sexually within courtship and had more casual and transitory dalliances. These changes, however, were caught within a web of familial politics. New England parents, realizing that it was difficult to prevent sexual activity, sought to control it. Young people were encouraged to engage in greater sexual freedom within the parental home, allowing parents to supervise and protect their children.[43]

The collapse of moral Puritanism, however, was not merely a reflection of the rise of capitalism. For Lawrence Stone, attitudes praising sexual pleasure and asserting the 'naturalness' of the body and sensuality were crucial. A loss of religious sense that sins of the flesh were important and the emergence of new ideas about the need to cultivate 'human nature' overthrew the strict moral austerity of Puritan England and Catholic Europe. Thus, for Stone, there was 'a release of libido from the age-old constraints of Christianity'. These attitudes first appeared amongst restricted court circles in England in the seventeenth century. Sexual libertinism and homoeroticism seem to have flourished amongst the courtiers in early-modern European and English Court society.[44]

In the post-Restoration Court 'sexual promiscuity became the hallmark of fashion', adultery was common and men of the upper classes were expected to have many mistresses and produce numerous bastards, who suffered few social slights as a consequence of their illegitimacy. A rich literary tradition promoted the 'virtue' of the arts of seduction, and the lack of career opportunities for educated bourgeois women provided a ready supply of mistresses for wealthy men. Female fashions in the upper classes changed, promoting clothing that grossly accentuated female buttocks and exposed or lightly covered breasts. Male clubs opened up in London, where men could engage in sexual experimentation. Similar developments were apparent on the Continent, especially in Paris. Clubs, balls and masquerades all fostered an ethic of sexual licence. Dildos and condoms became common accessories for the libertine classes.[45]

For Stone, libertine attitudes originating in Court society slowly trickled down to other social groups. By the late-seventeenth century tolerance of sexual freedom was widespread amongst the wider squirearchy. During the eighteenth century such attitudes spread to the gentry, upper echelons of the 'middling sort' and down to the lower middling classes. Stone, for example, uncovers a fascinating libertine group amongst craftsmen and their wives in early-eighteenth-century Norwich. This small coterie, including a bookseller and book-binder, an artist, a weaver, a maid and the wife of the bookseller, engaged in many erotic games involving voyeurism, group sex, wife-swapping, trimming pubic hair and extensive bisexual flagellation.[46]

As cities like London and Paris grew to a significant size during the seventeenth and eighteenth centuries, labourers, sailors, tradesmen, and a host of others made a life for themselves in the teeming metropolis. This was a large culture of mobile men, freed from the social constraints of village life, who frequented pubs and brothels in large numbers. Women, similarly, were freer in the city to make their own way. Working life could be periodic and tenuous and casual prostitution was a means of supplementing inadequate wages. This was not so much a cultivated ethic as a mode of life produced by the social relationships of the emergent cities.[47] By the eighteenth century people from a broad cross section of the population began to consider the 'sins of the flesh' as harmless and natural.

The Enlightenment attack on the clerisy and religious doctrine, and the promotion of mechanical and natural law conceptions of the universe hastened the decline of religious authority and sexual Puritanism. Enlightenment philosophers condemned religious doctrine, and promoted nature, pleasure and passion as the sources of morality and guides to the conduct of life. These ideas spread rapidly amongst other classes. The dramatic increase in the publication and sale of pornography is one indicator of this diffusion of libertinism and the importance of obscenity in the creation of modernity. A note of caution is required. While the proliferation of pornography might indicate a loosening of sexual constraints, it also reflected profound changes in technologies of dissemination. Cheaper and quicker forms of printing, the increase in the number of booksellers, the spread of literacy, the accessibility of pamphlets, newspapers and books and the popularity of coffee houses promoting reading and discussion created a ready market for radical and subversive literatures.[48]

In challenging a dominant religious and secular culture that advocated narrow definitions of sex as procreation, libertines explored the limits of bodily sensations through oral, anal and other forms of sexual pleasure such as voyeurism, flagellation, bondage and coprophilia. Many of these are evident in the pornographic literature of the period. The Marquis de Sade is an example of the desire to push bodily sensation, and the writing about sex acts, to new extremes. His literary efforts point to the problems in Steven Marcus' rigid distinction between pornography and literature.[49] The work of de Sade is literary, political and philosophical as much as pornographic.[50]

An important dimension of libertinism, however, is the way it played with conventions of gender. Cross-dressing, masquerade and 'passing' were favourite pastimes of libertines. In a variety of public spaces men and women passed for the opposite sex, testing the boundaries between nature and culture, pushing against forms of social toleration and delighting in the capacity to live gender as fluid, malleable forms of theatre.[51] Cross-dressing and passing had been a feature of European culture for centuries, serving many functions and heightening cultural anxieties. It was a way for women to enter public spaces normally denied them. Equally it was a way for men and women seeking a life in a same-sex relationship to go out in public disguised as man and wife.[52] The prevalence of cross-dressing, masquerade and passing in eighteenth-century libertine circles suggests that these practices were also ways of exploring the cultural limits of gender, undermining conventions of appropriate behaviour. They were forms of play, fun and excitement that gave added flavour to forms of seduction and sexual excess. In 'turning the world upside down' libertines revealed the cultural rather the natural character of social identity, threatening the boundaries of social order.[53]

While libertinism may have expanded sexual opportunities for some women, it also constrained others. In emphasizing women's sexual excesses and availability, libertines also reduced women to the image of the whore, ever available and compliant in the satisfaction of man's needs. Some of the frankly celebratory histories of greater sexual freedom in the eighteenth century have been displaced by a far more critical historiography, which has focused on the ways in which libertine ideas reduced women to being sexual objects, limiting their capacity for sexual autonomy. Moreover, sexual liberty had no impact on social and political liberty for women. They remained legally, politically and socially subservient to men.[54]

Libertine practices, however, were far from dominant. Eighteenth-century ideas and sensibilities also promoted companionate marriage, romance and domesticity. Ideals of romantic love and domesticity sexualized marriage and made it a relationship in which people expected to satisfy desires for passion and companionship. The older patriarchal structures of the early-modern family in Europe and colonial America were undermined by a more egalitarian ethos.[55] Romantic ideas about the intimate relationship between nature and emotion, as elevated states of being, put love at the core of social and sexual life. Numerous advice manuals and tracts advocated marriage based on affection rather than alliance. On both sides of the Atlantic, marriage was idealized as a relationship of love, conducted within a secure domestic space, where both partners could find sexual fulfilment.[56] For Lawrence Stone, the great cultural divide between marriage for procreation and sexual companionship, which had been a feature of European sexual cultures for centuries, was slowly closed.[57] Stone's 'great transformation', however, has been questioned by historians, such as Ralph Houlbrooke, who stress the continuities in English family life. For Houlbrooke, close domestic relationships, familial affection, care for children and other attributes of Stone's 'affective' revolution, can be traced much earlier.[58]

Regardless of the roots of domesticity, historians have tended to see a heightened emphasis on emotion, sentiment and affective relations amongst the middling and patrician classes of the eighteenth century. There were many cultural and social tributaries feeding this revolution in sentiment. During the eighteenth century a new culture of sensibility arose, which promoted the idea that refined people, especially women, should cultivate a consciousness of one's own and others' feelings. This promoted ideals of domestic harmony, but also allowed women to assert a measure of power within the middle-class home.[59]

Allied to this was the growth of ideas of self-discipline and restraint. Instead of gratifying one's immediate desires, giving into emotion, the hallmark of refinement became the capacity to overcome instinct. In aristocratic circles, according to Norbert Elias, this meant new freedoms for women in marriage. It underpinned a new ethic granting greater equality for women within this relationship.[60] Similar developments underpinned bourgeois ideals of marriage. This union was now seen as fundamental to fostering self-discipline, refinement and civility. The ideal of marriage became more egalitarian and companionate, with husband and wife working harmoniously to provide a close-knit domestic space, a haven from the public world, for the satisfaction of needs and the rearing of children.[61]

Other historians, however, have questioned the egalitarian nature of Romantic ideals of marriage. Despite the ideology of companionship and growing intolerance of wife-beating, many historians have highlighted continuing patterns of marital violence, adultery and brutality, suggesting that the enforcement of patriarchal authority remained an important dimension of many marriages.[62] On both sides of the Atlantic the sexual division of labour was entrenched, confining women to a much narrower social and domestic sphere. Moreover, the majority of women in eighteenth-century Europe and America continued to live on farms and in small rural communities, denying access to the sexual, economic and social opportunities of the city.[63]

Even if Romantic and domestic ideals of marriage flourished, the consequences for women are in dispute. Jean-Louis Flandrin, for example, has argued that a new concern of husbands for the health and well-being of their wives underpinned the significant fall in the French birth rate from the 1780s. Men treated wives with greater gallantry and care, seeking to practise fertility control to save their wives from the dangers of childbirth.[64] In contrast Angus McLaren has argued that the same ideals in England led to continuing increases in the birth rate (which did not begin to fall until nearly a century later). More importantly he suggests that fertility control divided couples. In France women developed greater levels of solidarity to resist male sexual advances and control their own fertility, and thus carved out for themselves 'a less domestic, less fettered life'. In England the greater emphasis on domesticity and egalitarian marriage, ironically, constrained women. They were cut off from society, more closely confined to the domestic sphere and hence more dependent upon their husbands. For McLaren, 'romantic marriages' limited the freedom of women, promoting domesticity, but this meant they were less able to resist the sexual advances of husbands and control their own fertility, at considerable risk to their own lives.[65]

Sexual Difference

The historiography on fertility patterns, family formation, affection, sensibility and domestic ideals has greatly expanded our knowledge of both sexual ideas and practices in early-modern Europe and America. In terms of a larger historical narrative of sexuality, however, this work presents problems. Two tropes structure the work of historians like Stone, Shorter or Godbeer. For Stone and Shorter, in particular, concepts of repression and tolerance are integral to the historical analysis of sex. In this they echo the ideas of Steven Marcus and John Boswell, whose work we have examined at some length. All these historians see the history of sexuality as essentially cyclical – oscillating periods of repression and tolerance. Sex in this context is transhistorical and enters history because social circumstances determine its various forms. Another crucial concept in this historiography is that of sexual underworlds. Here historians, such as Richard Godbeer and G.S. Rousseau contrast official ideas of continence and domesticity with the abundant evidence for sexual transgression, disobedience and freedom. In some hands, notably Richard Godbeer's, such concepts structure a clear narrative of generational conflict, social change and the ways sexual practices were shaped by broader social, economic and political forces. This is illuminating work, but it ignores questions of sexual identity and deeper transformations in the ways sexuality has been understood, themes central to the historiography of sexuality.

Other historians, however, have taken up complex questions about sexual identity in early-modern Europe and America. For Thomas Laqueur, the idea of the one-sex body, which had dominated Western conceptions of sex and gender for over two millennia, was overthrown in the eighteenth century.[66] Instead of male and female bodies being seen as essentially the same, on a hierarchal continuum, they were now considered fundamentally different. Women's organs were no longer seen as lesser forms of the man's, but signifiers of completely distinct bodies. Organs that had shared a name were now distinguished. For example, the vagina had traditionally been referred to as the 'sheath' or 'scabbard' or by Latin terms such as *phuseos* that applied to both male and female anatomy. But in the late-seventeenth century anatomists such as William Crowther began to distinguish the female 'sheath' from the penis, referring to it as *vagina uteri*. Moreover, basic structures of the body thought common to men and women were now seen as distinctly male and female. Anatomists even came to see the essential differences between male and female bodies in the skeletal structure.[67]

In important ways bodies became emblematic of sexual difference at the deepest levels of biology. As Ludmilla Jordanova has argued, during the eighteenth century the nervous system was feminized and musculature was masculinized, thus grounding social and cultural differences in the body.[68] Under the Galenic system men and women had essentially similar anatomical structures; what distinguished them were different levels of heat and moistness. In the eighteenth century, however, differences between masculinity and femininity were present in the very structure of the body. Sex, rather than gender, became the foundation of difference. People were no longer distinguished by the presence or absence of heat, or by clearly designated gender roles, but by incommensurable differences of bodily structure and function. In place of the one-sex body emerged the idea of two distinct bodies – male and female.

This profound shift in understanding was not a consequence of scientific discoveries. Laqueur argues that there were no great scientific breakthroughs in anatomy or biology underpinning these changes.[69] What occurred was a new way of seeing the body. Anatomists, doctors and scholars looked at bodies and now saw fundamental difference where previously they had seen similarity. This led to increased interest in anatomy and physiology.[70] These developments had important consequences for understanding gender. Women's supposed greater gentleness and sentimentality, fondness of domesticity, relative muscular weakness and greater propensity for nervous illness were now rooted in their biology.

Such ideas also transformed the understanding of sex acts. Instead of being seen as a congress between an active and a passive partner, with the former bringing the latter to a state of heated excitement, sex became a conjunction of two very different bodies. Thus instead of sex being a distributive economy of fluids and heat across bodies, men and women came to have quite distinct sexual natures and functions. More significantly, Laqueur charts how female orgasm was no longer considered essential for conception to take place. If women were different they no longer had to resemble men in the sexual act to conceive.[71] But there is a danger in overemphasizing the depth of the rupture between the one-sex and the two-sex models. In important ways the pervasive metaphors of the traditional system of representation were reconfigured. Traditional ideas of the double standard became part of the two-sex system, with men being seen as naturally promiscuous and active and women as chaste and passive.[72]

For Laqueur, the origin of these profound changes in the understanding of sex lay in struggles over the constitution of an enlarged public.[73] During the eighteenth century gender was put at threat by the struggle for political and social rights based on claims of liberty and equality. Prominent women embraced new democratic movements, seeking to claim a measure of equality and rights for women. This represented a profound challenge to gender roles in European culture. Carole Pateman argues that democracy undermined older, patriarchal forms of political power (Kings, Lords), instituting new fraternal bonds of authority (between male citizens), effectively countering feminist claims for inclusion in the public sphere.[74] Emerging out of these political and ideological struggles was the assertion that women could not be included in the public sphere because they were fundamentally different to men. For Laqueur, ideas of sex difference became a way of supporting or denying 'all manner of claims in a variety of specific social, economic, political, cultural, or erotic contexts'. Although there were disputes over the nature of these sexed differences and their extent, the idea of difference became paradigmatic within European culture. Difference became a means for rewriting the foundations of moral order. Men could lay claim to political and cultural rights denied women because of their essential biological difference.[75]

Randolph Trumbach sees the emergence of new sexual identities as the site for the most profound changes in eighteenth-century European sexual cultures. At the end of the seventeenth century, he argues, a third gender appeared – the adult effeminate sodomite.[76] This group of 'mollies' was marked by effeminacy. They adopted distinctive habits of speech and dress, often dressing in women's clothes or 'foppish'

finery, and congregated in special clubs for drinking, dancing, flirta-
tion and sex, or frequented parks, public latrines, streets and arcades
looking for sexual partners. At the beginning of the eighteenth century
these men became the subject of greater public scrutiny and condemnation. Groups such as the Societies for the Reformation of Manners
attacked effeminate sodomites in print, and in so doing helped to construct the image of the 'molly' as a contemptible man, linking those who
flouted conventional codes of masculine behaviour with the idea that
such men favoured sex exclusively with other men.

Tim Hitchcock has argued that in the eighteenth century sodomy
was not viewed as serious or part of a subculture. Sodomy was acceptable amongst a small libertine elite frequenting 'molly' houses.[77] Rictor
Norton, however, has argued that the 'molly' subculture was extensive
and encompassed men from both the elite and the working classes.[78]
The greater public visibility of this subculture made men adopting
effeminate mannerisms increasingly vulnerable to persecution, black-
mail and punishment. In the eighteenth century increasing numbers
of men were arrested for sodomy and fined, imprisoned, sentenced to
the pillory or hanged. The persecution of sodomites in the eighteenth
century is well documented. Alan Bray has noted the intensification
in the policing of sodomites and out of these forms of legal regulation came a new focus on the idea of the sodomite as a distinct social
and sexual type. Before the late-seventeenth century words such as
sodomite and bugger signified behaviours that were frowned upon, but
such terms encompassed a range of acts (bestiality, oral as well as anal
sex) and could also include women who transgressed the law in the
act of having sex. By the early-eighteenth century, however, sodomite
became a term almost exclusively for the description of sexual acts
between men.[79]

Trumbach, however, argues that an equivalent lesbian subculture
did not really appear until the late-eighteenth century.[80] Other scholars disagree. Emma Donoghue and Valerie Traub have charted a very
visible female homoerotic culture in Europe from the sixteenth century.
There were well-known networks of women who resisted the imperative to marry. Instead they associated with other women and some were
known for their masculine demeanour. Although 'sapphists' were not
subject to the same legal persecution as 'mollies', representations of
such women established key stereotypes of female homoeroticism – the
tribade and friend – that in the nineteenth century became fundamental
to the way sexology pathologized lesbianism. Traub has also uncovered
a rich array of written and visual texts representing female intimacy and
homoeroticism well before the end of the eighteenth century.[81]

The fixing of the adult male effeminate role as the 'condition of all
males who engaged in sexual relations with other males', however, had

a marked effect on the conduct of male sexuality. For Trumbach, the appearance of this 'reviled type' forced men to assert their masculine status. It encouraged men, of all classes, to orient their sexual desire towards an exclusive focus on women, for fear of being condemned for effeminacy. Males were 'now obliged to present themselves as sexually active' rather than passive once they entered puberty. As a result the age-old European sexual culture that tolerated sexual relations between men and adolescent boys was undermined. These processes of social regulation, definition and persecution were complex. Trumbach shows that many boys and men charged with sodomy and sodomitical assault showed no conventional signs of effeminacy. But in their trial they were represented as 'mollies' and thus suffered the stigma of this identity and the harsh penal consequences of such an attribution.

The emergence of this third gender meant that increasingly men, out of fear, began to constitute themselves around the identity of being sexually interested only in women. Thus the specification of the third gender was integral to the emergence of the idea of a heterosexual identity. In this context sex ceased to be seen as something between an active and a passive partner, regardless of gender, but ideally as an act between men and women. Those who flouted this ideal risked legal and social retribution.

Conclusion

Randolph Trumbach's analysis of the emergence and effects of new sexual identities in early-modern Europe raises important questions for the history of sexuality. He has mapped significant and far-reaching transformations in the historical nature of homosexuality and heterosexuality. In a broader context, however, there are legitimate questions about whether the eighteenth century is a fundamental turning point in the making of heterosexuality. As we have seen, a number of historians have argued that distinct sexual identities emerged well before the eighteenth century. Guido Ruggerio has argued that the sodomite became a distinct sexual identity as early as the fourteenth century in Italy.[82] We can go back even further to the condemnation of the *cinaedi* in Rome in late antiquity, for the pathologization of effeminate males who seemed to prefer sex with men.[83] In later chapters we will discuss work on men who identified as heterosexual but engaged in sex with other men provided they were the active partner.

Was there anything really different about the persecution of effeminate sodomites in eighteenth-century Europe and America? The history of past male effeminate subcultures questions the uniqueness of eighteenth-century constructions of identity. Moreover, Halperin has argued that discourses on male effeminacy since antiquity are largely

about inversion not homosexuality. What most offended was the transgression of gender stereotypes not the nature of homoerotic sex.[84]

Trumbach's focus on how men responded to the persecution of
'mollies', however, indicates that something new was happening in European sexual culture. Why European men of the eighteenth century
responded to the moral panic of effeminacy by asserting a heterosexual identity, when men of earlier centuries had not, is far from clear.
The processes Trumbach sees as largely eighteenth-century may actually have taken centuries to evolve and may have continued to evolve
in the nineteenth and twentieth centuries. Nonetheless, when we see
Trumbach and Laqueur's work together some significant changes
do seem to have occurred in European sexual cultures. Although
Laqueur's focus is on the discourse of sex and Trumbach's concern is
gender, both presage the idea that a culture based on the dichotomy
of active and passive was gradually replaced by one structured round
difference – male and female, homosexual and heterosexual.

Chapter 6

VICTORIANISM

Only the nineteenth century has achieved the distinction of being a 'sexual epoch'. The Victorian era has found a central place in popular culture as a period of excessive sexual austerity, repression and prudery. In the pioneering histories of Steven Marcus, Eric Trudgill and Ronald Pearsall, Victorian sexuality was depicted as a period of Puritan moralism, an inevitable reaction against the aristocratic libertinism of the eighteenth century. Queen Victoria's insistence on propriety and respectability seemed, to nineteenth-century moral reformers and twentieth-century historians alike, to define the age that bore her name.

Victorian moral rectitude was not confined to England. These values and anxieties were shared on both sides of the Atlantic. For the early historians of Victorian sexuality, however, this was also an age of hypocrisy. Social conventions made discussion of sex, sexuality and bodily functions taboo, but at the same time pornography and prostitution flourished. For Marcus and Pearsall, the sexual puritanism of the middle classes drove sex underground, creating a split in Victorian culture. Public prudery masked a flourishing trade in vice. These historians see the new sexual morality as the creation of a sober, austere, self-controlled and frugal middle class, whose ideas gradually held sway over other classes in Britain, Europe and America. Victorianism came to dominate the ideas, habits and social conventions of the entire society but, for Marcus and others, sexual desire could never entirely be tamed. It found outlets in the flourishing vice trade.[1]

The views of early historians of Victorianism echoed those of earlier critics. At the end of the nineteenth and beginning of the twentieth centuries a host of influential doctors and reformers, such as Havelock Ellis, Margaret Sanger, Edward Carpenter, Richard von Krafft-Ebing, Sigmund Freud and Magnus Hirschfeld, diagnosed the consequences of sexual repression and pointed to Victorianism as an era of unhealthy sexual adjustment. They were advocates of sexual reform, urging greater frankness in sexual matters and tolerance of a diverse range of sexual practices. It was these critics who constructed the image of the Victorian era as a period of heightened repression. Sexual liberals promoted an ideal of greater sexual freedom, challenging the beliefs of moralists who saw sex as a threat to social and religious order.[2] Thus our sense of the nineteenth century as a distinct period of sexual history, marked by a single trajectory and voice, comes first from those Victorians who sought to escape the embrace of these mores. Later historians took these characterizations as if they were fact, perpetuating the idea of Victorianism as synonymous with repression.

Since the late 1970s revisionist historians have done much to dismantle this simplistic historical cliché. For Michel Foucault, the 'repressive hypothesis' became the critical point of departure for an investigation of the explosion of sexual discourses in the nineteenth century. These discourses, he argued, constructed sexuality as the central domain for the decipherment of the self in modern Western cultures. Far from repressing sex the Victorians invented sexuality.[3] Others, such as Jeffrey Weeks, Michael Mason, Helen Lefkowitz Horowitz and Peter Gay, also highlight a wide range of evidence that challenges the idea of excessive repression. In place of Victorianism we can see the emergence of a more complex account stressing the proliferation of sexual discourses and the clash of sexual cultures in the nineteenth century. Equally important, historians such as Nancy Cott, Mary Ryan and Carroll Smith-Rosenberg have situated discourses of sexuality and moral reform in a wider context of rapid social transformation and gender crisis.

These revisions are not just a matter of adding new 'facts'. Historians of the Victorian era have traditionally relied heavily on medical sources and pornography to write the narrative of sexual hypocrisy. Revisionist historians, however, have highlighted the importance of putting such evidence into a broader cultural context. The language of Victorianism was enacted in a larger symbolic sphere, constructing new identities and oppositions that transformed the way men and women understood sex. Other historians have turned to evidence, such as diaries, popular literature, magazines, and advertisements to explore the diverse class, gender and ethnic sexual cultures that shaped nineteenth-century sexual experience. As a consequence of this extensive new research it is now questionable whether the concept of 'Victorianism' can be sustained. The range of sexual ideas and customs within the Victorian era have been shown to be so broad, varied and even contradictory that the notion of a single, coherent sexual culture, developed by historians such as Marcus and Pearsall, seems overly narrow. Victorianism needs to be abandoned as a meaningful category, even though it remains a useful device for exploring the pitfalls of universalizing approaches to the history of sexuality.

Victorian Fertility

When did the Victorian sexual epoch begin? Despite the name it certainly does not correspond precisely to the reign of Queen Victoria (1837–1901), although there is a significant overlap. A more conventional answer might be to see the Victorian era as a synonym for the nineteenth century, or for some historians the years from the end of the Napoleonic Wars (1815) to the beginning of the Great War (1914).[4] But if so, what is it that makes this century distinctive in sexual terms? Should we take particular ideas and attitudes as the defining characteristic of Victorianism? If so, should it be dated to the early decades of the nineteenth century when the Evangelical revival in England and the Second Great Awakening in America were in full flower? If sexual moralism is the key, how do we accommodate the sexual libertinism of London radicals groups, such as those lead by Richard Carlile, which flourished in the 1820s and 1830s? Should we take the dramatic upsurge in the nineteenth century of tracts warning against the 'evils' of masturbation as a key indicator of a new sexual morality? Or should we take heed of the emergence of anxieties about the extent of masturbation from the mid-eighteenth century? Alternatively, we might take Victorianism as the period when ideas began to have significant social effects, such as a marked decline in the birth rate. If so, does Victorianism begin in the 1780s when birth rates start to fall in France, or 1850 when the rate commences its long period of decline in England?

Moreover, when does Victorianism end? Do we follow Steven Marcus and see Freud as the herald of the end of the era of sexual repression? Or should we see the work of Kinsey in the 1950s, or perhaps the sexual revolution of the 1960s, as the final overthrow of sexual puritanism? Different answers are again possible if we take sexual practices rather than ideas as the main signifier of Victorianism. Does the dramatic rise in the birth rate in Britain and America after World War II finally signal the end of Victorian reticence about sex?

At first glance, fertility decline would appear to be strong evidence for greater levels of sexual austerity. A number of historians, such as Daniel Scott Smith, Linda Gordon and Barry Smith, have argued that declining birth rates were largely the result of sexual abstinence.[5] Similarly, Simon Szreter has argued that coitus interruptus was merely one part of a larger 'culture of abstinence and sexual disinclination', where coital frequency dropped as couples actively negotiated to reduce the number of children they produced.[6] Moreover, a number of historians, such as Angus McLaren and Linda Gordon, have seen coitus interruptus as the major form of nineteenth-century contraception.[7] Szreter and other historians of abstinence have generally seen withdrawal as a form of 'sexual disinclination'. This link reflects the weight of nineteenth-century literature preaching the virtues of sexual continence. But seeing abstinence and withdrawal as similar practices is questionable. Withdrawal might equally suggest great interest in sex but a desire to avoid conception. Szreter's assumption requires more detailed investigation.

Religious injunctions to practice abstinence indicate an important transformation in Protestantism. Until the nineteenth century Protestant theology had idealized sexual relations within marriage. The popular idea of 'conjugal debt', where both husbands and wives had a right to demand intercourse, signified an acceptance of the naturalness of marital relations.[8] The Evangelical revival in late-eighteenth- and early-nineteenth-century England and the Second Great Awakening in early-nineteenth-century America, however, stressed the virtues of moral purity and sexual restraint. In the context of the perceived breakdown of older community bonds, the disruptions of war and revolution, urbanization and the emergence of large and visible centres of commercial vice, radical Protestant sects urged a moral renewal to combat social decay. Numerous organizations such as the English Society for the Suppression of Vice (1802) and the American Society for Female Moral Reform (1835), sought to reform manners, promote sexual restraint and stamp out vice.[9]

Evangelicals and radical Protestants were united in their view that the family had to become the main force for moral training. Their 'god-given' ideal was the bourgeois family, characterized by moral rectitude, piety, and cultivation of the sentiments and domestic harmony. Family life was structured around the separation of male and female spheres of influence. For prominent evangelicals and moral reformers, women were properly the guardians of the private sphere, managing domestic affairs, creating a harmonious home life, supporting and nurturing both husband and children.[10] Men devoted their lives to the world of public affairs – business, politics, empire, war, philanthropy.[11] In reality middle-class family structures were subject to wide regional and occupational variations. Moreover, the work of historians, such as Catharine Hall and Leonore Davidoff, has shown that the separate spheres were actually heavily interdependent. Men could not succeed in public life without the emotional and social support of their wives, and often craved home as a haven from the exertions of the world. Women played a crucial role in forging social networks and associations that supported the public careers of husbands. Ironically religion and philanthropy also offered middle-class women the opportunity for an active public career.[12]

Although domestic ideology and moral reform were influential on both sides of the Atlantic, there were some important differences in the shape of these new religious movements in England and America. Although there were prominent women, such as Hannah More and Mary

Carpenter in the English Evangelical revival, the leading figures in the Clapham sect were men. Powerful figures, such as William Wilberforce, dominated moral reform politics. Despite the Evangelical emphasis on moral probity and a strict interpretation of the gospels, the English movement was less theologically radical than the American sects that actively opposed ritualism, and encouraged individualism and mysticism. Equally important, although men were still prominent leaders in the Second Great Awakening, women dominated the American movement. They organized prayer meetings, pressuring merchants to close shops, and invading brothels to plead with prostitutes and admonish men.[13]

The more prominent place of women in the Evangelical revival in America might be one factor in the significant difference in the timing of the decline in the birth rate. Another factor might be the impact of democratic ideas of rights that flourished in the American colonies in the late-eighteenth and early-nineteenth century. While English women had to confront the backlash against the French Revolution, American women lived in a culture committed to revolutionary ideals. Although women lacked the political rights of their brothers, commitment to moral reform was a means for acceptable, female, political participation. In America, particularly the New England colonies, women were more forthright in claiming a voice in the public sphere. Nancy Cott has suggested that by the 1830s domestic ideals eventually subsumed the equalitarian aspirations of American women. But the 'bonds of womanhood' enhanced women's social role, giving them confidence that in matters of home and family their voice was paramount.[14] Although women in the southern colonies were constrained by the restrictive ideals of 'chivalry' and the 'Southern lady', in New England middle-class women had a prominent private role, one which also sanctioned their work as moral reformers.[15] As Mary Ryan has shown, in the 1820s and 1830s it was amongst this group of women that the decline in the birth rate was first evident.[16]

The belief that the respectable classes should lead by example in checking excessive fertility had secular support. In Britain the dramatic increase in fertility in the late-eighteenth century increased fears about whether society was able to bear the consequences of a significantly larger population. The most famous formulation of these anxieties, Thomas Malthus' *Essay on the Principle of Population* (1798), foretold a world where the rate of increase in population far outstripped the capacity of the land to sustain this number of people. In an interesting reading of this essay, Thomas Laqueur has argued that the influence of Malthus' essay arose because it knitted together an understanding of desire, the body and the economy.[17] For Malthus, the market economy was driven by the desire for material goods, social prestige and bodily pleasure, enticing men and women to labour to achieve these wants. This presented a social dilemma. If the market economy unleashed passions, dramatically increasing production and wealth, then the consequence of this unshackling of desire, increasing population, would have disastrous effects such as starvation, privation, unruliness and riot. This was a key problem for Victorian political economists and social reformers. How could one advance the market economy without exacerbating poverty and social unrest?[18]

Moral restraint was one answer. While Evangelical reformers saw sexual abstinence as morally uplifting, political economists saw control of fertility in social and economic terms. Malthus had little faith in the capacity to check human passions, and instead focused on the necessity for birth control, a solution embraced by a small but vigorous group of Neo-Malthusians in the late-nineteenth century. American and British Neo-Malthusians such as Henry Allbutt, A.S. Dyer, Charles Knowlton, Frederick Hollick, Edward Bliss Foote, George Drysdale, Charles Bradlaugh and Annie Besant, were fervent preachers of the family limitation message in the nineteenth century. Their tracts sold well. Barry Smith argues that such ideas emerged first amongst the 'self-instructed' classes but spread quickly to the middle classes. What is more certain is that these ideas circulated widely amongst the respectable working classes and all sections of the middle classes.[19]

In the second half of the nineteenth century the conjunction in Britain of a flourishing moral reform movement, socialism and Neo-Malthusianism propelled the case for birth control, restraint and abstinence. Moreover, by the middle of the century the work of social and moral investigators, such as Henry Mayhew, Frederick Engels, Mary Carpenter and James Kay Shuttleworth, and later Charles Booth, highlighted the threat of 'darkest London'.[20] To both secular and religious reformers the control of fertility was essential to arrest social decline, exploitation, vice and corruption. The influence of these ideas is most apparent in the dramatic decline in the English birth rate from the 1850s, a decline that had spread to most social classes by the end of the century. Neo-Malthusian ideas also spread to the Continent in the late-nineteenth century, at a time of rapid fertility decline in Germany, Italy and Spain.[21]

Other historians, however, have been more sceptical about the impact of ideas on fertility. New ideas took hold because social and economic circumstances impelled changes in fertility. In France the decline of the birth rate was most prevalent amongst the bourgeoisie, which sought to increase its disposable wealth, and the peasantry, which sought to prevent impoverishment by reducing the number of male heirs claiming a share of the farm.[22] In early-nineteenth-century America moral reform ideas were powerful, but Mary Ryan has also shown that decline of available land in the agricultural hinterland of New York lead to a rapid turnaround in fertility patterns. Without available land to expand family farms children became an economic burden, rather than an opportunity to increase wealth.[23] In the second half of the nineteenth century in England and Germany, the aspirations to respectability of the middle and skilled working classes and the regulations against child labour and vagaries of the labour market for the working classes, made the economics of smaller families more attractive.[24]

Abstinence and birth control, despite efforts to link them by historians such as Szreter, lead in very different directions in a history of sexuality. While sexual continence suggests that husbands and wives decided, singly or together, to refrain from intercourse, birth control presupposes couples actively engaged in sex, with at least one partner, and commonly both, resorting to measures to prevent conception. Although there is evidence, mainly in diaries and letters, that evangelical and Neo-Malthusian couples heeded the message of sexual austerity, there is also abundant evidence of the widespread resort to contraception. Most historians have pointed to the popularity of withdrawal, and even non-ejaculatory (coitus reservatus or 'karezza') methods of intercourse. Such techniques were far from foolproof. Artificial methods were thus common. Sponges, diaphragms and pessaries were widely advertised in the nineteenth century. Such techniques were more effective if used with douching. By the 1850s vulcanized rubber condoms were available, although priced out of reach of the working classes. In the late-nineteenth century, Neo-Malthusians, such as Henry Allbutt popularized cocoa butter, glycerine, acidic powder and jelly spermicides.[25]

Contraception often failed. Withdrawal was risky and accidents could always happen with mechanical devices. Efforts to time intercourse with a safe period were hampered by ignorance of ovulation. Until the 1920s most doctors wrongly believed that the middle of the cycle was safe. Moreover, despite the widespread advertisements for contraceptive devices, most were expensive and unreliable. Angus McLaren cites evidence that by the early-twentieth century only 16 percent of married couples used mechanical devices. Some American surveys of middle-class women in the late-nineteenth and early-twentieth centuries indicated much greater usage of contraception, commonly of equally unreliable methods such as douching.[26] Unwanted pregnancies were the consequence.

Historians, such as Szreter, have argued that the costs and unreliability of contraception mean that abstinence was the real cause of fertility decline, dismissing abortion as an alternative. Relying on survey evidence to show that few women, even working-class women, admitted to any knowledge of abortion, Szreter believes that this practice was a negligible factor in the declining birth rate.[27] Given the small sample of respondents and the stigma of abortion such statements may be unreliable and, more importantly, they run counter to the abundant evidence for a thriving abortion trade in the nineteenth century.

Other historians, relying on newspaper advertisements, quack practices, criminal court and prison records, as well as figures on maternal mortality (largely due to infections from botched abortions and induced miscarriages) which remained high long after infant mortality began to decline, have argued that abortion was a significant factor in fertility decline.[28] Divorce and criminal court records document numerous cases of wives resorting to abortion because husbands refused to 'restrain themselves'.[29] James Mohr has concluded that abortion was widely used by middle-class women in America before it was outlawed in the late-nineteenth century.[30]

Abortifacients were widely advertised. Traditional methods of abortion offered by midwives, such as herbal remedies – pennyroyal, tansy, ergot of rye and other emmenagogues – were well known. In the nineteenth century there was a thriving 'quack' business in new abortifacients, such as lead, steel and phosphorous pills. In 1898 one noted abortion business in England had a client list of 10,000. The use of instruments was widespread, with the increased availability of cheap catheters, sounds, probes and injections. By the late-nineteenth century doctors sought a share of this lucrative market, offering curettage as an alternative. In France, by the end of the nineteenth century, there were as many as 100,000 to 500,000 abortions a year.[31] There were, however, class and regional variations in the methods deployed. Some evidence indicates that women from the rural and urban poor, including African Americans, relied more heavily on herbal and drug abortions, while middle-class women resorted to more expensive, but also more dangerous, instrument methods.[32]

Another reason for disentangling abstinence and birth control is that contraception was embroiled in controversy. Despite the popularity of birth control measures many doctors, moral reformers and politicians sought to prevent their use. The sources of this opposition were diverse. Moral reformers feared that birth control encouraged moral indulgence. Doctors witnessed the serious consequences of botched abortions, leading to permanent infertility and sometimes death. Other doctors resented the loss of custom to 'quacks' and midwives. By the late-nineteenth century the conjunction of an active woman's movement and the declining birth rate fanned masculinist anxieties that women were refusing to accept their natural place in the private sphere. Moreover, in the last decades of the century, eugenicist fears that middle-class women were reducing their fertility, while those from the 'degenerate' classes were not, added weight to the conviction that birth control was a social menace.[33]

Throughout the nineteenth century there were efforts to prosecute abortionists and those who spread birth control advice. In 1873 the

American Congress passed the Comstock Law, which made the sending of birth control literature through the mail illegal. Four years later, English Neo-Malthusians Annie Besant and Charles Bradlaugh were put on trial for publishing Charles Knowlton's birth control tract. More importantly, abortion was made a criminal offence. Traditionally abortion had been acceptable if performed before 'quickening' (when mothers were supposed to be able to feel the foetus), roughly the fourth month of pregnancy. In 1803 this doctrine was abolished in England, abortion becoming illegal at any stage in the pregnancy. In America the concept of quickening remained current until the 1840s, but agitation by doctors and moral reformers lead to laws making abortion a criminal offence. The first was passed in Illinois in 1867 and other States soon followed. Similar efforts to make all abortions illegal occurred on the Continent in the late-nineteenth and early-twentieth centuries.[34]

Abortion and birth control may have become the object of greater legal regulation in the nineteenth century, but the enforcement of these laws was far from rigorous. While the passage of legislation highlights emergent public anxieties about lack of moral restraint, women's 'selfish' reproductive management and the decline in the birth rate, there were other male interests at play in the politics of birth control. Despite legal sanctions and occasional prosecutions birth control and abortion businesses continued to thrive. The rate of abortion appears to have increased across the Western world in the late-nineteenth and early-twentieth centuries, with a corresponding decline in post-natal practices such as infanticide and baby farming. Those most directly involved with policing the abortion trade – police, magistrates and local council and parish authorities, as well as the people who could report well-known local abortionists – did not always exhibit great enthusiasm for the task. Many of them were men conscious of the fact that abortionists assisted desperate single women, who were the victims of rape, seduction and abandonment. They were also aware that many couples were anxious to limit the number of children they produced. Sometimes they turned a 'blind eye', knowing that men of their acquaintance were the seducers or husbands who benefited from the availability of birth control and abortion.[35]

The dramatic decline in the birth rate in the West throughout the nineteenth century did not necessarily signify greater sexual repression. Although many middle-class couples adopted an ethic of restraint to better regulate fertility, abstinence itself, despite the claims of historians such as Simon Szreter, seems an inadequate explanation for fertility patterns. The widespread use of coitus interruptus, mechanical forms of birth control and abortion indicate that intercourse was widespread in the Victorian era. There were many sound economic reasons to have smaller families and women and couples of all classes acted to reduce the birth rate. Birth control and abstinence were different responses to this desire. Moreover, the politics of family limitation, birth control and abortion indicates that there were many different interests clamouring to control sex and its consequences.

Sexual Anxieties

Sex was dangerous. This was the message of a vast amount of nineteenth-century moral reform, social conduct, pedagogy, child-rearing and medical advice literature. This was literally so for the women who died in childbirth or from botched abortions. It was also harmful to the men, women and children afflicted with venereal diseases.[36] Increasing rates of literacy and the mass production of cheap pamphlets and books facilitated the growth of a popular medical advice market. This literature conjured up a larger world of threat. Sex could undermine a fragile nervous system and deplete the body. Medical practitioners and the plethora of pamphleteers who peddled medical, child-rearing and social conduct advice to a wide audience were, in the evocative phrase of Alex Comfort, 'anxiety makers'.[37] Despite this climate of threat early historians of Victorian sexuality, such as Marcus and Pearsall, were eager to point to extensive prostitution, the high incidence of venereal disease and the proliferation of pornography as evidence that Victorians flouted medical advice and social convention. Victorians preached restraint but practised vice. As we have seen, this led Marcus to diagnose a split in Victorian culture between official ideas and an underground sexual culture. Revisionist historians have questioned this clear divide.

Historians of Victorian sexuality have understandably paid considerable attention to medical evidence. The voluminous opinions of doctors and charlatans created much of the climate of danger that enveloped sex in the nineteenth century. Moreover, the increasing prestige of the medical profession legitimated medical opinion making it a powerful voice shaping attitudes to the body and sexuality. Prominent Victorian medical practitioners, such as William Acton, author of *The Functions and Disorders of the Reproductive Organs in Youth, in Adult Age and in Advanced Life* (1857), saw the body as a fixed system of sexual energy. Orgasm represented a loss of energy, and thus a drain on the vital reserves of the body. This hydraulic theory of sexuality, where sexual energy was a reservoir that was depleted and never replenished, shaped medical fears about infantile sexuality, masturbation, excessive coition and a range of other forms of sexuality.

Acton was not alone in these views. A rich array of medical and moral texts sought to warn of the dangers of sex outside marriage. This literature offered sober advice on the need to focus sexuality on reproduction, limit the frequency of sexual intercourse, prevent children from touching their genitals, and hide books and pictures that might excite delicate sensibilities. This advice was conveyed in a richly euphemistic vernacular of private parts, members, bushes, and fields, wandering hands, some of which crossed over into pornographic literature.[38]

One of the most prevalent themes in this advice literature was the evil of masturbation. This fear can be dated fairly precisely. Tissot's famous treatise *On Onania* (1760) was one of the first of many European and American tracts arguing that masturbation caused general debility, nervousness, and a host of other disorders, even madness. This increasing obsession with the deleterious effects of masturbation has puzzled historians. Although Christian churches had condemned masturbation for centuries because it did not lead to procreation, before the late-eighteenth century there was remarkably little comment on 'self abuse' as threatening to health. Some historians, such as Edward Shorter and Jean-Louis Flandrin, have concluded that masturbation was almost unknown before the late-eighteenth century.[39] Other studies question this direct correlation between prohibitions and actual practice. For example, Tim Hitchcock has shown that masturbation was a common resort of young men, part of the courtship ritual enabling couples to defer marriage.[40] In a wider culture increasingly interested in promoting the virtues of individual self-control, productivity, saving, restraint and prosperity, however, masturbation came to be seen as waste, improvidence and moral weakness.[41]

These ideas were amplified and widely publicized in the nineteenth century by numerous doctors, charlatans and moral reformers. One of the great anxieties fanned by these writings was that masturbation caused impotence. Even sexual radicals, such as Richard Carlile, considered masturbation a threat to 'the nature of human solidarity'.[42] By the mid-nineteenth century medical practitioners had defined a specific condition arising from excessive loss of semen, spermatorrhoea, characterized by nervous debility and lethargy. Later in the century, another common nervous condition, neurasthenia, was defined by similar symptoms.[43]

These masturbation diseases fostered a large market in medical and quack cures for the 'depleted male system'. Rest, mountain walks, spas, herbal remedies, electrical stimulation belts and baths were just some of the many cures offered the sufferers of these conditions. Similar fears attended female masturbation. The belief in the greater vulnerability of women to nervous illness overlapped concerns about the effects of 'self abuse' on women. Masturbation exacerbated nervousness in women, undermining their desire to reproduce. Doctors advised rest and health spas for nervous women. A number also advocated extreme surgical measures, such as clitoridectomies, to stop female masturbation.[44] Parents were encouraged to be vigilant where children were concerned, and advised to use mechanical restraining devices to ensure that 'wandering hands' did not excite sexual organs during the night. Vigorous exercise, cold baths and the like were prescribed as excellent preventive measures.[45] Embedded in this literature were prevalent gender anxieties. Women who masturbated flouted the ideal of female 'passionlessness'.[46] While men were thought to have strong natural desires, 'real men' were considered capable of controlling these urges.[47]

The argument that medical practitioners were influential 'anxiety makers' has been challenged in recent years. While many doctors did not subscribe to all of Acton's views, Lesley Hall has argued that his views on the dangers of sexual excess were widely shared.[48] Other historians disagree, arguing that Acton was neither influential nor representative. They point to many respected authorities with very different views to Acton. For example, Jeanne Petersen has cited prominent doctors, such as Sir James Paget, who thought that masturbation was harmless. Political economist and liberal Jacob Bright dismissed Acton as illogical. Some of his claims about the health of prostitutes were dismissed as fanciful by influential sections of the medical profession. Many American and British doctors, feminists, radicals and moral reformers, such as Richard Carlile, Clelia Mosher, Alice Stockman, George Napheys, Elizabeth Cady Stanton and Elizabeth Blackwell, stoutly rejected Acton's views on female sexuality, claiming that the sexual passions were as strong in women as they were in men. This argument was endorsed by the *London Medical Review*.[49]

The anxiety thesis has also been questioned by studies of the dissemination of medical ideas. The marshalling of different views and opinions from a range of medical, political, religious and philanthropic authorities has its own pitfalls. While it fosters a sense of diversity, breaking down the monolithic entity of Victorianism, it cannot by itself give us an accurate picture of the influence of these ideas. Some of the major texts on sexuality in the nineteenth century sold very well. Charles Knowlton's *Fruits of Philosophy* (1876) sold over 165,000 copies, while Charles Drysdale's *Elements of Social Science* (1854) went to over 25 editions and sold as many if not more copies than Knowlton. Samuel Soloman's *Guide to Health, or Advice to Both Sexes* (1782) ran to 66 editions by 1817 and was still being printed in the 1870s. In America Edward Bliss Foote's *Medical Common Sense* (1858) sold 250,000 copies.[50] But regardless of these impressive sales figures, best sellers were probably not the main way in which the bulk of the population sought and obtained information about sex practices, orgasm, bodies, intercourse and sexual diseases.

Far more significant, particularly for the skilled and semi-skilled working classes, struggling petit bourgeoisie, and emergent lower professional and white collar classes, were the numerous journals, magazines, news sheets, advertisements, cheap advice guides and pamphlets. These popular writings, usually written by charlatans and medical hacks, distilled much of the reputable medical literature for a wider audience. Like Acton and other doctors, these charlatan tracts preyed on anxieties about impotence, sterility, menstruation and the pox. At the same time they 'titillated sexual curiosity', provided rudimentary physiological information and acquainted readers with basic information about sex and copulation. They also alerted readers to the existence of 'medical authorities' (mainly charlatans and quacks) prepared to offer further advice upon consultation.[51]

In addition, Victorians also attended cheap lectures, travelling medicine shows and popular museums of anatomy for instruction in elementary physiology. These performances and displays offered up a rich smorgasbord of often-contradictory advice. While much of it stressed the evils of 'over indulgence' and masturbation, other doctors and charlatans advised on ways of increasing potency. Similarly, while many pamphlets, journals and charlatans repeated the standard medical view that female orgasm was unnecessary for conception, other charlatans asserted that female orgasm was essential. Some doctors and charlatans advised on the need for men to have intercourse a few times a week, others as little as once or twice a year, and many found a figure somewhere between these extremes. As Roy Porter and Lesley Hall argue, there was a polyphony of voices on matters of sex in the nineteenth century.[52]

Helen Lefkowitz Horowitz has given the argument about diverse voices within Victorian sexual culture a sharper edge. Her illuminating account argues that there were four major sexual cultures in Victorian America, each imagining sex differently and jostling for supremacy. The first was a rich vernacular culture, which drew on traditional humeral ideas of the body and grounded in an 'earthy acceptance of sex and desire as vital parts of life for men and women'. Evangelical Christianity, however, held a 'deep distrust of the flesh' and advocated sexual continence. A third framework in Victorian culture was 'reform physiology'. Doctors and sexual radicals sought to enlighten people about modern knowledge of sexual functions and the body. They focused on reproductive organs, the nervous system, intricate relations between mind and body and the ways of living a healthy sexual life. Even Christian ministers and moralists slowly accepted new medical ideas of the body and sought to tie them to notions of moral restraint, sobriety, decorum and romantic love. For Horowitz, while Christians and freethinkers shared a common 'reform physiology' emphasis on health, this framework was sharply divided between those who saw sex as healthy and moralists who urged restraint to preserve health. The final Victorian framework grew out of 'reform physiology' but pushed it in more radical directions.

Emerging out of the free love movement were powerful voices, such as Victoria Woodhull and Ezra Heywood, who argued that sexual freedom and liberty were 'the most vital aspect of life'. They put sex at the centre of ideals of the self.[53]

Horowitz provides a striking critique of the idea of Victorianism. Her emphasis on battles between different Victorian cultures, with distinct understandings of the body and sex, highlights the limitations of the idea of a singular sexual epoch. Moreover, she argues forcefully that these were not merely differences of opinion but intensely political struggles. Using the law sexual moralists sought to suppress popular and radical sexual ideals. The campaigns against pornography, abortion, birth control, blasphemy, masturbation and obscenity were fought out in the courts. Equally important, these suppression efforts were contested and subverted. Horowitz's argument, however, is marred by a shallow and simplistic critique of Foucauldian approaches. According to Horowitz, Foucault characterizes Victorianism as a contest between expression and repression, glossing over Foucault's critique of both expression and repression and ignoring his work on the construction of sexual identities.

Nonetheless, her focus on the clash of diverse sexual cultures challenges the arguments of historians like Laqueur, who see a sharp rupture between traditional ideas of the body, going back millennia, and new notions of the one-sex body. Horowitz charts the persistence of older ideas well into the late-nineteenth century, raising questions about the formation of new sexual identities in the late-nineteenth century. Did the new identities constructed by the emerging sexual sciences of the late-nineteenth century have a significant impact on the vernacular tradition? Were such identities as homosexual, heterosexual, pervert or sadist as pervasive as historians like Foucault and Halperin supposed? We will return to this question in a later chapter.

One of the striking aspects of the Victorian literature on sex and the body is its medicalization.[54] Religious, moral and philosophical injunctions never disappeared, but they were swamped by the proliferation of medical texts on sex, the body, nervousness and venereal disease. Indeed, as Horowitz demonstrates, moralists gradually adopted medical ideas to argue for sexual restraint. The significant growth in the number of books and pamphlets by quacks, charlatans and doctors on the fringes of the profession reinforces the point. They sought legitimacy and credibility in a pseudo-medical language. It is not surprising then that historians have based many of their studies of Victorian sexuality on these medical and pseudo-medical sources. In doing so they have generally read them as mediums for imposing medical ideas of varying quality on an ignorant populace hungry for enlightenment.[55]

Horowitz's emphasis on the strength of vernacular sexual culture challenges the idea of medical hegemony. Michael Mason similarly has questioned the impact of new medical ideas. But unlike Horowitz, who sees the vernacular culture and reform physiology as frameworks in conflict, Mason sees them as intricately related. In Victorian England medical practitioners, particularly the great mass of general practitioners, were in a very competitive market, not only amongst themselves but also with the huge army of charlatans who peddled their cures with few impediments. In a tight market few doctors or charlatans could afford to stray too far from conventional wisdom in matters of sexual health. If doctors provided advice patients did not find palatable or acceptable, patients sought assistance from others.

Far from bringing the populace up to date, Mason argues that general practitioners continued to peddle obsolete ideas well into the late-nineteenth century. For example, although by the 1830s physicians, the elite of the profession, had concluded that ovulation was spontaneous and independent of female orgasm, general practitioners continued to advise patients that female orgasm was essential to conception until the late-nineteenth century. Similarly traditional doctrines, such as menstrual libido, disappointed pregnancy and uterine physiology, dismissed by Victorian physicians, were still found in nineteenth-century medical literature aimed at a popular market. Mason concludes that much of the medical profession, rather than interfering moralistically into the sexuality of patients, were actually the captives of lay opinions and prejudices. Medical sources, he argues, instead of masking or destroying common beliefs, could be a means of uncovering a rich history of popular attitudes to sexuality.[56]

Medical opinion may have been far from uniform in its attitude to sex, orgasm and masturbation, but underlying the polyphony of voices on Victorian sexuality lay pervasive attitudes to masculinity and femininity. Historians of Victorian sexuality have devoted considerable attention to the ways in which medical and moral advice constructed gender. William Acton is famous for declaring that 'the majority of women are not much troubled by sexual feeling of any kind'.[57] American pamphleteers echoed these sentiments. In 1875 one declared that 'women are innocent of the faintest ray of sexual pleasure'. In contrast men were possessed of natural animal appetites. Even women took up these ideas to proclaim woman's essential difference to man. For American Eliza Duffy 'the passions of men are much stronger and more easily inflamed' than those of women.[58] These attitudes shaped much sex education literature. In the late-nineteenth century Dr Alice Stockman declared that 'we teach the girl repression, the boy expression'.[59]

A few Victorian feminists did believe that women were 'passionate'. Elizabeth Blackwell and Elizabeth Cady Stanton, among others, argued that the passions of women were as strong as men's but considered them fundamentally different in nature. Where men's desires were urgent, strong, insistent and animal, women's were emotional, compassionate and accommodating. As we shall see in a later chapter such ideas became the basis for feminist demands for a distinctive place in the public sphere.[60] For the majority of Victorian medical and moral commentators, however, the idea of the different sexual natures of men and women was beyond question. Where men were virile, active, forceful and controlled, women were slower to arouse, more gentle, nurturing and passive. These differences were the basis for advice about how men and women should behave. Masculinity involved the mastery of desire and self-restraint, while femininity required decorum and the concealment of interest in the opposite sex. Codes of masculinity and femininity required mutual restraint within marriage. One of the fascinating dimensions of Victorian medical discourse is the way traditional ideas about gender (hot/cold, active/passive) stretching back nearly three millennia were mapped onto the sexed bodies of men and women.[61]

Historians of gender have also been attracted to medical evidence because it highlights the instability of prevailing codes of gender. While advice literature prescribed desirable codes of behaviour, bodies and desires had ways of disrupting expectations and beliefs. Running counter to ideals of sexual difference were other discourses on the vulnerability of middle-class women to nervous stress and debility, and more troubling conditions such as erotomania and nymphomania.[62] Some medical and scientific experiments uncovered disturbing evidence of female 'passion'.

In the 1840s and 1850s, attempts to use ether and chloroform as forms of anaesthesia in surgery drew strange reactions from patients. Women in particular seemed to writhe suggestively and mimic sexual excitement under chloroform, a reaction that doctors feared would undermine the legitimacy of their practice. Such responses also raised questions about women's true nature – were women's animal appetites actually stronger than those of men. The history of anaesthesia, argues Mary Poovey, involved a struggle between masculine medical dominance and the capacity of women's bodies to resist their incorporation into a narrative of medical advance.[63] Similarly, the credibility of mesmerism was undermined not just by instances of medical practitioners of this new science taking advantage of unsuspecting female patients, but more disconcertingly and controversially, by female subjects under influence who attempted to seduce doctors.[64]

The ideological counterpoint to the chaste middle-class matron was the fallen woman. Prostitution flourished throughout nineteenth-century Britain, Europe and America. By some estimates there were at least 50,000 prostitutes in Victorian London alone. Moreover, as we shall see in a later chapter, there was a measure of tolerance of the practice by governments and military authorities. Underpinning this tolerance was an acceptance that, while moral restraint was advisable, men's animal drives could not be completely contained. If the ideal marriage was restrained, then prostitution became a necessary evil. Even doctors and advocates of moral restraint like William Acton, who was also active in publicizing the dangers of venereal infection, seemed to accept that prostitution was inevitable. In this context many doctors concluded that the only recourse was to remove diseased prostitutes from the streets, not eradicate prostitution altogether.[65]

Such attitudes carried an enormous cost. The extent of venereal disease is unknown, but all the evidence suggests that it was widespread. In the early-twentieth century when tests for syphilis were first developed, prisoners and inmates of lunatic asylums had high rates of venereal disease.[66] Some American doctors, such as Prince Morrow, estimated that as many as three-quarters of all adult men had a history of venereal infection.[67] This figure might be an exaggeration, but there is little doubt that venereal disease was a serious health issue, with clients and prostitutes one of the main sources of infection. More importantly for Morrow, clients brought these infections home to wives exacting a cruel toll on their bodies, evident in the increased incidence of sterility.

If the desirable state of domestic femininity was 'passionlessness', then 'fallen women' were their mirror opposite, voracious, insatiable and morally corrupt. These were women who had fallen from grace. It was important to maintain a rigid distinction between the two. For example, America reformer John Kellogg believed that humans should follow the example of animals, pursuing intercourse only for procreation, denouncing men who tried to use their wives for pleasure, as one would a 'harlot'.[68]

Prostitutes were the objects of extraordinary ambivalence, entwined in contradictory and competing narratives. Some doctors and moral reformers argued that the body of the prostitute was a rotten, foul-smelling cesspool of corruption. Whores were seen as denizens of back streets, children of the slum bred to a life of vice. Others, however, saw them as innocent girls seduced and abandoned by aristocratic libertines and kept in bondage by middle-class customers. Prominent Victorians, like British Prime Minister William Gladstone, journalist W.T. Stead, and American anti-prostitution campaigner Clifford Roe, saw prostitutes as the victims of avaricious exploiters, and devoted their energies to publicizing the evils of prostitution and promoting rescue work.[69] Prostitutes were 'magdalens', capable of a life of purity and sacrifice if brought to the light.[70]

In the last decade of the nineteenth century and the first decade of the twentieth, social purity crusaders highlighted the perils of 'white slavery'. Abolitionists and social purity activists argued that innocent young girls were being induced into prostitution by an unscrupulous international traffic in women. Historians have argued that this moral panic touched on wider anxieties about immigration, the growth of ethnic ghettoes, the increasing incidence of venereal diseases and parental anxieties about the 'sexual liberty' of their children. White slavery symbolized these diverse fears and focused enormous public energy on the eradication of prostitution and increasing forms of regulation over sexual commerce.[71] David Pivar has contested this emphasis on white slavery as a symbolic movement fostering social control, arguing that social purity was also a form of social justice for women.[72]

Nonetheless, the regulation of prostitution did increase. In America government 'vice' commissions, new laws and local government regulations empowered police to make more arrests for prostitution-related offences. New red-light abatement laws allowed private citizens to report prostitution activity. Greater police and municipal regulation of prostitution, however, changed the shape of the commercial sex industry. Tougher regulation made freelance work more difficult, promoting the creation of a permanent workforce. Prostitutes had to find sufficient money to pay fines and bribe corrupt police and officials. Many turned to pimps and brothel keepers seeking protection and more secure income, and in return they had to take on the job full-time. While police and councils closed down brothels, street walking flourished. Efforts to remove white women from 'vicious associations' increased the numbers of African American and Asian women in prostitution.[73]

Understandably, prostitution, given its prevalence and the outrage it inspired, has been the focus of much historical research. While this research has focused on ideologies of purity and the politics of reform evident in the white slavery movement, important research has attempted to move beyond moralism to the political economy of commercialized sex and the daily lives of prostitutes. The work of historians such as Ruth Rosen, Timothy Guilfoyle, Judith Walkowitz, Frances Finnegan and Joanne Meyerowitz, for example, has highlighted the interconnections between prostitutes and working-class women.[74] Prostitution was a common resort of impoverished women, married and single, struggling to put bread on the table. In a context of labour market volatility it was a common means of gaining a livelihood. These historians have depicted prostitution as a form of women's work, breaking down the boundaries erected by Puritans between respectable and immoral working-class women. In seeking to break away from Victorian ideas that prostitution was a form of sexual pathology, historians have turned prostitution into an industry.

The historiography on prostitution as work has opened up important new perspectives on commercialized sex. But in focusing on prostitution as an industry historians have inadvertently removed it from the field of sexual history. They have overlooked how prostitution and sexuality are intertwined. While prostitution might say very little about female sexuality, it stands to tell us a great deal about male sexuality. As we shall see in a later chapter, gay historians have placed commercial sex at the centre of a history of homosexuality. Ironically feminists, in rescuing prostitutes from the masculine gaze and restoring this 'lost sisterhood' to history, have overlooked the sexual questions which lie at the heart of prostitution.

Challenging the Repressive Hypothesis

The idea of Victorianism has begun to unravel in recent years. A number of historians have questioned the characterization of Victorian sexuality as prudish, repressive and hypocritical. It is now clear that there was no single, or dominant, sexual ideology. Instead there were debates, disputes and differences of opinion over questions such as the need for orgasm to ensure conception, the physical and mental effects of masturbation, the existence of female passion, the desirability of regular 'sexual congress', the causes of venereal disease and the capacity of men to exercise sexual restraint. As we have seen, medical and moral advice literature was widely disseminated. Although some historians have explored how medical discourses on sexuality constructed ideas about gender and sexuality, Michael Mason has also suggested that these ideas did not just shape opinion, but also reflected popular attitudes and beliefs. But did people take this advice to heart? In what ways were attitudes and sexual practices transformed by Victorian discourses? Were there differences in the class, ethnic and regional responses to these Victorian ideas?

These types of questions have shaped important work in the history of sexuality. In moving beyond moral reform, medical and literary texts some historians have turned to private sources to explore Victorian sexuality. For example, Peter Gay's reading of diaries and travel journals has provided a startling new picture of sexual practices amongst the Victorian middle classes. Many historians have cited the unhappy marital sexual experiences and wedding night traumas of prominent Victorians, such as John Ruskin and J.A. Symonds, as evidence of the ways Victorian ideas of sexual guilt, prudery and ignorance invaded and destroyed the sexual experience of the middle classes. Gay argues, however, that these experiences were the exception not the rule. He analyses the diaries of Mabel Loomis Todd, a prominent New England wife and hostess, and intimate of poet Emily Dickinson. This diary reveals a culture of sexual knowledge and passion. Middle-class women like Todd placed a high price on sexual experience, seeking satisfaction of their own needs. They sought erotic and orgasmic intensity in their relations with men, and confided their desires to friends and close relatives. Far from being a culture of reticence and propriety, the Victorian middle classes exhibited detailed knowledge of sexual practices and a fondness for erotic life.[75]

Gay places Todd in a larger picture of Victorian sublimation. He proposes a psychoanalytic analysis of nineteenth-century middle-class culture. For Gay, sexual passion was a key dimension of this culture, but passion was usually in conflict with social codes of respectability and larger impulses of 'civilization'. Thus desire was sublimated into love, romanticism, art, sentiment and even aggression, class conflict and war. But within this larger struggle between instinct and culture, Gay uncovers a rich vein of sexual passion. Desire may have been sublimated in many things, but it also found genuine outlets in sexual practices. Although Gay shares many assumptions with Marcus and other Freudian scholars of Victorianism, he offers a far more sophisticated picture of Victorian sexuality. This was not simply repression but a field constrained by culture and convention in which men and women nevertheless managed to find satisfaction in physical passion.[76]

Sexual survey evidence also highlights the extent to which Victorian men and women found sexual pleasure in marriage. The early-twentieth-century surveys of American women by Katherine Bement Davis and Clelia Mosher, exploring the sexual attitudes and practices of women born after 1850, uncovered a world removed from that of William Acton. The majority of these women practised some form of contraception and found sexual intercourse agreeable. A third of Davis' respondents thought their desire was as strong as that of their husband. Many admitted to masturbation, and the overwhelming majority claimed they often experienced orgasm. In Davis' study two-fifths of these women had intercourse at least twice a week, four-fifths at least weekly. John D'Emilio and Estelle Freedman also highlight the ways Victorian prudery insinuated itself into the ideas and practices of these women, with most believing the main reason for intercourse was procreation. This wasn't always the case in practice. Although the surveys of Davis and Mosher were very limited, they indicate that some middle-class women lived active sexual lives characterized by frequent intercourse and widespread use of contraception. Many of these women found sex pleasurable, indicating that some Victorian women lived outside the prescriptions of doctors and moralists.[77]

The attitudes and sexual practices of working-class Victorians are more difficult to uncover. They have left fewer diaries and letters, but historians have used other sources to explore their lives. Historians such as Judith Walkowitz, Timothy Guilfoyle and Helen Lefkowitz Horowitz have uncovered vibrant narratives of sexual danger and a rich culture of erotica, obscene publications, clubs, saloons, cabarets, music halls, balls, brothels and streetwalkers in nineteenth-century London and New York. This culture horrified reformers and excited 'grub street' journalists who titillated readers with stories of 'darkest London', the 'alarming evils of New York', sexual excess and teeming masses of 'depraved women'. Cities such as London, New York and Paris drew young men and women away from towns and villages and into a larger world of economic struggle and sexual experimentation.[78]

There have also been excellent studies of working-class women, especially in America, using court, prison and welfare sources, which illuminate this sexual world of the urban lower classes. The late-nineteenth-century campaigns to eliminate vice, encourage temperance, raise the age of consent and prevent 'white slavery' caught many young women in criminal and welfare nets, subjecting them to greater forms of scrutiny and institutionalization. The work of historians, such as Mary Odem, Ruth Alexander and Kathy Peiss, has indicated, however, that working-class girls flouted the rules of moralists, helping create an urban sexual culture.[79] Many of these girls were immigrants, whose embrace of the new American urban culture of pleasure horrified parents. There was a marked generational conflict over the behaviour of girls who rebelled against rigid family, ethnic and social conventions. Within this culture some working-class girls sought steady boyfriends and others embraced all the sexual opportunities afforded by the proliferation of clubs, amusement halls and fun palaces in cities such as New York, Chicago and Los Angeles. Others used sex in order to survive in the face of poverty, abuse and family hardship. While some lived at home and went out for their pleasures, others moved to cheap apartments to gain their independence. These women were part of a wave of what D'Emilio and Freedman call 'sexual liberalism' that transformed Victorian sexual culture. This new culture asserted an ethic of individual sexual pleasure against the constraints of domestic ideology and self-sacrifice.[80]

In contrast British historians have drawn a very different picture of working-class life. They have challenged conventional views of slum life as morally corrupt and sexually licentious. Michael Mason, for example, reading social reform texts against the grain and exploring new sources such as working-class autobiographies, hospital and welfare records, has argued that there was a growing culture of respectability amongst Victorians of all classes by the mid-nineteenth century. This ethic was even evident amongst the urban working classes. Working-class parental reticence on sex in front of children was very marked by the end of the century. More significantly, Mason discerns different trajectories in the ethic of sexual moralism amongst the middle and working classes. While sexual moralism may have intensified amongst the middle classes in the early-nineteenth century, Mason discerns a loosening of restrictions after the 1860s, and a growing freedom for young women of the middle and professional classes. At the same time, moral codes strengthened for the working classes, with a greater focus on 'intense courtship', rather than promiscuous play.[81]

The idea of Victorianism has begun to crumble in other ways. Detailed analyses of class, region and sexuality, like that of Mason, have disrupted any sense that the trajectory of Victorian sexual history moves in a uniform way. Some of this research has highlighted divisions within social classes based on occupation, religion, politics and region. The work of Davidoff and Hall on the provincial middle classes is exemplary. They chart a diverse set of social groups, differing in political allegiance, religious affiliation, level of education, wealth, aspiration and number of servants. Although the middle class was united in its commitment to piety and domestic ideology, with home as the hallmark of respectability, there were many divisions within this group. Most importantly, these social differences affected the course of middle-class domestic ideology, with its stress on evangelical piety, modesty, restraint and the relegation of sexuality to the inner core of marriage. These ideas advanced more quickly in some sections of the middling ranks than others.[82]

Similarly, there were many different fractions of the working classes. Slum denizens were hardly the same as members of the labour aristocracy. There were clear divisions between skilled and unskilled workers, and some of these differences were reflected in the commitment to an ethic of respectability and sexual restraint within marriage. While Mason has argued that respectability gained wider credence within the working class by the end of the century, the urban under classes were largely outside this labour culture.[83] On the other hand, the increasing impact of ideas of respectability and sexual restraint crossed political lines within the labour movement. While there were vast differences between radical, socialist and more conservative elements of the working classes, as Barbara Taylor shows, even radicals were inclined to believe that women's place was in the home supporting men.[84]

Through this work we get a more complex picture of the relationship between class and sexuality. On the one hand, there were clear class and regional differences in the commitment to sexual moralism. Some of this was a matter of timing, with some classes and regional areas coming under the sway of ideals of respectability before others. On the other hand, ideals of respectability, fertility control and restraint crossed class barriers and were adopted by sections of the working class by the end of the nineteenth century.

Even the sense of Victorianism as an easily definable historical period has been challenged. Although the Victorian era has become a synonym for the nineteenth century, when we examine sexuality this chronology does not always work. There are distinct differences in the chronology of Victorianism between Britain and America, despite the power of domestic ideology on both sides of the Atlantic. As we have seen, in America the decline in the birth rate began around 1800 and continued apace throughout the nineteenth century. The breakdown of the older patriarchal family and the emergence of equalitarian ideas of family life were evident earlier in America than Britain. Moreover, the emergence of sexual liberalism amongst urban working class and ethnic social groups was more established there than in Britain by the end of the century.

British historians, however, have pinpointed a crucial shift in Victorian culture around the middle of the century. This is evident in demographic patterns. In Britain, and other parts of the continent except France, the decline in the birth rate did not really take off until the 1850s. Davidoff and Hall's history of middle-class domestic ideology, which framed Victorian sexual ideology, suggests that the idea of moral restraint advanced slowly through the middling ranks, only becoming dominant by the 1840s. Until then many sections of the middle classes juggled the contradictory messages of Romanticism and Evangelicalism.[85]

Moreover, John Tosh argues that after the 1850s middle-class men began to revolt against the strictures of domestic ideology. They increasingly sought out a public and homosocial world of manly endeavour, in preference to the stultifying feminine sphere of the hearth and home. This masculine revolt against the domestic ideology that had previously united the middling sort demonstrates that gender was a fundamental social division within Victorian sexual culture. It also suggests that at the moment of triumph for sexual moralism in Britain, domestic ideology and the sexual culture it supported began to decay.[86]

Conclusion

In a variety of ways then, historians have challenged the coherence of the nineteenth century as a specific period in the history of sexuality. There is clear dispute over what constitutes Victorianism. Is this a period of sexual puritanism or sexual hypocrisy? Is it an age of sexual restraint and the decline in the birth rate? Or is it an era when the masculine split between the chaste domesticated wife and the eroticized 'fallen woman' is strengthened? Is this a time when sex is repressed or where the proliferation of discourses on sex constructs sexuality? Even if we could arrive at a uniform definition of what characterized Victorianism, its chronology might vary significantly depending on the country chosen. For France it might begin in the 1780s, in New England in the 1800s, but for Britain, Germany and the Southern States of America the 1850s and 1860s might be a more useful starting point. In the light of such questions the concept of Victorianism now looks decidedly shaky.

Chapter 7

DOMINANCE AND DESIRE

In seventeenth-century Virginia, planter and promoter Robert Beverley offered visitors a 'brace of young Beautiful Virgins' to wait upon these 'happy gentlemen' when they retired to their quarters for the night. The women offered to guests were native Americans, whom Beverley thought 'generally beautiful'.[1] In eighteenth-century Jamaica slave overseer Thomas Thistlewood lost few opportunities to entice and, if necessary, force local slaves to engage in sex. The outposts of European colonization presented bountiful opportunities for sex and he meticulously recorded these conquests in an extensive diary. One of the obvious attractions of the frontier was sex, particularly with 'exotic' men and women. Other colonists generally tolerated these 'manly' exploits.[2] Planters, overseers, traders, soldiers and merchants were often in a position to insist that the slaves and indigenous people under their rule obey and serve the needs of masters.

Back in the metropolitan centres of European civilization, however, there were still opportunities for sexual conquest. One of the most famous pornographic texts of the Victorian era, *My Secret Life* (c. 1882) overflows with stories of Walter's 'erotic whims'. Little excited the gentleman hero of these 'sexual tales' more than young virgins, especially maids and serving girls. For Walter, getting one maid to hold down a young girl while he went about his business was enough to make him 'spend without a touch'.[3] American poet Walt Whitman delighted in bringing home young working-class men from New York, the 'city of orgies, walks and joys'.[4]

Many Europeans and Americans took the trouble to record how people of different races and lower classes could excite their sexual sensibilities. In the creative imagination and daily lives of Westerners cultural difference had powerful erotic overtones. Men more than women had the power to capitalize on these desires. On the other hand, these class and race boundaries could be fraught with anxiety.

In 'Jim Crow' America, Southerners pursued a savage policy of violent suppression of any blacks who threatened the sexual hegemony of white men. There were widespread fears that marauding blacks with insatiable sexual appetites were raping and violating young white women. As Georgia reformer Rebecca Felton declared, 'the brutal lust of these half-civilized gorillas seems to be inflamed to madness'.[5] Lynchings were a common solution. Similarly, just after World War I, German returned officers resorted to violence and murder to ensure that the nation did not fall into the hands of communist forces. Leading Freikorps officers imagined their enemy in very sexual terms, as castrating rifle-carrying 'red' women.[6]

In recent years, some of the most important work in the history of sexuality has explored the interconnections between sex, gender, race, class and nation. Sex rarely sits alone within Western culture. It is embedded in wider contexts of power and dominance, sometimes reinforcing oppression, at other times moderating it. Desire gained sustenance and form from the European engagement with different cultures and classes. Much of the scholarship on the intersection of desire with other social structures has explored how sex was a tool of oppression and dominance, maintaining hierarchies of class and race. Few would question the brutality and violence of Western conquest and domination.[7] These are vital dimensions of the historical experience of cultural clash. Sex, however, also complicated conquest and compromised dispossession. More importantly, it produced 'mestizo' cultures, peoples in-between cultures who sought to create new identities.[8]

Historians have begun to explore sexual borders between classes and races as places of resistance, danger and desire. The links between pleasure and danger and the ways the 'exotic' has become associated with eroticism have become important themes within European and American cultural history.[9] Sexual desire could create a space in which transgression and subversion flourished, where men and women crossed the lines of class, race and gender and broke with the social conventions that governed their lives. In doing so they challenged those conventions, sometimes at great personal cost. These potential crossings fanned the determination of others to prevent cultural and political 'contamination'. Sexual, racial and class borders are sites of contest and desire. Here we will explore a small sample of this rich body of work in an effort to highlight some of the different ways historians have tried to see connections between sex and power.

Sexuality and Class

In the eighteenth and nineteenth centuries doctors, moral reformers and polite society viewed the bodies of working-class women and girls with a mixture of horror, fear, contempt and lofty sympathy. Scientific, medical, religious and literary texts pathologized the 'fallen woman'. Prostitutes were seen as the site of disease, degeneration and corruption, their bodies represented as sites of suppurating sores, foul odours and polluting secretions. Worse, doctors and reformers, such as Frederick Hollick, Michael Ryan, Edward Tilt and George Napheys, argued that the wear and tear of excessive sexual intercourse, the mixing of so many different types of semen and the lack of 'feeling' for customers generally rendered prostitutes barren. In doing so doctors displaced a disease transmitted by both men and women into something quintessentially feminine.[10] This scientific effort was part of a larger cultural revulsion at the sights and sounds of the urban under-class going about its business. For example, in 1851 George Templeton Strong complained about the 'whorearchy' that populated the streets of New York. Everywhere he went there was 'some hideous troop of ragged girls...with thief written in their cunning eyes and whore on their depraved faces...such a group is...the most revolting object that the social diseases of a great city can produce'.[11]

The attitudes of men like Strong towards women of the streets were commonplace. They fuelled nineteenth-century social purity and abolitionist campaigns for the eradication of prostitution.[12] In the evolving medical and reform literatures on the evils of prostitution, however, the marks of this 'foul disease' were difficult to distinguish from those of ordinary working-class women. When Strong and other Victorian social investigators and reformers strolled down the streets of major American and European cities they collapsed the distinctions between women who earned their livelihood as laundresses, maids, flower girls, milliners, factory workers and shop assistants and those who plied their trade as prostitutes. This is not altogether surprising. Some working women supplemented their inadequate wages with earnings from casual prostitution. Other working-class girls, however, clung to notions of respectability. Moreover, the pioneering social surveys of London and New York, by men like Henry Mayhew, Robert Hartley, Jacob Riis and B.O. Flower, created a nightmare world of the 'social cellar' for an avid middle-class audience. In this context working-class girls in the cities were caught within a bourgeois discourse of moral corruption whether they were prostitutes or not.[13]

The association of moral depravity, sexual diseases and prostitution with working-class women was a double-edged sword. Such images stood in marked contrast to middle-class ideals of domestic femininity, with their emphasis on passionlessness, purity, restraint, moral uplift, domesticity, motherhood and nurture.[14] Although middle-class women, such as Laura Lyman and Mabel Loomis Todd, expressed ardent sexual desires in private, there was a rich cultural association between middle-class purity and working-class depravity.[15] In a bourgeois culture that disavowed any link between respectability and sensual pleasure, working-class women became major signifiers of depravity and eroticism.

The sensual delights of working-class women, especially prostitutes were the staple of eighteenth- and nineteenth-century pornography and obscenity. Although there were pornographic traditions of the aristocratic libertine seductress and the respectable virgin, whose chasteness was compromised by the adventurous man, Helen Lefkowitz Horowitz has argued that John Cleland's *Fanny Hill* (1748) became the '*ur*-text' for erotic writing in Victorian America. This was the story of a spirited prostitute who enjoyed sex in all situations and positions. Erotic books, magazines and journals circulated widely in Europe and America, conjuring up a world of wayward, insatiable women who experienced overwhelming orgasms at the hands of inexhaustible men.[16]

In these texts maids, servants and prostitutes featured heavily as willing companions in sexual escapades. Walter's *My Secret Life*, for example, is an extraordinary compendium of chance assignations, furtive encounters and endlessly repetitive sensual pleasures. The bulk of Walter's 'adventures' were with maids, servants, farm girls, prostitutes – 'lewd and bawdy wenches' – who occasionally feigned resistance but always gave in to his advances. Victorian pornography paraded an array of working-class girls as the objects of erotic life, the opposite to the stifling maternalism of the bourgeois home.[17]

There is more than literary evidence to support this association between class and desire. Some men actively lived the eroticism of difference. The attractions of working-class women are very evident in the extensive papers of Arthur J. Munby, civil servant, teacher, poet and artist. In a rich archive of diaries, letters, photographs and drawings, Munby recorded in intricate detail the elaborate fantasies and games he enacted with his country-born servant, and later wife, Hannah Cullwick. In return Hannah recorded for Munby her own memoirs, detailing her conditions of work, wages, hours, recreations and the relationships among the other servants.

The richly detailed Munby papers have offered historians, such as Leonore Davidoff, a means of exploring the intimate world of class relations and sexuality in Victorian England. Davidoff highlights the differences in station of Arthur and Hannah, but pushes on beyond the issue of social status to examine how the private world created by Munby and Cullwick was saturated with questions of dominance and subordination, strength and weakness, autonomy and dependence. Munby was obsessed with issues of dirt, manual work, lowliness, degradation and love. Munby used Cullwick to perform various tableaux – she would become the country wench tilling the fields, the abject servant washing the steps, the wretched chimney sweep covered in ashes, or the poor girl begging for mercy. Munby also persuaded Cullwick to dress as a man, an angel or very occasionally as a middle-class lady.[18]

Davidoff sees in this relationship a complex play on class. It was commonplace in music hall and popular entertainment to reverse social roles – and have men play women, women play men, working girls play ladies or adults play children. Such entertainments were designed to mock, amuse and equally importantly reinforce the social character of status and hierarchy. Munby's elaborate performances drew upon a repertoire of popular theatrical devices. But Davidoff also detects deeper cultural roots in these games. Munby was fixated on the bodies of working girls, for him they conjured up strength, work, abjection, servitude, qualities that he found deeply erotic. Although there are doubts about whether his relationship with Hannah was consummated, the sensuality of the writings and pictures leaves little doubt about their sexual nature. Davidoff also speculates that Munby's obsessions arose from a deep fixation on his nanny, who was, as for so many middle-class men, his primary carer as a child. This childhood association fostered a sexual fixation on working women.

The attempt by Davidoff to uncover the psychic origins of Munby's erotic interests is the most speculative part of her argument. More convincing is her demonstration that for Munby love and inner worth was associated with outer abjection, lowliness and servitude. Davidoff argues that although there were signs of Hannah's independence, Munby kept forcing her back into child-like dependency. For Davidoff, issues of authority and domination were crucial dynamics in Munby's sexual fantasies. Thus pervasive structures of class and gender in Victorian society helped construct personality and shape unconscious desires. For Davidoff, middle-class men were able to live a life of privilege and authority, commanding others, particularly working-class women in servant positions. This authority and subservience in the close confines of domestic spaces had the potential to become highly eroticized. Thus through sexual fantasy middle-class men were able to enact dominance through sex. Class relations could heighten and give form to sexual desire and sexual desire could cement social relations of dominance and submission.

Anne McClintock and Liz Stanley, however, argue that Davidoff relies too heavily on the diaries of Munby. Cullwick's writings paint a very different picture of the relationship, one of domestic sado-masochism, in which power and authority was not conferred by social status but negotiated through performance. Thus Cullwick enacted submission as a way of gaining control over Munby, and ritual control over her own social disempowerment. This alternative reading of Munby and Cullwick is less about sources than interpretation. McClintock suggests that Davidoff imposed structures of class and gender upon the evidence. As a consequence Davidoff sees the Munby archive as illustrative of Victorian social structure. Munby's writings demonstrate the class and gender dynamics that Davidoff expects to find in Victorian culture. In contrast McClintock and Stanley attempt to uncover the deeper cultural struggles embedded within these literary texts. Far from the writings of Arthur and Hannah enacting class and gender dominance, these texts reveal that domination and subordination were contested. Hannah may have been the servant but through her participation in erotic games she gained a measure of control.[19]

McClintock also highlights other dimensions overlooked by Davidoff. For McClintock there was a strong strand of race fetishism in Munby's sexual games. Cullwick chose to address Munby by the imperial title 'Massa', wore a 'slave band' and often dressed as a slave. In addition she would kneel, lick his boots and wash his feet to profess her love and servitude.[20] The roles of slave and master were central dynamics in their play. Thus the politics of race and Empire created a vital part of the symbolic field in which gender and class struggles could be enacted. Through these means the game of master and servant became a sado-masochistic ritual, where the positions of dominance and subservience were ambiguous and contested. Central to the 'empire of the home', to use McClintock's evocative phrase, were erotic struggles over power and authority that were grounded in larger social and symbolic structures of race as much as class and gender.

Orientalism and Desire

Sex was a crucial part of Western expansion, settlement and colonization. In the quest for economic riches, strategic outposts and safe trade routes, Europeans explored other lands, traded around the world and conquered vast territories in Asia, Africa, America, Australia and the Pacific. Waves of Europeans left Britain and the Continent for new worlds, settling there and creating diverse societies. The maintenance of effective control over territories and peoples required the deployment of troops and a significant European corps of administrators, police, magistrates, judges and trading agents. Imperialism also involved the movement of subject peoples. Africans and Pacific Islanders were captured, bribed and enticed to provide the essential slave labour force for European expansion in the Caribbean, South Africa, America and Australia. Asians also moved in large numbers as servants, slaves, prostitutes and indentured labourers around the British, Dutch, Portuguese and French Empires. European expansion from the sixteenth to the twentieth century involved a momentous and far-reaching clash of cultures. Mestizo cultures and Western anxieties about miscegenation were testament to the sexual dynamics of empire.

European expansion and colonization was fought out in a number of spheres. It is evident in the clash of bodies and the incidence of disease, enslavement and economic exploitation. It also shaped the Western imagination. Over the last few decades, historians, anthropologists, literary and social theorists have begun to look more closely at the intellectual frameworks that justified domination and promoted racism. Close scrutiny of major European texts, from Jane Austen to Verdi, reveals a rich sub-text of race and empire in Western culture. These cultural concerns also shaped Western sexuality.[21]

Edward Said's path-breaking work *Orientalism* (1978) has set much of the framework for the analysis of the interrelationships between imperialism and culture. Said argued that British, European and American anthropology, philology, science, literature and art systematically represented the East as the polar opposite of the West. Where the West was rational, scientific, ordered, modern, organized, vigorous and systematic, the East was chaotic, debilitating, irrational, backward, mystical and sensual. The East was 'the other' that helped define the distinctiveness and superiority of the West. These Orientalist discourses did not explain the East in its own terms, but instead provided an elaborate but ultimately distorting lens through which the West could view and understand the East. In other words, 'orientalizing' knowledges were powerful cultural forces explaining and justifying European imperialism and colonialism.[22]

Orientalist discourse had an explicit gender dynamic. For Said, it was a 'male power-fantasy' that sexualized a feminized Orient, making it available for Western domination and exploitation. The imperial frontier was in some contexts virgin land, or in others hot, sensual and exotic, while the West was enshrined in masculine metaphors of coldness, hardness and vigour. A key dynamic of imperialism was the sexual subjection of oriental women by Western men. Sex was both a signifier and a practice for asserting dominion over other peoples. For Said, imperialism and colonialism became 'an exclusively male province' for Western domination.[23] Said's depiction of Orientalism as dominant and hegemonic, however, has been contested by other scholars. Ann Laura Stoler and Homi Bhabha suggest that Said underestimates the active resistance to Western colonialist and Orientalist discourses.[24] Anne McClintock argues that Said fails to see that gender and sexuality are constitutive not just representative of dominance.[25]

Moreover, Said tends to see gender and sexuality in largely male and female terms, ignoring same-sex relationships across races. He also places the homosocial dynamics of imperialism, which promoted intense bonds amongst Empire builders and encouraged feelings of contempt for the men subject to their authority, at the margins of his analysis.[26] Other historians have seen such processes as more central. For example, Mrinilini Sinha has shown that masculinity was an important part of Orientalist discourse. Imperialists drew a sharp distinction between manly Englishmen, rightfully in a position of natural dominance over effeminate Bengali men.[27] Other work has shown how women were active producers of Western ideas and representations that sit outside frameworks established by Said. While women writers, artists and scientists generally worked within an Orientalist tradition, they often focused on different aspects of the imperial experience – the subjection of women and children, social customs, travel discomforts, the picturesque, distinctive flora. Their picture of the Orient sometimes cut across masculine fascination with the sublime, exotic harems and the passive Eastern man. In doing so women indicated the instability and fragility of masculine representations of the East.[28]

Sexuality has become a key theme in the analysis of how Western culture shaped the experience of colonialism and imperialism. Cultural historians in particular have stressed the differences in the way colonial discourses on sexuality functioned in different parts of Europe's empires. Although one of the key themes of Said's Orientalism is the alluring, seductive East, this trope was by no means universal. Colonial frontiers, particularly areas opened up to new conquest, such as Australia and Africa, could be sexually threatening – feminized spaces devouring men.[29] Equally there was a clear contrast in the way Europeans understood Asian and African male sexuality. Orientalist discourses on Asia represented the East as a place of exotic women. Female sexuality was at the centre of these representations, while Asian male sexuality was ignored or seen as dissolute and passive. In contrast African men were invested with considerable sexual prowess, making them a disturbing and threatening presence on the frontier.[30]

Orientalism, however, was not just an imposition on the colonized. Ideas and practices born in the colonies moved back to the metropolitan centres, shaping Western culture in profound ways. In this context a number of scholars have explored how the Orient, the empire, 'exotic races' and other tropes functioned within nineteenth-century Western culture to signify sexuality. For example, Joanna de Groot has analysed images of the 'harem', 'dancing girls' and the 'slave market', common within Victorian visual and literary culture. Idealized representations of exotic otherness were saturated in sexual metaphors of allure, domination, temptation, luxury, voluptuousness and death. These images depicted the East as a place of erotic fantasy and fulfilment, cementing the image of the Orient as a feminized and sexualized world, completely other to the chaste domestic world of European middle-class maternalism. Race and sex reinforced each other to conjure up a European male fantasy world.[31]

Sander Gilman has taken this argument further. He examines the ways in which 'black bodies', most importantly the Hottentot female, became a central part of European iconography. Black women often featured in European paintings, usually as background characters and Gilman argues that their presence served to sexualize the scene. More importantly, key elements of the repertoire of signs for the Hottentot female were incorporated into representations of European women, signifying them as prostitutes, courtesans and other types of 'loose women'. Thus it became unnecessary to paint black women to make the visual field sexual. Instead certain gestures, poses and body shapes, derived from black bodies, became a visual language to represent European women as sexual.[32] A powerful link between sexuality and exotic others was forged within Western culture.

Sex and Race

Although the sexualized cultural frameworks through which the West asserted its domination have a central place in contemporary scholarship many historians have also sought to uncover the ways sex operated in colonial encounters. The brute facts of European expansion have been extensively documented over many decades and more recently historians have uncovered the ways sexual relations operated on colonial frontiers. Men populated Western frontiers. As soldiers, administrators, governors, slave owners, overseers, police, traders, pastoralists, workers and civil servants, Western men asserted their entitlement to sex with prostitutes, slaves and local women and men. Later, in many colonies, Europeans moved out as family groups, creating a gender balance in the colonizer population, although one which did not necessarily end 'inter-racial sex'. A considerable body of scholarship has documented sexual violence and coercion on the frontier. Soldiers, traders and masters raped slaves, servants and indigenous peoples. They also forced, beat and demanded sexual services from those under their control. There were few impediments to such practices. While men might run the risk of indigenous reprisals for rape and violence, few Western authorities were prepared to curb such practices.[33]

Indeed there is abundant evidence that throughout America, Australia, Africa and Asia sexual relations with women of other races was widely tolerated. Settlers in the West Indies, Richard Godbeer has argued, made no secret of their 'infatuated attachments to black women' and men who frowned on these relationships were thought to be 'blockheads'.[34] Equally important, some colonists, such as eighteenth-century Virginia planter William Byrd, used their sexual mastery to construct a self-image of benevolent gentlemen masters.[35] Slave owners in the American South, however, were generally more circumspect. Although many communities indulged, and even prided themselves on the sexual licentiousness of their young men, indiscriminate sex with slaves

threatened the 'property' of other slave owners. Through property laws
there were efforts to regulate inter-racial sex. Moreover, women colonists used slander and ideals of piety to undermine the reputations of
men whose indiscretions were too public.[36]

Although mindful of the underlying structures of coercion that
shaped frontier sexual relations, in recent years some of the more
interesting studies have focused on dimensions of colonial sexuality
that went against the grain of brutal domination. Seventeenth- and
eighteenth-century colonists sometimes established relatively stable
and permanent relationships with slaves and indigenous women, conferring a higher status on these women. More interesting, because
they undermine one-dimensional representations of the frontier as
places of racist domination, have been studies of white women who
had relationships with black slaves and indigenous men. There is also
evidence of permanent relationships between indigenous people and
slaves. Another important, but rarely glimpsed, aspect of the homosocial world of frontier society are same-sex relationships between masters, masters and slaves and amongst mobile groups of men, such as
soldiers, sailors and traders. Such studies highlight the fluidity of race,
gender and sexual hierarchies in frontier contexts. While male colonists
asserted their sexual dominion over other races, slaves and indigenous
peoples forged lives with each other and with masters that compromised these racial hierarchies. Sex could subvert authority conferring
a small measure of autonomy and status on those normally subject to
coercion and violence.[37]

One of the central questions in the historiography of colonial sexuality has been whether attitudes to inter-racial sex gradually became
less tolerant. Some of the evidence, as we have seen, suggests that relationships between white masters and servants and slaves were commonplace and widely accepted. Men may not have introduced their black
and indigenous lovers into polite society, but these liaisons were usually widely known and rarely resulted in any loss of social status. But
throughout the eighteenth and nineteenth centuries attitudes began
to harden and laws were introduced to govern inter-racial sex. Some of
this related to the protection of property, but historians have generally
seen increasing racism in the relations between whites and other races
especially by the late-nineteenth century. In South Africa, Australia and
the American South, in particular, race relations took on a harder edge
and anxieties about miscegenation fostered harsher punishments for
those who engaged in sex across racial boundaries.[38]

The source of this increasing intolerance has been disputed. The
growth of moral puritanism within British and American culture is one
factor. Missionaries on the frontier, as well as social purity campaigners, moral reformers and abolitionists, created a climate increasingly

intolerant of licentiousness, sexual exploitation, concubinage and prostitution both at home and abroad.[39] Catherine Clinton and Michele
Gillespie, however, have argued more convincingly that the 'spreading
stratification' accompanying a more balanced colonial sex-ratio made
racial, sexual and gender roles more rigid.[40] By the late-nineteenth
century social Darwinist ideas of racial fitness and degeneration convinced many commentators that miscegenation was a threat to 'racial
fitness'. Harsher attitudes also fanned anxieties about the threat to
white supremacy from blacks and coloureds who might covet white
women. The apotheosis of these cultural shifts was 'Jim Crow' America
and apartheid South Africa. For historian George Frederickson, these
regimes were ones rooted in a genuinely racist belief in the immutable
genetic inferiority of non-white races.[41]

The scholarship on miscegenation and metis populations in the
nineteenth and twentieth centuries has pointed to the widespread 'racial
fears' of inter-racial sex. 'Jim Crow' America was only the most extreme
case of the sexual anxieties about the mixing of races. Historians of social
purity and abolitionism have pointed to the ways that laws and regulations governing rape, sexual violence, the age of consent and prostitution were also aimed at policing miscegenation. Importantly, while
some of these reformers saw female sexual promiscuity as the source of
social pollution, recent work has pointed to widespread concern about
unchecked white male sexuality. For some social purity campaigners regulations were needed to prevent men from exploiting women of other
classes and races. [42]

Historians of 'Jim Crow' America, in particular, have highlighted
the importance of sexual anxiety in the escalating violence against
African Americans in the Southern States. The response of white
Southerners to black emancipation was brutal. Laws enforced rigid
separation of the races, blacks were subjected to humiliating and
demeaning laws and regulations restricting their rights, forms of association, freedom of expression and capacity to contract as free labourers. They were widely condemned as racial inferiors, and constructed
as subservient, loyal 'darkies' and 'mammies' or vicious, savage, sexually voracious animals. As Grace Elizabeth Hale has argued, the culture of segregation in the South after Reconstruction was central to
the formation of 'whiteness' and the ethic of white American egalitarianism.[43] In such a context inter-racial sex was the source of considerable anxiety. Black men suspected of sexual interest in white women
were beaten, lynched and burnt by local whites and organized groups
such as the Ku Klux Klan.

The violence of the Jim Crow South has rightly been the focus of
considerable attention. More recently, however, historians have explored
the longer history of illicit inter-racial sex in colonial America. Although

the first law condemning inter-racial sex was passed in Virginia as early as 1662, as we have seen relations between white masters and black slaves were tolerated, at least until emancipation. On the other hand, relations between white women and black men were the source of concern and criminal prosecution from the 1690s.[44] Despite racist antipathy to inter-racial sex, the illuminating work of Martha Hodes has demonstrated that relationships between black men and white women gained a small measure of tolerance in the antebellum South.

This tolerance dissipated on emancipation. The penalties for such relationships were severe. Nonetheless, Hodes explores the ways black men and white women sustained sexual relationships under the most adverse circumstances. Running counter to the ethos of 'Jim Crow' were the desires of ordinary men and women.[45] Similarly, Glenda Elizabeth Gilmore explores how white separatism also fostered black political mobilization. African American women slowly forged a political voice, linking with Northern white women's groups around questions of male sexual exploitation, to create a larger Progressive movement challenging the culture of southern white supremacy.[46]

Sexual Dynamics of Empire

Despite the proliferation of recent studies of colonialism and sexuality significant works of synthesis have been rare. One of the few exceptions is Ronald Hyam's study of sex and the British Empire. For Hyam, British imperialism and sexuality were intricately linked, but the sexual dynamics of empire changed through the course of the nineteenth century.[47] He sees two crucial phases in the sexual history of Empire – relative tolerance followed by racist social puritanism. The timing of this shift varied across the Empire. It was evident in India by the early-nineteenth century, but occurred later in the century in Africa and the Pacific. India is Hyam's key example. Eighteenth-century Englishmen, he argues, had relatively consensual sexual relations with 'natives'. There, many traders and officials of the East India Company used prostitutes but also formed permanent concubinage relationships with native women.

These English 'nabobs' acknowledged their Indian wives and children, and some brought their 'native' families home on their return to Britain. Such unions developed during a period when English merchants and companies sought Indian cooperation and support for their commercial enterprises. Moreover, many eighteenth-century scholars and writers admired the richness and sophistication of Indian civilization. From the 1790s, however, tensions between rival European powers and wars between the East India Company and Indian states resulted in effective British political dominion over India. Attitudes to these now subject peoples began to change. Increasing missionary activity and a growing

Christian distaste for pagan Indian culture led to official condemnation of concubinage relationships and repudiation of 'Eurasians'.

For Hyam, like earlier scholars such as T.G.P. Spear, the arrival of greater numbers of British women in India further undermined the legitimacy of inter-racial unions.[48] Memsahibs transmitted and enforced Victorian ideals of respectability, restraint, social purity and domesticity. Inter-racial sex became increasingly illicit, forced or more formally organized through prostitution. Of course, officialdom turned a blind eye to practices such as prostitution, but colonial discourses governing sexuality gradually became more puritan, racist and harsh.

At the same time, Hyam also sees the empire as an outlet for male sexual energies. The growth of social purity campaigns in Britain, particularly from the 1880s, reduced sexual opportunities for men at home, encouraging them to see the Empire as a place for sexual adventure. In a climate of growing intolerance of male same-sex relationships, especially after the 1880 Labouchere amendment outlawed many types of sexual activity between males, the homosocial world of the Empire afforded men greater opportunities to share their lives with other men – European and 'native'. Some colonizers took the opportunity to have active same-sex erotic relationships, others were predominantly, in Hyam's words, asexual, but felt far more comfortable in largely male company. Thus, for Hyam, there was a central tension between the forces of erotic adventure and social purity in Victorian culture.

Sexual repression at home made the Empire the natural site for sexual expression. Hyam's analysis, however, rests on a rather mechanistic notion of male sexuality. In seeing erotic desire as a need that has to find an outlet Hyam reproduces the 'hydraulic' theories characteristic of Victorians such as William Acton. Moreover, his view of the Empire as bountiful place for sexual opportunity ignores the dynamics of sexual and political domination. Hyam romanticizes a 'golden period' of supposed sexual tolerance and demonizes the middle-class women and missionaries who, in his view, were the purveyors of puritanism. Such a conclusion ignores the broader cultural, political and economic contexts that fostered antagonism towards the 'Orient'. Moreover, it underplays the crucial role of European men in enforcing sexual puritanism, as well as the importance of social Darwinist ideas in pathologizing inter-racial sex.

Hyam's account also suffers from crucial tensions in the argument. On the one hand, he argues that sexual repression at home drove men to the frontier, while on the other, he highlights how ideals of restraint encouraged imperial male sexual sublimation in work, military aggression and staunch puritanism. Missing from Hyam's sexual dynamics of the Empire is a detailed analysis of rape and other forms of sexual violence on the frontier. Moreover, Hyam doesn't adequately distinguish between discourses of social purity and how men responded to these ideas. Although social purity campaigns were active in Britain, they did not extinguish the prostitution industry or the growth of dancing halls, parlours and clubs, where a lively culture of eroticized heterosexual and same-sex interactions thrived. In other words, men did not need to go to the imperial frontier for illicit sex. Something more powerful drove them there. Hyam's analysis is too focused on a narrow definition of sex as an 'outlet', and fails to situate both Empire and sexuality in a wider gender context.[49]

In contrast, historians of gender and imperial enthusiasm, such as John Tosh and Graham Dawson, see the flight to the frontier as a product of a Victorian crisis of masculinity. They argue that the cult of domesticity at home emasculated men and fostered a fantasy of the Empire as a place of manly endeavour. Middle-class men increasingly sought to escape the strictures of domesticity through the homosocial world of Empire. Here was a place of adventure, excitement, travel and achievement.[50] Moreover, fears that modernity, sedentary occupations and urban dissipation were undermining the racial vigour of Western manhood, fuelled the promotion of ideals of muscular Christianity, action, vitality and imperial endeavour.

A rich variety of stories, lectures, images and tales of the Empire as a place of masculine achievement, adventure, excitement and challenge made it the imagined crucible of British manhood. Stories of great explorers, adventurers and soldiers, such as General Gordon, Stanley Livingstone, Henry Havelock, Captain Waverley, later Scott of the Antarctic and Lawrence of Arabia, and imagined heroes, such as Horatio Hornblower, Allan Quatermain, and Biggles, promoted the image of war, adventure and sacrifice. These were noble ideals to inspire generations of boys. Sexual conquest was woven into this larger masculine narrative in subtle ways, but it remained a central element of the larger fantasy. The ideal of the exotic frontier, or metaphors such as virgin lands waiting to be subdued, were saturated in masculinist and sexual imagery that added to the allure of imperial adventure.[51]

The existence of large numbers of single men, however, posed acute problems for colonial policy making. As Gayatri Spivak has argued, colonial discourses were always intimately tied to problems of government.[52] Frontiers may have been places of sexual adventure, but the daily realities of Empire ensured that they were also places of sexual exploitation. Administrators believed that stability depended on serving the 'needs' of Empire builders. Prostitution was tolerated and even accommodated by British colonial authorities as a legitimate means of regulating the sexual needs of the colonizers – to protect their health, act as an outlet for natural desires and ensure social order. Colonial administrators also had to balance the needs of colonizing men against the demands of ruling 'native' populations. Sometimes this meant enforcing European sexual norms, such as monogamy, on subject populations. At other times it meant legislating 'protections' to prevent excessive sexual exploitation of slaves, servants and 'native' peoples. A number of historians have focused on the dynamics of sexual regulation in the outposts of European Empires, investigating the policing of such practices as prostitution, polygamy, age of consent and inter-racial marriage.[53]

These studies highlight the importance of regulating sexual relations in the imposition of colonial order. The mechanisms of colonial policy were diverse and local studies have stressed regional peculiarities. Some of the best work has also examined how the government of sex was integrally related to questions of class and race. For example, Lenore Manderson's study of prostitution in 'British Malaya' demonstrates that class hierarchies and racial stereotypes shaped policies on prostitution. The colonial population was not homogenous, but divided by class and status differences – there were officers and ordinary soldiers, senior administrators and lower ranks of civil servants, plantation managers, major traders and lesser merchants, clerks, sailors and workers. Moreover, there was a large group of imported workers from other parts of the Empire whose task was to do the menial chores of imperial exploitation. Colonial authorities regulated prostitution through brothel licences and registration for each of these groups of men, but perceptions about racial differences influenced decisions about the appropriate consorts. Malay and Japanese women were seen as clean and free of disease and hence suitable for the 'colonial aristocracy', English district officers and plantation managers. Chinese women and poor European women (mainly Jews) were seen as dirty and diseased, but suitable for the lower ranks. Tamil women were imported exclusively for Tamil workers.[54]

The Empire offered more than an opportunity for sexual outlet or a place to live out manly ideals. It also made possible the construction of new identities. One of the great fantasies and anxieties of colonial culture was the phenomenon of 'passing'. The idea that the boundaries between colonizer and colonized could be fluid was both alluring and threatening. Although 'passing' was traditionally associated with the transgression of gender stereotypes, on colonial frontiers passing was more often about race. [55] The idea that some men could go 'native', dress, talk and act as the other, and pass undetected amongst colonized peoples threatened the rigid boundaries between races erected by European 'racial science'.

In the imperial context passing posed special dilemmas. Notable 'passers', such as explorer, scholar and diplomat, Richard Burton and soldier T.E. Lawrence, were viewed with both admiration and suspicion. The capacity to move across cultural borders conferred great authority, but at the same time it conjured up the idea that 'civilized men' might revert to the 'primitive', undermining claims to cultural and racial superiority. There was an intense cultural and psychological anxiety about the potential loss of self involved in 'going over'. Underpinning this was a concern that the allure of the East might be too powerful and that return would be impossible. Such fears were saturated in sexual imagery of a debilitating, enervating, feminizing East. Here men might lose their manhood. The sexual violation of T.E. Lawrence by Turkish soldiers after his capture, encapsulated some of these fears for a wider audience and led to an intense personal sense of 'splitting apart' for Lawrence.[56]

Rudyard Kipling's novel *Kim* (1901), similarly, presents the idea of a boy caught 'between two worlds' as both enticing and threatening. Kipling resolves this tension by having Kim disavow the feminine East and return to the masculine West.[57] But 'passing' was not just a cultural, sexual and psychological threat to the Empire ideal. It also conjured up the spectre that people from the East might pass as Westerners. Here lay some of the intense cultural ambivalence about the Westernized elites produced by the Empire. Although there were many efforts to convert, reform and educate colonized peoples, turning them into, in Homi Bhabha's memorable phrase, 'mimic men', the members of these new colonial groups were consistently denied the status of Westerners. Mimicry, however, could also imply that the habits of Empire were the product of education and training rather than racial superiority. While critics of colonialism, such as Frantz Fanon, condemned those with 'black skins and white masks', adopting Western life styles and political ideologies also challenged the legitimacy of colonial discourses.[58]

Postcolonial Identities

Imperialism and colonialism destroyed, suppressed and transformed other economies and cultures, but also produced new peoples and identities. The children of inter-racial frontier unions, the metis populations of the Americas, Africa and Asia were literally in-between cultures. Over the last few decades a number of historians have studied the emergence of these mixed cultures and their assertion of distinct social and political identities. In Canada, in particular, the metis became a powerful and distinct social and political force. As we have seen, throughout the nineteenth century 'miscegenation' also became the object of greater regulation and condemnation. Moreover, the populations of most concern also changed. In eighteenth-century America, native Americans and slaves were the most common sexual partners for men on the frontier. By the early-twentieth century freed blacks and Asians were the source of widespread white American fears about the threat to racial purity. In Australia Asians, Pacific Islanders and Aborigines were the source of most concern. In India and other parts of Asia, however, the issue was less miscegenation than the aspirations of the emerging indigenous elites. A rich historiography has developed around the position of these peoples on the borders of the Empire. Much of this work has highlighted the central place of sex in Western anxieties about cultural boundaries.

Postcolonial theorists have been prominent in the debates about the relationship between colonialism, sexuality and identity. Such studies have highlighted the social and psychic tensions for colonized peoples who were made the 'subjects and objects of modernity'.[59] Some of this work, following Foucault, has explored how colonial discourses produced new social groups (classes, families, racial types) and subjectivities (housewife, Western educated man, waged worker) amongst colonized populations. New Westernized identities were created by the 'compelling seductions of colonial power'. There was, as Leela Gandhi has argued, a 'relationship of reciprocal antagonism and desire between colonizer and colonized'.[60]

Colonialism forged hybrid social groups and identities. The new social elites amongst the colonized – civil servants, soldiers, traders and lower professionals – adopted European languages, habits, customs and culture, mixing them with indigenous cultural customs and attributes. They were educated in European ways and were conversant with European ideologies of nationalism, liberalism and democracy. In this context postcolonial historians have provided a more critical account of indigenous elites than earlier studies, which depicted them as bearers of an inevitable modernity, courageous leaders of nationalist struggles and the creators of new, dynamic cultures. Homi Bhabha's concepts of mimicry and hybridity highlight the processes whereby emergent indigenous middle classes adopted Western social habits, styles of dress and liberal democratic political ideologies. These groups inhabited a zone in-between colonizer and colonized and were powerful forces in the nationalist struggles that eventually toppled empires.[61]

But the understanding of European culture produced by these new groups chafed against the reality of their position. They were denied full access to the rights and privileges of the colonizer, marginalized and denigrated by racist ideologies and practices, made the victim of sexual exploitation and robbed of the full fruits of their labour. Bhabha utilizes Freudian ideas of fantasy to theorize how these people are 'caught *inappropriately*, between the unconscious and the preconscious, making problematic, like mimicry, the very notion of origins'. Bhabha draws an analogy between the structure of the unconscious and the formation of particular colonial types who have no point of origin in an indigenous culture and forever sit between cultures. These concepts help open up

new understandings of the ways colonialism both suppressed indigenous practices and transformed them in the production of new identities and cultures.[62]

Similarly, there has been important work on groups outside the
colonized elite. For example, the 'subaltern studies' group has pioneered the analysis of 'the people' in colonized cultures – the urban
and rural poor, the emergent working classes and other marginalized groups, who challenged colonial powers and the nationalist elites
transforming colonial society and politics.[63] Critics, such as Spivak,
have raised important questions about the dilemmas for historians
involved in trying to uncover the voices of subaltern groups. She warns
that, in recovering and explaining these forms of resistance, historians
have translated subaltern struggles into the language of the colonizer,
entrapping the subaltern in new networks of knowledge and power.[64]
Nevertheless, subaltern studies have opened up new perspectives on
the relationships between colonizer and colonized, shifting focus away
from an exclusive concentration on elites.

Western-educated elites, however, were major forces driving nationalism in the colonial world. Subaltern groups were important forces of
resistance to both colonialism and elite nationalism, but it was the elites
who articulated a dominant nationalist discourse, one that incorporated
and subverted subaltern aims. Within these nationalist struggles Third
world ideologies of colonial liberation became, like their European
counterparts, highly gendered discourses.[65] Indigenous male elites represented themselves as the saviours of 'mother' nations, harking back
to often imagined traditions thought to be strong before the arrival of
Europeans. Part of their appeal to a larger populace was the promise
of a return to the past. They sought to reclaim their women from the
colonizer and often sought a return to traditional cultural practices of
female submission as an integral part of national renewal, thus stifling
some of the indigenous feminist movements that were beginning to
emerge in parts of the empire.[66] At the same time they inspired others
through a vision of a bright future as a modern nation. There were complex tensions between these divergent futures. And in this cultural and
political flux race, gender, sexual and class conflicts intermeshed and
shaped national political transformations.

Some of the most interesting work on colonialism and sexuality, however, has been on the ways racial ideologies and identities were subverted
and undermined. Historians of colonialism have often turned to literary
texts for evidence of the ambivalent and contested boundaries of empire.
There has been interesting work on writers between worlds such as Rabind-
ranath Tagore, Frantz Fanon, V.S. Naipaul, Salman Rushdie and Oswald
Mtshali. This work has highlighted the ways indigenous elites, metis and
other emergent social groups under European rule exposed the moral

and political hypocrisy of imperialism and the private and public struggles embedded in the colonial rule. The majority of literary studies, however, have explored the conflicts, tensions and ambivalent responses by
Europeans in the colonial situation. The work of European writers such
as E.M. Forster, Rudyard Kipling, George Orwell, and Olive Schreiner
has commanded attention. Careful readings of these texts reveal complex
gender and sexual dynamics in the colonial imagination.

One example of the utility of literary analysis in the history of sexuality is Pamela Pattynama's fascinating study of Louis Couperus' novel
of Dutch colonial culture in Indonesia at the end of the nineteenth
century. *The Hidden Force* (1900) explores inter-racial sexuality, miscegenation and the decline of empire. This story of a Dutch colonial
family weaves a complex narrative web around a series of inter-racial
and incestuous relationships: a stepson is involved with his creole stepmother, and a daughter and the stepmother also vie for the affections of
a Eurasian man. At the same time tensions escalate between the father
and the local Javanese regent. Mysterious forces attack the house of the
Dutch family, stones are hurled, letters sent accusing family members
of indecency, betel juice spat at them – signifying a larger confronta-
tion between European rationalism and Eastern spiritualism. The family begins to disintegrate under these diverse tensions. The wife returns
to Paris, the children leave and the father remains, living in a native
village with a local woman. The novel exposes sexual, gender and class
frictions within the colonial community and in doing so suggests a collapse of faith in the colonial enterprise. More intriguingly, the narrative develops an indigenous female viewpoint – the Javanese maid acts
as a point of observation for the collapse of this colonial family.[67] For
Couperus, the fate of this Dutch family was a metaphor for the decline
of Europe's imperial fantasy.

Much of the historiography of sex and colonialism has focused on
the ways sexuality undermined imperial domination. It examines the
history of the colonizers, the sexual drives impelling imperialism and
the processes that lead to the collapse of Western domination. Other
work, however, has begun to examine the transformations wrought by
the West in Eastern sexual cultures. In the first volume of *The History of
Sexuality* Michel Foucault drew a distinction between a Western concern
with the science of sex and an Eastern tradition of *ars erotica* devoted to
the uncovering of truth through pleasure.[68]

This distinction has shaped the historiography of non-Western sexuality. Historians of Eastern sexual cultures have highlighted how, in
many Asian and Middle Eastern traditions, sex was not an independent feature of life but an integral part of being. In many Asian cultures,
in particular, concepts of sexual orientation did not exist. Nonetheless,
within Eastern cultures increasing contact with the West led to transfor-

mations within religious doctrines, notably 'neo-Confucianization' and Chinese Buddhism, which stressed sexual abstinence and the avoidance of women as a bulwark against religious and social decline. These responses to the West began as early as the thirteenth century.[69]

More recently there has been considerable work on how traditional Eastern sexual identities were transformed by colonialism. As with debates over Western sexuality the existence of Asian homosexual cultures has been the subject of considerable debate. Some historians, for example Bret Hinsch, have attempted to uncover a long tradition of 'gay' cultures in the East, stretching back millennia. In these works Western homophobia was imposed on indigenous cultures of tolerance and respect for same-sex desire.[70] In contrast, other historians have argued that while same-sex cultures flourished in Asia for centuries, homosexual identities are a recent phenomenon.

In this context, however, there is considerable debate over the timing of the emergence of Western sexual identities in the East. Some historians and social scientists have argued that the emergence of Western-style gay and lesbian identities, particularly in Asia, are of very recent origin, the product of a global 'queering' of contemporary culture.[71] Others have stressed the historical roots for these new identities. Throughout Asia urban sexual cultures of gays, lesbians, effeminates and transsexuals developed in the nineteenth and twentieth centuries catering to the sexual demands of colonizers. These cultures developed their own dynamics and codes and laid the foundations for the more confident and self-conscious modern global sexual identities of the late-twentieth and early-twenty-first centuries.[72]

Nationalism and Sexuality

Sexuality has rarely figured in the study of nationalism. More commonly historians have studied the political, economic, social, racial and imperial contexts which forged European nationalism. For historians such as Benedict Anderson and Ernest Gellner, modern European nationalism, which began to emerge in the sixteenth and seventeenth centuries, was also a creative cultural act. People began to imagine themselves as part of a larger social entity – the nation. For Anderson this leap of imagination required the spread of vernacular languages and the means for mass communication (the printing press, newspapers, broadsheets, journals and magazines) to facilitate a sense of common purpose amongst people of different social groups spread over vast tracts of land. Only when people sensed a common connection with each other did they band together through the political ideology of nationalism into the new social formation of the nation.[73] Gellner has stressed that nations are created as particular correlations of culture and polity.

Although nations were very new entities, national histories naturalized these political and social structures, giving them a lineage and a sense of timeless inevitability.[74]

Thus nations were seen as the realization of inherent possibilities, hitherto stifled by wars, rivalries, hereditary aristocracies and kingship. Nations were also invested with a sense that they were the expression of distinct racial and social groups, marked off from each other by fundamental differences. Nationalism was also produced in the heat of battle. Wars of national liberation aimed to throw off the yoke of foreign or aristocratic domination. Wars between nations, over disputed territories and peoples, helped foster a sense of identity, patriotism and loyalty. Although the debate over the political and cultural origins, characteristics and motivating forces of nationalism is very extensive, a few historians have also ventured to argue that sexuality was a factor in the emergence of nationalism.

The key question for historians of nationalism and sexuality has been how to connect sexuality and a mass political movement and ideology. One notable answer has been Peter Gay's attempt to place nineteenth-century nationalism into a larger history of 'aggression'. Aggression is part of Gay's broader examination of the tensions between the sex instinct and the civilizing impulse within Victorian culture. Gay's explicitly Freudian theory posits libido as a natural instinct that needs to be tamed for society and culture to flourish. Similarly, aggression is instinctual. Thus the nineteenth century, for Gay, becomes 'a measure of collaboration and clashes' between the sexual and aggressive instincts. For Gay, aggression was a fundamental fuel for wars, class struggles and the hatred generated by nationalism and imperialism. His study of aggressiveness in the nineteenth century covers a very broad canvas – from duelling, corporal punishment and satire to execution, feminism, education and war.

In this context nationalism was a complex response to the epic upheavals of industrialization, urbanization, individualism and the French Revolution. It was conflict-ridden and emotional in nature. Nationalist movements may have evolved in 'highly individual ways' but at their heart was 'a potent amalgam of libido and aggression'. As we have seen, Gay moves away from a simplistic account of culture as repression. Instead he explores the ways instincts are sublimated and thus fuel culture. Aggression could be driven by frustration, and thus was a means for libido to find expression. The passionate intensity of much aggression derived from its capacity to harness sexual drives to its purposes. Although Victorians found some forms of aggression threatening and unacceptable (duelling, crime, class struggle) and sought to police these practices, there were other forms, notably nationalism, which were prized. Thus Victorian culture was not marked by the eradication of aggression, but by a struggle over what constituted acceptable avenues for its expression. For Gay, like Freud, sublimation of aggression could fuel such virtues as aesthetic appreciation, scientific productivity, pacifism or patriotism. Ironically nationalism, a form of aggression much praised in the nineteenth century, could also lead to the murderous destructiveness of World War I.[75]

George Mosse, like Gay, sees nationalism and respectability as safety valves, harnessing the power of sexuality to political and social ends. For Mosse, male friendship was a driving force within nineteenth-century nationalism. Close male bonding carried the threat of sexuality. He highlights the homosexual and homosocial dimensions of many of the social organizations integral to nineteenth-century German nationalism. Through a close examination of the diverse youth, nudist, life-reform and *volkish* movements of the nineteenth century, Mosse maps how the promotion of close male bonds, veneration of the body, nature and physical exercise, and ideals of masculinity gave these organizations their appeal and emotional strength. There was a strong strand of homoeroticism to many of these groups, such as the coterie around the German poet Stefan George. A few of these male youth groups were rocked by homosexual scandals. But, for Mosse, this erotic potential was sublimated in an ethic of respectable manliness. Respectability and nationalism were the 'bulwark against sexual passion'.

These proto-nationalist youth organizations were largely exclusive, admitting only men. Young men and their mentors found their sense of self in an explicit rejection of feminine virtues of domesticity, physical weakness, spirituality and sentimentality. Such movements gained their definition through the construction of a sharp distinction between the sexes. Women were naturally respectable and placed on a social pedestal – an ideal to live and die for, but one emotionally distant from the masculine world of the youth movements. Moreover, these movements often linked nationalism to feminine respectability. Women were the embodiment of the nation, the thing men defended and protected. Thus homosocial bonds were reinforced by a disavowal of female sexuality. Women were virtuous mothers and pure maidens.[76]

Although less explicit than Gay, Mosse clearly draws on Freudian ideas of desire. His argument that respectability, manliness and nationalism were forms of sublimation strikes a chord with Gay's notion that the battle between sexual instinct and culture creates many of the major institutions, ideas and habits of Victorian social life. But Gay's account, for all its depth and sophistication, lacks a clear historical grounding. Little attention is paid to why the timeless struggle between aggression and culture should take the forms that it did in the nineteenth century. Gay describes the diverse manifestations of aggression with great insight, but fails to explain why the nineteenth century sanctioned outlets for aggression that were different to those of earlier periods of European history. Instead he falls back on the assumption that they reflected larger social and political changes. This view is plausible, but the precise links between social change and forms of aggression are vague, and derive their force from conjunction rather than a theory of causation.

In contrast, Mosse specifies a direct link between sexuality and nationalism. He argues that Victorian homoerotic movements coincide with the emerging focus on homosexuality as a form of abnormal sexuality. The rise of sexology and theories of degeneration defined a range of homoerotic desires and behaviours as pathological, forcing men to sublimate homoeroticism into the nationalist, youth, body cult movements of the nineteenth century. These were regarded as acceptable and respectable outlets for feelings that were troubling and increasingly the subject of medical and political regulation. Yet at the same time this form of sublimation made the homosocial world of the *volkish* organizations the seedbed for nationalist fervour.

Another important study of a homosocial world riddled with sexual anxieties is Klaus Theweleit's exhilarating two-volume study *Male Fantasies* (1987). Although ostensibly a specific study of a small group of Freikorps officers in Germany in the first few years after World War I, *Male Fantasies* is an extraordinarily detailed exploration of the fragile emotional world of proto-fascist bourgeois nationalists. The Freikorps officers admired respectable middle-class women, especially their wives, and adored the nation, but had no real emotional connection to the women in their lives. They were much more comfortable in the world of male comrades. Time and again these men disavowed sexuality, skirting around the issue or avoiding it altogether, even in their most private records.

This was a sexless world of virtuous women and chaste men committed to the cause of saving the nation from the threat of bolshevism, class struggle, feminism and Jewish financiers. But it was also a vulnerable world, driven by anger and frustration about Germany's 'betrayal' and loss. Theweleit brilliantly elucidates the private and public culture of this small world, revealing the sexual fears that drove its politics. These men were obsessed with being overwhelmed and destroyed by fantastic figures such as rifle-carrying bolshevik women, nurses, and floods of threatening social forces. They feared sexual passion, the touch of bodies and were disturbed by profound castration anxieties.[77]

It is hard to do justice to the richness of Theweleit's account, a complex mix of cultural history, political analysis and the history of ideas. It is also a detailed psychological portrait of a social group. Although there is no explicit reference to psychoanalysis, Theweleit's elucidation of an anxious world that disavows passion, and promotes male bonding, violence, nationalism and hatred of the forces that oppose it has its roots in ideas of repression and sublimation. More importantly, Theweleit resists the temptation to reduce these diverse currents of desire and anxiety to a reflection of social, economic and political forces. Although he highlights the precise cultural context of postwar, returned soldier anger and German political upheaval, what carries Theweleit's analysis is the detailed ethnographic and psychoanalytic reconstruction of personal conflict and struggle. Like many of the texts examined in this chapter, it explores the fraught emotional and sexual character of forms of social domination.

Conclusion

As we have seen, the boundaries of gender, class, race and sex relations are structured around historically contested and changing forms of domination. Although it is possible to analyse nation, race, class and gender as political, social, cultural and economic phenomena, historians of sexuality and gender have sought to uncover the sexual anxieties and emotional investments that underpinned larger social institutions. These relationships of domination were often ambiguous and sexually charged: sites of attractions and repulsions.

In these contexts the search for the innermost forces impelling these social passions has brought many historians to an interest in psychological theories. These carry a risk of making historical events the product of universal psychological struggles. But they also offer the possibility of explaining why people have fought and died for ideals of class, Empire and nation. More importantly, historians of sexuality have uncovered a rich history of transgression. While sexual desire and anxiety could support forms of domination, they were also points of contest. Men and women who crossed the race barrier in their sexual relationships, and slaves, servants and concubines who used sex to claim a measure of power and control, subverted dominant structures of power.

Chapter 8

FEMINISM AND FRIENDSHIP

In 1870 Josephine Butler, prominent English campaigner against the 1866 Contagious Diseases Acts, published 'An Appeal to the People of England on the Recognition and Superintendence of Prostitution by Governments', condemning the Acts as 'deeply degrading' because they assumed that men were 'utterly and hopelessly slaves of their own passions'.[1] The Acts governed naval ports and cities with military garrisons, allowing for the compulsory medical examination and incarceration of prostitutes. For Butler and her fellow campaigners, these Acts sanctioned prostitution as a necessary evil to meet the imperative sexual demands of soldiers and sailors. Instead, Butler proposed that 'adulterous husbands and fathers' abstain from fornication.

Similarly, in America, there were many late-nineteenth and early-twentieth century moral reform and anti-vice movements opposed to the legalization of prostitution or the introduction of contagious diseases regulations. The leaders of these organizations were politicians and moral reformers such as Anthony Comstock and Charles Parkhurst, but women, such as Charlotte Perkins Gilman, Jane Ellice Hopkins, Anna Powell, Frances Willard and Lavinia Dock, were also at the forefront of societies for moral purity and the eradication of prostitution. The 'new abolitionists', as historian David Pivar has described them, believed that men had to accept woman's standard of morality.[2]

The assertion that men had to conform to a stricter morality went against the grain of 'commonsense' understandings of male sexuality. As Helen Lefkowitz Horowitz has argued, there was a rich nineteenth-century sexual popular culture that saw obscenity, ribaldry, prostitution and illicit sexual intercourse as natural.[3] The idea that masculine sexual needs were imperative, however, crossed class boundaries. Many in the respectable working and middle classes believed that all men possessed a natural appetite for sex that had to find an outlet, preferably in marriage, but often outside it. Such attitudes underpinned the widespread acceptance of prostitution and adultery, as long as it remained private. These simple faiths also framed the opposition of many parliamentarians to efforts to raise the age of consent for women, as they feared that such a step might punish the 'natural and harmless' immorality of young men. Prominent medical authorities, such as Sir James Paget, saw continence as equally harmful to the male system as over-indulgence.[4]

The reputations of the Victorian abolitionists and feminists who challenged the inevitability of male sexual needs have had a chequered history. Some contemporaries ridiculed them as pleasure-hating spinsters and religious fanatics. Such assessments were perpetuated by generations of historians who regarded feminist moral reformers in particular as middle-class puritans campaigning against simple working-class pleasures, unwitting accomplices of a larger movement towards increased state regulation of morality.[5] But the attitudes of woman movement activists of the nineteenth century to sex have also troubled feminist historians. A number have seen the nineteenth-century campaigns for social purity led by reformers like Josephine Butler, Elizabeth Wolstenholme Elmy and Jane Addams as socially and sexually conservative.[6] Moreover, the argument of prominent suffragists on both sides of the Atlantic, such as Emmeline Pankhurst, Millicent Garrett Fawcett, Butler herself, Charlotte Perkins Gilman and many others, that essential differences between men and women were the basis for women's political rights, has been seen by some historians as a dead-end for feminist politics.[7]

These women have been characterized as middle-class reformers who failed to understand the need for more fundamental social change, which could address the real differences between women, based on class and race.[8] Some prominent feminist historians, such as Nancy Cott, have seen these reformers as leaders of a 'woman movement', one that spoke of women as a unified category, insensitive to the differences between them. Instead, Cott argues that feminism was born in the early years of the twentieth century, when its leaders began to advocate 'female individuality, political participation, economic independence and sexual freedom'. This represented a real challenge to masculine social order.[9] Other historians who have argued that nineteenth-century suffragists, new abolitionists and purity campaigners were grappling with some of the fundamental dilemmas of feminist politics – oppression and similarities and differences between the sexes – have contested such assessments.[10]

How should we understand these campaigns around sex in the nineteenth and early-twentieth centuries? The debate about the nature of Victorian feminism and the feminist movement of the early-twentieth century highlights important dimensions of Victorian sexual culture. While popular working-class attitudes sustained an older tradition of both male and female desire, middle-class Victorians came to see sexuality as inevitably shaped by gender. As we have seen in earlier chapters, men were believed to have 'animal sexual appetites', while women's natural condition was chaste. The creation of separate and gendered sexual attributes allowed Victorians to talk about distinct sexed moralities – woman's was based on the transcendence of sex, man's was rooted in nature. The pervasiveness of these ideas shaped Victorian sexual politics. It was the basis for new abolitionists and feminists to claim that men had to accept a new standard of morality, a woman's standard. Nineteenth-century feminists were able to claim a right to citizenship, not because they were the same as men but because they were fundamentally different. Men could not possibly represent a constituency that was so foreign to their nature.

For historians, a gendered sexual culture raises the haunting spectre of anachronism. There is the ever-present danger of assessing Victorian attitudes to sexuality in the light of a set of assumptions bequeathed by the sexual revolution of the 1960s. The assertion that new abolitionists, social purity reformers and Victorian feminists were prudes is one example of this trap. Instead we have to see these reformers in their context. The campaigns of women like Butler, Elmy, Gilman and others, are examples of how sexual cultures can both silence some possibilities and develop others. Victorian sexual ideas provided a discourse and a set of tools which inhibited mobilization around female sexuality, but allowed reformers to contest the ideas of male sexuality that underlay men's sexual dominance. Reformers and feminists were bound by the assumptions of their time. But they were also able to break some of them, challenging beliefs that had hitherto been taken for granted.

Christine Stansell has described the break with Victorian feminism as the birth of 'sexual modernism'.[11] There were extraordinary changes in late-nineteenth and early-twentieth century understandings of sexuality, and women were active participants in these transformations. By the early-twentieth century new ideas about women's sexuality pioneered by sexologists and sex reformers, such as Sigmund Freud, undermined the idea of gendered sexual cultures. Women, as well as men, had a strong sexual drive. Modern sexual discourses transformed the perception of friendships between women, which were such an important part of the social and emotional life of many middle-class women.

New understandings of sexuality also raised important political questions for women, encouraging the generation of early-twentieth-century and inter-war feminists to develop ideas and strategies that were a significant departure from those of their nineteenth-century sisters. Embedded in the praise of the newer generation of feminists is an implicitly 'Whig' narrative. An essential part of our exploration of feminist understandings of sexuality is the requirement to step outside this framework to more closely examine feminist ideas and campaigns in their specific historical context and consider how those contexts and consequently politics changed. The historical debates around female friendships and feminist politics afford us an opportunity to explore the perils and possibilities in viewing a past so different from our own.

Female Friendships

In the eighteenth and nineteenth centuries the growth of a leisured middle class and the increasing emphasis on the domestic sphere as women's domain encouraged women to orient their social life towards home, church, child-rearing and visiting. It also afforded them the opportunity to develop close relationships with other women in similar circumstances. The popularity of diary, journal and letter writing has left historians a rich archive for examining the feelings and emotions of these women. But it also poses a dilemma for modern historians. Making sense of these writings, with their specific conventions, forms of address and modes of expression, is difficult, especially after Freud has encouraged us to see sexual desire in so much of everyday life. This temptation is even greater for those historians writing after the 1960s, when lesbianism became a public, and for many, a relatively acceptable practice. The protestations of love and the profusion of emotion that characterizes much Victorian correspondence inevitably raises questions about the nature of these female friendships.

It was commonplace for female friends in the Victorian era to address each other as 'my darling' or 'my dearest', even 'my dearest, dearest lover'. Their letters were liberally sprinkled with statements such as 'a thousand kisses – I love you with my whole soul' or 'imagine yourself kissed many times by one who loved you so dearly'. Of course, the existence of these letters in archives and libraries is dependent on the fact that author and the recipient were apart, but the correspondence and diaries also refer to the warm embraces when friends met. Middle-class women often took vacations together. Some unmarried women shared houses after parents died. Even women who married sometimes moved in with a friend when their husbands were away. There were plenty of opportunities for intimate contact, and the diaries often refer to kisses, embraces and the sharing of beds during these visits.[12]

Is this evidence of a significant lesbian culture in nineteenth-century Europe and America? Some historians, notably Carroll Smith-Rosenberg and Lillian Faderman, have counselled against reading the evidence in such a way, arguing that it imposes the present on the past. Instead, they see these relationships as passionate emotional commitments that were intimate, but not necessarily sexual. While Faderman accepts that some of these friendships involved sex, she concludes that Victorian codes of reticence and respectability inhibited sexual activity. More important was nurturing and loving companionship between women. These relationships were essentially romantic friendships not lesbian sexual relationships.[13] Smith-Rosenberg and Faderman point to the fact that these friendships were common, openly professed and widely accepted by families, husbands and friends. Such women did not live in a lesbian subculture but freely and openly expressed their love. These historians argue that we need to put such relationships in their cultural and social setting and not impose a modern psychosexual perspective on the past.

Instead, Smith-Rosenberg and Faderman argue that the rigid distinction between the public and the private spheres in Victorian middle-class culture created significant social barriers between the sexes. There were very severe social restrictions on intimacy between young men and women. They largely inhabited different social worlds, encouraging close friendships with those of their own sex. Intimate mother–daughter relationships were the foundation for this enclosed female world. Other women, usually from extensive kinship networks, were then incorporated into this social circle providing mutual support, comfort and social advice. Moreover, Victorian romanticism provided a language of high emotion, sensibility and passion for expressing everyday feelings of affection. Women 'lived in close emotional proximity with each other…[and] friendships and intimacies followed the biological ebb and flow of women's lives'.[14]

Moreover, close examination of these relationships suggests that sexual contact between female friends was rare, even when women lived together. This was so, despite appearances, even in those cases where one of the women in the couple adopted 'mannish' clothes and mannerisms. For example, Faderman finds no evidence of a sexual relationship in the loving friendship of Jane Pirie and Marianne Woods, even though they were accused of immoral conduct.[15] The term 'Boston marriages' was often used to describe female couples in which women referred to themselves as 'man and wife'. There were many of these marriages in Britain, Europe and the United States, and such women often held positions of authority and respect, such as school headmistress.[16] Even Sarah Ponsonby and Eleanor Butler, the 'Ladies of Llangollen', who ran away from Ireland in 1798 to live together thereafter in remote, rural north Wales, have been seen as romantic friends. Ponsonby and Butler shunned social contact, ostensibly conducted their relationship as a marriage and often dressed like men.[17]

For Smith-Rosenberg and Faderman, Victorian beliefs that women had a limited sexuality, largely focused on procreation, allowed women the freedom to explore intense emotional relationships with each other without social stigma. This was not a culture obsessed with the problem of 'deviant' sexuality. It was only later, with the work of late-nineteenth- and early-twentieth-century sexologists, that these behaviours and relationships were pathologized. Sexologists saw the 'mannish' woman as a voracious, licentious, unnaturally masculine type often suffering from an enlarged clitoris. Such women were accused of converting sexual innocents to a perverted lifestyle.[18]

The representation of relationships between women as forms of 'sexual inversion' or, later, lesbianism, drove women apart. They could no longer seek the loving support of friends without the risk of ostracism, innuendo and even medical intervention. For Smith-Rosenberg and Faderman, however, modern psychopathology should not lead us to take these relationships out of context. To do so risks imposing anachronistic readings on this female world of loving friendship.[19]

Despite the best efforts of Smith-Rosenberg and Faderman to place female friendships in a specific Victorian social context, other feminist historians have contested their conclusions. They have pointed to new evidence undermining the claim that these relationships were merely socially acceptable friendships. For example, the diaries of Anne Lister, part of the social circle of the 'Ladies of Llangollen', contains details of her on-going sexual relationship with a married woman and several affairs, 'sexual conquests' that definitely involved genital contact.[20] Moreover, other evidence shows that contemporaries saw some of these friendships, such as that of Ponsonby and Butler, as unnatural. Diarist Hester Thrale Piozzi, called them 'damned sapphists', and claimed that literary women were reluctant to stay the night unless accompanied by their husband.[21] While a few nineteenth-century women, such as soldiers Loreta Velazquez and Sarah Seelye and doctor, Mary Walker, 'passed' as men to escape the limitations imposed on women, others such as Mary Anderson and artist Carolina Hall, were renowned for their sexual interest in women.[22]

More importantly, critics have accused Faderman and Smith-Rosenberg of falling into the trap of imposing the present on the past, the very thing they had tried to avoid. Liz Stanley has pointed to the dangers of determining the 'nature' of a relationship *post hoc* with the partial and limited materials historians have to work with. She points to the flaws in Faderman's narrow definition of sexuality, as an act involving genital contact.[23] Such a definition is riddled with questionable assumptions. It goes against the grain of influential theorists and historians, such as Adrienne Rich and Blanche Wiesen Cook, who have suggested that there is no single lesbian attribute or sexual behaviour, but rather a continuum of women-identified practices and lifestyles that constitute lesbianism. Cook forcefully argues that 'women who love women, who choose women to nurture and support and to create a living environment in which to work creatively and independently, are lesbians'.[24]

Similarly, Sheila Jeffreys sees these relationships as genuinely passionate, and the issue of genital sex entirely irrelevant, especially given the widespread nineteenth-century feminist belief in 'psychic love'.[25] It is essential to see, as Stanley suggests, that lesbianism may have been understood and expressed differently in the past. To have a single modern definition of lesbian to measure the past might be just as anachronistic as failing to see relationships in their specific historical context.[26]

Much of the best recent work on nineteenth-century female friendships has stressed their rich diversity. Martha Vicinus, in an insightful review of the field, has argued that historians of lesbianism should explore a variety of relationships, including 'teenage crushes, romantic friendships, Boston marriages, theatrical cross-dressing, passing women, bulldykes and prostitutes, butches and femmes, and numerous other identifications, which may – and may not – include genital sex'.[27] Vicinus adopts a position close to that of Rich and Cook, suggesting that what happened in bed is less important than the engagement in a woman-identified life. Such an approach helps break down the unhelpful dichotomy between romantic friendship and lesbianism erected by Faderman and Smith-Rosenberg. Instead we can start to distinguish between different types of friendship. Female relationships were a continuum – with formal friendship at one end and active genital sexual relationships at the other; and many gradations in between.

Women, who married, had children and enjoyed the comforts of a large family circle, even if they maintained close romantic relationships with women, are probably more easily categorized as friends. But the many professional and bohemian women who usually supported themselves, did not marry and shared their social lives, and often their homes, with other women, fit more closely the definition of lesbian advanced by Blanche Wiesen Cook. These were women who embraced a world of female companionship largely free from that of men. Even so there were significant grey areas. For example, in 1859 Mary Sidgwick married her cousin Edward White Benson, scholar, headmaster and later Archbishop of Canterbury, and bore him six children. But she claimed to lack his 'strong human passion', and her recollections of the marriage bed indicate a troubled and rather one-sided sexual life. In her mid-thirties Mary developed a succession of loving attachments to women, and eventually fell in love with one, who shared her bed after Benson died.[28]

The problems involved in categorizing the nature of personal relationships between women in the Victorian era highlights the difficulties historians face. History is never simply uncovering the past. It requires judgements about the appropriate contexts in which to make sense of the evidence. While Faderman and Smith-Rosenberg stress the importance of understanding the conventions of women's culture and social life in the nineteenth century, other historians have argued that this social focus glosses over the need to define sex more broadly. It runs the risk of misunderstanding the nature of these friendships. We cannot put these relationships in a social context without some concept of what actually constitutes a sexual relationship. Do we take sexual intercourse or other forms of genital contact as the signifiers of sex acts? Or should we expand the category of sex to incorporate a large range of sensual and erotic acts and experiences? If the latter, how far do we go in expanding the definition before it loses all meaning, and we begin to fundamentally misunderstand the nature of some significant relationships in the past?

Victorian Feminism and the Critique of Sexuality

Suffrage has loomed large in studies of Victorian feminism. It was, as one of its first historians Ray Strachey declared, 'the cause'.[29] The struggle for the right to vote was a point of unity for feminists, although there were sharp differences over strategies and tactics. A sense of grievance that women were denied citizenship and a voice in the emergent Western democracies had been evident from the late-eighteenth century.[30] The assertion of women's rights, to be recognized as much as the 'rights of man', fired the writings of women such as Mary Wollstonecraft and Olympe de Gouges. They diagnosed the hypocrisy of movements for democratic rights, which in reality shunned universal rights and instead conferred them on the basis of gender. The democratic revolutions of the late-eighteenth and early-nineteenth centuries were, as Carol Pateman has argued, fraternal social contracts.[31]

Men had gendered citizenship and ironically this became the ground on which women could struggle for the vote. The Victorian campaign for female suffrage took as its rationale the idea that while women were similar to men in some respects, particularly intellectually and morally, there were fundamental differences between the sexes in experience. Women, claimed suffragists, had different views, ideas and interests and thus men could not possibly represent them in Parliament. If democracy was about a legitimate forum for 'the people', then women's voice needed to influence who would be chosen as their representatives. In other words they took the prevailing ideology of gender difference and used it as an argument in favour of the right to vote.[32]

This embrace of a fundamental tenet of Victorian sexual ideology did not insulate suffragists from criticism and entrenched opposition. Conservative anti-suffragists condemned the effort of women to enter the public sphere as ridiculous. They marshalled an array of arguments against female suffrage, beginning with the view that husbands and fathers were perfectly capable of representing the views of women and insisting that women were too emotional and sentimental to influence important matters of state. Women by nature, they asserted, were more fitted for the home. Women would be too easily swayed to cast their vote for the wrong interests.[33]

On the left, trade union, labour and socialist groups were often equally ambivalent about a movement dominated by middle-class women. They feared that feminist campaigns for women's right to work would undermine their struggle for a 'breadwinner's wage'. Radical elements of the labour movement criticized feminism as a bourgeois movement that threatened to deflect working-class women from the 'more important' class struggle. There were intense struggles between feminists on the left over the relationship between the struggle for suffrage and socialism. For example, German socialist feminist Lily Braun spoke in favour of suffrage, but Clara Zetkin condemned separate feminist organizations as 'fuzzy stupid dreams', asserting that women could only be emancipated if they tied their struggle to that of social democratic parties.[34]

The emphasis that the suffrage campaign placed on arguments of difference rather than equality has troubled later feminist historians. The idea of difference seemed a political dead-end for early 'second wave feminists', condemning women forever to being seen as weaker, less able and requiring men to protect them.[35] There were other features of Victorian feminism that disturbed feminist scholars in the 1970s. Middle-class women dominated the movement, marginalizing the voices and interests of working-class women. Their claim that the denial of citizenship put respectable women on a par with the poor, criminals and blacks was seen as evidence of a prevalent racist and class bias in the suffrage movement. Moreover, the involvement of many suffragists in movements for the regulation of the working classes, such as temperance, social purity and philanthropy, have lead some historians to conclude that Victorian feminism was an effort to impose evangelical and bourgeois ideals of respectability and domesticity on the wider populace.[36]

Suffrage, however, was not just an end in itself but a means to an end. It was a vehicle for ensuring the success of feminist social reforms, particularly in the area of sexual relations. Feminist support for new abolitionist and social purity campaigns such as the Comstock Act (1873) in America, their opposition to the Contagious Disease Acts, support for raising the age of consent for women, and their involvement in rescuing 'fallen women' and encouraging moral self-restraint have been seen as puritanical. Historians have highlighted the strong evangelical and social purity beliefs of many feminists.[37] Worse, while social purity provided feminists with a language to challenge male authority, it also put these reformers into a larger framework of medico-moral ideas and practices, which constructed a dominant discourse of sexuality with distinctive 'class articulations'.[38]

In America social hygiene campaigns of the late-nineteenth and early-twentieth centuries were also entwined with the politics of race. Progressive and feminist efforts to regulate prostitution and venereal disease were energized by pervasive fears about the threat to social order posed by immigrants and African Americans. Reformers feared that white slavery and racial minorities promoted venereal disease, rape and inter-racial sex. As a bulwark against these threats they promoted images of white purity. Racist anxieties underpinned feminist sexual conservatism.[39]

This characterization of feminist campaigns for abolition, social purity and suffrage has been challenged. A number of historians, such as Sheila Jeffreys, Margaret Jackson and Lucy Bland, have argued that there were radical and genuinely feminist aims within these campaigns. As Jackson argues, 'the fact that both feminists and conservatives shared a common sexual vocabulary has tended to obscure their political differences'. Feminists and conservatives alike may have embraced 'chastity', 'vice', 'purity' and 'continence' but there were differences in their aims and objectives.[40]

These revisionist historians have argued that there was a significant and radical feminist strand within the social purity movement devoted to controlling male sexuality.[41] Some social purity feminists, such as Josephine Butler, Jane Ellice Hopkins, Elizabeth Blackwell and Wolstenholme Elmy, campaigned against what they saw as the rising tide of sexual abuse of women, evident in the efforts to regulate rather than prevent prostitution. Moreover, Helen Lefkowitz Horowitz has argued that ironically the feminist interest in social purity put sex 'at the core of being'. American feminists drew on a range of ideas, from Spiritualism, reform physiology, Fourierism and Utopianism, to make sexuality central to spiritual and social emancipation, an idea pursued vigorously by feminist sexual modernists.[42] Similarly, John D'Emilio and Estelle Freedman stress the double-sided nature of Victorian feminism, sexually conservative and at the same time a radical critique of masculine sexual prerogatives.[43]

Feminists saw an affinity between their concerns and those of moral reformers. In Britain and Europe prominent advocates of the emancipation saw sexual morality as a key issue in women's oppression. They added their voice to that of other organizations seeking moral reform. In the 1870s European feminists, such as Anna Maria Mozzoni, were fierce opponents of the efforts of many Continental governments to register prostitutes and incarcerate those found to be suffering from venereal diseases. Others such as Aimé Humbert, Emilie de Morsier and Maria Deraismes, helped form the British and Continental Federation against the State Regulation of Vice. Similarly, while the British Social Purity Alliance, established in 1873, was led by men wishing to transform the conduct of men through the eradication of prostitution and the promotion of self-restraint, women were also prominent in the Alliance.[44]

The British social purity movement was given a significant boost in 1885 by W.T. Stead's sensational disclosures, 'The Maiden Tribute in Modern Babylon', which detailed the extensive sexual exploitation of young girls as prostitutes.[45] During the late-nineteenth and early-twentieth centuries a number of other organizations, such as the Church of England Purity Society, White Cross League, Moral Reform Union, England Purity Society, and the National Vigilance Association, also appeared to direct the movement for social purity. Evangelical reformers were attracted to the ideal of purification and moral uplift. But feminists, according to Jeffreys, also saw social purity as a vehicle to make their influence felt.[46]

In other words, there were different strands to the social purity campaigns. The conservative, evangelical element of the social purity movement was largely concerned to eliminate vice through 'protective' legislation for stricter policing of prostitutes, the closure of brothels, and tougher penalties for the publication and sale of obscene material. Such campaigns punished women who were reliant on prostitution for their livelihood. Feminists focused more on the problems of the sexual double standard and enforced 'sex slavery' for women.

Many American feminists also became involved in social purity, temperance and welfare work. Prostitution was a key issue. Enforced medical treatment of prostitutes and the widespread use of municipal regulations to create 'red-light' districts in many cities were seen by American abolitionists as sanctioning male lust at the expense of women's bodies. While women such as Jane Addams, Charlotte Perkins Gilman, Kate Bushnell, Harriet Burton Laidlaw and Rose Livingston, were prominent in organizations such as the National Purity Congress and the White Ribbon campaigns, they were fiercely opposed to the regulation of prostitution. They were instrumental in challenging the support of sections of the medical profession for 'red-light' districts.

Prominent doctors believed safe areas were the best means of preventing the spread of venereal diseases. Feminists insisted that such districts encouraged white slavery and demanded abolition rather than regulation. They received support from some doctors. In the early-twentieth century Prince Morrow concluded that disease rates increased rather than decreased in cities with 'red-light' districts. But, as David Pivar has shown, in the inter-war years the alliance forged between feminists and doctors collapsed and doctors increasingly supported social hygiene campaigns to 'clean up' prostitutes. As a result many feminists resigned from purity and hygiene organizations because hygienists refused to see that the most serious disease problem was the male client not the female prostitute.[47]

The Contagious Diseases Acts highlighted the issue of the sexual double standard for many British feminists. The opposition to these Acts was followed closely by feminists in Europe and America, helping to shape their own campaigns against vice. In the 1860s these Acts attempted to safeguard men from venereal infections. In certain towns and ports, where soldiers and sailors were stationed, police were empowered to detain prostitutes and subject them to medical examination. If they were found to have venereal diseases they could be detained in lock hospitals for up to nine months. Opponents of these Acts claimed that such legislation condoned prostitution. The British Parliament, the Army and Navy, and many doctors who supported this legislation assumed that men had sexual needs and prostitution was a necessary and inevitable 'evil'. The key issue for these authorities was to prevent the spread of disease, not improve the morality of society.

As we have seen, Josephine Butler was a leading campaigner against these Acts. In her 1870 'Appeal' we can glimpse some of the difficulties historians face in disentangling the feminist and moral reform strands of her argument. On the one hand, she wrote in the name of 'thoughtful and Christian women of England', and talked at length about the need for religious principle, moral persuasion, self-restraint and the fear of a bureaucracy that would imperil free people. She also adopted the patronizing tone of Victorian philanthropy, referring to prostitutes as 'unfortunates' and the need for 'reclamation of the fallen'.

On the other hand, there is an impassioned critique of legislation that 'treats as a crime *only* in one sex, and *only* among the *poor* of that sex'. For Butler and her feminist supporters these Acts sacrificed the 'souls and bodies of tens of thousands of women' to the 'supposed necessity' of men's passions. They made the 'path of the fornicator safe' while at the same time punishing impoverished women driven to a life of vice, and subjecting them to loss of self-respect and the indignities of the 'dissecting room'.[48] At the heart of their concerns was the sex slavery enforced on women by the assumption that men had stronger sexual instincts.

The Contagious Diseases Acts were repealed in 1885. But feminists became involved in a host of other struggles over sexuality and morality in the late-nineteenth and early-twentieth centuries. Raising the age of consent, in an effort to protect young girls from seduction and sexual abuse, was one. After Stead's sensational revelations feminists and new abolitionists succeeded in raising the age for sexual intercourse in England from 13 to 16 years in 1885, although it remained at 13 years for sexual assault. In the 1880s and 1890s American purity groups succeeded in raising the age of consent from as low as 10 in some States to between 14 and 18 years.[49] Other campaigns focused on the problem of incest (outlawed in Britain in 1908), and the need for

women doctors, police and prison guards to safeguard prostitutes from
the degradation involved in being searched, interrogated and imprisoned by men. Underpinning all these feminist campaigns was the idea
that men assumed sexual rights over women, demanded sexual services, and enacted laws to protect their access to clean women. For feminists, it was necessary to demand that men reform themselves.

Feminists considered women naturally chaste, more moral and civilized than men. It was the task of men to bring themselves up to the
level of women. In making masculinity the central issue feminists turned
Victorian sexual ideology on its head, accepting its central premise,
but drawing a very different conclusion. Not all feminists, however,
accepted that women had weaker sexual inclinations. For example,
American medical pioneer Elizabeth Blackwell believed that the sexual
instinct was as strong in women as it was in men, but the conclusion she
drew on the basis of this 'fact' put her in the feminist mainstream. If
women had a powerful sex instinct and could tame it, then the obliga-
tion was on men to do likewise.[50] To this end feminists supported societies encouraging male chastity. They also resorted to such tactics as
picketing brothels and publishing the names of prominent male clients
of such establishments, to shame the hypocrites, embarrass the legisla-
tors and encourage male continence.

Feminists also campaigned against the 'sex slavery' of marriage.
Prominent British, European and American feminists, such as Olive
Schreiner, Cicely Hamilton, Concepcion Arenal and Charlotte Perkins
Gilman, argued that marriage was a degraded relationship largely
based on economic need. Because women were denied work and adequate wages they were forced to sell their bodies, labour and emotional
resources in return for room and board. Men purchased the sexual
services of women and used them to nurture their heirs, while women
were compelled to marry otherwise they risked poverty, and social
ostracism as 'old maids'. Overcoming the inequalities in the institution of marriage became a central plank of Victorian feminism.

A key strategy in this broader campaign was to create opportunities
for the economic independence of women. Feminists campaigned for
the right of women to retain their property after marriage and equal
rights to sue for divorce (in Britain and Australia men could divorce for
adultery alone, women were required to have additional grounds such
as cruelty or desertion). Equally significant were campaigns to foster
respectable employment and adequate wages for women workers. Economic independence would enable women to escape sexual slavery.

Other feminists, however, believed that the problem was deeper than
economic inequality. They saw male sexual dominance as the root cause
of women's oppression. A few feminists condemned marriage as bondage, advocating free love to give women the opportunity to choose their

own sexual partners. Others highlighted the consequences of man's assumed right of control over the body of his wife. Frances Power Cobbe publicized the evils of domestic violence, where women were assaulted and murdered by husbands for trivial acts of disobedience. Courts were generally lenient in such cases. For feminists, these examples were clear instances of how marriage institutionalized male power over women.[51]

Defining Victorian feminism and distinguishing it from a host of new abolitionist, social purity, temperance and middle-class reform movements has proven difficult. Moreover, the intersections between Victorian feminism and these other movements has lead to contrary assessments of the nature of the nineteenth-century woman move-ment. While historians have highlighted the ways male sexuality was at the heart of Victorian feminist concerns, the strategies feminists used have led to disputes over the nature of this movement. In their cam-paigns to tackle the consequences of male lust and vice, some feminists aligned themselves with moral reform and philanthropic movements that focused on such themes as morality, depravity, drink and poverty rather than women. While some feminists saw a link between these con-cerns and the problems of women, others were determined that fem-inist concerns with male sexual dominance and female slavery were distinctive. Thus there was no single feminist voice and no clear differ-ences amongst feminists over strategies and tactics and fundamental issues such as female sexuality (was it as strong as men's or not?).

In this context the analysis of what constitutes Victorian feminism is as difficult as understanding its diverse politics, philosophies and tactics. This was a shifting and fluid world of alliances and interventions. Vic-torian feminists shared much with evangelical moral reformers. Some also accepted key tenets of Victorian sexual ideas, while others contested them. Sheila Jeffreys is forthright in her assessment that the women who contested male sexual dominance were genuinely radical and feminist. Their campaigns for continence in men and the promotion of inde-pendent chaste lives for women represented a profound challenge to male power.[52] Others are more circumspect. Lucy Bland and Barbara Caine, for example, focus on the contradictions in Victorian feminism, the ways in which feminists both challenged and were embroiled in their times. Victorian women may have grappled with fundamental feminist dilemmas of equality and difference, but their answers were often repres-sive, condescending in matters of class and race and rooted in a Victo-rian belief that the sex instinct could be overcome.

Feminism and Sexual Modernism

In the late-nineteenth and early-twentieth centuries sexology and psy-choanalysis transformed the terms of debate about sexuality. The ideas of theorists, such as Havelock Ellis, Iwan Bloch, Augustin Forel, Magnus Hirschfeld, Edward Carpenter and Sigmund Freud, had a profound impact on feminist ideas, objectives and strategies in Britain, Europe and North America. Sexology and psychoanalysis eroded feminist beliefs in women's sexual difference, purity and continence. Although there had been a few Victorian feminists, like Elizabeth Blackwell, who believed that women possessed sexual passions, their conclusion that women (and men) could triumph over animal appetites was also challenged by the new sexology.

Havelock Ellis, in particular, saw sexuality as integral to personal identity and fulfilment. In his view, satisfying sexual relations were essential for emotional balance and mental health, especially for women whose 'passions' had been denied for so long. More significantly, Sigmund Freud's theory of libido not only asserted forcefully that everyone had a sexual instinct, it also undermined the idea that men or women could overcome these drives. For Freud, the sex instinct never disappeared but was transformed through sublimation into positive attributes such as artistic expression, the work ethic and philanthropy, or more disastrously into neurosis. The high incidence of women suffering hysteria was taken as evidence that the 'excessive' repression of female sex instincts was unhealthy.[53]

In this landscape new generations of feminists had to grapple with the 'reality' of sexuality. Sexology exacerbated tensions within Victorian feminism. By the 1890s the 'new woman' had emerged as a figure in both fiction and non-fiction to describe 'what many regarded as the worrying changes in the behaviour, the activities and the demeanour of women'. This economically independent, socially active, athletic, politically forthright 'modern girl' rejected marriage as sexual slavery in favour of sexual freedom. Although some saw the 'new woman' as synonymous with feminism, this figure was the source of considerable dispute within the woman movement.[54]

While condemnation of the 'double standard' and marriage as slavery represented a point of continuity between nineteenth-century feminism and the emergent 'new feminism' of the twentieth century, older campaigners such as Millicent Garrett Fawcett, Frances Power Cobbe and some younger suffragists, such as Edith Watson and Christabel Pankhurst, retained their faith in the right of women to refuse intercourse as the solution to female sexual oppression. But for a newer generation, such as Olive Schreiner, Mona Caird, Stella Browne, Madeline Pelletier, Rebecca West, Ellen Key, Margaret Sanger and Dora Marsden, the very idea of freedom included sexual freedom.[55]

These 'sexual moderns' demanded sexual pleasure for women and an end to the 'myth of female sexual passivity'. Many of the disputes over sexuality were fought out in the pages of new journals such as *Freewoman* in England and *The Woman Rebel* in America. In these forums feminists debated the question of the harmfulness of abstinence, the benefits of pleasure and issues such as auto-eroticism and inversion. Contributors frequently invoked the 'scientific truths' advanced by sexologists like Ellis. Libertarians, such as Edward Carpenter and H.G. Wells, also contributed to these journals.[56] The idea of the 'new woman' also became a source of intense cultural debate outside feminist circles. Henrik Ibsen's character Nora, in *A Doll's House* (1889), played out the dilemmas of a woman trapped in marriage and desiring the freedom to pursue her desires. In art, literature and theatre the independent new woman was praised or condemned, and historians such as Bram Dijkstra have argued that the theme of 'sex war' was pervasive in turn of the century European culture.[57]

The conflict over sex was part of a larger transformation within feminism. At the turn of the century the emergence of the term 'suffragette', particularly in Britain, heralded a new militancy in feminist politics. Feminist groups, most notably the Women's Social and Political Union (WSPU), lead by Emmeline and Christabel Pankhurst, and others such as Anne Kenney, moved the campaign for the vote into the streets, publicly demonstrating for suffrage, disrupting political meetings, chaining themselves to gates and holding huge processions through towns and cities. Some were arrested and imprisoned, and went on hunger strikes to publicize their cause. These tactics were widely admired on the Continent inspiring activists such as Madeline Pelletier, Hubertine Auclert and Clara Zetkin.[58] In America the National Women's Party took to the street, picketing the White House in 1917 and campaigning more vigorously for women's rights.[59]

The most radical suffrage activists were British. Although small in number, the energy and enthusiasm of the WSPU invigorated the movement, leading to a significant increase in membership of women's groups and an increasing willingness to publicize feminist demands. The umbrella organization, the National Union of Women's Suffrage Societies, quadrupled its membership just before the outbreak of war in 1914. But the increasing militancy of the WSPU polarized English feminists. While many young women were attracted to the dramatic tactics of the militants, others gravitated towards more moderate groups campaigning for the vote.

Suffrage had been seen by most Victorian feminists as a means to ensure women's freedom rather than an end in itself. As the suffrage campaign intensified, feminists did not lose sight of the broader emancipatory objectives of the movement and younger generations of feminists added sexual freedom to an older agenda of sexual protection, economic independence and women's education. In the early years of the twentieth century American bohemian and socialist feminists, such as Crystal Eastman, Emma Goldman, Henrietta Rodman, Beatrice Hinkle and Marjery Dell, flocked to Greenwich Village in New York in pursuit of sexual equality and social reform. They followed the lead of earlier advocates of 'free love', such as Victoria Woodhull, and were inspired by the work of Swedish sex reformer Ellen Key, promoting the ideal of 'free love'. In 1914 they established a new feminist club 'Heterodoxy', promoting free speech, sexual autonomy and sexual equality.[60]

By the late-nineteenth century women socialists were also becoming active around issues such as divorce, childcare and sexuality. Prominent socialists such as Stella Browne, Margaret Llewellyn Davies, Clementina Black and Ada Nield Chew, protested the costs of sexual hierarchy. Some, like Browne, tried to put issues such as birth control and abortion onto the socialist agenda. Although some socialists, notably Edward Carpenter, supported suffrage and sexual freedom, the questioning of women's role in the family brought socialist feminists into conflict with men in the labour movement. Although socialist feminists and middle-class suffragists shared many agendas, there were also tensions between them, made more intense by the labour movement's demand that solving class conflict came first.[61] What appears in the early-twentieth century is a growing fissure in international feminism, between Victorians committed to sexual abstinence and restraint as the means of escaping sex dominance and moderns who sought to claim sexual equality as the means to emancipation.

The First World War fuelled change. Widespread disillusionment with the 'old men' who could wilfully sacrifice Western youth exacerbated generational tensions. In the 1920s the popularity of urban pleasures, such as dancing halls, jazz clubs, amusement parks and dating, signified a loosening of constraints on relations between the sexes. Fashion, notably that of the flappers, challenged Victorian notions of femininity. In this context of postwar hedonism and greater sexual freedom, the ideas of sexologists began to spread. Their work was popularized in magazines and journals for a mass audience.

Although feminist activism in areas like wages, childcare, divorce, social policy and family endowment remained strong, in the area of sexuality the voices of women like Marie Stopes and Margaret Sanger came to dominate. Stopes, in particular, commanded a wide audience for her message of sexual pleasure. Like Ellis and other sexologists, Stopes believed that women had a right to sexual pleasure and her best-selling books – *Married Love* (1918), *Wise Parenthood* (1918) and *Enduring Passion* (1928) – advised on techniques for pleasure as well as providing guidance for rearing children. Stopes and Sanger advocated birth control to free women of anxieties that inhibited sexual pleasure and to enable them to determine when they wished to reproduce. They envisioned a world where women were no longer slaves to repeated pregnancies and denied a world of sensual pleasure and conjugal harmony. In the inter-war years birth control became a major feminist demand, something that indicates the gulf that had appeared between 'new feminists' and their Victorian counterparts.[62]

Feminist arguments for sexual pleasure and birth control were often intertwined with eugenic discourses on racial fitness. This unpalatable language was part and parcel of late-nineteenth- and early-twentieth-century sexology and social reform. It has led some historians, nota-bly Jeffrey Weeks, to highlight the conservative, class-bound and racist dimensions of some of these campaigns for sex reform.[63] Nonetheless, there is much support amongst historians for seeing new feminist atti-tudes to sexuality as a decided advance on the prudery of the Victorian era. The embrace of ideas of female sexuality heralded a 'demystification of women's bodies', freeing them from the tyrannies of the past.[64] D'Emilio and Freedman see this as the beginnings of an age of 'sexual liberalism'.[65]

Other feminist historians, however, have criticized the account of sexology as a story of sexual enlightenment. Two of the most vigorous critics have been Sheila Jeffreys and Margaret Jackson. Both see the feminist embrace of sexology in the inter-war years as a set-back for feminist politics. They highlight the conservative dimensions of sexol-ogy, not just in class terms but in feminist terms. For Jeffreys in particu-lar, sex reform was anti-feminist. These historians focus on the idea of sex complementarity embedded in the theories of prominent sexolo-gists such as Havelock Ellis. In Ellis' sexology women and men both had sexual natures, but man's was more virile and forceful, while woman's was submissive and sensual. Ideally sexual relations should be the com-bination of these different principles into a greater whole.

For Jeffreys and Jackson, these theories were an explicit reworking of the sexual double standard that had been the brunt of feminist cri-tique for over a century. Worse, sexology pathologized women's sexual-ity. The focus of this new science became women's sexual dysfunction and concepts such as frigidity made female rather than male sexuality the problem. This represented a defeat for the radical sexual critique of Victorian feminism. Where Victorian feminists were able to problema-tize male sexuality and envisage a world for women free of the bonds of heterosexual oppression, inter-war feminists and their message of sexual pleasure locked women into compulsory heterosexuality.

Finally, for these historians, sexologists undermined the female cul-ture of the Victorian era that sustained intimate relationships between women. The work of Ellis on 'sexual inversion' and Edward Carpen-ter on the 'intermediate sex' contributed to ideas that women of manly dress and appearance, or those who expressed love for other women, were in fact part of a distinct 'sexual species'. These friendships could now be seen in a new light – as forms of sexuality rather than relation-ships between friends. As we shall see in the next chapter, the emerging sexology was highly normative. Ideals of sexual health revolved around heterosexual companionate marriage; although individual sexologists were often advocates of tolerance for those who did not conform to these sexual norms, they erected an elaborate framework geared to the diagnosis of sexual deviancy. Women who lived in 'Boston marriages' and adopted mannish attire were increasingly seen as sexually devi-ant. Such ideas made close friendships socially unacceptable and more difficult to pursue. For Jeffreys and Jackson, sexology and feminist sex reform represented not only a defeat of a more radical Victorian femi-nist tradition, but also an attack on those spinsters who had struggled to live outside the culture of 'compulsory heterosexuality'.[66]

Jeffreys and Jackson raise fundamental issues about what consti-tutes a feminist politics of sexuality. Nonetheless, a number of histori-ans have pointed to flaws in their picture of feminist collaboration with sexology. Barbara Caine and Nancy Cott have argued that many inter-war feminists in Britain and America did not wholeheartedly embrace the message of sexology and generally thought issues such as birth con-trol and abortion marginal to the main feminist agenda of sex equality, wages, work and social reform.[67] Others have also contested the simplis-tic picture of sexology and feminism advanced by Jeffreys and Jackson. For example, Lesley Hall and Lucy Bland argue that many feminists were disturbed by the emphasis of sexology on female submission to the virile male and instead sought to turn the 'facts' of female sexual-ity towards more feminist ends, emphasizing the capacity of women for sexual independence. Feminist understandings of sexology represented a critical engagement with these theories, not unwitting acceptance and blindness to the masculine bias of sexology. Equally important, sexol-ogy itself was not monolithic, and 'few accepted conventional assump-tions about sexual difference'.[68]

Hall's analysis of Stella Browne is an excellent case in point. Browne, a prominent socialist feminist and abortion activist, initially accepted key dimensions of Ellis' work. In struggling to find a sexual vocabu-lary for women's sexuality she often fell back on traditional ideas of women as cold and men as hot. Her initial concern was to find a space for women to seek pleasure within heterosexual relationships. But her ideas changed. Gradually she became interested in bisexuality as a nat-ural condition for both sexes, and even came to see lesbianism as a form of legitimate relationship. Feminists may have taken key ideas and con-cepts from sexology, but often reworked them in feminist ways.[69]

The pathologization of female friendships is likewise more com-plex than Jeffreys or Jackson allow. While sexology did serve to make certain types of female friendship into forms of deviancy, providing a

lexicography of behaviours, fashions, and modes of address for diag-
nosing such 'conditions', Ellis and other sexologists viewed sexual
inverts with a great deal of sympathy (Ellis himself married a prominent lesbian). More important, sexology was not just an imposition of
conservative heterosexual ideas on homosexuals and lesbians. On the
contrary, many homosexuals and lesbians embraced the new sexology
because it gave them an explicit identity previously denied them.

Socialist and sex reformer Edward Carpenter, himself homosexual,
was very active in publicizing the idea of inversion and his own notion of
the intermediate sex as a means of legitimizing this desire. He and Ellis
received letters from grateful inverts who felt that at last they understood who they really were.[70] Similarly, Radclyffe Hall's sensational
novel, *The Well of Loneliness* (1928), was in part a plea for sympathy and
tolerance of female inversion. The central character, Stephen Gordon,
closely modelled on many of Havelock Ellis' case studies, struck a chord
with many readers. Despite the sense of tragedy that enveloped and
ennobled Gordon, some 'inverts' were grateful that their condition had
been revealed.[71]

Conclusion

The historical debates about the nature of sexology and its effects on
feminism highlight the contradictory ways new sexual discourses shaped
early-twentieth-century Western sexual politics. In naming sexual desires
and behaviours sexology subjected effeminate men and mannish women
to moral regulation, medical scrutiny and marginalization. But equally
many homosexuals and lesbians felt acutely the problem of silence. Silence
may have guaranteed a degree of freedom, but it also robbed them of an
identity they craved. Distinct identities allowed 'sexual deviants' to name
and acknowledge others of their kind and eventually to mobilize as a
political force. Sexology gave gays and lesbians another voice.

In the last analysis feminists had to work with the tools provided by
their culture. When it was possible to see women as outside of sexuality
they were able to turn this central tenet of Victorian culture into a radical critique of male sexuality and female oppression. These ideas created considerable space for women to explore a variety of relationships
with each other, free of the fear of social ostracism. It also condemned
those who sought sexual intimacy within these relationships to public
silence. The new sexology transformed understandings of female sexuality. Remaining wedded to an ideal of female continence ran the risk of
making feminism anachronistic. Feminists had to move with the times,
and work with the new sexual culture emerging in the early-twentieth
century. This was a complicated task, running the risk of making them
captive to ideas advanced by scientists who were not always in sympathy

with feminist aims. Scientific theories brought female relationships into a new light, making them far more vulnerable to medical and social regulation. But it also gave feminists the opportunity to mobilize around new causes relevant to women, such as abortion. It gave them the capacity to theorize sexuality in radically new ways, highlighting the sexual oppressions of heterosexuality in a more sustained way than before. There were gains and losses in these historical transformations.

Chapter 9

IMAGINING PERVERSION

Richard von Krafft-Ebing, in his influential study of perversion *Psychopathia Sexualis* (1886), pleaded 'few people ever fully appreciate the powerful influence that sexuality exercises over feeling, thought, and conduct'. 'The importance of the subject demands', he explained, 'that it should be examined scientifically.'[1] Many took up his challenge. By some estimates there were more than 10,000 monographs and articles relating to sexuality published in German alone between 1886 and 1933, 1,000 on homosexuality between 1898 and 1908.[2] In turn the late-nineteenth and early-twentieth centuries have been of intense interest for historians of sexuality. For Steven Marcus, this period represents the moment when Freud was able to wash away the ignorance of the Victorian repression. Commonly historians have seen the pioneers of sexology, such as Krafft-Ebing, Havelock Ellis, Magnus Hirschfeld and Sigmund Freud, as the progenitors of modern scientific understandings of sexuality.[3] More recently, historians such as John D'Emilio and Estelle Freedman, have seen this period ushering in the 'sexual liberalism' of the 1920s.[4]

Other historians, however, have questioned the idea of a decisive break between Victorian ignorance and a new age of 'scientific' understandings of sex. Frank Sulloway, for example, has argued that Freud was deeply influenced by the vast range of pseudo-scientific ideas that were popular in nineteenth-century Europe and America.[5] More importantly, Michel Foucault has argued that the fundamental tools of psychoanalytic practice – talking, transference, dream analysis and free association – have their roots in older technologies of confession rather than a new scientific approach to sex.[6]

Foucault's reappraisal of Freud's significance sits within a larger argument about the making of sexuality. For Foucault, the Victorian era was not an age of silence about sexuality but one of 'increasing incitement' to put sex into discourse. What emerged was 'a science of sexuality'. Where

previously matters of sex had been the subject of religious or moral regulation and criminal injunction, in the nineteenth century sex became a
subject of enquiry within a range of emerging disciplines, notably demography, pedagogy, medicine, psychiatry, psychology, biology and eugenics.
More significantly sex emerged as a distinct domain of scientific inquiry,
spawning its own discipline – sexology.

These disciplines were made possible by new institutions and practices. The growth and development of schools, asylums, bureaucracies,
factories, prisons, medical clinics and laboratories in the Victorian era
made available distinct populations for scientific inquiry. The nineteenth
century, suggests Foucault, far from being an age of sexual repression
put 'into operation an entire machinery for producing true discourses'
about sex. The scientists investigating sex deployed techniques such
as interviews, consultations, the case study, clinical diagnosis, statistics,
questionnaires and surveys – an 'obligatory and exhaustive' injunction
to confess – in their quest for knowledge. Sex became a transfer point for
knowledge and power. What these sciences produced was 'sexuality'.[7]

Foucault's argument that sexuality was a product of nineteenth-century scientific discourses has been influential. Following Foucault, historians such as Vernon Rosario, Arnold Davidson, Jennifer Terry and
David Halperin, have seen the late-nineteenth century as the period
when homosexuality emerged as a specific identity, marked not merely
by sexual orientation but also by particular lifestyles, codes of dress and
bodily gestures. The idea that some individuals were innately attracted
to others of the same sex only emerged in scientific literature in the second half of the nineteenth century. Concepts such as contrary sexual
feeling, uranism, inversion, the intermediate sex and eventually homosexuality were efforts to define a distinct species of sexuality.

As we have seen, this does not mean that same-sex acts escaped
serious scrutiny before the Victorian era. But the way in which these
sexual acts were understood and treated changed significantly in the
nineteenth century. Previously the term 'sodomite' had designated the
perpetrator of an offence against nature. It did not necessarily signify
someone whose object of sexual desire was of the same sex. The sodomite was a sinner or criminal deserving punishment. They were not seen
as the bearers of a deeper pathology. The new language of sexuality,
however, did not necessarily entail acceptance of homosexual identities
and practices. In the nineteenth and twentieth centuries homosexuals
were still subject to arrest and punishment although psychiatrists and
sexologists argued that perverts were not criminals but sexually 'abnormal', requiring treatment rather than incarceration. Sexology helped to
fix the homosexual as a distinct type of sexuality.[8]

The homosexual was only one part of a much wider scientific inquiry
into different sexual types. Sexology produced a vast catalogue of 'per-

versions' and figures such as the sado-masochist, the fetishist, the transvestite and the sexual hermaphrodite crossed the borders, back and
forth, between scientific literature and popular culture. Doctors and
sexologists diagnosed numerous forms of sexual abnormality producing vast compendiums of sexual deviancy. The social visibility of perversions, however, depended on the willingness of people to confess
their desires. Sexology was not just a way of producing and regulating sexuality, but was also a form of collaboration in the production of
new identities. But the idea of sexual 'deviancy' crucially depended on
a concept of 'normality'. As Jonathan Ned Katz has argued, the explosion of scientific interest in sexual perversion was part of a larger 'invention of heterosexuality'.[9] Late-nineteenth- and early-twentieth-century
sexual sciences constructed ideals of normality and perversion and
bequeathed a discourse of sexuality, forms of treatment, practices of
self-examination and sexual typologies that have shaped sexual modernity in profound ways.

The Making of Sexology

There were many factors shaping the emergence of a distinct discourse
of sexuality in the late-nineteenth century. The evolution of medical practices and ideas, the creation of institutional populations that
could be subjected to scientific investigation and wider cultural anxieties about social progress, civilization, degeneracy, racial fitness and
women's emancipation all contributed to the production of new ways
of seeing sex. As Foucault has argued, discourses are intimately tied to
social practices. In other words, ideas and concepts did not appear in
a vacuum, they were forged in specific contexts. Forms of social action
produced new ideas and ideas in turn shaped social action.[10] The intersections between ideas and practices shaped Victorian and Edwardian
sexology.

Changes in the organization of medical markets were important
in fostering greater medical interest in sex problems. In the early-
nineteenth century doctors were in fierce competition with midwives,
charlatans and quacks for lucrative markets in surgery and general
practice – including not only childbirth and birth control but also a
wide range of nervous and behavioural disorders. The masturbation
anxieties peddled by charlatans and doctors alike created a large market of those suffering nervous debility, exhaustion, 'spermatorrhoea'
and hysteria. Doctors sought a larger slice of these markets, promoting proper medical training and credentials as the basis for the right to
practise medicine and lobbying governments to make quackery illegal.
They also worked hard to assert the superiority of medical treatment
over alternatives such as midwifery and homoeopathy. These were long

struggles, but by the late-nineteenth century the prestige, status and authority of the medical profession was widely accepted.[11]

Although there was still a flourishing market of treatment alternatives, doctors by the late-nineteenth century commanded the most profitable aristocratic, middle-class and respectable working-class sectors. Moreover, doctors and patients alike were interested in specific diseases of 'civilization', most importantly nerve complaints, which were widely thought to be the products of the increasing pace of urban living and the pressures of mental labour. While some feared that modern life excited constitutional defects, doctors advocated a variety of therapies, such as rest cures, drugs, electrical stimulation, hypnosis, suggestion and surgery, for these modern diseases. Nervous illness became the signature of the leisured middle classes and doctors clamoured for a slice of this lucrative market.[12]

At the same time the emergence of institutional forms of treatment for criminals, juvenile delinquents and lunatics created new populations for observation and classification. Large institutions created laboratories for scientists to investigate social pathologies, opportunities that had not existed before. For example, in the eighteenth century there were few large asylums and most lunatics were treated at home, in charitable and Poor Law institutions or in small private 'mad-houses'. Reformers, however, believed institutional care was preferable and advocated the establishment of large institutions where patients could be restored to health through moral reform. Although these reformers were often evangelicals, doctors began to take control of the burgeoning nineteenth-century asylum system. There was a massive expansion in the lunatic asylum population, considerable overcrowding and widespread dismay at the accumulation of chronic patients.

In this context alienists (the nineteenth-century term for psychiatrist) sought to differentiate the incurable, best treated in asylums, from the curable who were more effectively treated in the early stages of their illness.[13] Thus psychiatrists began to establish lucrative private practices in the hope of stemming the rising tide of lunacy. While asylums became repositories for psychotics and chronic patients, in private practices and clinics psychiatrists treated patients afflicted with anxiety and depression, often arising from sexual misery.[14]

The changes in the treatment of criminals were equally dramatic. Until the late-eighteenth century criminal justice was founded on a principle of exemplary punishment. There were few police forces (except in France and Ireland) and those in England and America were mainly private. Magistrates often bestowed mercy on defendants as an encouragement to reform, and the few sentenced were subject to horrendous physical punishments, such as whipping and hanging, or transported to the ends of the world as a warning to others of the consequences of criminality. The focus of criminal justice was deterrence. Towards the end of the eighteenth century, however, reformers, such as Cesare Beccaria and Jeremy Bentham, advocated reforms such as police forces, sentences that fitted the severity of each crime and imprisonment as a means of reforming the criminal.

In the nineteenth century these reforms made headway. Police forces were established, bringing more criminals before the courts than ever before. Penitentiaries were established for the incarceration of offenders. This brought a substantial population of criminals together, allowing observation and study. The science of criminology was born out of investigations into the common characteristics of prisoners undertaken by scientists such as Cesare Lombroso in Italy and Alexandre Lacassagne in France.[15]

The court system also brought doctors into the criminal justice system. In the nineteenth century determining responsibility for criminal acts became an important issue in criminal trials. In 1843 British courts established the McNaghten Rules in an effort to identify criminals suffering insanity and therefore not responsible for their acts. Similar legal criteria were widely adopted in European and American jurisdictions. In trials doctors were called upon to help make decisions about criminal culpability.[16] Thus by the late-nineteenth century, doctors, particularly psychiatrists, had extensive experience in the observation and treatment of criminals and those suffering nervous illness. Forensic medicine became a legitimate area of medical specialization. What doctors observed was disturbing. In the courts they examined rapists, paedophiles and compulsive sex criminals. They also investigated the cases of brutal murderers and serial killers, such as 'Bluebeard', Mary Ann Cotton and Dr Thomas Cream, who seemed motivated by strange sexual compulsions and homicidal impulses.[17]

Another key factor shaping the emergence of sexology was the increasing visibility of sexual subcultures. Since antiquity large urban centres had proved to be havens for sexual underworlds. For example, Enlightenment London had a rich underground culture of brothels, gin palaces, music halls and 'molly' clubs.[18] The unprecedented growth of large cities in nineteenth-century Europe and America provided the conditions for the proliferation of sexual subcultures catering for the varied tastes of a large clientele from different classes. Municipal regulations sanctioning red-light districts assisted the growth of these services. Moreover, the Victorian passion for social surveys, evident in the work of Henry Mayhew and Charles Booth in England and Jacob Riis in America, brought these urban underworlds to light as never before. Clubs catering for homosexuals were an integral part of these red-light districts. For example, George Chauncey's path-breaking study of late-nineteenth- and early-twentieth-century gay New York, uncovers a rich culture of clubs, bars and dance halls where cross-dressers, inverts and effeminates mixed freely and openly. In the urban vernacular they were well known as 'fairies' and 'queers' – objects of ridicule but familiar to other inhabitants of the city.[19]

Perversion and decadence also became more explicit in literature. The voices of novelists, writers and classicists provided a repertoire of sexually ambiguous characters helping to shape representations of sexual perversion for a wider audience. In European universities the cult of Hellenism promoted appreciation of classical Greece and the cult of pederasty. At Oxford and Cambridge Uranian societies promoted male love and comradeship on the Greek model. 'Decadent' writers, such as Joris Karl Huysmans and Oscar Wilde, explored an ethic of heightened aesthetic appreciation, presenting effeminate male characters committed to a life of culture, provocatively challenging prevailing masculine ideals of muscular Christianity.

Some Victorian sexologists drew inspiration from this literature. For example, Richard von Krafft-Ebing, Professor of Psychiatry and Neurology at the University of Vienna, was heavily influenced by eighteenth-century writers such as Jean-Jacques Rousseau and the Marquis de Sade as well as more contemporary authors, such as Marcel Proust, Colette, Fedor Dostoevsky, George Sand, Louis Couperus and Emile Zola. Many of these writers were avid consumers of the new sexology. Krafft-Ebing found Leopold Sacher-Masoch's novella *Venus in Furs* (1870) particularly important, inspiring his concept of masochism.[20]

Finally, it is important to acknowledge the role of patients themselves in shaping sexology. Foucault's argument about confession becoming a key technique through which people came to understand sexual subjectivity is pertinent. Although there were sharp differences between the psychological theories of psychoanalysis and the biological orientation of most sexologists they shared a common interest in producing detailed individual case histories. Freud described psychoanalysis as the 'talking cure' and other psychiatrists relied heavily on detailed case notes taken during interviews with patients.

Asking patients about their problems, putting these afflictions in context, classifying the condition and offering a cure were common methods of diagnosis and treatment. Such methods were dependent on the willingness of patients to undergo medical treatment. While Freud famously analysed the ways patients resisted interrogation and offered techniques such as transference for overcoming this reticence, the success of his practice and that of other sexologists relied on people seeking help, paying fees and answering questions. In the nineteenth century an increasing number of wealthy middle-class patients, troubled by sexual anxieties and fixations, sought help in understanding their condition and entered into therapeutic compacts with the growing number of doctors who specialized in sexual and nervous diseases.[21]

Thus in literature and in courts, prisons, hospitals, clinics and private practice, doctors were confronted with the spectacle of criminals and patients exhibiting perverse desires and suffering sexual fixations. This was the seedbed for sexology. Prominent psychiatrists, such as Krafft-Ebing, were scrupulous accumulators of case details. Over time Krafft-Ebing produced a portfolio of 'strange cases' – men and women who could only be sexually excited by particular types of clothes or hair, being whipped or humiliated, or humiliating others, or by seeing animals slaughtered. They documented those who sought out sexual satisfaction with children or animals. Some patients only seemed attracted to people of the same sex and others found themselves aroused if they dressed as the opposite sex. Krafft-Ebing took a forensic interest in these cases, inventing a range of new terms, such as fetishism, sadism and masochism and popularizing others such as sexual hermaphroditism, to describe the various classes of 'perversion' he found. His concept of 'the psychopath', someone unaffected by moral scruples and constitutionally or psychologically driven to perversion, gained wide currency in the early-twentieth century. His path-breaking *Psychopathia Sexualis* was an immediate sensation, going through numerous greatly expanded editions and being translated into many languages. Krafft-Ebing received thousands of letters from those offering insights into their 'condition' and seeking his help.[22]

Krafft-Ebing was not alone. There was a small but active group of doctors and social reformers in Britain, Europe and America interested in sex perversions. On the Continent sexologists, such as Iwan Bloch, Wilhelm Stekel, Alfred Moll and Magnus Hirschfeld, conducted detailed research into sexual aberrations. Hirschfeld moved beyond patient case studies, utilizing such techniques as questionnaires to expand the scope of his investigations, and his concept of congenital sexual intermediacy to explain same-sex desire proved to be influential amongst sexologists such as Edward Carpenter, Havelock Ellis, Moll and Stekel.

Another key figure in the evolution of sexology, although one at odds with the biological school of thought, was Sigmund Freud, who developed his theories of general mental function through the careful analysis of individual cases of hysteria, obsession, sexual fixation and neurosis. In Britain Havelock Ellis was a great popularizer of European research. He was largely responsible for introducing the ideas of Italian criminologist Lombroso to an English-speaking audience and also publicized the work of Freud and European sexologists such as Hirschfeld. Ellis accumulated his own detailed case studies of sexual pathology, developing elaborate classification systems using such concepts as auto-eroticism, eonism and sexual inversion. Psychiatrists and psychologists in America, such as Eugene Fuller, William Healy, G. Frank Lydston, Abraham Meyerson and Elmer Southard, were active investigators of sexual dysfunction, adolescent sexual delinquency and psychopathology.[23]

The science of sexual pathology, however, was controversial. Krafft-Ebing wrote some sections of his treatise in Latin, partly to shore up claims to scientific authority and partly to disguise the sensational aspects of his cases. This did not stop some reviewers from declaring his work 'repulsive' and 'nauseous'. Freud faced continued criticism throughout his career from sections of the medical profession, which condemned his obsession with childhood sexuality and the sexual origin of neurosis. Havelock Ellis struggled to find a publisher for his work on sexual inversion, and after its publication *The Lancet* declared it 'odious'. A few years later George Bedborough, Secretary of a free-thought group, the Legitimation League, was prosecuted for selling a copy of Ellis' 'lewd, wicked, bawdy' *Sexual Inversion* (1897).

Slowly sexology made headway. Ellis' seven-volume *Studies in the Psychology of Sex* (1897–1928) found an appreciative audience and he was widely praised for his pioneering efforts. Sex researchers, such as Bloch, Moll and Stekel, commanded respect and journals and monographs in sexology proliferated. In 1911 Hirschfeld established an Institute for Sexual Science in Germany and three years later The British Society for the Study of Sex Psychology was founded. In 1921 the first of a series of World Congresses on Sex Reform met, and in 1928 the World League for Sexual Reform was established. Similarly, the International Psychoanalytical Association thrived between the wars and found strong adherents, especially in America in the 1930s.[24]

Sexology may have grown out of forensic medicine and psychiatry, but its popularity and significance was an aspect of a much larger 'crisis of modernity'. Historians of *fin-de-siècle* Europe, Britain and America have highlighted the dramatic contrast between Western economic, political and cultural mastery of the world and the pervasive sense that Western civilization was imperilled by corrosive social, political and biological forces. As Eugene Weber has argued, this was an era of 'material progress and spiritual dejection'. Advocates of crisis pointed to evidence of decline: persistent urban poverty, rising rates of crime, the accumulation of lunatics and prisoners in institutions, growing international tensions over imperial expansion, race antagonisms, the decline in the birth rate, the epidemic of nervous diseases, the rise of the labour movement and the agitation of woman movement activists. The emergence of 'mass society', with its 'disturbing' crowds of socialist, anarchist and feminist agitators challenging bourgeois culture and politics suggested to many that confident Victorian assumptions about social progress were increasingly untenable.[25]

The responses to this sense of crisis were enormously varied. While some doctors, politicians and reformers, especially in Progressive America, retained a great faith in the capacity of social action, urban renewal, philanthropy, muscular Christianity and strong family ties to effect social progress, other commentators believed that the ills of modernity arose from biological and hereditary imperfections. Influential doomsayers publicized the plight of civilization. For example, Albert Morel's *Treatise on Decadence* (1857) and Max Nordau's *Degeneration* (1892) highlighted the threat of moral degeneracy. Nordau argued that the modern age was characterized by enervation, exhaustion, hysteria, egotism and inertia, and laid the blame for this at the door of 'degenerate' artists and writers. Perverse sexuality was seen as a symptom of a larger moral decay. Otto Weininger's misogynist and anti-Semitic tract *Sex and Character* (1903) declared that all organisms were fundamentally bisexual and sexual union was akin to murder. The only solution was to transcend sexuality.[26]

Those who spread the message of moral, social and sexual decline supported reforms to root out the deficiencies that threatened Western civilization. For example, criminologists, such as Lombroso, considered the criminal an evolutionary atavism, a survivor of an earlier stage of human evolution poorly adapted to modern life. Similarly alienists, such as Henry Maudsley, argued forcefully that many criminals and lunatics suffered from hereditary deficiencies, requiring permanent incarceration rather than reform or treatment. An influential movement in late-nineteenth and early-twentieth century Britain, Europe and America to arrest the perceived decline in racial fitness was eugenics, an outgrowth of the social Darwinist faith in the 'survival of the fittest'. Drawing on biological research into the mechanisms of heredity, such as August Weismann's theory of germ plasm, eugenicists challenged the neo-Lamarckian faith in the transmission of acquired characteristics. The future of the race could not be shaped by adaptation but instead depended on the survival of those best adapted. Eugenicists, such as Francis Galton, Karl Pearson, Benjamin Kidd and Charles Davenport, preached the message that societies needed to promote the fertility of the racially fit and prevent, through sterilization, segregation or extermination, the reproduction of the unfit. Sexologists, such as Krafft-Ebing and Havelock Ellis, were vitally interested in eugenics.[27]

The interest of sexology in sexuality, neurosis and sexual pathology put doctors at the centre of debates about social decline. Sexologists were surrounded by evidence of sexual 'pathology' and they laid claim to authority in the diagnosis and treatment of these 'endemic social problems'. The streets and haunts of the demi-monde, and respectable people of their acquaintance, revealed flourishing underground worlds of sexual 'deviancy'. Patients brought 'bizarre' stories of sexual fixation, obsession and misery and their adventures in these subcultures. Much of the character of new sexual sciences grew out of what historian Kurt Danziger has called 'reflections on practice'. Sexologists attempted to observe and explain and their work was shaped not only by the wider climate of opinion but also the concrete experience of daily clinical work.[28] How, then, did sexologists respond to the evidence before them and the broader cultural climate that framed their inquiries? How did they explain sexual pathologies and what were the consequences of their conclusions?

Sexology and Perversion

Sexology was not a unified movement. This is especially evident in theorizations of same-sex relations. A number of early theorists of homosexuality, such as Karl Heinrich Ulrichs and Carl Westphal writing in the 1860s and John Addington Symonds in the 1890s, relied on classical analogies to conceptualize 'contrary sexual feeling'. Ulrichs, in particular, drew on Platonic ideas, naming this sexual inclination Urning. John Addington Symonds, Ellis' original collaborator on *Sexual Inversion*, and himself an 'invert', celebrated the manly love of comrades in pre-historic Hellas. Symonds argued that Greek history demonstrated that 'inversion' was really a product of cultural environment, in contrast to the determinist orientation of most sexology.[29]

The majority of doctors attracted to the study of sexual pathology in the late-nineteenth and early-twentieth centuries, however, had been trained in a discipline increasingly concerned with the physical and somatic basis of mental phenomena. The growing fascination with medical explanations for social problems, such as crime and lunacy, fostered the idea that sexual pathology was an affliction to be treated. Patients visited doctors to be cured and successful practices were built upon efficacious therapy. Thus at the heart of sexology was the question of disease and its cure.[30]

Sexology research was vitally interested in the problem of heredity and environment. The key question for many sexologists was the extent to which perversions were innate or acquired. Were perverts the victims of heredity or was their 'illness' environmental or psychological maladjustment or personal and familial trauma? While biological theories supported hereditarian conclusions, medical injunctions to cure fostered a faith in the capacity of sexologists to treat sexual afflictions. Sexology was polarized. On one side, there were strong adherents of congenital perversion, such as Krafft-Ebing and Havelock Ellis and on the other, psychoanalysts and other advocates of psychotherapy such as Carl Jung, Stekel, Alfred Adler, Wilhelm Reich and William Healy who emphasized the psychological dimensions of sexual development.[31]

Some historians, however, have challenged the idea of distinct schools of sexology. For example, Renate Hauser has suggested that

Krafft-Ebing's understanding of sexual pathology underwent subtle changes after the publication of *Psychopathia Sexualis*. Krafft-Ebing's reading of literature and anthropology challenged simple assessments of congenital perversion. Moreover, his growing interest in hypnosis as a form of therapy suggested that some perversions were psychological rather than physiological. These ideas about psychological pathologies shaped new interpretations of some of his fundamental concepts. By the 1890s he began to argue that fetishism was not so much pathological as an element in all sexual attraction. Krafft-Ebing had shifted towards a psychological theory of pathology by the time of his death.[32]

In contrast other historians have sought to highlight the biological basis to psychoanalytic ideas. Frank Sulloway's controversial reassessment of Freud argues that psychoanalysis was rooted in a genetic psychobiology. Rather than representing a break with social Darwinist and other hereditarian theories of sexual development, Sulloway examines how Freud, through his reading of sexologists such as Krafft-Ebing, adapted evolutionary concepts to his theory of psychosexuality.[33] This is an interesting interpretation of Freud, highlighting hidden dimensions of psychoanalytic theory, but it does not entirely demolish the distinction between psychological, physiological and hereditarian theories of sexual pathology. While Freud may have drawn heavily from his early medical training he took biological concepts and radically transformed them into a dynamic psychological framework that shaped many subsequent approaches to the problem of psychopathology.[34] What Hauser and Sulloway indicate, however, is that the discourse of sexology was a diverse field of intellectual inquiry and debate. It encompassed both theories of psychological and congenital causation, and many sexologists adopted elements of both.

There were also national differences in the relative strength of psychological and congenital theories. The heartland of theories of psychopathology was Germany, although the work of scholars such as Krafft-Ebing, Bloch and Hirschfeld was influential throughout the West. Continental Europe, more generally, was marked by clear disputes over the relative merits of psychoanalysis and theories of hereditary deficiency, with pockets of strength varying from country to country. Moreover, the early-twentieth century witnessed a fracturing of the psychological school, with major theorists such as Jung, Stekel, Wilhelm Reich and Alfred Adler, breaking away from Freud to develop their own theories of psychosexual development. British sexology, however, was dominated by the socially liberal but essentially hereditarian ideas of Havelock Ellis. Although Freud had his followers, they were on the margins of British debates on psychopathology. Psychoanalysis more commonly made its way into British psychology and psychiatry in bowdlerized forms.[35]

In the United States, although eugenics and social Darwinist thought was strong, psychoanalysis and psychological psychiatry were more influential than in Britain.[36] While there were plenty of alarmists, such as G. Frank Lydston, who claimed there were over 200,000 degenerates in the USA, leading psychiatrists, notably Adolf Meyer and Karl Menninger, brought a rich European tradition of dynamic psychology to America and married it to the pragmatism of William James.[37] Many American psychiatrists embraced dynamic psychological approaches because they offered therapeutic hope, and situated individual psychosexual development in precise social and familial environments that were amenable to therapeutic intervention. This optimism was welcomed by 'progressive era' Americans who maintained a strong faith in social progress. As a consequence psychological categories such as 'neuropath' and 'psychopath' were common in American forensic psychiatry by the 1920s. In contrast, British criminology stuck to eugenic notions of moral imbecility until the 1940s.[38] In some American States, such as New York and Massachusetts, psychological assessment of criminals and delinquents was commonplace by 1920.[39]

Many sexologists sought to move beyond a narrow focus on psychopathology to explore the general implications of their work. Havelock Ellis, for example, was an advocate of eugenics and hereditarian theories of crime and insanity. He was also interested in the biological theories of Patrick Geddes and J. Arthur Thompson, whose *The Evolution of Sex* (1889), was published in a series edited by Ellis. Geddes and Thompson's influential but contentious work proposed that in the world of animals there were two fundamental types, 'the "anabolic" or constructive and conservative energies of the female, and the "katabolic" or disruptive and destructive energies of the male'. Thus there were fundamental biological differences between men and women. Ellis transformed these ideas into a theory of sexual complementarity. Women's sexuality was largely responsive to the active male.[40] Similarly Krafft-Ebing's investigation of a wide range of fetishes and perversions increasingly lead him to theorize such problems as sexual dependence, concluding that the mechanisms of psychological attachment in perverts were remarkably similar to those amongst heterosexuals.[41]

Despite the seemingly rigid biological basis to Ellis' sexology his conclusions lead in surprising directions. On the one hand, Ellis justified a fundamental sexual difference between the sexes but, on the other, argued that women had sexual passions and 'erotic rights', advocating a more sexually egalitarian relationship between the sexes. At the same time, although he argued that autoeroticism might foster 'morbid self consciousness', in moderation it was harmless as it was common amongst 'all the higher animals'. Nature and culture could operate in diverse ways to justify a range of conclusions. Ellis became a voice for 'sexual liberalism' in Britain and America, challenging Victorian ideas that women were asexual. Instead he supported campaigns for effective birth control, partly on eugenic grounds, but also to enable women to experience sexual pleasure without the fear of pregnancy.[42]

A number of sexologists, despite their belief in congenital perversion, were at the forefront of movements agitating for more tolerant attitudes towards homosexuals. Prominent sexologists such as Ulrichs, Symonds, Edward Carpenter and Hirschfeld were themselves homosexual and anxious to eliminate popular prejudices and repeal laws criminalizing same-sex love. Hirschfeld was a central figure in the European homosexual rights movement establishing the Scientific-Humanitarian Committee in 1897, with a view to removing social discrimination and repealing the German sodomy statute.[43]

Personal sexual preferences, however, were not the only factors underpinning the sexual liberalism of many sexologists. Havelock Ellis, although married to a lesbian, was not homosexual. Moreover, it is a mistake to categorize hereditarians as inevitably conservative and environmentalists as sexual liberals. Biological theories could and did shape liberal conclusions. For example, Ellis argued that inversion was a congenital abnormality involving 'a modification of the secondary sexual characteristics'. If inversion was congenital then the sufferers could not be blamed for their condition and moreover, he concluded, many influential and intelligent people were inverts and thus it could not be characterized as degenerate. Ellis became a critic of 'degeneration' theories and a firm proponent of social tolerance for 'deviants'.[44] For sexologists like Carpenter, Hirschfeld and Ellis, biological determinism was a reason for social tolerance. If homosexuality was sanctioned by nature then it should not be punished.

The language of affliction, disease and treatment, however, indicates the paternalism inherent in much sexology. Although many sexologists were socially radical in their conclusions, advocating decriminalization of sodomy and tolerance for inverts and other 'perverts' there was a patronizing tone to their claims, born of a sense of therapeutic mastery. Equally important, wider social discourses, particularly those on gender, shaped biological sexology in fundamental ways. The category of sexual inversion exemplifies how sexology could simultaneously illuminate and deceive.

A number of historians have argued that when Ulrichs, Westphal, Krafft-Ebing and Ellis and others, sought to understand the 'pathology' of people attracted to the same sex they interpreted this phenomenon through the lens of gender rather than sex. What they found noteworthy in their patients, and the writings they consulted, was the effeminate man and the mannish woman, each attracted to members of the same sex. In this framework, pathology was evident in the transgression of gender roles. This concern with gender transgression was central to early attempts to theorize same-sex behaviour. In 1864 Karl Heinrich Ulrichs described those with a 'female psyche confined in a male body' as Urnings. Five years later Karl Westphal introduced the diagnosis 'contrary sexual feeling'.[45]

More common, however, was the idea of inversion, characterized by effeminacy in men and mannishness in women. For Ellis, Carpenter, Symonds and others, this was a phenomenon worthy of sympathy, but inversion transposed the issue of same-sex desire into one of gendered physical attributes, behaviours and forms of dress. Thus sexologists collapsed into one category a range of sexual orientations that we would now distinguish – such as transvestism, transsexuality and homosexuality. Moreover, David Halperin argues that sexologists like Krafft-Ebing drew distinctions between perversion and perversity. Men who penetrated other men were seen as merely perpetrators of perverse acts, prone to vice, but largely normal. Inverts, however, because they flouted gender norms by parading effeminacy, cross-dressing and preferring to be penetrated, suffered from perversion.[46]

Although some homosexuals embraced the concept of inversion as recognizing their identity, others grappled with its limitations. Edward Carpenter came to favour concepts such as homogenic, or later the intermediate sex, trying to see same-sex desire as not so much inversion of norms but as a complex mixture of gendered attributes. Sexologists also had to confront the anomalies produced by their cases. When Krafft-Ebing's patients reported that they lived with another of the same-sex 'as man and wife' it became necessary to theorize both participants in this relationship and the concept of inversion largely described only one. By the early-twentieth century sexologists were beginning to define 'inversion' more in terms of same-sex desire and increasingly the concept of 'homosexuality' was adopted as a more accurate concept encompassing the variety of same-sex orientations that sexologists confronted in their clinical practice.[47]

Psychoanalysis also played a part in shifting the focus from contrary gender behaviour to the diversity of same-sex desires and practices. Although some sexologists between the wars continued to believe that inversion was congenital, Freud's theory of homosexuality as 'arrested psychosexual development', while equally problematical (representing it as an inadequate form of sexuality), shifted the terms of the debate away from gender transgression towards sexual object choice as the defining characteristic of homosexuality. By the 1920s inversion began to disappear from mainstream sexology literature. The shifting terminology for same-sex desire highlights more profound shifts in the way homosexuality was theorized. Equally important, it indicates how sexology was a dynamic interaction between the discipline and its patients. Experience, individual cases and the cut and thrust of research and critical debate brought to the fore new ways of seeing sexual 'perversion'.[48]

The role of sexology in constructing new homosexual identities has been the subject of extensive historiographical debate. For Lillian Faderman, like Margaret Jackson and Sheila Jeffreys, sexology represented a sustained attack on the female romantic friendship. In the nineteenth century, as we have seen, intense emotional relationships between middle-class women were commonplace and widely accepted. In the second half of the nineteenth century, however, sexologists became increasingly concerned at the sexual liberties of young men and women who lived in European and American cities. The culture of pleasure pursued by the urban working classes and the sexual underworlds that flourished in large cities were increasingly seen as 'degenerate' by doctors and social reformers. Faderman argues that ideas of female same-sex pathology were first developed in relation to working-class women. But by the end of the nineteenth century the 'morbidification' of same-sex relationships between women began to shape perceptions of the relationships between middle-class women. Increasingly romantic friendships were seen as forms of 'deviant' lesbian sexuality. Sexology drove same-sex love between women underground, creating a lesbian identity.[49]

Other historians, however, have questioned Faderman's characterization of sexology as an ideological imposition on women's relationships. While Jennifer Terry, Leila Rupp and George Chauncey agree that medical ideas constructed same-sex relationships as pathological, they also explore the complex interconnections between feminism, urban subcultures and the production of knowledge. For Rupp and Chauncey, in particular, there were active urban gay and lesbian subcultures in many cities. Sexologists were acute observers of these cultures. While they diagnosed many of the common behaviours in these underworlds as pathological, gay and lesbian identities existed long before the work of sexologists constructed them as disease categories. What they chart is the back and forth between the social world of subcultures, in which sexual 'deviancy' was normal, and the evolution of medical concepts from inversion to homosexuality.[50]

Jennifer Terry points to the significant number of homosexuals who gravitated towards sexology. She explores the ambivalent relationship between sexology and sexual practice in the evolution of concepts of inversion and homosexuality. While many 'inverts' eagerly embraced the idea that same-sex love was congenital as a way of explaining and justifying their desires, the acceptance of sexual pathology made homosexuals and lesbians more vulnerable to social prejudice, arrest, psychiatric incarceration and clinical treatment.

Terry explores with great insight the ways in which medical ideas helped construct social and sexual identities, giving greater cohesion to existing subcultures and a point of orientation for the members of these subcultures.[51] While Faderman accepts that some homosexuals found the 'congenital' theory attractive, she argues that nineteenth-century homosexual subcultures were predominantly male. Lesbian subcultures were largely the product of the pathologization of romantic friendships.[52] Chauncey and Rupp disagree. They map a rich history of both gay and lesbian subcultures, arguing that the intersections between homosexual and lesbian ways of life and medical ideas shaped the emergence of distinct gay and lesbian identities.[53]

Although sexology was grounded in clinical research and critical reflection, historians have also attempted to highlight the specific social and political dimensions of the new sexual sciences. Sexologists were active in sex politics. Practitioners used their status and knowledge to support particular ideologies and reforms, such as social Darwinism or eugenics. Sheila Jeffreys and Margaret Jackson, for instance, have seen sexology as part of an anti-feminist backlash, forcing women into compulsory heterosexuality.[54] Some sexologists were extreme. Otto Weininger believed that feminism was a manifestation of 'decadence'. Nevertheless, his belief in a fundamental bisexuality presented masculinity and femininity as ideal types. Masculinity was the highest type (and thus the masculine lesbian the highest form of woman). Weininger often seems to confuse sex and gender, sometimes denying sexual difference and then making it the centrepiece of his argument. Women, for Weininger, were creatures purely of sex and reproduction, mothers or whores, incapable of transcending sexuality. Only men had the capacity to overcome nature, through force of will, and thus only men could be fully human.[55]

Lesley Hall's studies of British sexology indicate that even liberals like Havelock Ellis were ambivalent about feminism. Although Ellis was sympathetic to the idea of social and erotic rights for women, he feared challenges to sexual difference. Thus he promoted the idea of different male and female principles that needed to be brought together in sexual union to make a sum greater than the parts. Ellis's belief in masculinity as the active principle and femininity as the passive perpetuated Victorian ideas of sexual difference. Radical egalitarian feminists of the 1920s, such as Marie Stopes and Stella Browne, criticized his limited understanding of sexuality, arguing instead that women had an active sexuality. They took some of Ellis' key ideas on sex complementarity and turned them in new directions to argue for greater sexual autonomy for women.[56]

Another focus of historical debate has been the relationship between sexology and race. The links between sexology and eugenics were close, and American eugenicists, through concepts of hereditary perversion, mental deficiency and psychopathology, helped justify prejudice against supposedly inferior African Americans and Hispanics.[57] Sexology was largely the study of white middle-class sexual dysfunction or the sexual pathologies of sex criminals. Nonetheless, there has been important work on how sexual scientists wrestled with race even though they rarely explicitly analysed the relationship between sex and race. Sander Gilman has provided a fascinating analysis of Freud's efforts to position himself in relation to the strengthening anti-Semitism of the late-nineteenth and early-twentieth centuries. In *fin-de-siècle* Europe, particularly within medical literature, there was a growing association between Jews and sex crimes, incest, prostitution, effeminacy and perversion. Jews were seen as decadent, sensual types, prone to sexual psychopathology. Latent criminality, argues Gilman, 'became a common mental construction of the Jews'.

A few sexologists such as Havelock Ellis denied the association between Jews and sexual perversion, but it was a prevalent belief in European medical sexology and criminology. Freud, a Jew, read this literature carefully and developed some of his theories of the relationship between civilization and sexual morality as a rebuttal. He emphasized the harmful effects of civilization on sexual life, repressing the debate on Jewish psychopathology, and shifting the terms of analysis to ones of human civilization, morality and the psychic costs of sexual repression. Gilman also argues that Freud displaced the distinction between the Aryan and the Jewish male body onto a reading of the female body as undeveloped. Instead of the castrated Jew, Freud theorized female penis envy. Gilman's provocative reading of key psychoanalytic concepts opens up fruitful insights into the relationship between sexual science and broader social and political contexts.[58]

Psychological theories of sexuality, perversion and criminality did not necessarily mean more enlightened or sympathetic attitudes to 'deviants'. Many sexologists may have been sexual liberals but this was most evident in their attitude to people of their own class. Tolerance was less evident in relation to criminals. Sexologists and forensic criminologists, however, facilitated a shift in the focus of policing from 'deviant acts' to personality types. If sexual perversions, and other products of psychopathology such as crime, were the result of particular psychological predispositions, then psychiatry offered a technique to identify and treat social threats at an early stage, before they became serious. It also offered a means for identifying those criminals and perverts whose condition required extended incarceration and treatment to 'safeguard' society. Psychiatric theories of sexual psychopathology justified extended periods of incarceration for 'perverts'.[59]

Estelle Freedman's examination of the 'social panic' about 'perverts' in mid-twentieth-century America remains one of the best accounts of this process. For Freedman, psychiatric theory fanned anxieties about the menace of over-sexed and uninhibited sexual psychopaths – violent sex criminals, voyeurs, child molesters, rapists and homosexuals – who threatened innocent boys, women and children. From the late 1930s a number of States passed 'sex psychopath' laws, mandating extended incarceration for men convicted of these crimes. This panic, fanned by numerous stories about sexual psychopaths in newspapers and popular magazines, helped educate the public in what constituted 'normal' and 'abnormal', by associating perversion with violence and degeneracy.[60]

Freedman suggests that much of the concern about sex psychopaths was a code for deeper anxieties about homosexuality. Other historians, such as Stephen Robertson, have questioned this emphasis. Although homosexuality was central, Robertson sees the idea of the sex psychopath as a response to a wider range of anxieties. For Robertson, these laws also grew out of changing discourses on childhood and adolescent sexuality. Psychiatric discourses helped sexualize the young and made them a source of heightened anxiety. Doctors feared that overtures from perverts and attacks by sex criminals would arrest proper psychosexual development in children, making them the psychopaths of the future.[61] In particular contexts psychiatric theories of sexuality – rather than breaking down the distinctions between heterosexuality and homosexuality, fostering tolerance, as Havelock Ellis hoped – hardened divisions and assisted in the greater policing and persecution of sex criminals and homosexual subcultures.

Psychoanalysis and Sexology

The place of Freud in the history of sexuality and sexual science has been the source of considerable dispute. Unlike the work of other early sexual theorists, such as Ellis, Hirschfeld, Weininger, Marie Stopes or Krafft-Ebing, which remain the focus of largely historical interest, psychoanalysis continues to command contemporary authority and relevance. There are, of course, many recent critics of Freud who argue that psychoanalysis is unscientific, and a fiction that has polluted literary and critical theory.[62] As we have also seen, historians such as Frank Sulloway have argued that psychoanalysis is tainted by nineteenth-century biological determinism. It was not a genuine break with Victorian medicine. Similarly, poststructuralist and feminist theorists have interrogated the masculinist structures of Freudianism.[63]

Despite these critiques psychoanalysis remains a thriving branch of psychological medicine. Equally significant, it has exerted enormous influence over the humanities and social sciences, providing important theoretical concepts for poststructuralist, feminist and Marxist scholars in cultural studies, anthropology, history, literary criticism and postcolonial studies.[64]

Unlike many sexologists Freud did not confine his focus to the diagnosis and treatment of neurosis and perversions, rather he used his analysis of these problems to advance a general theory of mental functioning. In this context he bequeathed a powerful and influential language of the unconscious, ego, superego, repression, sublimation, displacement, fixation and Oedipus complex, which has shaped modern theories of sexuality and psychosexual development. Freud's theory that all sexual life, not just perversions and nervous illness, was the product of unconscious conflicts between instincts and society, has been a profound influence on theories of sexuality.

The centrality of Freud to contemporary theories of sexuality, however, puts historians in a difficult position. How should we position him historically? As we have seen, some of the earliest historians of sexuality, such as Steven Marcus, took Freud as the crucial turning point in the history of sexuality. Before Freud was unhealthy Victorian repression and sexual hypocrisy. After him we understood how sexuality was made and that excessive repression was harmful. Thus psychoanalysis divided the history of sexuality into two major epochs.[65] Most subsequent historians have been more circumspect. They have tried to place psychoanalysis in its specific historical context. For example, Jeffrey Weeks analyses the ambiguities in Freud's theorization of the relationship between masculinity and femininity, and suggests that there is an incipient biologism in psychoanalysis. For Weeks, this is a serious flaw in the theory, symptomatic of the close relationship between Freud and sexology. Nonetheless, he still sees Freud's dynamic theory of sexual development as a positive and fundamental break with the biological essentialism of Havelock Ellis.[66]

Similarly, Elaine Showalter charts Freud's 'blindness' in his understanding of female hysteria and the increasing rigidity in his theories. Showalter concludes that through Freud 'women's voices, stories, memories, dreams and fantasies enter the medical record', creating dialogues between hysterical women and male psychiatrists. Psychoanalysis 'offered a considerable advance over biological determinism and moralism in Darwinian psychiatry'. Nonetheless, she concludes that Freud interpreted hysteria through a masculine lens, seeing the struggles of women for sexual expression within masculinist culture as largely pathological.[67] Likewise Angus McLaren tries to put Freud firmly in the context of the late-nineteenth and early-twentieth centuries, arguing that the 'real interest of psychoanalysis resided in the fact that it drew on contemporary sexological investigations and many... common sexual preoccupations'. Nevertheless, like Weeks and Showalter, for McLaren, Freud was a break with sexology, 'making normal sexuality the object of scientific investigation'.[68]

Foucault marks a departure from these efforts to see Freud as a flawed but important break with Victorian biological sexology. For Foucault, as we have seen, the Victorian era was not characterized by repression but by an explosion in discourses about sex. Thus Freud did not signify a new direction in sexology but another instance of the effort to produce truths about sex. Moreover, psychoanalytic techniques such as talking, dream analysis and transference, were part of a longer history of technologies for enabling sex to be regulated, prescribed and confined. Foucault traces the slow secularization of confessional techniques, and how they become harnessed to a range of power/knowledge practices – state regulation of populations, medical scrutiny of perversion and the self-government of sexuality. In other words, Freud was part of a longer lineage of discourses and confessional practices for governing the production and regulation of sex.[69]

Conclusion

Despite sharp differences between biological sexology and psychoanalysis, their shared interest in sexual perversion was integral to the emergence of concepts of sexuality. Discourses of sexuality made sexual orientation a key element of modern social identity. Many historians have charted the relationships between the diverse subcultures, which harboured 'perverts', and the scientists who sought to make sense of the inhabitants of these worlds. Foucault's critique of psychoanalysis and its place in the history of sexuality has helped open up important questions about the historicity of sexuality and the construction of sexual identities. In these terms the invention of perversions in the late-nineteenth and early-twentieth centuries was one step in a larger process of producing sexuality. But Foucault underestimates Freud's significance. While Freud can be usefully situated as part of nineteenth and early-twentieth century sexology, his emphasis on the psychosexual basis of perversion and his interest in charting a general theory of mental development was a significant departure. It facilitated a growing interest in 'normal' sexuality, relegating the study of perversions to disciplines such as forensic criminology. Increasingly the sex sciences sought to investigate the sexual behaviours of ordinary men and women.

Chapter 10

NORMALIZING SEXUALITY

Historian Vern L. Bullough has argued that what differentiated early-twentieth-century sex research in America from that in Britain and Europe was its focus on heterosexual problems.[1] Obviously there are exceptions to Bullough's generalization. American psychiatrists and criminologists, such as Frank Lydston, Adolf Meyer and William Healy, were at the forefront of investigations into degeneracy, delinquency and sexual psychopathology. There were also major American studies of 'perversions', notably the 1935 New York Sex Variants survey.[2] Moreover, continuing media fascination with sexual notoriety, such as the transsexual Christine Jorgensen's famous announcement in 1952 that she had undergone sex change surgery, kept 'deviancy' in the news.[3]

On the other side of Bullough's equation, British sexologists such as Marie Stopes, Havelock Ellis and Norman Haire, made significant contributions to research through their best-selling sexual advice books and articles, aimed largely at heterosexual couples. Moreover, European psychotherapists, such as Sigmund Freud, Carl Jung, Alfred Adler and Wilhelm Reich, may have begun by researching neurosis, anxiety and depression but moved from there to investigations of the structure of mental processes, collective psychological phenomena and the problems of general sexual misery.[4]

Despite these exceptions Bullough has highlighted something important in twentieth-century sex research. Although some of the pioneering sexologists focused on the diagnosis, classification and treatment of perversions, others sought to examine 'normal sexuality'. Some of this research was driven by the desire to chart the anatomy and physiology of human sexual response. But there were other avenues of inquiry directed towards the links between psychopathology, sexuality and normal mental functioning. For example, social hygienists, criminologists, police and psychiatrists became interested in the role of sexuality in the propensity to juvenile delinquency, prostitution and criminality. They promoted extensive inquiries into the social and sexual mores of the 'dangerous classes'. This research threw up interesting questions and problems. To what extent were the sexual habits of these 'deviant' classes actually 'abnormal'?

Another important force driving twentieth-century sex research was the emergence of medical practices devoted to the treatment of sexual unhappiness. Sexologists found that large numbers of their patients suffered few overt perversions, but expressed considerable dissatisfaction with their sexual lives. Was sexual dysfunction the lot of a few or the many? What were the causes of this misery? The answer to such questions involved knowledge of the sexual habits of ordinary citizens. Mapping the boundaries between normal and abnormal became a central preoccupation of sexology. In America, in particular, significant resources were devoted to treating sexual problems and charting the contours of everyday sexual experience. Large surveys set out to establish the range and variety of sexual practices in the general population. Such surveys have proved to be invaluable sources for historians of sexuality seeking to chart changing sexual habits, practices and beliefs over the twentieth century. Equally important, the results of these surveys were often surprising, challenging prevailing discourses on sexuality in fundamental ways.

Sex Research

In the nineteenth century the treatment of sexual problems proved to be a source of considerable profit. The thriving market in charlatan remedies for spermatorrhoea and hysteria is testament to the demand. By the second half of the century the growing middle-class market in nervous and sexual illnesses sustained the emergence of psychotherapy and sexology. Many of the patients who sought out sexologists and therapists often suffered from extreme sexual misery, anxiety, frustration and guilt. Although many of the patients of doctors and sexologists, such as Krafft-Ebing, Magnus Hirschfeld, Iwan Bloch, Havelock Ellis and Freud, came from respectable backgrounds they were deeply troubled by strange and unconventional impulses. As we have seen, sexology was founded on the inquiry into perversity. But by the inter-war years a number of sexologists and therapists began to focus more on the sexual problems of heterosexuals, married couples in particular. Havelock Ellis had long advocated the need for harmonious marital relations based on mutual sexual satisfaction. In the 1920s and 1930s, however, writers such as Theodore van de Velde and Marie Stopes in Europe and Britain, and Emanuel Haldeman-Julius, Margaret Sanger and Max Exner in America, spread the message of marital sexual pleasure.[5]

Their books, articles and talks reached a wide audience, and the extensive correspondence generated by their work indicates that many women and men were keen for advice on how to improve their sex lives. This work was controversial. Sex reformers such as Stopes and Sanger, for example, supported birth control, insisting that sex should be for pleasure as much as procreation, effective prevention easing anxiety about the possible consequences of intercourse, a view condemned by religious and moral authorities. Both Stopes and Sanger were prosecuted for sending 'offensive' material through the mails and faced civil actions attempting to drive them out of business. Despite continued opposition and criticism the movement for greater marital sexual pleasure and fertility control gathered momentum. Effective birth control allowed couples to explore the pleasures of the marital bed and many of the popular sex advice books, such as Stopes' *Enduring Passion* (1928), focused on techniques for achieving sexual fulfilment.[6]

A number of historians have pointed to the early-twentieth century as a time of significant change in sexual practices and public discourses on sex. For some, such as Kevin White, this was a revolt against Victorianism, when sexual liberals broke the 'conspiracy of silence' surrounding sex.[7] White, however, is too focused on ideas and the heroic struggles of significant sexual radicals, failing to see the broader social and cultural contexts underpinning the emergence of sexual liberalism. Other historians, such as Steven Seidman, Kathy Peiss, Jeffrey Weeks, John D'Emilio and Estelle Freedman, have argued that liberal sexual attitudes spread rapidly through the growth in mass media. The availability and popularity of radio, newspapers, cheap marriage manuals and advice magazines all served to advertise the importance of sexual pleasure, birth control, marital happiness and the importance of sexual attraction in love.[8]

But the effective spread of these ideas required an appreciative audience. Historians have stressed such factors as the declining birth rate, the higher age of marriage, the significant number of women delaying marriage and entering college and the growth of large cities where urban workers could earn a wage and live away from home, in creating a youthful culture oriented towards leisure and unchaperoned mixing of the sexes. The rigid Victorian separation of the spheres began to erode. Men and women were increasingly freed from parental and local community scrutiny and could enjoy an abundance of city pleasures – dances, amusement halls, bars, theatres and night clubs – which brought young men and women together. In this context love, as Seidman has argued, was sexualized and sex eroticized.[9]

The shift to sexual modernity, characterized by love, sexual pleasure and individual satisfaction, however, was protracted and contested. While reformers like Sanger and Stopes were active public figures commanding a wide audience, there were many religious, temperance and social purity groups that stoutly opposed what they saw as a dangerous decline in moral standards. From the 1910s to the 1930s antiprostitution

and other social purity campaigns remained active. There were also continuing efforts to stamp out vice, regulate dance halls more closely and,
in the 1930s, attempts to censor magazines, books and films, to safeguard moral standards. Similarly, eugenicists warned of the dangers of
indiscriminate sex amongst the 'unfit' and inhabitants of inner city tenements. In some jurisdictions laws were enacted to prevent intercourse
with 'deficients' and efforts to sterilize and segregate the unfit resulted
in closer scrutiny of the lives of the 'lower orders'.[10]

These contests over sexual morality raise important questions for
historians. Was there a general transition towards sexual modernity in
the twentieth century? While most historians point to increasing liberalization in ideas and practices how far these extended is open to question. While modern attitudes were prevalent in cities such as London,
Berlin, Paris and New York, these ideas and practices do not seem to
have spread at the same rate elsewhere. Is it possible to make a general
claim for a transition in sexual attitudes with so many potential regional
differences? Or were the frameworks for sexual modernity, as the important work of historians such as Beth Bailey suggests, shaped as much by
local circumstances as the ideas of sexologists and sex reformers?[11]

Equally, historians also dispute the chronology of sexual modernity.
While some point to the new woman of the 1890s as a crucial starting
point, others have pinpointed different times.[12] Christine Stansell, for
example, focuses on the Greenwich Village radicals of the first two decades of the twentieth century.[13] D'Emilio and Freedman see sexual liberalism taking off in the 1920s.[14] Others, as we shall see, consider the
Kinsey reports of the 1950s as the crucial turning point in American sexual history.[15] A few see the sexual revolution of the 1960s as the significant
break with the Victorian past.[16]

Such differences reflect the difficulties inherent in defining sexual
modernity. This is very evident when it comes to the ideas of leading sexual moderns. While some recent studies have stressed the political and
social radicalism of sexology, other historians have tended to focus on
the limitations and conservatism of sexual liberals.[17] There were clear
links for instance between eugenics and sexology.[18] Havelock Ellis and
Marie Stopes may have stressed the necessity for women to experience
sexual pleasure, but they did so within very limited contexts. As we have
seen, Ellis believed in tolerance but, nonetheless, saw perverts as unfortunates who required sympathy and treatment. Although he supported
ideals of companionate marriage this bond was 'natural' because of the
inherent differences between active masculine attributes and passive
feminine sexual propensities. Similarly, Stopes stressed the importance
of sexual pleasure within marriage rather than pleasure itself. More fundamentally for these sex researchers (as for many subsequent historians),
sex and heterosexuality were synonymous with intercourse. For histori-

ans like Carroll Smith-Rosenberg, the sexual bohemians and feminists of early-twentieth-century America may have developed a radical new language of heterosexual relations, staking a claim for sexual equality, but they failed to overturn the entrenched masculine relations of power that subjugated women.[19]

Nonetheless, sexologists, sex reformers and scientists interested in the nature of sex and sexuality were instrumental in developing new discourses about sex of enormous significance in the twentieth century. Patients, however, were also crucial to sex research. The growing emphasis on sexual companionship in public media highlighted widespread sexual dissatisfaction. Disgruntled seekers of sexual satisfaction went to doctors complaining about their sexual lives. Many women reported that they failed to achieve orgasm and found intercourse distasteful. Men were frustrated about impotence, unresponsive wives and infrequency of sex within marriage. Sexologists sought to explore the roots of sexual dysfunction and many of the answers they found dramatically changed ideas about sex and sexuality.

These investigations were also shaped by ideas about gender. The focus on heterosexuality and its discontents was framed by research in many disciplines in which sex and gender became crucial explanatory frameworks. For example, in the inter-war years endocrinologists in Europe and America first isolated sex hormones, fostering new insights into sex, the menstrual cycle, puberty and menopause. Such research suggested that the sex drive was 'natural' and biological. More importantly, doctors were able to specify the 'safe period' in the menstrual cycle, assisting couples in regulating reproduction. The discovery of hormones, however, both confirmed and challenged pervasive ideas that there were fundamental differences between the sexes. While endocrinology indicated that there were male and female hormones, some researchers concluded that they were mixed in a fluid system of internal secretions, suggesting that sex differences were matters of degree rather than absolute difference. Hormonal research also fostered the idea that sexual dysfunction, and possibly perversion, was a consequence of imbalances or deficiencies in these secretions.[20]

Similarly, other disciplines such as psychological testing, most importantly the work of Lewis Terman and Catharine Miles, blurred the boundaries between the sexes. Their masculinity/femininity index suggested that personalities were mixed in their characteristics, with subjects exhibiting a preponderance of either masculine or feminine traits but never absolutely one or the other. This suggested that 'sex variants' had 'inverted' personality types, but these types were matters of degree rather than complete reversal. Moreover, some psychologists saw personality types as the product of complex interactions between constitutional tendencies and specific social circumstances.[21]

Gynaecological research also reshaped ideas about sexuality. In the 1920s Robert Latou Dickinson investigated the physiology of intercourse, observing the vaginas of women who masturbated. Similarly, Ernst Boas plotted pulse rates during intercourse. Research into the physiology of sex indicated that masturbation did not impair, but actually enhanced the capacity for orgasm during intercourse. Such conclusions raised interesting questions about female sexual response – was penetration essential for female satisfaction? Were women sexually unresponsive or did the fault lie with men failing to take female arousal seriously? More radically, some physiologists asked whether female sexual response was more determined by culture than biology?

Other disciplines also stressed the cultural dimensions of sex. Social science research raised questions about the relationship between modern life, morality and sexuality. For example, anthropologists, such as Bronislaw Malinowski and Margaret Mead, studied Pacific Island communities and claimed to find havens of sexual freedom. Here young men and women supposedly grew to sexual maturity free of the excessive repression of Christian sexual morality. This anthropological research suggested that morality, gender and what constituted acceptable sexual practices were bound more by custom than nature.[22]

Sex research led in many directions. It promoted new ways of seeing perversions and homosexuality. Equally important, it blurred the boundaries between normal and abnormal, masculinity and femininity. Sexologists faced the difficult task of promoting sexual adjustment in the context of increasingly fractured and contested discourses of sexuality. While psychiatrists pursued diverse therapies for sexual pathologies (psychoanalysis, hypnosis, counselling, personality testing, and hormone adjustments) other sexologists focused on education and information for the sexually miserable. Their aim was to overcome ignorance and misinformation by fostering an understanding of bodies, sexual organs and processes for enhancing sexual excitement and satisfaction.

In America, in particular, the influential mental hygiene movement also spread the message of normal sexual adjustment. Mental hygienists, heavily influenced by psychiatric, sociological and criminological ideas, advocated the principles of healthy minds and bodies. They stressed the importance of sex education and instruction to encourage young men and women to pursue healthy outlets for sexual drives. Education was a bulwark against sexual psychopathology.[23] While many mental hygienists, psychiatrists, sexologists and sex reformers accepted and promoted the idea of sexual difference between men and women, they also urged men to be more caring in their sexual overtures and women to be more demanding. Margaret Sanger proposed that women had a right to sexual expression and it 'was none of Society's business what a woman shall do with her body'.[24] To claim this right women and men had to be freed from guilt, superstition and ignorance.

There was much advice in books and popular magazines on what to do to and how to do it well. For advice-givers like Stopes, nature could not take its course; people had to be instructed in sexual techniques. This advice was framed as much by prejudice, ideology and tradition as it was by science. It was full of overblown rhetoric about jangled nerves, heightened sensation and the mingling of bodily juices. Although Stopes condemned prostitution and was a savage critic of the idea of man's marital rights, she maintained that men and women were fundamentally different in the form of their desire. Women's desire waxed and waned in a regular cycle, men's was more constant, and thus sexual life was a matter of bringing two different principles together without crushing one or the other. The advice of Stopes, and others, was often contradictory, at times radical, at others accepting of the double standard. For instance, Stopes suggested that male ejaculation was secondary to 'soothing the nerves', but she also advocated the idea that coitus was the inevitable point of sensual play.[25]

Despite all the advice it was evident that sexual misery persisted. This demanded explanation. Almost all sexologists, including Freud, accepted that genital intercourse was the signifier of normal sexual development. Although much of the research of doctors like Dickinson, Ellis and Freud indicated that the clitoris was the primary site of female sexual pleasure, this ran counter to the idea that coitus was the most significant sexual act. Freud argued that women had to 'give up' the clitoris and advance to the stage where the vagina and the reproductive function was the basis for pleasure. Medical scientists promoted the importance of vaginal orgasm, despite the fact that there was no anatomical or physiological research that could confirm the existence of this event.[26] Some historians, such as Thomas Laqueur, have suggested that Freud differed from the biological determinism of most of his contemporaries, theorizing that vaginal pleasure was learned, a 'narrative of culture in anatomical disguise'. But whether it was inherent or learned, sexologists commonly believed in vaginal orgasm and the primacy of sexual intercourse in 'normal' sexual development.[27]

The importance of vaginal orgasm shaped another key concern in mainstream sex research. In the inter-war years sexologists and advice givers, such as Wilhelm Stekel, Havelock Ellis, Weith Knudsen, Charlotte Haldane and Theodore van de Velde, developed the concept of the 'frigid woman' to explain the resistance of women to marriage and their lack of interest in intercourse. Estimates of the extent of frigidity in married women varied from as low as 10 percent to as high as 60 percent. One of the keys to sex therapy and advice became the need to overcome 'sexphobia' in women. In the context of high rates of postwar marriage and declining birth rates, the refusal of women to submit to the demands of 'nature' seemed decidedly pathological. As we have seen in an earlier chapter, radical feminist historians, such as Sheila Jeffreys, Lillian Faderman and Margaret Jackson, have pointed to discourses on frigidity and vaginal orgasm as further evidence for their argument that sexology was conservative and heterosexist. For them, sexology pathologized spinsters and reluctant women, depoliticizing forms of resistance to the 'heterosexual coital imperative'.[28]

This powerful critique uncovers some of the key ideological assumptions underpinning inter-war sexology. But Jeffreys, Faderman and Jackson overplay their hand. They lump all expressions of female sexual dissatisfaction with heterosexuality into forms of resistance, despite the evidence that many women were troubled by their sexual life and sought advice from experts to improve it.[29] Moreover, not all sexologists laid the blame on women. By the late 1930s sexologists, such as Norman Haire, influenced by their reading of anthropological literature, saw men's ignorance of women's sexual needs as the cause of frigidity. Western men, Haire argued, needed to adopt the practices of 'savages' and make the sexual satisfaction of women their primary sexual aim. He drew on an array of ethnographies to document the wide variety of sexual techniques employed by men from 'primitive cultures' to ensure that women achieved orgasm.[30] This may have left the distinction between the sexes intact, but Haire and others, like Dickinson, focused more on men's than women's failings.

Surveying Sex

In the inter-war years, forensic criminologists, sexologists and social investigators became important producers of knowledge about sexual practices through new survey techniques. Although doctors, psychotherapists, criminologists and sexologists continued to emphasize the importance of individual case studies a few ventured more widely in an attempt to investigate the prevalence of specific sexual behaviours and practices. As we have seen in the previous chapter, the roots of social investigation go back into the nineteenth century. Police, philanthropists, journalists, urban investigators and city missionaries sought to uncover life in the 'social cellar'. Henry Mayhew and Robert Hartley in the 1840s and 1850s, and later in the century, Jacob Riis, Charles Booth, W.H. Stead, Charles Loring Brace, Sophonisba Breckinridge and many others produced a rich archive of information on 'Darkest London and New York'. They created images of urban underworlds characterized by poverty, overcrowding, and high rates of crime, prostitution, perversion, child labour, white slavery, illegitimacy and delinquency.

Urban criminal subcultures, however, were a source of social and scientific debate. What produced these undesirable places and people? For some, as we have seen, the origin of crime and sexual perversions was degeneracy. The denizens of these underworlds were inherently depraved. By the late-nineteenth and early-twentieth centuries such conclusions were given sharper focus by the growing popularity of the eugenic theories of Francis Galton, Karl Pearson, Robert Dugdale and Lewis Terman. The belief that social inefficiencies and psychopathology was the consequence of the spread of hereditary deficiencies led to calls for permanent segregation, sterilization and even extermination of the racially unfit.[31]

Others, however, drew different conclusions, believing that impoverished social environments bred crime and vice. Social imperialists in Britain and Progressives in America supported renewed efforts at social amelioration and reform. These beliefs were stronger in America where social reformers and philanthropists vigorously promoted 'social diagnosis' and new forms of treatment for delinquent families. This required, according to influential America social worker Mary Ellen Richmond, 'the gathering of social evidence', so that reformers would have a precise understanding of the social, familial and psychological influences that created delinquency.[32]

In the early-twentieth century a small number of reformers and psychiatrists sought to better individualize the treatment of delinquents by developing 'life histories'. In 1912, the Superintendent of Bedford Hills Reformatory for Women in New York, Katharine Bement Davis, established a Laboratory of Social Hygiene, funded by the Rockefeller Foundation, to investigate the causes of female delinquency. A few years later the Rockefeller Foundation, through its Bureau of Social Hygiene, established a Classification Clinic at Sing Sing Prison, under the control of psychiatrist, Bernard Glueck. Similarly, in Chicago, and later Boston, psychiatrist William Healy, influenced by the ideas of Austrian criminologist Hans Gross, undertook extensive investigations of the character and circumstances of children brought before the juvenile courts.[33]

At these and other institutions psychiatrists headed teams of doctors, psychologists and social workers, who examined the social environment of the delinquent, their physical health (especially venereal diseases), mental capacities and psychological character. Davis developed extensive questionnaires (with from four to eight pages of questions) for inmates and their parents, focusing in minute detail on prenatal, natal, early childhood and adolescent events, as well as details of narcotic, alcohol and sex habits. Similar techniques were also utilized at the classification clinics at Sing Sing and many other prisons and reformatories in the inter-war years. The questions on sex focused on such issues as when did the inmate get their first instruction in sex and from whom, when did intercourse start, with whom, was it with consent, when did the inmate enter prostitution, if married why did they marry, were there any sex deviations. Through the combination of life histories, mental tests and psychiatric interview the mentally deficient could be separated from those whose delinquency was caused by an impoverished social environment. In charting the specific familial and social circumstances of the 'curable' inmates investigators hoped to facilitate correct diagnosis and treatment.

The inmates were remarkably frank about their sexual history, creating an extraordinary archive of information. Psychiatrists and reformers learned that many young men and women began having sex as early as 8 years of age, although more commonly between 14 and 17 years, most had masturbated, and many were initiated into sex by older neighbourhood children. A number of female delinquents admitted that their first experience of intercourse was 'without consent', although many said they subsequently went out with the person responsible. There was a substantial incidence of older male relatives being the first 'sexual experience'. A high proportion suffered repeated bouts of venereal disease (one Bedford Hills girl believed that intercourse was the only cure for gonorrhoea). The majority of girls admitted to prostitution, although many of these drew a distinction between those they charged and boys who they would do it with for love. A few admitted to homosexual encounters. Although many of these delinquents lived in tenements, a sizeable proportion held jobs and lived at home.[34]

The unabashed evidence of active sexual lives amongst juvenile delinquents confirmed a suspicion that lack of adequate moral authority in the home was a primary cause of delinquency. Sex activity became a signifier of moral waywardness. The increasing scrutiny of delinquency, particularly female delinquency, has produced a rich historiography on the efforts of urban working-class girls to forge independent lives, the anxieties of parents about this independence and the struggles of reformers, police and scientists to protect and morally reform wayward girls. American historians, such as Ruth Alexander, Mary Odem and Kathy Peiss, have charted the complex battles over the emerging urban sexual culture that working-class girls forged in the early-twentieth century. While these historians uncover the rich culture of urban pleasure and sexual experimentation embraced by young urban working women they also highlight the generational conflicts within families over the sexual independence of daughters and the increasing measures of coercive surveillance and control that emerged to govern female sexuality.[35]

The interest of both reformers and historians in female delinquency reflects the centrality of sexuality in defining 'deviancy' in women. While Victorian and Edwardian reformers and doctors saw sexual expression as natural for men, female sexuality disturbed ideals of appropriate female behaviour. For historians this represents an opportunity to explore the ways in which reformers, sexologists, criminologists and psychiatrists problematized female sexuality. Medical and criminological discourses on female sexuality in the early decades of the twentieth century were shaped by two pervading tropes – the 'frigid' middle-class woman and the promiscuous working-class girl. Both required correction. As Elizabeth Lunbeck has argued, no matter how much psychiatrists sought to normalize female sexuality, their efforts to do so 'located it in the hypersexual one moment, in the hysteric the next'.[36]

But the foundations for these distinctions began to erode in the interwar years. The rise of the flapper and the jazz age signalled a new sexual freedom for middle-class women. Increasingly the idea that pleasure and sexual freedom were signifiers of deviancy collapsed. Ruth Alexander has argued that the 'narrative of female adolescence written by mental hygienists…stressed young women's needs for sexual and social autonomy'.[37] Sex researchers came to see sexual companionship and expression as a normal part of women's social and sexual adjustment.

Other efforts to chart the incidence and nature of deviancy also threw up surprising insights. Jennifer Terry's insightful analysis of the 1935 New York Sex Variants study highlights the ways notions of normality and abnormality were complicated by survey research. Psychiatrist George Henry's path-breaking survey of homosexuals and lesbians revealed that homosexuality was more widespread than had previously been accepted. Equally important, it was not the preserve of a deviant fringe. Men and women of the professional classes actively engaged in homosexual and lesbian sex. While Henry assumed that hereditary and psychological factors influenced sex variation, and believed that such 'substitute' relationships had to be relinquished for more healthy heterosexuality, the survey evidence complicated such assumptions. Henry uncovered a wide variety of homosexual types, many with 'intermediate characteristics', and men and women who expressed greater sexual satisfaction in encounters with the same sex than they did in heterosexual relationships. More controversially, he concluded that 'homosexuals offered a model of greater emotional and sexual satisfaction compared to heterosexuals'.

Terry highlights a number of important dimensions of this research. Homosexuals and lesbians embraced the opportunity to influence the survey, hoping that it would offer the opportunity to justify their sexual choice and lead to greater social tolerance. Similarly, investigations of sex variation helped construct homosexual and lesbian identities, defining the social, sexual and cultural characteristics of a range of types. But, as Terry shows, psychiatrists such as Henry also used the evidence about homosexual and lesbian sexual satisfaction to highlight problems in the

sex lives of heterosexual Americans.[38] The more researchers focused
on deviants the more the question of what actually constituted sexual
pathology came to the fore. How unusual were female sexual delinquents? To answer this required a clear understanding of what was sexually normal.

While there was continuing interest in sexual deviancy, the focus of
twentieth-century sex research became the sex lives of ordinary people. What were the sexual habits of the population? This was the question taken up by a number of researchers in the early-twentieth century.
Dr Clelia Mosher, a feminist sex hygienist, undertook one of the first
surveys. From the 1890s to the 1920s Mosher asked her patients to fill
in questionnaires about their marriages to assist in the provision of
informed advice. Although she discovered sexual ignorance amongst
respectable women, more surprisingly many of these women considered sexual fulfilment an integral part of marriage.

Mosher's survey evidence has been the source of dispute amongst
historians. Carl Degler has used the Mosher survey to critique the idea
of Victorian repression. Degler highlights the importance of sex in
marriage and the frequency with which married women in the Mosher
sample engaged in marital sex. For him, sexual modernity could be
found in the Victorian era when many of Mosher's patients came to
sexual maturity.[39] Steven Seidman has questioned Degler's revisionist
interpretation. He points to the limitations of Mosher's survey; fewer
than 50 women filled out the survey. More importantly, he notes that
of the women surveyed those born earlier were more likely to consider
sex less important in marriage. In other words, Seidman argues for a
decided shift from Victorianism to modernity in the sexual attitudes of
the women surveyed by Mosher.[40]

The different interpretations of the Mosher survey point to the problems historians face using survey evidence. While sex surveys are a rich
source of evidence about sex, poor sampling techniques, vague definitions
and ambiguities in the findings mar many of the studies. Moreover, as the
debate between Degler and Seidman shows, the same evidence can lead
to very different conclusions. Nonetheless, the proliferation of sex surveys in the twentieth century represent an important means for historians
to move beyond medical discourses and advice literature to explore the
sexual practices of ordinary people. Early sex research, however, is also
a means of exploring how sexologists, psychiatrists, hygienists, sociologists and reformers constructed commonplace knowledge about sex. Surveys provided detailed information on sex habits and practices that made
concepts such as frigidity, sex variation and satisfaction key elements in
the public discussion of sex. Moreover, information on the incidence of
such things as masturbation, oral sex and orgasm helped shape public
and scientific perceptions of normality and abnormality.

The findings of many of the early surveys ran against the grain of moral reform discourses that condemned sex outside marriage and urged sexual restraint within marriage. Sex research became an integral part of sexual modernity. For example, pioneering gynaecologist Robert Latou Dickinson asked all his patients to answer a series of questions about their sexual and family history. He also drew and photographed their sexual organs. By 1923 he had collected 5000 cases, later published as *A Thousand Marriages* (1931) and *The Single Woman* (1934). Dickinson's study was skewed towards women with gynaecological problems, but in this sample he found that the average frequency of marital intercourse was two to three times a week. He also found a high incidence of masturbation, although this was more common in married women, over ten percent of his patients had venereal diseases and a small number had had lesbian experiences. Such controversial findings were couched in careful scientific language to avoid offending moral reformers, but the evidence that many people were ignoring the message of sexual restraint was clear.[41]

In the 1920s Katharine Bement Davis and the Bureau of Social Hygiene became convinced of the need to undertake a large-scale study of human sexuality. A year later the National Research Council established a Committee for Research in the Problems of Sex. These organizations funded some of the early sex survey work in America. Gilbert Hamilton's survey of 200 married men and women, published in 1929, used a combination of questionnaire and interview. He found a wide range of sexual activity, including masturbation, premarital sex and homoeroticism, amongst white, college-educated men and women and he also reported the existence of multiple orgasms in women.

Davis herself undertook a major survey, published as *Factors in the Sex Life of Twenty-Two Hundred Women* (1929), based on extensive questionnaires, covering such issues as contraception, frequency of intercourse, masturbation and lesbianism, and completed mainly by alumni of leading women's colleges. This was hardly a broad sample, but it did address the social group of most interest to new sex researchers. Her findings were controversial. Nearly two-thirds of unmarried and two-fifths of married women surveyed admitted to masturbation. Very few women had intercourse before marriage, but after marriage most women had intercourse once or twice a week, ten percent of married women had had an abortion, and half admitted to 'intense emotional relationships with women'.[42]

In the 1930s further surveys were undertaken. Dorothy Bromley and F.H. Britten, two journalists, interviewed over 200 college students at campuses across the country and a further 1000 students completed a questionnaire. Although this survey was again restricted to a narrow sample its finding that young men and women were engaged in much more sexual activity than had previously been expected received wide publicity. Others such as Lewis Terman and Catharine Miles used larger surveys to speculate on the relationship between psychological factors and sexual behaviour. Although they added further weight to the mounting evidence for extensive premarital sexual activity amongst college-educated Americans, they sought to move on beyond mere description to explore sexual dispositions amongst different psychological types based on their masculinity/femininity scale.[43]

By the 1940s interest in the sexuality of the broader population was also evident in Britain, well after survey research had been established in America. The social disruptions of war in Britain, however, encouraged interest in the habits of the population. Eliot Slater and Moya Woodside, for example, studied the marital relationships of 200 working-class soldiers hospitalized with war neurosis. This was a limited study, not published until 1951, but it pointed to an increasing resort to birth control within marriage and a belief that sex was an important part of marriage.[44] The major vehicle for examining British society during the war was Mass Observation, a research group of sociologists and anthropologists established in 1937 to investigate the details of 'ordinary lives at home'. During the war this group undertook extensive investigations into social life and morale. Some of their projects raised important issues about sexuality. For example, they studied Bolton workers holidaying in Blackpool, finding that much sexual activity was in public places and seen as legitimate and sanctioned by parents and friends. An integral part of the holiday experience was the possibility of illicit sexual activity, although little of it 'went all the way'.[45]

Another wartime project was a study of public attitudes to government campaigns to prevent the spread of venereal diseases. Mass Observation researchers found that few people considered such diseases either serious or shameful. More importantly, they investigated the decline in the birth rate, arguing that women's attitudes to marriage and child-rearing were changing. Fewer women wanted to be tied down like their mothers and many indicated that they wanted to improve their living conditions and have more time for leisure. Women were deliberately spacing births to achieve these ends. Further extensive sex survey work in Britain did not take place until after the war. In 1949 Mass Observation undertook a large survey of sexual attitudes and behaviours, known as 'Little Kinsey', largely aimed at exploring how young men and women found out about the facts of life. It was more concerned with sex education, marriage and fertility than questioning how sexuality had been understood.[46] Its inspiration, however, was the path-breaking Kinsey Report on male sexual behaviour published the year before. Kinsey's work, described as 'the most talked about book of the twentieth century', transformed debates about sexual behaviour in fundamental ways.[47]

Kinsey

While European and British historians have tended to see Sigmund Freud as the crucial figure in the emergence of modern sexual discourses, Alfred Kinsey has loomed larger within American historiography. Kinsey, an Indiana University entomologist and gall wasp expert, began researching sex in the late 1930s. His two major publications, *Sexual Behavior of the Human Male* (1948) and *Sexual Behavior of the Human Female* (1953), excited extraordinary scientific and popular attention. These studies were based on an unprecedented sample of 18,000 cases, compiled largely through extensive interviews, covering more or less the full social spectrum, unlike earlier studies which had usually be confined to one social group, most commonly college students. Within weeks of publication the male volume was on the best seller lists. The findings were controversial. Religious groups and conservatives decried the volume's 'disgusting prurience', declaring it to be an 'attack on the Western family' and Kinsey a 'menace to society'.

The criticism was not confined to moral conservatives. A few sociologists disputed the interview and statistical methodologies that framed the findings and psychoanalysts generally criticized the arid 'materialism' of the analysis, which challenged psychological theories of sexuality. Prominent literary critic and liberal social commentator, Lionel Trilling, argued that while Kinsey's work purported to be scientific, 'it editorialised freely' and was actually 'full of assumption and conclusion'. In the US Congress Kinsey was condemned as a communist, and there were efforts to have the Postmaster General ban the transmission of the Female Report through the mail. In 1954, at the height of the McCarthy era, Congressional efforts to investigate the financial aid provided by the Rockefeller Foundation for Kinsey's research, led to the cancellation of this source of funding. Kinsey, deeply embittered, died two years later.[48]

Kinsey remains a contentious figure. Although there were fervent critics, many contemporary scientists and sex researchers considered Kinsey's work path-breaking. Pioneering sex researcher Robert Latou Dickinson wrote 'Glory to God!' on receiving his copy of the male volume. Later he declared that in matters of sex 'America, hereafter [would] speak of the Pre-Kinsey and Post-Kinsey eras'.[49] Subsequent historians have tended to echo this judgement. Vern Bullough has argued that Kinsey established the study of sex as a genuinely scientific discipline, challenging medical dominance of the field and opening it up to other disciplines.[50] Others, such as Paul Robinson, Regina Morantz, Carolyn Dean and Edward Brecher, have presented Kinsey as an 'heroic figure' in intellectual history battling against the weight of American moral conservatism. For them, Kinsey fundamentally changed the way we view sex. The difficult circumstances of Kinsey's final years are, of course, ripe for a tragic narrative, shaping much of the commentary on his scientific findings.[51]

This mixing of the life and the work is equally evident in some of the recent critical accounts of Kinsey. Judith Reisman and Edward Eichel, in a generally shallow and unsympathetic analysis of the Reports, dismiss Kinsey's research as unscientific, unreliable and fraudulent.[52] These sentiments have been echoed by one of Kinsey's biographers, James Jones, who accuses Kinsey of being a masochistic homosexual living in a open marriage, whose methodology and research ethics were suspect. Crucially, Jones claims that Kinsey distorted his findings to fit his prejudices. For Jones, the life invalidates the work.[53] Jonathan Gathorne-Hardy's more balanced portrait of Kinsey challenges some of Jones' more extreme claims, without undermining the complex and contradictory nature of Kinsey's life, work and personality. But Gathorne-Hardy's account is marred by the effort to counter the claims of Jones. In effect he is as locked into defending the life as Jones is in attacking it.[54] It is a measure of Kinsey's cultural significance that his life and his work have melded together in so much of the historiography. Disentangling Kinsey's ideas from his life complicates assessments of the impact and significance of his theories.

Although Kinsey liked to represent himself as a humble seeker of the objective facts of sexual life, Paul Robinson's argument that he was not a simple empiricist rings true.[55] Kinsey shaped his research findings by drawing on concepts from the natural sciences. For Kinsey, sex was intrinsic to nature and measurable. Orgasm was a simple and objective indicator of sexual activity. If this was the case, Kinsey argued, then the scientific study of climax could monitor two factors – outlet and frequency. There were six main outlets for orgasm – masturbation, nocturnal emissions, heterosexual petting, heterosexual intercourse, homosexual relations and intercourse with animals or other species. Frequency had two valencies – the frequency associated with each outlet and the total number of orgasms from all sources (which could also be mapped over time). On this basis Kinsey challenged prevailing distinctions between heterosexuals, homosexuals and bisexuals. Instead he proposed a seven point classification system – ranging from exclusively heterosexual to exclusively homosexual with various mixes of the two in between (equally heterosexual and homosexual being the mid-point in this scale).

There are some bold and contestable assumptions here. Sex, for Kinsey, was largely about sexual arousal and climax, and thus physically, in their sexual response, men and women were identical. He ignored completely sexual experiences that did not end in orgasm. Equally important, by focusing solely on orgasm he adopted a stance of 'moral relativism' refusing to give priority to any particular sexual outlet, thus challenging assumptions about normal and abnormal sexuality. Like Havelock Ellis and Freud, he saw sexuality more as a continuum than a sharp division between distinct sexual identities. But unlike them, Kinsey rejected the notion of identity altogether, seeing most people as inherently bisexual (something he thought was confirmed by observations of the mammalian world) with differences only in degree. Unlike Victorians who believed that sex involved the overcoming of nature, Kinsey took the rejection of this nineteenth-century ethic to a new level. Civilization interfered with sexual response; so efforts to enhance satisfaction involved a challenge to morality and a return to natural practices.[56]

Kinsey, having established a supposedly objective measure for sexual activity, could then correlate outlet and frequency to a range of social indicators, such as gender (the basis of the division between the two volumes), age, age at puberty, residence, religion, education and class. Kinsey sought to assess the extent to which social factors affected the frequency of orgasm and the choice of outlet. As critics have noted, there were flaws in his methods. The reliance on interviews, despite his meticulous attention to their proper conduct, crosschecking of information and sensitive interpretation, was always fraught with problems. The relative skill of the interviewer, the tricks of memory, and the desire to impress, were subtle and incalculable influences on the outcomes. Moreover, despite Kinsey's attention to a broad cross-section of subjects, there were biases in the sample (too many prisoners, homosexuals and Midwesterners). Perhaps the most glaring flaw was the fact that few African Americans were included in the final findings. Kinsey, ever the rigorous scientist, believed he did not have a big enough sample of blacks. He also failed to employ a black interviewer. It was white sexual behaviour that was the subject of his study.[57]

Despite these flaws the findings were startling and influential. According to Kinsey, marriage accounted for considerably less of men's sexual activity than religious and moral authorities presumed. By taking into account all sexual outlets the male volume concluded that 95 percent of men had by conventional legal and moral standards engaged in illegal or immoral sexual activity (most commonly masturbation). Most had established a regular sexual outlet by the age of 15, over 80 percent had engaged in premarital sexual intercourse, half had extramarital intercourse and heterosexual petting was nearly universal, much of it to orgasm. For married men only 85 percent of their orgasms came from intercourse. Social environment and age also influenced frequency. Religious piety lead to a decline in frequency of about 30 percent. The frequency of orgasm in men peaked in the late teens and then declined steadily throughout life. Perhaps the most controversial finding was that 37 percent of men had had a homosexual encounter involving orgasm.

Some of the most interesting sections of the male volume concern class differences. The report identified two basic patterns. Working-class men had higher rates of premarital intercourse and homosexual experience; they shunned foreplay, oral sex, kissing and nudity, masturbated less frequently, and were generally more promiscuous when adolescents and more monogamous later in life. In contrast middle-class men tended to defer intercourse seeking other outlets before marriage. Thus they masturbated more frequently, engaged in more non-genital activities, placed greater store on foreplay and sexual sophistication, but were more likely to be promiscuous after marriage.[58]

The female volume, despite Kinsey's assertions that in terms of sexual response men and women were no different, devoted less attention to orgasm. In part this was because Kinsey took the opportunity to refine some of his assumptions. But it also reflected what the evidence indicated. Kinsey found fewer class differences in the sexual behaviour of women, noting merely that, like men, working-class women had less extramarital sex, while middle-class women were more likely to have had homosexual relations. Instead his primary focus was on the differences between men and women. Although Kinsey had originally theorized female orgasm as clitoro-vulvar and occasionally vulvic, in the female volume he abandoned the idea of a vaginal response, arguing that women only achieved orgasm through clitoral stimulation. Kinsey, in a direct attack on psychoanalysis, argued that the vaginal orgasm was a myth. Women, he concluded, had greater erotic range while their frequency of outlet was less. Although women wished for and enjoyed orgasm just as intensely as men, they masturbated less often. He noted that women were far less likely to be aroused by visual stimuli or fantasy, but more commonly found continued physical stimulation important for orgasm. Kinsey concluded that female sexuality was primarily physical and responsive, while men's was psychological and active.[59]

Kinsey has left an ambiguous legacy. On the one hand, his evidence challenged pervasive moral precepts, the reason for much of the opposition to his work. More importantly, it undermined one of the fundamental concepts of sexology – the distinction between normal and perverted sexuality. The interviews suggested that a range of illicit sexual practices were commonplace, natural and by implication acceptable. Kinsey sought to shift the whole ground of debate away from metaphors of illness and perversion, towards a critique of the social, religious and moral injunctions that inhibited the fulfilment of natural instincts. His work showed that people commonly found a range of sexual outlets, so the effect of moral prohibitions was to create guilt and sexual misery. He asserted that healthy sexual expression in adolescence enhanced rather than undermined marriage. Worse, puritan moralism pathologized and criminalized common sexual outlets such as homosexuality.

The Kinsey Reports represented an attack on the sexual psychopath laws, making them look ridiculous in the light of evidence that suggested that the majority of the population might be classified as sexually psychopathic. This evidence provided the 'facts' for a range of sexual libertarian groups to press for the decriminalization of 'abnormal' sexual behaviours in the coming decades. His critique of the 'vaginal orgasm' also became an integral part of later feminist critiques of Freud and sexology. The Kinsey Reports became important weapons in the fight for sexual liberalism.[60]

In many respects Kinsey was a radical thinker. Historians such as Jeffrey Weeks have argued that, in the short term, Kinsey's claim that many men had engaged in same-sex practices leading to orgasm challenged claims that homosexuality was the preserve of a perverted minority. More importantly, Weeks suggests that Kinsey undermined the concept of normality as a natural and innate disposition.[61] Some historians, however, have questioned Kinsey's radicalism. Angus McLaren argues that Kinsey saw his work as a support for marriage. More importantly for McLaren, Kinsey's stress on sexual behaviour sidelined the tenuous movements for sexual rights in the 1950s, such as the emerging homophile movement.[62] On the other hand, Kinsey's critique of sexual identity and his stress on sexual behaviour as a continuum rather than a fixed point of natural orientation might be seen as very radical, anticipating later Foucauldian critiques of identity politics.

Kinsey's attitude to class and sexuality is also in dispute. Paul Robinson suggests that, although Kinsey criticized the 'narrowness' of working-class ideas, he was sympathetic to the directness of 'lower class sexual habits'. He approved of their preference for intercourse and their tolerance of homosexuality. In contrast Kinsey thought the sexual sophistication of the middle classes was superstitious, fetishized the female breast unnecessarily and inhibited orgasm during intercourse in women.[63] McLaren, however, argues that Kinsey found middle-class sexual sophistication healthier and in Kinsey's stress on social factors shaping sexual behaviour he detects a residue of eugenic thinking.[64]

Feminists have found other tensions in Kinsey's theories. Janice Irvine and Lynne Segal have argued that Kinsey smuggled sexual difference back into sexology. Segal notes that all his evidence actually confirmed 'sexual dissimilarity'. Women had far fewer orgasms than men, especially after marriage. Although he supported marriage the evidence indicated that intercourse was largely irrelevant to women's sexual response. Thus there was an inconsistency between his support for marriage and his belief that social institutions and morality inhibited sexual outlet and frequency. Kinsey's refusal to abandon a commitment to marriage blunted the radical implications of his findings.[65]

There were other blind spots. He ignored men's sexual coercion of women and children. Similarly, Irvine demonstrates that Kinsey's focus on the different forms of sexual response of men and women (male as psychological, female as physical) was not grounded in a theory of socialization. Instead he sought biological roots for these differences. In doing so he 'naturalized' gender differences in sexual response. His 'biologically deterministic theory of sexual capacity supported the very stereotypes about female sexual indifference of which Kinsey was so critical'.[66]

Conclusion

Kinsey transformed the discipline of sex research. Although subsequent researchers were often critical of his methods and interpretations, Kinsey's concepts and conclusions captured them. Much of the sex research of the next few decades was dedicated to confirming, refining or refuting his findings. To do this many later sex researchers engaged in large-scale sample surveys of broad cross sections of the population, much as Kinsey had done. Thus Kinsey's methods and questions came to shape the direction of both supporters and critics.

Other researchers, however, went in a different direction. In the 1960s William Masters and Virginia Johnson focused more closely on exploring the physiology of female orgasm. Their biological research observed individual patients in a clinical setting. Although they, like Kinsey, argued that female orgasm was clitoral not vaginal, Masters and Johnson stressed quality rather than quantity of orgasm. They pioneered a thriving sex therapy industry in the 1960s and 1970s primarily interested in improving rates of female orgasm within heterosexual relationships. Masters and Johnson stressed the importance of foreplay and clitoral stimulation in female orgasm. Historians, such as McLaren and Irvine, however, point to the limitations in the physical and biological emphasis of sex therapy research. Sex therapy might have been a radical critique of women's experience of heterosexuality, but in trying to fix this experience therapy made sexual dissatisfaction an individual failing rather than a symptom of the wider power relationships that shaped relationships between men and women.[67]

Another important development in sexology, however, was the increasing significance of women in sex research. In the 1970s some of the most important sex survey research was undertaken by women such as Mary Sherfey, Lonnie Barbach, Mary Calderone and Helen Singer. This work sought to redress the 'harmful' view of female sexual passivity that had been the focus of twentieth-century sexology. Some feminist sex research, notably Shere Hite's, was also critical of Kinsey's conclusion about the biological differences between men and women. Hite worked from an assumption that women had an equal sexual capacity to men, investigating women as independent sexual agents. She stressed, more than Kinsey did, the importance of clitoral stimulation and the capacity of women for multiple orgasm. She also concluded that women were frustrated in their sexual relationships with men. For Hite, it was not the different sexual response of women that explained fewer orgasms, but the failure of men to understand female sexuality. Women lived in a culture that fostered dependence rather than autonomy. Thus, for Hite, the problem for female sexuality was cultural rather than biological.[68]

Lynne Segal argues, however, that this feminist critique of female sexuality itself remained mired in Kinsey's framework. For Hite, the key indicator of female sexual autonomy was orgasm, the same measure that Kinsey used. Yet this criterion ignored her own evidence. Hite's respondents generally reported that they found penetration psychologically and sexually very pleasurable, even if it did not lead in itself to orgasm. For these women, penetration was an integral part of sexual satisfaction. Hite ignores this evidence, returning time and again to female orgasm and its discontents. For Segal, this is an indication that Hite's work replicated 'the limitations of prevailing theory'. Hite, like Kinsey, reduces sex to the biological quantum of orgasm, almost suggesting that sex is merely a form of clitoral masturbation. This ignores the psychological and fantasy elements of sexuality. Hite fails to overturn pervasive theoretical problems within sex research, reducing a larger world of sensuality to a mechanistic search for orgasm. Rather than breaking with Kinsey, feminist sexology remained trapped within his paradigm. Segal concludes that sexological research has 'at times facilitated, but more often merely reflected or tried to contain, women's long struggle for control over their lives and sexuality'.[69]

Chapter 11

SEXUAL REVOLUTION

In 1962 journalist Helen Gurley Brown advised 'nice single girls' to say yes to sex. Men, she declared, were 'a lot more fun by the dozen'. Similarly Hugh Hefner, publisher of *Playboy*, attacked the 'ferocious antisexuality' and 'dark antieroticism' in America, trumpeting the 'end of Puritanism'.[1] One of the most popular cultural narratives of the late-twentieth century has been the 1960s and 1970s as an age of 'sexual revolution'. In the 1960s sexual liberalism may have became a very public discourse, but as historians such as David Allyn have argued the nature and forms of this revolution were contested.

For Brown, Hefner and others, the 'sexual revolution' became an advertising slogan and a source of great profit. Their magazines, journals, clubs and advice manuals sold in the millions to avid consumers of a fantasy of guilt-free sex, now possible with the invention of 'the pill'. Hippies, however, challenged the conventional gender stereotypes implicit in the libertinism of Brown and Hefner. They promoted a new androgynous, pansexual 'turn-on, tune-in, drop-out' ethic. Other counter-culture groups, such as the 'underground' and the 'yippies', were more conventionally political, tying sexual revolution to a larger campaign of social revolt. For them, sexual libertinism was just one part of a wider protest against racism, middle-class respectability, the Vietnam War, colonialism, class oppression and educational conservatism. Graffiti and slogans, such as 'make love not war' or 'the more I revolt the more I make love', became forthright declarations of a new link between sex and politics.[2]

In this context the 'personal is political' became a popular catch-cry. New movements mobilized critiques of sexual oppression. Feminist activists of the 1960s and 1970s, such as Shulamith Firestone, advocated the 'ultimate revolution'; to free women from the tyranny of biology, end the nuclear family, return to polymorphously perverse sexuality, and allow women and children to do whatever they wished sexually.[3]

Similarly, gays and lesbians took to the streets publicly protesting the medicalization and criminalization of their legitimate sexual rights. They were 'coming out' and in the process declaring that they were 'not lonesome deviants...but rather oppressed victims of a society that is itself in need of basic change'.[4] For French gay activist, Guy Hocquenghem, the 1960s and 1970s presented an opportunity for a 'revolution of desire' through the disappearance of sexual repression.[5]

Historians, however, have begun to question this 'revolution'. Robert Nye has argued that it is 'by no means certain that the events of those years were either revolutionary or particularly deep and long-lasting'.[6] Similarly, Angus McLaren sees it as a 'myth', not so much a 'simple liberation as the emergence and clash of a variety of different sexual agendas and cultures'.[7] David Allyn also highlights the range and variety of groups struggling to define 'the sexual revolution'. Although Allyn is more inclined to see the 1960s and 1970s as a time of revolutionary change, when established sexual codes were attacked and sexual behaviour underwent significant liberalization, his stress on the multiplicity of 'revolutions' complicates any simple notion of a unified revolt against the prevailing sexual order.[8]

Some historians have also tried to undermine the uniqueness of the 1960s and 1970s by putting it into a much longer context of 'sexual revolutions'. They have described the 1960s as the 'second sexual revolution', highlighting the 1920s as an earlier and, in some senses, more profound transformation in sexual attitudes and practices.[9] As we have seen in earlier chapters, the idea of an early revolution is also contested. While some historians have supported the idea of sexual modernity as an early-twentieth-century development, others argue that sexual modernity was characteristic of Victorians. Richard Godbeer even uncovers a 'sexual revolution' in the eighteenth century.[10]

Much of this debate about revolution arises because of the difficulties inherent in defining sexual modernity. Is it best characterized by the emergence of heterosexuality as a distinct identity, the freedom of people to chose sexual partners based on affection rather than social ties or the idea that men and women should both have a right to sexual pleasure? Any, or all, of these criteria have a claim to being the defining characteristic of modernity. Moreover, many have sought to tie sexual modernity to broader social and cultural developments. Thus historians such as Pamela Hagg have argued that this longer history of sexual modernity was intimately intertwined with political and economic modernity stretching back over many decades. The emergence of an individualist, consumer society constructed a sexual culture oriented towards gratification and the pursuit of pleasure.[11]

The historiography of sexual revolutions has commonly focused on the ideas of sexual liberals and reformers, such as Margaret Sanger and Alfred Kinsey. These reformers were undoubtedly influential. But when Kinsey came to chart American sexual habits he was really coming after the event. People had forged their own distinct sexual cultures long before Kinsey's findings 'shocked' the reading public. Recent research using police, court and prison archives, and more importantly the increasingly rich twentieth-century oral history record, has enabled historians to explore a range of hitherto barely glimpsed sexual cultures. This work has uncovered many sexual subcultures, in cities and rural areas, which forged networks of relationships and sexual practices that defied, parodied and sometimes ignored the ideas of both middle-class moralists and sexual reformers.

Some of this historical research indicates that there were profound and complex transformations in sexual practices taking place in different times and different places throughout the twentieth century. Many of the sex researchers who sought to chart shifting patterns of sexual behaviour captured slices of these deeper changes, but some of these practices slipped through the sexology net to be uncovered later by historians. Such research throws up important questions about whether the concept of revolution itself, either a single revolt or a series of them, is an adequate metaphor to encapsulate the history of late-twentieth-century sexuality.

Sexual Liberalism

In the 1940s and 1950s when sexologists began to survey large numbers of Americans and Britons they detected a shift in sexual habits. Alfred Kinsey found evidence for a marked sexual liberalization especially amongst women born after 1900: the incidence of masturbation, petting and premarital intercourse increased dramatically, especially after World War I. He attributed this 'new libidinousness' in women to the 'purity' and feminist campaigns against prostitution, which encouraged men to seek sexual satisfaction during courtship and marriage, and the influence of sexual modernists like Havelock Ellis, Marie Stopes and Sigmund Freud, whose ideas about the importance of sex to physical and mental wellbeing were widespread in the media.[12] Another sex survey pioneer, Eustace Chesser, found a similar pattern. His survey of the sexual relationships of English women uncovered a trebling in the incidence of petting leading to orgasm amongst women born from 1904 to 1914, over those born before 1904. There were significant increases in other practices. Surveys indicated that the rate of premarital sexual intercourse had nearly doubled in the inter-war years on both sides of the Atlantic.[13]

Early-twentieth-century social commentators did not need sexual surveys to convince them that there were troubling transformations in sexual customs. In the inter-war years American College youth began replacing supervised courtship with dating. There was a weakening in the authority of parents. In both Europe and America the 'jazz age' and the flapper were just the most visible symbols of a new mood of sexual hedonism. Films, music halls, dance clubs and advertisers identified this new market and sought to exploit it, until moralists sought to censor this sexual rebelliousness in the 1930s. In England another contributing factor to the increase in premarital sexual experimentation was the emergence of 'the amateur'. Doctors, reformers and military authorities were alarmed at the number of girls who offered their 'favours' to soldiers for free.[14]

As we have seen in earlier chapters, some historians have seen the culture of cheap amusements and sexual experimentation as originally a working-class phenomenon. In the late-nineteenth and early-twentieth centuries, white and black youths in large towns and cities dropped out of school and began earning wages. Some married early, but increasing numbers used their new financial freedom to explore the pleasures of dance halls, jazz clubs, and Coney Island. In the inter-war years movie palaces, bowling alleys and skating rinks, and later bars, provided opportunities for youths and girls to meet.[15] In London also, 'gents', 'swells', barmaids, 'self-possessed working women' and 'music hall ladies' resisted middle-class moralizing, exploring the sexual opportunities provided by the East End.[16]

By the 1920s, however, widespread discussion of the amateur, dating and petting was an indication of an emerging sexualization of middle-class women. Where previously Victorian ideals of separate spheres encouraged middle-class men to find sexual outlets (to use Kinsey's term) with prostitutes, by the inter-war years they were also pursuing sex play (petting, mutual masturbation and intercourse) with women of their own class. Many historians see this early-twentieth-century revolution as largely confined to the middle classes.[17] John D'Emilio and Estelle Freedman argue it was also an urban phenomenon. Dating opportunities were fewer amongst youths in rural areas. Blacks in the American South from families of moderate wealth and status also faced a strict moral code. Youths in small towns and rural areas, black and white, had less mobility, little access to the new urban pleasures and little opportunity to 'date'.[18]

More recent research, however, has qualified this claim. Local studies, notably Beth Bailey's history of Lawrence, Kansas, and Sharon Ullman's examination of early-twentieth-century Sacramento, have explored the ways the 'first sexual revolution' gradually worked its way into small town and rural America. These studies suggest that the timing of the 'revolution' varied considerably across different parts of the country. In Kansas the major change was really several revolutions wrought not by the first

World War but by the second. The nationalizing and internationalizing forces of federal government, global trade, consumer society, and mass media undermined the ability of local elites to control the boundaries of their communities, propelling the spread of new sexual customs to small towns. Rather than a revolution, sexual modernity seeped gradually throughout American society.[19]

Outside of the metropolitan centres working-class sexual customs moved to a different historical rhythm to that of their urban confreres and the local middle class. In the rural South, for example, African Americans and poor whites faced 'few sanctions against premarital intercourse'. Sex play was commonplace amongst blacks and whites in the South, as Kinsey was to later discover. Rural isolation fostered the development of independent sexual customs, many of which anticipated the supposed middle-class revolutions later in the twentieth century.

As a public phenomenon early-twentieth-century liberalization was also largely heterosexual. For homosexuals, sexual liberalism was a two-edged sword. On the one hand, flourishing urban cultures of pleasure provided a space for gays and lesbians to congregate and create a vibrant community of interest. On the other, growing visibility carried the risk of easier persecution and discrimination. A key question for gay and lesbian historians has been the chronology of these processes. When did visible gay and lesbian subcultures emerge? What were the patterns of tolerance and persecution arising from the emergence of large communities of gays and lesbians?

John D'Emilio has argued that World War II was the crucial turning point in the development of a 'gay subculture'. The War freed many men and women from small town and family supervision and introduced them to a same-sex environment and urban life. After the War many stayed on in the cities, joining the burgeoning gay and lesbian worlds of bars, clubs and bathhouses.[20] The increasing visibility of urban gay and lesbian subcultures and concern about homosexuals infiltrating positions of power prompted a McCarthyist crackdown on gays in government, the bureaucracy, the unions and Hollywood and stricter policing of gay and lesbian nightlife.[21]

Other historians, notably David Greenberg, Jonathan Ned Katz and Jeffrey Weeks, situate the growing intolerance of gay and lesbian subcultures earlier in the century. For these historians, the medicalization of homosexuality and the increasing emphasis in criminology and sexology on psychopathology, inversion and degeneracy created a climate that fostered greater police and judicial scrutiny of homosexuality. Increasingly authorities came to see homosexuality as a crime rather than a sin.[22] George Chauncey, however, argues that medicalization was only one part of a larger movement seeking to destroy urban sexual underworlds which for moralists had become too visible by the inter-war years.

In America an anti-gay backlash accelerated in the 1930s, with a host of new censorship regulations, municipal codes and greater police regulation aimed at suppressing gay life. He concludes that 'gay life in New York was less tolerated, less visible to outsiders, and more rigidly segregated in the second third of the century than the first'.[23]

In contrast to historians who see World War II as the moment when a gay subculture emerged, Chauncey and Leila Rupp uncover thriving late-nineteenth- and early-twentieth-century urban gay and lesbian cultures that were well known and tolerated. By the 1890s there were distinct centres of gay life in New York, popular drag balls, clubs and bathhouses, which created a sense of community and social support networks that sustained gays. Through these clubs, resorts, balls and parades, gay men were a visible and relatively tolerated part of urban culture. There were limitations to visibility. Gays and lesbians developed a sophisticated system of cultural codes of dress and speech that enabled them to recognize each other. Despite the fact that many were arrested for minor street offences, New York society viewed the dramatic manifestations of gay life as part of the city's spectacle.[24]

Chauncey's detailed ethnographic reconstruction of this urban gay culture, in particular, highlights the complexity of sexual identity in the late-nineteenth and early-twentieth century. A diverse range of groups with distinct styles and identities inhabited the emerging urban gay cultures of the big cities. There were also 'normals' and 'wolves' who shunned the gay lifestyle but sought sex with 'fairies'. Effeminate 'queers' and 'fairies', however, were an acknowledged and recognizable part of city life.[25]

Chauncey also argues that gay New York was initially a working-class culture. While middle-class men and women visited these urban underworlds in search of sexual adventure, these subcultures were largely situated in African American, Irish and Italian immigrant neighbourhoods, industrial areas and docks. Local working-class neighbours generally tolerated the effeminates and mannish women in their midst. By the 1920s, however, there were middle-class enclaves of gays and lesbians in Greenwich Village. Similar subcultures emerged in other American cities such as Chicago, Philadelphia and St Louis and major cities such as London, Paris and Berlin. The spread of gay and lesbian cultures outside of working-class enclaves was one factor in the growing intolerance and increased policing of the 1930s.[26]

This urban gay and lesbian culture often paraded itself through appropriation and parody of dominant cultural norms. Although some gays shunned effeminacy, it was through this performance that many gay men asserted their identity. Similarly, 'mannish' women played with gender stereotypes, allowing them to 'pass' in mainstream culture and represent their difference. Equally important, many of these men and women refused to accept medical and criminological representations of homosexuals as deviant or sick. They asserted their right to pleasure. At the same time many men who rejected 'effeminate' behaviour and had sex with other men did not see themselves as 'queers' or 'fairies' as long as they were the 'active' partners.

As we have seen, the belief that men should be active penetrating partners was a very old one. Historians have attempted to pinpoint when ideas of active/passive were supplanted by a culture of homosexual and heterosexual identities. For Randolph Trumbach the eighteenth century was the crucial turning point. In contrast David Halperin sees the late-nineteenth century as the period when sexology constructed the idea of the homosexual.[27] Chauncey's research indicates, however, that an active/passive culture of 'wolves' and 'fairies' was flourishing in early-twentieth-century New York. Within this culture 'wolves' were not characterized as deviants. Transgression of gender stereotypes, effeminacy in men and mannish women, remained major signifiers of sexual pathology.[28]

Gay and lesbian cultures also shaped twentieth-century heterosexual relations. For Chauncey and Rupp, sex with men was not necessarily seen as compromising masculinity until the inter-war years. After World War I the growing visibility of gay and lesbian cultures forced heterosexuals to differentiate themselves more clearly than ever before. Gender stereotypes became more central to heterosexual identity. Men were more inclined to assert their difference from gays, by 'eschewing anything that might mark them as queer'. The homosexual type, according to Chauncey, was not the product of sexologists but of gays themselves. The emergence of this figure forced 'straights' to adopt styles of dress, speech and walking that clearly distinguished them from gays. Moreover, the emerging gap forged between 'normals' and 'gays' fostered increasing intolerance and more intensive policing. Rupp has called this the 'heterosexualization' of American culture, making exclusive desire for the opposite sex the key to gender identity. In this context the growing popularity of premarital sexual intercourse amongst middle-class men and women, uncovered in the surveys of researchers like Kinsey and Chesser, might be seen as in part a response to the shifting boundaries of what constituted gay and lesbian life.[29]

Historians of homosexuality have concentrated on urban gay and lesbian cultures. These were the identities and practices that were most visible and the intense twentieth-century policing of gays and lesbians has produced a rich archive for historians to chart the contours of gay culture. For historians, twentieth-century gays and lesbians have left an extraordinary number of personal reminiscences, facilitating the production of detailed reconstructions of sexual communities. Much of this evidence has focused on the urban sexual minorities, usually in the larger American and European metropolises. While urban gay and lesbian cultures attracted men and women from small towns, villages and isolated districts, gay and lesbian life in rural America, Britain and Europe has, until recently, largely escaped notice. Oral history research, however, has helped overcome this silence.

John Howard's innovative history of 'queers' in the American South traces a very different world to that of gay New York. Here men did not openly proclaim their queer identity, but instead used the cover of silence to pursue their desires. In the South sexual and gender experimentation by boys and youths was sanctioned, and there was a larger culture of 'clandestine, but commonplace adult and intergenerational queer acts'. Boys, youths and men 'did it' in hotels, churches, fields, roadside parks and workplaces. Their diverse and scattered sexual networks were characterized by circulation rather than congregation. African Americans in the South pursued similar styles of homosexual interaction, although segregation ensured that their networks rarely overlapped with those of whites. These rural practices complicate historical narratives of homosexuality in America. For Howard, unlike Chauncey, D'Emilio or Rupp, the 1950s was a period of relative tolerance for 'queers' in the South. Only with the 'coming out' of gays and the visible presence of homosexuals in the civil rights movement in the 1960s did Southern queers face heightened persecution.[30]

Sex Radicals

The important historical work on the emergence of sexual modernity in nineteenth- and twentieth-century Britain and America suggests that the 1960s and 1970s sexual revolution was less revolutionary than its most fervent prophets claimed. While historians differ over the definition, timing and impact of various forms of sexual modernity, it seems clear that there were vibrant and active homosexual and heterosexual cultures, committed to an ethic of sexual pleasure well before the 'sexual revolution'. The increased incidence of petting and premarital sex amongst college-educated men and women also suggests that modern ideas and practices, born in urban subcultures, were spreading into the middle-class mainstream through the twentieth century.

Nevertheless, the sexual revolution associated with 'the pill and permissiveness' does stand out as an unprecedented moment of cultural spectacle. Sex came to the forefront of public debate in the 1960s and 1970s. Angus McLaren has argued that the most important dimension of the 'sexual revolution' was the emergence and clash of new sexual scripts.[31] For McLaren, the most important of these were feminism, sexual revolution and gay liberation. These scripts, however, did not spring forth spontaneously. There were important antecedents that laid the groundwork for the activists of the 'second sexual revolution'.

As we have seen, the new generation of inter-war feminists in Britain and Europe found the sexual theories of Victorian feminists unrealistic. Influenced by the sexology of Havelock Ellis and others, they accepted that passion was the preserve of women as well as men. For feminists between the wars, like Marie Stopes and Margaret Sanger, women were entitled to sexual pleasure within marriage, although a few radicals, such as Stella Browne and some Greenwich Village bohemian feminists felt that satisfaction might be found outside marriage.[32]

In contrast the 1940s and 1950s have been seen as the 'nadir of feminism'.[33] More recent research, however, has indicated that feminist activism did not disappear after World War II. In the postwar media there was much discussion of the 'woman question' as women sought greater opportunities in the workforce. Feminists continued to press for legal and economic rights for women. But some historians have suggested that there was a sharp break between the legal and political emancipation concerns of these feminists and the personal liberation ethics of 1970s women's liberation.[34]

More significantly, many of the leaders of a revitalized feminist movement of the 1960s and 1970s defined themselves against the liberal reformist agenda of the past.[35] Major texts such as Simone de Beauvoir's *The Second Sex* (1949) and Betty Friedan's *Feminine Mystique* (1963) highlighted for a new generation of women systemic obstacles to emancipation. The evident failure of women's right to vote in over-coming some of the most glaring disadvantages facing women (poorer wages, fewer employment opportunities, and sexual violence) drove home the limitations of incremental legal reform. Men's investment in power over women became increasingly apparent and was the spring-board for a more radical theory and politics of sexual oppression.[36]

The birth of 'gay liberation' after the 1969 Stonewall riots in Green-wich Village has obscured the longer history of movements for homo-sexual rights. Many of the forces that sought to oppress homosexuals and lesbians – homophobia, censorship, and policing – made political mobilization difficult. Another factor in the historical silence of gays and lesbians was the complex and ambivalent relationship between sexology and homosexuality. The names 'invert', 'lesbian' and 'homo-sexual', however, were embraced by some prominent 'inverts', such as Edward Carpenter and Radclyffe Hall, as a means of stripping away the silence that masked their lives. A definable identity gave gays and lesbians a point of identification, a means of acknowledging their com-munity with others.[37] But a name also made them more vulnerable to police and medical surveillance and incarceration. New discourses of degeneracy constructed same-sex desire as pathological, an illness to be cured.[38] George Chauncey, however, has argued that many gays in New York resisted the efforts of doctors to describe them as sick and deviant.[39] As Teresa de Lauretis has argued, such identities are 'neither innate nor *simply* acquired...but dynamically (re)structured by forms of fantasy both private and public...and historically specific'.[40]

As we have seen, sexologists such as Havelock Ellis believed that homosexuals and lesbians deserved sympathy and tolerance. The idea that their condition was not of their own making, fostered a belief that homosexuals should not be subject to police and criminal regulation. Sexologists became prominent members of reform societies seeking to repeal laws that punished homosexuality. As we have seen, prominent sexologists, such as Edward Carpenter, Magnus Hirschfeld and Norman Haire, were themselves homosexual. While the embrace of a homosexual identity made gays and lesbians more vulnerable to forms of social surveillance these identities also became a point for political mobilization. Jeffrey Weeks, John D'Emilio and other historians have charted the emergence of early homosexual rights movements in America, Britain and Europe.[41]

Magnus Hirschfeld was a major figure in homosexual emancipation. In 1897 he founded the Scientific-Humanitarian Committee in Charlottenburg in Germany, and branches were later established in Munich, Leipzig, Hanover and Amsterdam. The Committee publicized research on homosexuality and was very active in petitioning for the decriminalization of homosexuality in Germany and the Continent. In 1914 the British Society for the Study of Sex Psychology (later the British Sexology Society) was established. Like Hirschfeld's Committee it devoted itself to publicizing the findings of sexology and pressing for repeal of the 1885 Criminal Law Amendment Act sections on homosexuality. Some reformers, like Carpenter, explored other strategies. He sought to publicize the contribution of homosexual writers and painters, suggesting that homosexuals had produced many of the fruits of Western culture. Others stressed the classical tradition of Greek pederasty as justification for reform. From these different justifications for tolerance emerged numerous groups such as the Order of Chaeronea, the French Sexological Society and the America Society for Human Rights, pushing the cause of homosexual law reform. In addition, forums such as the World League for Sex Reform, attempted to coordinate the efforts of different groups in Britain, Europe and America. Some of these efforts were crushed by Fascist and Stalinist persecution. Nazi authorities burned Hirschfeld's books and closed his Institute.[42]

After the War there were efforts by reformers such as Haire to revive the educative and reform role of sexology. These efforts were short-lived. The focus of reform efforts shifted to America. In the 1940s and 1950s groups such as the Mattachine Society, Homophile Action League and the Janus Society, attempted to promote tolerance of homosexuality. Their aim was to encourage acceptance of homosexuality, and to this end they publicized the cultural significance of homosexuals and highlighted the links between classical Greece and modern homosexuality. Lesbians were less visible and suffered fewer legal restrictions. Their lack of recognition, however, promoted efforts, such as those of the Daughters of Bilitis, to make lesbianism respectable along the lines of the homophile societies.[43]

In the context of rampant homophobia and severe persecution of homosexuals after the War these were brave and pioneering efforts. The heightened persecution of homosexuality also aided their cause. In Britain a series of arrests of prominent actors, artists, civil servants and politicians, prompted reformers to establish the Homosexual Law Reform Society in 1958. They pressured governments for reform and were partly successful with the 1967 Sexual Offences Act, which decriminalized homosexual activities in private for adults.

Historians of these early reform movements have stressed the tensions between these societies and groups. More importantly, although these homophile groups of the 1940s and 1950s appear relatively conservative in comparison to the later gay liberation movement, their efforts to create an 'ethical homosexual culture' was a vital foundation for later radicalism. In challenging the medicalization that made homosexuality a 'shameful illness' and proclaiming same-sex desire as a higher form of love they sought to create a proud homosexual community. These homophile groups sought to make homosexuality acceptable and remove some of the worst forms of legal persecution. They helped foster a climate of sympathy for homosexuality amongst liberals and sexologists and gave voice to a movement that was in its infancy.[44]

Another powerful force driving new sexual agendas was the emergence of a small group of sexual radicals who vigorously attacked sexual conservatism. A number of studies have analysed the lives and thought of inter-war and early postwar sexual radicals. Most were influenced by psychoanalysis. The psychoanalytic dramaturgy of a struggle between unconscious instincts and morality fought out in the ego shaped the radical agenda. While Freud and most of his fellow psychoanalysts, saw the 'superego' or the demands of civilized morality as a universal and necessary force, a few, notably Wilhelm Reich, Geza Roheim and Herbert Marcuse, saw sexual repression as a major mechanism of capitalist political domination. They insisted that modern civilization demanded excessive sexual repression, rendering individuals passive consumers of broader conservative social forces. Reich and Marcuse, in particular, sought to forge a link between psychoanalysis and Marxism. Thus modern capitalism and the patriarchal family were structures which alienated people from themselves.[45]

The pursuit of sexual pleasure then, became a means of resisting capitalist domination. In the hands of Reich this degenerated into a simplistic evocation of the mystical properties of genital orgasm. Marcuse, however, developed a subtle and influential analysis of how capitalist culture constructed 'repressive needs' and permitted through 'repressive desublimation' areas of sexual expression that supported the dominant order. Marcuse advocated a release of erotic energies as a means of curtailing the aggression at the heart of economic exploitation.

The idea of 'excessive repression' and sexual pleasure as a form of revolution and resistance to the dominant social order inspired libertarian and bohemian groups in the 1950s. American psychotherapists, such as Fritz Perls and Norman O. Brown, also wrote influential books on the 'evils' of sexual repression. Like Marcuse they proclaimed the importance of 'resexualizing the body' as a strategy of resistance against the effects of capitalist modernity. Such arguments laid the theoretical foundation for the sexual revolution of the 1960s. These theorists were widely read and their ideas were used to support new doctrines of sexual permissiveness and social revolution. Although Marcuse expressed some ambivalence about the sexual revolution, the tradition of sexual radicalism, born in a marriage of Marxism and psychoanalysis, was an important influence on many of the radical leaders of sexual revolution in the 1960s and 1970s.[46]

The Sexual Revolution?

The maelstrom of the 1960s and 1970s has achieved mythical status. The major events of the era have entered popular consciousness in profound and contradictory ways – May 1968 in Paris, the *Oz* trial in London, the student demonstrations at Berkeley, the assassinations of the Kennedys, the civil rights movement, opposition to war in Vietnam, the Chicago Eight, Stonewall and Woodstock – to name but a few, have been told and retold. These events can strike a chord of dismay or nostalgia in different audiences. For some, permissiveness, rock music, student and anti-war protest, radical feminism, gay liberation and the brazen embrace of drugs were symptoms of 'moral decay' in modern culture. For others they represent once buoyant hopes and their betrayal – a glorious heyday crushed by political and sexual conservatism, mass culture and consumerism.[47] For David Allyn, this was a 'deeply American revolution...spiritual yet secular, idealistic yet commercial, driven by science yet coloured by a romantic view of nature'.[48] This is illuminating, but too parochial. While America was at the centre of permissiveness and revolt, these movements were widespread and global in their effects.

Historians have begun to step outside narratives for or against the sexual revolution of the 1960s and 1970s arguing that it was not a single, uniform protest but a series of competing struggles, each with different agendas and widely varying results. At the same time the revolution was a dramatic transformation in attitudes. Nudity, free love, androgyny, wife swapping, more explicit erotica in the mass media, all marked out a significant liberalization in public attitudes to sex.[49] As David Allyn has argued, the difficulty in defining the nature of the sexual revolution reflects the fact that it embraced contradictory meanings – formal and conscious revolt against authority and general social transformations in attitudes and behaviours.[50] Sex was central to both. Sexual permissiveness was a major signifier of a shift in public attitudes towards greater tolerance of sexual expression. Sex was also a vital part of emancipatory struggles, such as those opposing censorship, homophobia, colonialism, sexism and capitalism. Integral to many of these protest and emancipation movements were contests over knowledge and authority; were doctors, criminologists and therapists the purveyors of truth or agents for capitalist, homophobic and misogynist authorities. Radical movements recast the language of therapy, adjustment and individualization as social control. Within this context sex was a tool of social oppression and a means of liberation.

The so-called 'sexual revolution' actually had two faces. There was the ersatz revolution of Helen Gurley Brown and Hugh Hefner – a fantasy world of ever-willing bodies with infinite sexual capacities, very like the Victorian 'pornotopia' analysed by Steven Marcus, but now popularized, commercialized, and integrated into mainstream culture. This sexual libertarianism was masculinist, and originated in the 1950s as an assertion of a bachelor culture alternative to the marital and suburban domesticity promoted by conservative opinion makers and commercial media. In many respects it built upon the revolution in heterosexual relations, as mapped by Kinsey, that had been taking place since the 1910s. But this consumerist sexual culture also tapped into important social transformations of the postwar years. In the 1960s and 1970s the average age at marriage began to rise again, while the birth rate began to decline after the postwar baby boom. Men and women were spending a larger part of their lives as 'singles'. There was a large market of increasingly prosperous sexually available people. Similarly, rising divorce rates meant that nearly half of all marriages would end up with the participants on the 'market' for sexual adventure and companionship.

The world of multiple sexual partners, 'swingers', wife swapping and easy promiscuity promoted by the commercial sex media, legitimized permissiveness as a way of life. Moreover, the invention of the contraceptive pill in 1960 promoted a belief that permissiveness could be practised without unwanted consequences. By 1970 nearly two-thirds of married women relied on the pill, IUDs or sterilization for contraception. These practices were common across all classes. Abortion reform also meant women had relatively greater access to birth control services when contraception failed. Reliable contraception fostered permissiveness. Genital intercourse, however, was no longer the hallmark of sexual liberalism. The new permissive culture promoted extended foreplay, and a host of previously 'perverse' practices such as oral and anal sex, and to a lesser extent bondage and discipline, as legitimate forms of sex play for heterosexuals.[51]

Sexual radicals, however, condemned Hefner and Brown, as 'false prophets of Eros'. Leading figures of the 'counter-culture' promoted the idea of a 'genuine sexual revolution', shorn of 'playboy bromides'. Prominent advocates of 'underground sexual morality', such as Australian journalist Richard Neville and 'counter-culture' theorist Theodore Roszak, pushed the idea of an alternative culture, expanding consciousness through drugs and adopting a guilt-free and direct approach to sex. If two people liked each other they went to bed.[52] For Neville the false, moralistic arts of 'seduction' were dead, to be replaced by uninhibited carnality. The 'underground' and counter culture identified sexual freedom with total freedom. It was a world free of pornography and prostitution. Drawing on the work of Marcuse and Reich, advocates of the 'underground' saw freedom from inhibition as the first step to a 'new, freer, happier civilization'.[53] But radical critics and subsequent historians have pointed to the severe limitations of this 'revolution'. The links sexual radicals made between sexual freedom and political revolution were vague and based on poorly digested lumps of Marx, Marcuse and Reich. Much of the supposed radicalism of the 'underground' was subsumed in a wider, largely apolitical celebration of a 'drugs, sex and rock and roll' culture that lacked a coherent political program and was easily appropriated by commercial interests.[54]

Another critical voice was feminism. Advocates of women's liberation condemned both the 'playboy fantasy world' of mainstream culture and the sexual politics of supposed revolutionaries. The sexism of counter-culture advocates and the broader New Left, alienated many radical women. Black Power activist Stokeley Carmichael's famous statement that 'the position of women in the movement was prone' was only one example of the pervasive misogyny of prominent men on the left. In his best selling *Playpower* (1971) Richard Neville's celebration of gang rape and evocation of an idyllic world of freely available 14-year-old girls, reveals a radical politics that had manifestly failed to theorize sexual power relations.[55] Part of the impetus for second wave feminism was the failure of the New Left to give space to the ideas, experiences and perspectives of women. Revolution seemed to some women to be sexual freedom for men and a new form of slavery for women.

The relationship between second wave feminism and earlier feminisms has been a source of considerable historical debate. Did second wave feminism represent a radical break with the past? Certainly in terms of tone and style 'women's liberation' was a conscious effort to overcome the limitations of past feminist practice, although it did echo some of the efforts of earlier suffrage militants. A wonderfully combative and confrontational politics emerged – street protests, marches, picketing beauty pageants and other male festivals, the establishment of political lobby groups, the exposé of institutions such as *Playboy*, burning bras, supporting abortion clinics and high profile media reports of prominent women's liberationists – thrusting feminism to the forefront of popular consciousness in the early 1970s.

A flurry of major texts, such as Kate Millett's *Sexual Politics* (1970), Germaine Greer's *The Female Eunuch* (1970) and Shulamith Firestone's *The Dialectic of Sex* (1970), savagely attacked male sexism and patriarchal culture, demanding sexual liberation for women and freedom from the burdens of reproduction, childcare and domestic enslavement. Moreover, women's liberationists, through consciousness raising groups and arguments about 'the personal is political', focused more than ever before on the direct relations of domination and subordination in the everyday life of women. Where earlier feminists had concentrated on formal legal and political issues such as suffrage, property, custody, divorce and welfare reform, women's liberationists explored the politics of the bed, the nursery and the kitchen.[56]

Prominent feminist historians and theorists of the 1970s, such as Sheila Rowbotham, Ellen DuBois and Juliet Mitchell, highlighted the break between the socialist and revolutionary character of women's liberation and the bourgeois feminism of the past.[57] Historians such as Nancy Cott have also stressed the sharp disjuncture between modern feminism and the Victorian woman movement.[58] Other assessments of the history of feminism, however, have stressed the continuities between 'women's liberation' and earlier feminisms.[59] Many of the central campaigns of 'women's liberation' – abortion rights, equal pay, male violence, pornography, childcare, employment opportunities – had first been proposed by earlier feminists. Equally, women's liberation in its insistence that women were oppressed as a sex, had striking parallels with Victorian feminist claims that women were fundamentally different and victims of 'man's passions'.

Moreover, these revisionist historians argue that Victorian feminists grappled with many of the same theoretical and political dilemmas as modern feminists. Should the basis for feminist politics be the claim that women are the same as men and deserving equal rights or were women fundamentally different requiring recognition of their specificity and the creation of social structures which acknowledge, accommodate and reward this difference?

The renewed historical debate over what constitutes feminism, and the relation between feminism and its past, reflected deeper fissures

within 'women's liberation'. Although many early women's liberationists proclaimed that women were united as a sex, there were significant
divisions over political strategies and priorities between radical, socialist and equality feminists. Increasingly radical critics of feminism and
feminists themselves highlighted that sex always intersected with structures of class and race and that women could not be seen as an undifferentiated group. Sexuality, however, remained a key defining point
for feminist theory. For radical feminists, such as Adrienne Rich, sex
was fundamental to male domination. The answer was complete sexual
autonomy for women. A feminist sexual revolution meant refusing the
patriarchal imperative of 'compulsory heterosexuality'. For Rich, heterosexuality was not innate. What was required was recognition of the
'lesbian continuum'.[60]

Similar arguments underpinned the sympathy feminist historians
like Sheila Jeffreys felt for Victorian feminists. They saw the embrace
of chastity by nineteenth-century feminists as more radical than the
efforts of inter-war feminists to improve sexual relations between men
and women.[61] Other feminists, however, did not consider lesbianism
the solution for the majority of women. The politics of heterosexuality
were at the centre of their concerns.

The surveys of women undertaken by feminist sexologists, such as
Shere Hite, suggested that women were chronically dissatisfied with
heterosexuality. How could one make it better? Here feminists faced
a dilemma. Was sex, as Kinsey, Masters and Johnson, Hite and other
sexologists implied, a matter of freeing women to enjoy orgasm? Or
did it involve grappling with more complex concepts of desire, fantasy,
pleasure, power, play and interaction? Moreover, how were feminists to
deal with issues such as rape, pornography, violence, paedophilia and
the 'coital imperative'? Many turned to gender and masculinity as a key
historical problem. History became a field in which some of these problems could be explored. Studies of the Victorian woman movement,
inter-war feminism and women's liberation offered a means of exploring complex theoretical problems about the nature of feminist politics
as well as the lessons of past political campaigns.[62]

Gay liberation was an unambiguous assertion of the importance of
sexuality in the achievement of political and social freedom. Although
there had been gay activists in the 1940s and 1950s working quietly away
on obscure journals and books trying to promote tolerance of homosexuality, in the 1960s these efforts became very public. Homosexuals formed
organizations to promote the cause of liberation. In June 1969 a police
raid on Stonewall Inn, a well-known homosexual bar in Greenwich Village, caused four days of rioting. There was a new gay self-assertiveness.
In America, Australia, England and Europe gay liberation groups were
established demanding recognition of homosexuality. They pressed for

decriminalization, the cessation of police harassment, the end of psychiatric constructions of homosexuality and lesbianism as a disease, and the right of gays and lesbians to kiss, hold hands and express affection in public just as heterosexuals did. They proclaimed that far from being just a sexual orientation, homosexuality constituted an identity, forged in the political struggle to overcome oppression. It was now a valid sexual identity and way of life.[63]

For some activists, promoting gay and lesbian identities had more radical implications than just tolerance of different sexual orientations. For Denis Altman, becoming gay meant rejecting 'the program for marriage/family/home that our society holds as normal'. Moreover, gay identity was also a rejection of behavioural theories of sexuality or 'Kinsey-like computations of orgasms'. For radical activists homosexuality was 'as much a matter of emotion as genital manipulation'. It was not a sin or a pathology, but just another way of 'ordering one's sexual drive'. Thus society was oriented towards repressing one way of sexual ordering and promoting another. Theorists like Altman argued that coming out and living a gay life were ways of undermining patriarchal and heterosexist social structures.[64]

The early optimism of gay liberation, however, was fractured by political and social dissension. Although some parts of the movement saw it as a step towards a deeper social transformation, others saw it as largely about personal liberation. John D'Emilio and Estelle Freedman have charted the demise of liberationist politics in America. It declined in part because the radical milieu that invigorated it lost its edge. Gay liberation instead recast itself as part of the long tradition of American reformism, focusing more on civil rights than sexuality.[65]

Similarly, Jeffrey Weeks has argued that four major splits undermined the radical liberationist politics of groups like the British Gay Liberation Front. First, there were differences between gays and lesbians. The movement was dominated by gays, and lesbians found it difficult to get their priorities accepted. They felt constrained by the male sexism of the gay movement and the exclusive focus on the gay/straight divide. The growth of feminism also gave lesbians an alternative forum in which to campaign for their rights. Secondly, feminist critiques of male sexuality challenged gays who were defending it. Thirdly, there were some gay liberationists concerned to link their struggle to that of all oppressed peoples. But there were counter-culture sections of the movement more interested in exploring drugs, personal liberation and sexual hedonism. Finally, gay liberation was built on the premise that it would become a mass movement. It was not, however, a stable basis for such a movement. Like feminism, gay liberation encompassed 'a host of conflicting class, cultural, sexual, political and social allegiances [that] tugged in increasingly divergent directions'.[66]

By the mid 1970s there was a shift away from liberation to a politics of legal reform, toleration and the creation of visible gay communities. This shift, however, had its radical dimensions. One of the outgrowths of 'gay pride' and the emergence of gay sexual identity was the collapse of the old homosexual and lesbian stereotypes of male effeminacy and the 'mannish' woman. Gay activists now felt confident about exploring a diversity of sexual performances, such as drag, working-class clones, 'dykes on bikes' and lesbian chic. The emphasis in gay and lesbian culture shifted from mass movement to diversity and variety. These performances of sexual identity were in part parodies of dominant gender stereotypes, thus undermining the essentialism of heterosexual masculinity and femininity. Moreover, prominent historians of gay and lesbian liberation, such as Leila Rupp, have argued that the shift from movement to community politics did not necessarily mean the decline of radicalism. For Rupp, this change is better understood as an evolution from a politics of liberation to a radical politics of representation.[67]

Conclusion

The sexual revolution certainly did not live up to the hopes of its early proponents. It did not become a mass political movement that fundamentally transformed the structures of social and sexual life. Internal conflicts undermined cohesiveness. The radical fervour of the period evaporated as disputes and splits indicated that sexual politics were far more complicated than radicals had supposed. Historians have understandably tended to stress the limitations of the movement.[68] Nonetheless, feminism and gay liberation made extraordinary strides in the 1970s. They transformed the social and sexual climate in profound ways, challenging the homophobia and misogyny that prevented women, lesbians and gays from exploring the sexual pleasures they desired. In the process there were important legal reforms which made it more possible for these groups to strive for sexual freedom. By the 1980s lesbians and gays, in particular, were able to live outside of the social norms of heterosexual culture more openly than ever before.

The enthusiasm for sexual revolution evaporated. In part this was a consequence of feminists, gays and lesbians developing more sophisticated critiques of the relationship between sexual identity, sexuality and politics. This involved new theories of the complex nexus between sexuality and forms of power. In the late 1980s and early 1990s the clash between essentialists and social constructionists that underpinned the growth of the discipline of sexual history was at the centre of these debates about power, knowledge, identity and politics. The shift to a politics of representation, as Rupp suggests, indicated a broader focus and the abandonment of simplistic notions that having sex was itself a radical act. Feminists and gays had made sex and sexuality a vital question for radical politics and critical theory.

Historians of the sexual revolution, however, have usually seen the 1980s and 1990s as a time of 'backlash'. The growing incidence of sexually transmitted diseases and, significantly, the appearance of HIV/AIDS brought home forcefully the potential consequences of unprotected promiscuity. More importantly, historians have detected a new sexual conservatism in the West. In significant parts of the popular media the 1960s revolution was increasingly depicted as a time of 'moral decay' leading to family breakdown, drug wars, rising rates of sexually transmitted diseases and social decline. The result, according to critics, was social and sexual misery, rampant sexual corruption, paedophilia scandals, rising rates of divorce and increasing social instability undermining the psychological health of children. There were calls for a return to a 'new moralism' and demands for stricter censorship controls, more policing of sexual deviancy and greater restrictions on access to abortion.[69]

We should not take evidence of 'backlash' too far. While the movement for a new sexual moralism gathered pace in the 1980s and 1990s, particularly in America, at the same time there are many indicators of increasing sexual liberalization. For example, the pornography industry continues to make enormous profits and through the internet has more outlets than ever before. Equally, a culture of ecstasy-fuelled dance clubs thrives, sex is more explicit in much mainstream media and gays and lesbians have achieved a new visibility and acceptance in films and television. While cultural critics have questioned the limited and stereotypical representations of gays and lesbians in these forums, the fact remains that homosexual characters have a new and in many instances favourable place in popular television and film. They are no longer in the closet but an acknowledged and sometimes central part of many popular programs.[70] Moreover, opinion polls suggest increasing public tolerance of teenage sexuality and alternative sexual lifestyles and identities. Even the supposed sexual conservatism of the 1980s and 1990s still situated sexuality as an issue of enormous significance. Sex and sexuality were no longer at the margins of science, politics or social identity. By the end of the twentieth century they were at the centre.

EPILOGUE

If by the late-twentieth century sexuality had become a major way men and women understood and marked their identity, would it continue to do so? An answer to that question depends in part on the historical narratives of sexuality that shape contemporary understandings of the interrelationships between sex and identity. Sex may be a biological drive but it is also a set of practices through which men and women shape and are shaped by culture. A careful examination of the history of sexuality suggests that sex has presented both possibilities and problems in many times and places. Sexual desire has been a way of cementing social bonds, asserting dominance and signifying status. It has also been seen as something that could unsettle the social order, a capacity that needed to be mastered, regulated and in some instances outlawed and punished.

For many historians the clash of instinct and culture suggests important continuities in the history of sexuality. This is most evident in the search for a gay and lesbian past. Historians have uncovered a rich history of same-sex practices across many times and places. Gay and lesbian history has attempted to uncover the contours of the struggle of homosexuals and lesbians to express desire and live in communities of those who share their passions. These efforts to enact sexuality are intimately linked to widespread concern about homosexuality. This type of love has been condemned, ridiculed, persecuted and punished. For many historians homophobia is a useful concept for charting this long history of antagonism to same-sex desires. The history of sexuality, then, can be seen as a clash of sexual identities, a dominant heterosexual culture oppressing alternatives such as homosexuality and lesbianism. What made sex historical was the alternation of periods of repression and tolerance in attitudes to sexuality.

Other historians, however, question whether same-sex desires (equally, opposite-sex desires) and sexuality are one and the same thing. While they acknowledge that men and women in the past have had sex with either their own or the opposite sex, and in many instances both, they insist that this does not necessarily represent the timeless presence of sexual identities in all cultures. Instead they have charted sexuality as historically specific forms of identity emerging, depending on the historian concerned, sometime from the fourteenth to the late-twentieth century. For these historians same-sex desire may have occurred in the past, but such desires did not necessarily create a homosexual identity any more than opposite-sex desire created heterosexual identity. Rather, desire was caught within a broader field of signification concerned with such things as citizenship, subservience, masculinity, femininity, self-mastery and control. For these historians past cultures did not divide the world of sex into straights and gays, but around different tropes such as active and passive, subject and object, citizen and slave. Antagonism to same-sex desire was not homophobia, but revulsion at people who flouted gender conventions and codes of active and passive.

According to these historians sexuality did not appear as an independent domain until people began to be classified as either heterosexual or pervert. This coincided with profound transformations in readings of human anatomy – from classical anatomical ideas, where women were seen as having undeveloped male bodies, to a modern view that the biology of men and women was fundamentally different. There were significant historical shifts – from seeing the sexual world as one based on social status and dominance, or active and passive partners, to one focused on heterosexuality and perversion, and a clear demarcation of male and female bodies. These transformations did not so much transform sexual identity as create it. Men and women began to see themselves as heterosexual or pervert, making sexual desire an independent arena. Thus sexuality was made into a self-conscious and distinct sphere for the first time.

The clash between these two different approaches to writing the story of sex stimulated and enlivened the emergence of sexuality as a major area of historical debate. The so-called essentialist and social constructionist debate shaped much of the discipline in the 1980s and 1990s. The struggle over whether sexual identities in the past were similar to those of the present day or radically different and specific to particular times and places created a significant body of scholarship. It also meant that much of the focus of sexual history was the history of homosexuality. This debate has generated an enormous body of evidence concerning the history of sex and sexuality and major concepts of enduring significance for the discipline.

Nonetheless, the sharp disjuncture between the emphasis on continuity or difference inhibits as much as illuminates the history of sexuality. It is important to recognize that there are themes of long duration and others of marked specificity in the history of sexuality. For example, the intersections between sexual practices and codes of gender have shaped the history of sexuality in profound ways. For millennia what seems to have troubled commentators on sex were men and women who transgressed ideals of masculinity and femininity in their dress, styles of speech and sexual preferences. The effeminate man who was the passive partner in the sexual act was the source of great opprobrium as was the mannish woman. Moreover, the shift to a world where sexual orientation, regardless of bodily presentation or role in the sexual act, mattered more than the transgression of gender roles does not mean that gender ceased to matter. On the contrary, it is significant that many of the sexual codes of antiquity (active, passive) persisted in early Christian and medieval Europe and in early-modern Europe and America. Moreover, ideas of active and passive shifted to signify gender (men as active, women as passive), shaping key dimensions of the emerging modern domain of sexuality. Traditions of Western sexual culture transmuted and persisted, shaping configurations of modern sexuality in important ways.

At the same time it is highly significant that the sexual cultures of classical antiquity did not condemn same-sex desire itself, but instead found the passive adult male citizen the source of greatest anxiety. This represents a fundamentally different sexual culture to that of modernity, where sexual orientation, regardless of whether one is the active or the passive partner, is an important defining characteristic of sexual identity. Others such as gender transgression (transgender) and passivity (masochism and fetishism) remain important sexual signifiers, but it is the heterosexual/homosexual divide that frames discussions of identity in modern sexual cultures. It is essential that historians grapple with these differences, and not fall into the trap of seeking convenient but misleading homologies between the past and the present.

Greater recognition of the complexity of sexual history, however, has undermined old antipathies between essentialism and constructionism. It is important to map both the continuities and differences in sexual history – the ways the past persists in the present as well as the chasms that separate sexual cultures. It is equally important to recognize the diversity of sexual cultures. The supposed shift to sexual modernity characterized by the creation of an independent domain of sexuality and a world divided along lines of sexual orientation rather than gender transgression, now appears to be more a series of local transformations and slow tectonic shifts. The early Christian condemnation of sodomy found both the active and the passive partner at fault, an important idea that took nearly two millennia to work its way into the centre of debates about identity. For some historians sexual modernity may have appeared in the early-eighteenth century in London, but an older culture of male effeminacy and masculine wolves was still apparent in New York in the early-twentieth century. Moreover, in the Southern States of America a radically different homosexual culture existed until the 1950s.

It is a sign of the growing maturity of sexual history that historians are now moving beyond conventional concerns with the history of inversion, effeminacy, homosexuality and heterosexuality. Sitting alongside the history of sexuality of course there have been other historiographies that have had a great deal to say about sexuality – the history of fertility, family formation, birth control, feminism and postcolonialism to name but a few. These historiographies have crossed over into the history of sexuality adding new questions and perspectives. But even within the sphere of sexual history more narrowly defined, there are historians like Regina Kunzel asking new questions about 'situational homosexuality' and Stephen Robertson about the intersections between age, childhood and sexuality, that promise to open up new areas of investigation and debate.

This brings us back to the question that began this epilogue. Is sexuality now an entrenched part of modern sexual culture and one likely to persist? Certainly historians such as Denis Altman have argued that sex has infiltrated every sphere of culture bringing the personal and the political together more intimately than ever before. For Altman, this is a global sexual culture where the commercialization of sex and the politics of epidemic disease, migration, sex slavery, tourism, popular culture, mass marketing and the information revolution have saturated every aspect of life in narratives of sexual desire and danger. In such a context sexual identity has become a very significant marker of personal identity.

In the late 1970s, however, theorists such as Michel Foucault warned of the dangers of sexual identity. Identities imprisoned sex, forcing it into specific channels, undermining the capacity to explore the diversity and polymorphous perversity of desire. The passionate embrace of one identity denied other potential identities, and if identity was constructed within specific contexts of power, knowledge, truth and freedom, then identities were not singular but multiple. The force of this critique has been taken up by a number of social theorists, largely from within gay and lesbian politics, who have argued for a shift from homosexual identities and camp sensibilities to queer politics. These theorists have explored the political and social limitations of sexual identities, advocating multiple, diverse and critical sexual interventions, stressing plurality, ambiguity and transgression rather than community and coherence. Queer theorists have challenged a conventional politics of sexual liberation and resisted the fixing of sexual desire around stable identities such as gay and straight.

Will the queer critique undermine the centrality of sexuality in modern culture? The signs are mixed. The capacity of modern commercial culture to appropriate radical critiques is astounding. Recent media representations of men who utilize effeminate attributes (camp style, jewellery, make-up) to signify a new hyper-masculinity or women who use male attire to create deeply eroticized images appealing to both men and women, point to the ways gender ambiguity has come to mark sexual allure. These images have been commercialized for a mass market. Sexual ambiguity, bisexuality, metrosexuality and the like have become commonplace discourses and representational practices within mass culture, suggesting that the queer critique may have lost its edge and become part of global sexual culture.

Equally, in some ways queer itself has become an identity, fixing in specific ways codes of sexual practice just as restrictive as the ones it sought to replace. On the other hand, queer theory has produced radically unsettling readings of contemporary culture and concepts which challenge the idea of identity itself. Will the critique of sexual identity become commodified and just another form of identity? Or are we poised at a moment when fixed sexual orientations will begin to fade as primary modes of modern identity, to be replaced by transgressive plurality and ambiguity? This will be a fascinating chapter for a future history of sexuality.

ENDNOTES

Chapter 1

1. See, for example, Howard Brown Woolston, *Prostitution in the USA*. I. *Prior to the Entrance of the United States into the World War* (Montclair, NJ: Patterson Smith, 1969 [c.1921]).

2. W.E.H. Lecky, *History of European Morals from Augustus to Charlemagne* (London: Longmans, Green, 1869).

3. Margaret Mead, *Coming of Age in Samoa: A Study of Adolescence and Sex in Primitive Societies* (Harmondsworth: Penguin Books, 1943 [1928]).

4. Norman Haire *et al.*, *The Encyclopedia of Sex Practice* (London: Encyclopaedic Press, 2nd edn, 1951 [1938]).

5. Hans Licht, *Sexual Life in Ancient Greece* (trans. J.H. Freese; London: Routledge, 1932).

6. Gordon Rattray Taylor, *Sex in History* (London: Thames & Hudson, 1953).

7. For useful overviews of sexual liberation movements see Jeffrey Weeks, *Sex, Politics and Society: The Regulation of Sexuality since 1800* (London: Longman, 2nd edition, 1989), pp. 249-72 and Angus McLaren, *Twentieth-Century Sexuality: A History* (Oxford: Basil Blackwell, 1999), pp. 166-67.

8. For some useful overviews of this debate see Jeffrey Weeks, *Making Sexual History* (Cambridge: Polity Press, 2000), pp. 1-13, Robert Padgug, 'Sexual Matters: On Conceptualizing Sexuality in History' in Edward Stein (ed.), *Forms of Desire: Sexual Orientation and the Social Constructionist Controversy* (New York: Routledge, 1992), pp. 43-67 and Domna C. Stanton, 'Introduction: The Subject of Sexuality' in Domna C. Stanton (ed.), *Discourses of Sexuality: From Aristotle to AIDS* (University of Michigan Press: Ann Arbor, 1992), pp. 1-46.

9. See Keith Thomas, 'The Double Standard', *Journal of the History of Ideas*, 20.2 (1959), pp. 195-216. For some of the early 'attitude' studies see David J. Pivar, *Purity Crusade: Sexual Morality and Social Control 1868–1900* (Westport: Greenwood Press, 1973), Michael Pearson, *The Age of Consent: Victorian Prostitution and its Enemies* (Newton Abbot: David & Charles,

1972) and Eric Trudgill, *Madonnas and Magdalens: The Origins and Development of Victorian Sexual Attitudes* (London: Heineman, 1976).

10. Steven Marcus, *The Other Victorians: A Study of Sexuality and Pornography in Mid-Nineteenth Century England* (New York: Basic Books, 1966 [1964]).

11. See, for example, Michael Mason, *The Making of Victorian Sexuality* (Oxford: Oxford University Press, 1994), pp. 175-215.

12. For some overviews of social role theory, labelling theory, social interactionism and symbolic interactionism see David R. Maines, *The Faultlines of Consciousness: A View of Interactionism* (New York: de Gruyter, 2001) and Ken Plummer, *Symbolic Interactionism* (Aldershot: Elgar, 1991).

13. Mary McIntosh, 'The Homosexual Role', *Social Problems* 16 (Fall 1968), pp. 182-92.

14. For a sympathetic and insightful assessment of the importance of McIntosh's work see Jeffrey Weeks, 'Mary McIntosh and the "Homosexual Role"', in Weeks, *Making Sexual History*, pp. 53-74.

15. See Weeks, *Making Sexual History*, pp. 53-74 and Kenneth Plummer (ed.), *The Making of the Modern Homosexual* (London: Hutchinson, 1981).

16. For some general overviews of the emergence and concerns of the new social history see Peter N. Stearns, 'The Old Social History and the New', in Mary Kupiec Cayton, Elliot J. Gorn and Peter W. Williams (eds.), *Encyclopedia of American Social History* (New York: Scribner, 1993) and Harold Perkin, 'Social History in Britain', *Journal of Social History* 10.2 (1976), pp. 129-43.

17. See such early social history contributions as Patricia Knight, 'Women and Abortion in Victorian and Edwardian England', *History Workshop* 4 (1977), pp. 57-69, Guido Ruggiero, 'Sexual Criminality in Early Renaissance Venice 1338–1358', *Journal of Social History* 8.4 (1974) and Carol Z. Wiener, 'Sex Roles and Crime in Late Elizabethan Hertfordshire', *Journal of Social History* 8.4 (1974), pp. 38-60.

18. Some of these early articles include Charlotte Wolf, 'Sex Roles as Portrayed in Marriage and the Family Textbooks: Contributions to the Status Quo', *Women's Studies* 3.1 (1975), pp. 45-60, Nancy Cott, 'Passionlessness: An Interpretation of Victorian Sexual Ideology', *Signs* 4.2 (1978), pp. 219-36 and Vern L. Bullough, 'Heresy, Witchcraft and Sexuality', *Journal of Homosexuality* 1.2 (1974), pp. 183-202.

19. See, for example, Boston Women's Health Book Collective, *Our Bodies, Ourselves: A Book by and for Women* (New York, 1973).

20. See the contributions of these scholars in Carol Vance (ed.), *Pleasure and Danger: Exploring Female Sexuality* (Boston: Routledge & Kegan Paul, 1984).

21. See Patricia Branca, *Women in Europe since 1750* (London: C. Helm, 1978) and Renate Bridenthal and Claudia Koonz (eds.), *Becoming Visible: Women in European History* (Boston: Houghton Mifflin, 1977).

22. See Linda Gordon, *Woman's Body, Women's Right: A Social History of Birth Control in America* (New York: Grossman, 1976), Judith Walkowitz, *Prostitu-*

tion and Victorian Society: Women, Class and the State (Cambridge: Cambridge University Press, 1980) and Ruth Rosen, *The Lost Sisterhood: Prostitution in America, 1900–1930* (Baltimore: The Johns Hopkins University Press, 1982).

23. The idea that prostitution is more about men than women was forcefully argued in Carole Pateman, *The Sexual Contract* (Cambridge: Polity Press, 1988), pp. 189-209.

24. Jonathan Katz, *Gay American History: Lesbians and Gay Men in the USA* (New York: Cromwell, 1976). This project of recovery remains a very active area of scholarship. A recent notable addition to this corpus of work is Paul Knobel's *Encyclopedia of Male Homosexual Poetry*, CD-Rom (Sydney: Homo Poetry, 2002), which contains 6,300 detailed entries. Knobel's *Encyclopedia of Male Homosexual Art* is nearing completion.

25. For some useful overviews of this trend see George Chauncey Jr, Martin Duberman and Martha Vicinus (eds.), *Hidden from History: Reclaiming the Gay and Lesbian Past* (New York: New American Library, 1989).

26. Jeffrey Weeks, *Sex, Politics and Society* and John D'Emilio and Estelle B. Freedman, *Intimate Matters: A History of Sexuality in America* (New York: Harper & Row, 1988).

27. Michel Foucault, *The History of Sexuality*. I. *An Introduction* (trans. Robert Hurley; New York: Random House, 1978).

28. For example, 'The Confession of the Flesh', in Colin Gordon (ed.), *Power/Knowledge: Selected Interviews and Other Writings 1972–1977 by Michel Foucault* (New York: Harvester Wheatsheaf, 1980), pp. 194-228. Foucault was also closely associated with another significant effort to undermine the legacy of Freud, and more specifically Lacan, notably Gilles Deleuze and Felix Guattari, *Anti-Oedipus: Capitalism and Schizophrenia* (trans. Robert Hurley, Mark Seem and Helen R. Lane; New York: Viking Press, 1977).

29. David Halperin has also been very assiduous in pointing to the ways in which historians have misconstrued Foucault's arguments (in part to set up a straw scholar to advance their own arguments). See David M. Halperin, 'Forgetting Foucault: Acts, Identities, and the History of Sexuality', *Representations* 63 (Spring 1998), pp. 93-120.

30. See 'The Ethics of the concern of the Self as a Practice of Freedom', in Paul Rabinow (ed.), *Michel Foucault: Ethics – Subjectivity and Truth* (London: Allen Lane, 1997), pp. 281-83.

31. See especially 'Technologies of the Self', in Rabinow (ed.), *Michel Foucault: Ethics – Subjectivity and Truth*, pp. 223-51.

32. For an argument about this controversy and the 'triumph' of social constructionism at the Amsterdam Conference see Weeks, *Making Sexual History*, pp. 125-41.

33. See Rictor Norton, *The Myth of the Modern Homosexual: Queer History and the Search for Cultural Unity* (London: Cassell, 1997).

34. For a discussion of these early movements see Norton, *The Myth of the Modern Homosexual*, pp. 160-79.

35. See Steven Epstein, 'Gay Politics, Ethnic Identity: The Limits of Social Constructionism', *Socialist Review* 93-94 (May–August 1987), pp. 9-54, Jeffrey Weeks, *Coming Out: Homosexual Politics in Britain since the Nineteenth Century* (London: Quartet Books, 1990), and Norton, *The Myth of the Modern Homosexual*, pp. 34-60.

36. John Boswell, *Christianity, Social Tolerance, and Homosexuality: Gay People in Western Europe from the Beginning of the Christian Era to the Fourteenth Century* (Chicago: Chicago University Press, 1980).

37. For Foucault's generally sympathetic appreciation of Boswell's work see James O'Higgins, 'Sexual Choice, Sexual Act: An Interview with Michel Foucault', *Salmagundi* 58-59 (Fall 1982–Winter 1983), pp. 10-12. For some critical reviews of Boswell's work see David Halperin, *One Hundred Years of Homosexuality and Other Essays on Greek Love* (New York: Routledge, 1990).

38. John Boswell, 'Revolutions, Universals and Sexual Categories', *Salmagundi* 58-59 (Fall 1982–Winter 1983), pp. 89-113. See also John Boswell, 'Categories, Experience and Sexuality', in Stein (ed.), *Forms of Desire*, pp. 133-73.

39. John Boswell, *Same-Sex Unions in Pre-Modern Europe* (New York: Villard Books, 1994).

40. Some of their more important works include Weeks, *Sex, Politics and Society*; Weeks, *Coming Out*; Weeks, *Sexuality and its Discontents: Meanings, Myths and Modern Sexualities* (London: Routledge & Kegan Paul, 1985); Weeks, *Against Nature: Essays on History, Sexuality and Identity* (London: Rivers Oram Press, 1991); Kenneth Plummer, *Sexual Stigma: An Interactionist Account* (London: Routledge & Kegan Paul, 1975); Plummer (ed.), *The Making of the Modern Homosexual* (London: Hutchinson, 1981); Plummer, *Telling Sexual Stories: Power, Change and Social Worlds* (London: Routledge, 1995) and D'Emilio and Freedman, *Intimate Matters*.

41. See also John D'Emilio, *Sexual Politics, Sexual Communities: The Making of the Homosexual Minority in the United States, 1940–1970* (Chicago: University of Chicago Press, 2nd edn, 1998) and George Chauncey Jr, *Gay New York: Gender, Urban Culture, and the Making of the Gay Male World, 1890–1940* (New York: Basic Books, 1994).

42. Weeks, *Making Sexual History*, p. vii.

43. Chauncey, *Gay New York*, pp. 1-29.

44. See his important article 'Foucault for Historians', *History Workshop Journal* 14 (Autumn 1982).

45. For example, see Foucault's essays in Graham Burchill, Colin Gordon and Peter Miller (eds.), *The Foucault Effect: Studies in Governmentality* (Chicago: University of Chicago Press, 1991).

46. See John J. Winkler, *The Constraints of Desire: The Anthropology of Sex and Gender in Ancient Greece* (New York: Rouledge, 1990), David M. Halperin, John J. Winkler and Froma I. Zeitlin (eds.), *Before Sexuality: The Construction of Erotic Experience in the Ancient Greek World* (Princeton: Princeton

University Press, 1990) and Arnold I. Davidson, *The Emergence of Sexuality: Historical Epistemology and the Formation of Concepts* (Cambridge, MA: Harvard University Press, 2001).

47. Padgug, 'Sexual Matters: On Conceptualizing Sexuality in History', pp. 43-67.

48. Halperin, 'Forgetting Foucault: Acts, Identities and the History of Sexuality', pp. 93-120. An interesting point in Halperin's discussion is the issue of identity. He points out that this concept is not used by Foucault and points to some of the difficulties in its deployment.

49. Some of his most important contributions include *One Hundred Years of Homosexuality* and *Saint Foucault: Towards a Gay Hagiography* (New York: Oxford University Press, 1995).

50. Ann Laura Stoler, *Race and the Education of Desire: Foucault's History of Sexuality and the Colonial Order of Things* (Durham, NC: Duke University Press, 1995).

51. For a few representative works see Anne McClintock, *Imperial Leather: Race, Gender and Sexuality in the Colonial Contest* (London: Routledge, 1995) and Frederick Cooper and Ann Laura Stoler (eds.), *Tensions of Empire: Colonial Cultures in a Bourgeois World* (Berkeley; London: University of California Press, 1997).

52. Michel Foucault, *The Use of Pleasure: The History of Sexuality* (trans. Robert Hurley; New York: Random House, 1985), II, pp. 1-13.

53. Catharine A MacKinnon, 'Does Sexuality Have a History?', in Stanton, *Discourses of Sexuality*, pp. 117-36.

54. Gayle Rubin, 'Thinking Sex: Notes for a Radical Theory of the Politics of Sexuality', in Vance (ed.), *Pleasure and Danger*, pp. 267-319.

55. Teresa de Lauretis, *Technologies of Gender: Essays on Theory, Film and Fiction* (Bloomington: Indiana University Press, 1987), p. 3.

56. See Carolyn J. Dean, 'The Productive Hypothesis: Foucault, Gender and the History of Sexuality', *History and Theory* 33.3 (1994), pp. 271-96, Lynn Hunt, 'Foucault's Subject in the *History of Sexuality*', in Stanton, *Discourses of Sexuality*, pp. 78-93 and Eloise A. Bruker, 'Hidden Desires and Missing Persons: A feminist Deconstruction of Foucault', *Western Political Quarterly* 43.4 (1990), pp. 811-32.

57. For some good overviews of this huge field of scholarship and some of the earlier feminist collections see Martha Vicinus, 'Sexuality and Power: A Review of Current Work in the History of Sexuality', *Feminist Studies* 8 (1982), pp. 134-56; B. Ruby Rich, 'Feminism and Sexuality in the 1980s', *Feminist Studies* 12 (1986), pp. 525-61; Ann Snitow, Christine Stansell and Sharon Thompson (eds.), *Powers of Desire: The Politics of Sexuality* (New York: Monthly Review Press, 1983) and Kathy Peiss and Christina Simmons (eds.), *Passion and Power: Sexuality in History* (Philadelphia: Temple University Press, 1989).

58. Judith Butler, 'Against Proper Objects', *Differences: A Journal of Feminist Cultural Studies* 6.2-3 (1995), pp. 1-26.

59. Joan W. Scott, 'Gender as a Useful Category of Analysis', in *idem*, *Gender and the Politics of History* (New York: Columbia University Press, 1988), pp. 28-52.

60. Butler, 'Against Proper Objects', pp. 1-26 and Biddy Martin, 'Sexualities without Genders and other Queer Utopias', *Diacritics* 24.2-3 (1994), pp. 104-21.

61. Foucault, *The History of Sexuality*, I, pp. 75-160.

62. See Judith Butler, *Gender Trouble: Feminism and the Subversion of Identity* (New York: Routledge, 1990), *Bodies that Matter: On the Discursive Limits of 'Sex'* (New York: Routledge, 1993) and 'Against Proper Objects', pp. 1-26. See also Teresa de Lauretis, *The Practice of Love: Lesbian Sexuality and Perverse Desire* (Bloomington: Indiana University Press, 1994).

63. See Caroline Walker Bynum, *Fragmentation and Redemption: Essays on Gender and the Human Body in Medieval Religion* (Cambridge, MA: Harvard University Press, 1992), pp. 19-20 and James R. Farr, *Authority and Sexuality in Early Modern Burgundy, 1550–1730* (Oxford: Oxford University Press, 1995), pp. 6-7.

64. See, for example, Gisela Bock and Susan James (eds.), *Beyond Equality and Difference: Citizenship, Feminist Politics and Subjectivity* (London: Routledge, 1992), Nancy Duncan (ed.), *BodySpace: Destabilising Geographies of Gender and Sexuality* (London: Routledge, 1996) and Jeffret T. Nealon, *Alterity Politics: Ethics and Performative Subjectivity* (Durham, NC; London: Duke University Press, 1998).

65. Eve Kosofsky Sedgwick, *Epistemology of the Closet* (Berkeley, CA: University of California Press, 1990), pp. 1-66.

66. See E.A. Grosz, *Volatile Bodies: Toward a Corporeal Feminism* (Bloomington: Indiana University Press, 1994) and *Space, Time, and Perversion: The Politics of Bodies* (New York: Routledge, 1995).

67. Robert A. Nye (ed.), *Sexuality* (Oxford: Oxford University Press, 1999), p. 10.

68. David M. Halperin, 'In Defense of Historicism' in *idem*, *How to Do the History of Homosexuality* (Chicago: Chicago University Press, 2002), p. 12.

69. David M. Halperin, 'How to Do the History of Male Homosexuality', in *How to Do the History of Homosexuality*, pp. 104-37.

Chapter 2

1. I am not suggesting here that Greek and Roman antiquity was necessarily the 'cradle of civilization'. In recent years a number of scholars, notably Martin Bernal and Paul Cartledge, have questioned this traditional assumption. Nonetheless, classical civilization has traditionally been considered, by scholars and popular commentators alike, one of the most important sources for key elements of Western culture. See, in particular, Paul Cartledge, *The Greeks: A Portrait of Self and Others* (Oxford: Oxford University Press, 1993), pp. 1-7.

2. David M. Halperin, John J. Winkler and Froma I. Zeitlin (eds.), *Before Sexuality: The Construction of Erotic Experience in the Ancient Greek World*

(Princeton: Princeton University Press, 1990), pp. 3-20 and Hans Licht, *Sexual Life in Ancient Greece* (trans. J.H. Freese; London: Routledge, 1932).

3. J.Z. Eglinton, *Greek Love* (New York: O. Layton Press, 1964).

4. K.J. Dover, *Greek Homosexuality* (London: Duckworth, 1978).

5. Eva C. Keuls, *The Reign of the Phallus* (New York: Harper & Row, 1985).

6. Dover, *Greek Homosexuality*, pp. vii-viii and 1-3.

7. Sigmund Freud, *On Sexuality: Pelican Freud Library Volume 7* (trans. James Strachey; Harmondsworth: Penguin, 1977), p. 61.

8. David M. Halperin, *One Hundred Years of Homosexuality and Other Essays on Greek Love* (New York: Routledge, 1990) and Paul Veyne, 'Homosexuality in Ancient Rome', in Philippe Aries and André Béjin (eds.), *Western Sexuality: Practice and Precept in Past and Present Times* (Oxford: Basil Blackwell, 1985), pp. 26-35.

9. John J. Winkler, *The Constraints of Desire: The Anthropology of Sex and Gender in Ancient Greece* (New York: Routledge, 1990), pp. 45-70.

10. Mary Lefkowitz, *Women in Greek Myth* (Baltimore: The Johns Hopkins University Press, 1986).

11. Daniel A. Garrison, *Sexual Culture in Ancient Greece* (Norman: University of Oklahoma Press, 2000).

12. For example, at the siege of Perusia, Perusians fired sling bullets inscribed with sexual taunts about Octavian's effeminacy and love of sodomy. See Judith P. Hallett, 'Perjusinae Glandes and the Changing Image of Augustus', *American Journal of Ancient History* 2 (1977), pp. 151-71.

13. Danielle Allen, *The World of Prometheus: The Politics of Punishment in Democratic Athens* (Princeton: Princeton University Press, 2000), pp. 214-15.

14. See Cartledge, *The Greeks*, pp. 63-90 and Dover, *Greek Homosexuality*, pp. 81-110.

15. Eva Cantarella, *Bisexuality in the Ancient World* (trans. Cormac O Cuilleanain; New Haven: Yale University Press, 2nd edn, 2002), pp. ix-x.

16. David M. Halperin, 'Why is Diotima a Woman? Platonic *Eros* and the Figuration of Gender', in Halperin, Winkler and Zeitlin, *Before Sexuality*, pp. 257-308.

17. David Cohen, *Law, Sexuality and Society: The Enforcement of Morals in Classical Athens* (Cambridge: Cambridge University Press, 1991), pp. 180-85 and *Law, Violence and Community in Classical Athens* (Cambridge: Cambridge University Press, 1995), pp. 186-87.

18. Cantarella, *Bisexuality in the Ancient World*, pp. 156-64.

19. Martha Nussbaum has highlighted the complex ethical considerations surrounding pederasty, arguing that Foucault has not fully recognized the problems arising in such relationships. See Martha Nussbaum, 'Eros and Ethical Norms: Philosophers Respond to a Cultural Dilemma' in Martha C. Nussbaum and Juha Sihvola (eds.), *The Sleep of Reason: Erotic Experience and Sexual Ethics in Ancient Greece and Rome* (Chicago: Chicago University Press, 2002), pp. 55-94.

20. Cantarella, *Bisexuality in the Ancient World*.

21. Michel Foucault, *The Use of Pleasure: The History of Sexuality* (trans. Robert Hurley; New York: Random House, 1985), II, pp. 187-203.

22. Foucault, *The Use of Pleasure* and *The Care of the Self: The History of Sexuality*, III (trans. Robert Hurley; New York: Random House, 1986). On the rise of interest in continence see also Aline Rousselle, *Porneia: On Desire and the Body in Antiquity* (trans. Felicia Pheasant; Oxford: Basil Blackwell, 1988), pp. 129-59.

23. See some of the articles in the excellent collection, Judith P. Hallett and Marilyn B. Skinner (eds.), *Roman Sexualities* (Princeton: Princeton University Press, 1997).

24. For the greater social status of Roman women see Beryl Rawson (ed.), *The Family in Ancient Rome: New Perspectives* (London: Croom Helm, 1992).

25. See Bernadette J. Brooten, *Love between Women: Early Christian Responses to Female Homoeroticism* (Chicago: Chicago University Press, 1996), pp. 190-91.

26. Lesley Dean-Jones, *Women's Bodies in Classical Greek Science* (Oxford: Clarendon Press, 1994), pp. 247-48.

27. Winkler, *Constraints of Desire*, pp. 188-209. See also Christopher A. Faraone, 'Agents and Victims: Constructions of Gender and Desire in Ancient Greek Love Magic', in Nussbaum and Sihvola (eds.), *The Sleep of Reason*, pp. 400-26.

28. See Helene P. Foley (ed.), *Reflections of Women in Antiquity* (New York: Gordon and Breach, 1981), Averil Cameron and Amelie Kuhrt (eds.), *Images of Women in Antiquity* (London: Croom Helm, 1983) and Eva Cantarella, *Pandora's Daughters: The Role and Status of Women in Greek and Roman Antiquity* (Baltimore: The Johns Hopkins University Press, 1987).

29. David M. Halperin, 'Homosexuality', in Simon Hornblower and Anthony Spawforth (eds.), *Oxford Companion to Classical Civilisation* (Oxford: Oxford University Press, 1998), pp. 353-54.

30. See Maarit Kaimio, 'Erotic Experience in the Conjugal Bed: Good Wives in Greek Tragedy', in Nussbaum and Sihvola (eds.), *The Sleep of Reason*, pp. 95-119.

31. See Lin Foxall, 'Pandora Unbound: A Feminist Critique of Foucault's *History of Sexuality*', in David H.J. Larmour, Paul Allen Miller and Charles Platter (eds.), *Rethinking Sexuality* (Princeton: Princeton University Press, 1998), pp. 132-33 and Susan G. Cole, 'Greek Sanctions against Sexual Assault', *Classical Philology* 79 (1984), pp. 111-13.

32. Winkler, *Constraints of Desire*, pp. 129-209.

33. Foxall, 'Pandora Unbound', pp. 132-33, John Boswell, *Christianity, Social Tolerance and Homosexuality: Gay People in Western Europe from the Beginning of the Christian Era to the Fourteenth Century* (Chicago: Chicago University Press, 1980), pp. 220-21 and *idem*, *Same-Sex Unions in Premodern Europe* (New York: Villard Books, 1994), p. 71.

34. See Dean-Jones, *Women's Bodies in Classical Greek Science*, pp. 225-29 and

Helen King, *Hippocrates' Women: Reading the Female Body in Ancient Greece* (London: Routledge, 1998).

35. Thomas Laqueur, *Making Sex: Body and Gender from the Greeks to Freud* (Cambridge, MA: Harvard University Press, 1990), pp. 25-62.

36. John Thorp, 'The Social Construction of Homosexuality', *Phoenix* 46 (1992), pp. 54-61 and Cohen, *Law, Sexuality and Society*, pp. 171-202.

37. Cantarella, *Bisexuality in the Ancient World*, pp. viii-ix.

38. Boswell, *Same-Sex Unions in Premodern Europe*, pp. 53-107.

39. David Leitao, 'The Legend of the Sacred Band' in Nussbaum and Sihvola (eds.), *The Sleep of Reason*, pp. 143-69.

40. David M. Halperin, 'How to Do the History of Male Homosexuality', in *How to Do the History of Homosexuality*, pp. 104-37.

41. Williams, *Roman Homosexuality*, pp. 225-29.

42. Foxall, 'Pandora Unbound', pp. 134-35.

43. Maud W. Gleason, *Making Men: Sophists and Self-Presentation in Ancient Rome* (Princeton: Princeton University Press, 1995) and 'The Semiotics of Gender: Physiognomy and Self-Fashioning in the Second Century C.E.', in Halperin, Winkler and Zeitlin, *Before Sexuality*, pp. 389-415.

44. Amy Richlin, 'Not before Homosexuality: The Materiality of *Cinaedus* and the Roman Law against Love between Men', *Journal of the History of Sexuality* 3.4 (1993), pp. 523-73, *The Garden of Priapus: Sexuality and Aggression in Roman Humor* (New York: Oxford University Press, 2nd edn, 1992) and *Pornography and Representation in Greece and Rome* (New York: Oxford University Press, 1992).

45. David M. Halperin, 'Forgetting Foucault: Acts, Identities and the History of Sexuality', *Representations* 63 (Spring 1998), pp. 93-120.

46. Gleason, 'The Semiotics of Gender', and Craig A. Williams, *Roman Homosexuality: Ideologies of Masculinity in Classical Antiquity* (New York: Oxford University Press, 1999), pp. 160-224.

47. Michel Foucault, 'Afterword: The Subject and Power', in Hubert L. Dreyfus and Paul Rabinow, *Michel Foucault: Beyond Structuralism and Hermeneutics* (Brighton: Harvester, 1982), pp. 208-26.

48. Rabun Taylor, 'Two Pathic Subcultures in Ancient Rome', *Journal of the History of Sexuality* 7.3 (1997), pp. 319-71.

49. Halperin, 'How to Do the History of Male Homosexuality', pp. 87-124.

50. Veyne, 'Homosexuality in Rome'.

51. Williams, *Roman Homosexuality*, pp. 91-93.

52. Winkler, *Constraints of Desire*, pp. 45-70.

Chapter 3

1. Dominic Montserrat, *Sex and Society in Graeco-Roman Egypt* (London: Kegan Paul, 1996), pp. 163-66.

2. Dyan Elliott, *Spiritual Marriage: Sexual Abstinence in Medieval Wedlock* (Princeton: Princeton University Press, 1993), pp. 16-50. See also Uta Ranke-Heinemann, *Eunuchs for Heaven: The Catholic Church and Sexuality* (trans. John Brownjohn; London: Deutsch, 1990), pp. 62-83.

3. Michel Foucault, *The Use of Pleasure: The History of Sexuality* (trans. Robert Hurley; New York: Random House, 1985), II, pp. 33-93.

4. Quoted in Vern L. Bullough, 'Introduction: The Christian Inheritance', in Vern L. Bullough and James Brundage (eds.), *Sexual Practices and the Medieval Church* (Buffalo: Prometheus Books, 1982), p. 3.

5. Lesley Dean-Jones, *Women's Bodies in Classical Greek Science* (Oxford: Clarendon Press, 1994), pp. 225-50.

6. Ranke-Heinemann, *Eunuchs for Heaven*, pp. 12-17 and 35-50.

7. Peter Brown, *The Body and Society: Men, Women and Sexual Renunciation in Early Christianity* (New York: Columbia University Press, 1988), pp. 213-40.

8. See Peter Brown, *Religion and Society in the Age of Saint Augustine* (New York: Harper & Row, 1972), p. 17.

9. Elizabeth A. Clark, *Ascetic Piety and Women's Faith: Essays on Late Ancient Christianity* (Lewiston: E. Mellen Press, 1986). See also Karen Jo Torjesen, *When Women were Priests: Women's Leadership in the Early Church and the Scandal of their Subordination in the Rise of Christianity* (New York: Harper & Row, 1995) and M.H. King, *The Desert Mothers* (Toronto: Toronto University Press, 2nd edn, 1989).

10. See Bullough, 'Introduction: The Christian Inheritance', pp. 1-12. For an argument that early Christians 'misconstrued' the teachings of Christ, promoting anti-sexual ideas and practices in the context of their own struggle for power and influence see Ranke-Heinemann, *Eunuchs for Heaven*, pp. 18-34.

11. Ranke-Heinemann, *Sexual Eunuchs*, p. 9.

12. Elliott, *Spiritual Marriage*, pp. 16-50.

13. Most of these examples are taken from Ranke-Heinemann, *Eunuchs for Heaven*, pp. 1-50. The examples of Cato and Laelius are from Foucault, *The Use of Pleasure*, pp. 17-18.

14. Elaine Pagels, *Adam, Eve and the Serpent* (New York: Random House, 1988).

15. See for example Aline Rousselle, *Porneia: On Desire and the Body in Antiquity* (trans. Felicia Pheasant; Oxford: Basil Blackwell, 1988), Halvor Moxnes (ed.), *Constructing Early Christian Families* (London: Routledge, 1997) and Patrick D.G. Riley, *Civilising Sex: On Chastity and the Common Good* (Edinburgh: T. & T. Clark, 2000).

16. John Boswell, *Same-Sex Unions in Premodern Europe* (New York: Villard Books, 1994), pp. 108-13.

17. Boswell, *Same-Sex Unions*, pp. 108-109.

18. Bernadette J. Brooten, *Love between Women: Early Christian Responses to Female Homoeroticism* (Chicago: Chicago University Press, 1996).

19. Brooten, *Love between Women*, pp. 1-26.

20. David M. Halperin, 'The First Homosexuality?', in *idem, How to Do the History of Homosexuality* (Chicago: Chicago University Press, 2002), pp. 48-80.

21. Brooten, *Love between Women*, p. 17.

22. Halperin, 'The First Homosexuality?', pp. 48-80.

23. One of the best introductions to this subtle shift in emphasis and concern from power/knowledge to truth, freedom and the subject is Michel Foucault, 'Afterword: The Subject and Power', in Hubert L. Dreyfus and Paul Rabinow, *Michel Foucault: Beyond Structuralism and Hermeneutics* (Brighton: Harvester, 1982), pp. 208-26.

24. For a general discussion of the larger project and its rationale see Foucault, *The Use of Pleasure*, pp. 3-24.

25. See for example Eva Cantarella, *Bisexuality in the Ancient World* (trans. Cormac O. Cuilleanain; New Haven, Yale University Press, 2nd edn, 2002), pp. ix-x, John Thorp, 'The Social Construction of Homosexuality', *Phoenix* 46 (1992), p. 61 and Amy Richlin, 'Not before Homosexuality: The Materiality of *Cinaedus* and the Roman Law against Love between Men', *Journal of the History of Sexuality* 3.4 (1993), pp. 523-73.

26. Michel Foucault, *The Care of the Self: The History of Sexuality* (trans. Robert Hurley; New York: Random House, 1986), III, p. 240.

27. See Richard Saller, 'Men's Age at Marriage and its Consequences for the Roman Family', *Classical Philology* 82 (1987), pp. 21-34 and Susan Treggiari, *Roman Marriage: Iusti Coniuges from the Time of Cicero to the Time of Ulpian* (Oxford: Clarendon Press, 1991).

28. See Eva Cantarella, 'Marriage and Sexuality in Republican Rome: A Roman Conjugal Love Story', in Martha C. Nussbaum and Juha Sihvola (eds.), *The Sleep of Reason: Erotic Experience and Sexual Ethics in Ancient Greece and Rome* (Chicago: Chicago University Press, 2002), pp. 269-82 and Keith R. Bradley, *Discovering the Roman Family: Studies in Roman Social History* (New York: Oxford University Press, 1991).

29. See David Cohen and Richard Saller, 'Foucault on Sexuality in Greco-Roman Antiquity', in Jan Goldstein (ed.), *Foucault and the Writing of History* (Oxford: Basil Blackwell, 1994), pp. 35-59 and David H.J. Larmour, Paul Allen Miller and Charles Platter, 'Introduction', in *idem* (eds.), *Rethinking Sexuality* (Princeton: Princeton University Press, 1998), pp. 26-28.

30. See Craig A. Williams, *Roman Homosexuality: Ideologies of Masculinity in Classical Antiquity* (New York: Oxford University Press, 1999), pp. 3-8.

31. Eva Cantarella, *Bisexuality in the Ancient World*, pp. 156-64.

32. See the entries on 'Augustus', 'marriage law' and 'women' in Simon Hornblower and Anthony Spawforth (eds.), *The Oxford Companion to Classical Civilisation* (Oxford: Oxford University Press, 1998).

33. Hornblower and Spawforth (eds.), *Classical Civilisation*, pp. 235-40.

34. Brown, *Body and Society*, see especially the Preface and the Epilogue.

35. Peter Brown, 'Bodies and Minds: Sexuality and Renunciation in Early Christianity', in David M. Halperin, John J. Winkler and Froma I. Zeitlin (eds.), *Before Sexuality: The Construction of Erotic Experience in the Ancient Greek World* (Princeton: Princeton University Press, 1990), p. 481.

36. See also Richard Sennett, *Flesh and Stone: The Body and the City in Western Civilization* (London: Faber, 1994), pp. 124-48.

37. Erin Sawyer, 'Celibate Pleasures: Masculinity, Desire, and Asceticism in Augustine', *Journal of the History of Sexuality* 6.1 (1995), pp. 1-29 and Kim Power, *Veiled Desire: Augustine's Writing on Women* (London: Longman & Todd, 1995).

38. Brown, *Body and Society*, p. 393.

39. Brown, *Body and Society*, p. 430.

40. Boswell, *Same-Sex Unions*, chapter 5.

41. Boswell, *Same-Sex Unions*, p. 109.

42. James Brundage, *Sex, Law and Marriage in the Middle Ages* (Brookfield: Variorum, 1993), pp. 361-85.

43. Vern L. Bullough, 'The Formation of Medieval Ideals: Christian Theory and Christian Practice' in Bullough and Brundage (eds.), *Sexual Practices and the Medieval Church*, pp. 14-21.

44. Brundage, *Sex, Law and Marriage in the Middle Ages*, pp. 195-210.

Chapter 4

1. For a brilliant evocation of the Inquisition and the clash between Church teachings and folk ideas see Carlo Ginsburg, *The Cheese and the Worms: The Cosmos and a Sixteenth-Century Miller* (trans. John and Anne Tedeschi; London: Routledge & Kegan Paul, 1980). For the wider context of heresy and witchcraft see Malcolm Lambert, *Medieval Heresy: Popular Movements from the Gregorian Reform to the Reformation* (Oxford: Basil Blackwell, 2nd edn, 1977); Jeffrey Burton Russell, *Witchcraft in the Middle Ages* (Ithaca: Cornell University Press, 1972); Robin Briggs, *Witches and Neighbors: The Social and Cultural Context of European Witchcraft* (New York: Penguin, 1996) and Lyndal Roper, *Oedipus and the Devil: Witchcraft, Sexuality and Religion in Early Modern Europe* (London: Routledge, 1994).

2. For further discussion on these teachings, in addition to sources cited in the previous chapter, see Dyan Elliott, *Fallen Bodies: Pollution, Sexuality and Demonology in the Middle Ages* (Philadelphia: University of Pennsylvania Press, 1999), Merry E. Wiesner-Hanks, *Christianity and Sexuality in the Early Modern World: Regulating Desire, Reforming Practice* (London: Routledge, 2000), pp. 21-58 and Dale B. Martin, 'Paul without Passion: On Paul's Rejection of Desire in Sex and Marriage', in Halvor Moxnes (ed.), *Constructing Early Christian Families: Family as Social Reality and Metaphor* (London: Routledge, 1997), pp. 201-15.

3. Elliott, *Fallen Bodies*, p. 82

4. See Marina Warner, *Alone of All Her Sex: The Myth and Cult of the Virgin Mary* (New York: Knopf, 1976).

5. Carolinne White, *Christian Friendship in the Fourth Century* (Cambridge: Cambridge University Press, 1992).

6. See John Boswell, *Same-Sex Unions in Premodern Europe* (New York: Villard Books, 1994), p. 109.

7. See R.I. Moore, *The Formation of a Persecuting Society: Power and Deviance in Western Europe, 950–1250* (Oxford: Basil Blackwell, 1987); Thomas N.

Tentler, *Sin and Confession on the Eve of the Reformation* (Princeton: Princeton University Press, 1977); Elliott, *Fallen Bodies*, pp. 81-126 and Wiesner-Hanks, *Christianity and Sexuality*, pp. 34-44.

8. See Mark D. Jordan, *The Invention of Sodomy in Christian Theology* (Chicago: Chicago University Press, 1997). See also, Elliott, *Fallen Bodies*, pp. 14-60; Dyan Elliott, *Spiritual Marriage: Sexual Abstinence in Medieval Wedlock* (Princeton: Princeton University Press, 1993), pp. 16-50; Kim Power, *Veiled Desire: Augustine's Writings on Women* (London: Darton, Longman & Todd, 1995) and Wiesner-Hanks, *Christianity and Sexuality*, pp. 34-44.

9. See Aline Rousselle, *Porneia: Desire and the Body in Antiquity* (trans. Felicia Pheasant; Oxford: Basil Blackwell, 1988), and Bernadette J. Brooten, *Love between Women: Early Christian Responses to Female Homoeroticism* (Chicago: Chicago University Press, 1996), pp. 271-80.

10. See for example Jeffrey Richards, *Sex, Dissidence and Damnation: Minority Groups in the Middle Ages* (London: Routledge, 1991), pp. 1-41, Georges Duby, *The Knight, the Lady and the Priest: The Making of Modern Marriage in Medieval France* (trans. Barbara Bray; Harmondsworth: Penguin, 1984) and Tentler, *Sin and the Confession*.

11. Pierre Payer, *Sex and the Penitentials* (Toronto: University of Toronto Press, 1984), p. 121. Payer provides a very useful and insightful overview of the history of penitentials. Other interesting accounts of how the church sought to govern sexuality through the technique of the confessional and penitentials include Stephen Haliczer, *Sexuality in the Confessional: A Sacrament Profaned* (New York: Oxford University Press, 1996) and Julie Ann Smith, *Ordering Women's Lives: Penitentials and Nunnery Rules in the Early Medieval West* (Aldershot: Ashgate, 2001).

12. See Carolyn Dinshaw, *Getting Medieval: Sexualities and Communities, Pre and Postmodern* (Durham, NC: Duke University Press, 1999), pp. 55-99.

13. Elizabeth Makowski, *Canon Law and Cloistered Women: Periculoso and its Commentators, 1298–1545* (Washington, DC: Catholic University Press, 1997), p. 71.

14. Wiesner-Hanks, *Christianity and Sexuality*, pp. 118-21.

15. Guido Ruggiero, *The Boundaries of Eros: Sex, Crime and Sexuality in Renaissance Venice* (Oxford: Oxford University Press, 1985), pp. 115-16.

16. Mary Elizabeth Perry, 'The "Nefarious Sin" in Early Modern Seville', in Kent Gerard and Gert Hekma (eds.), *The Pursuit of Sodomy: Male Homosexuality in Renaissance and Enlightenment Europe* (New York: Harrington Park Press, 1989), pp. 67-90.

17. Judith Brown, *Immodest Acts: The Life of a Lesbian Nun in Renaissance Italy* (New York: Oxford University Press, 1986).

18. See, for example, Elizabeth A. Clark, *Ascetic Piety and Women's Faith: Essays in Late Ancient Christianity* (Lewiston: E. Mellen Press, 1986), Susanna Elm, *'Virgins of God': The Making of Asceticism in Late Antiquity* (Oxford: Oxford University Press, 1996) and Jane Schulenburg, *Forgetful of their Sex: Female Sanctity and Society ca. 500–1100* (Chicago: University of Chicago Press, 1998).

19. See Sabina Flanagan, *Hildegard of Bingen, 1098–1179* (London: Routledge, 1989) and Maud Burnett McInerney, *Hildegard of Bingen* (New York: Garland, 1998).

20. Most notably in Caroline Walker Bynum, *Fragmentation and Redemption: Essays on Gender and the Human Body in Medieval Religion* (Cambridge, MA: Harvard University Press, 1991).

21. Bynum, *Fragmentation and Redemption*, pp. 181-238.

22. See Margaret McGlynn and Richard J. Moll, 'Chaste Marriage in the Middle Ages: "It were to hire a greet merite"'; Jacqueline Murray, 'Hiding Behind the Universal Man: Male Sexuality in the Middle Ages', in Vern L. Bullough and James A. Brundage (eds.), *Handbook of Medieval Sexuality* (New York: Garland, 1996), pp. 103-47; Henry Ansgar Kelly, *Love and Marriage in the Age of Chaucer* (Ithaca: Cornell University Press, 1975); John Baldwin, *The Language of Sex: Five Voices from Northern France around 1200* (Chicago: Chicago University Press, 1994) and Dinshaw, *Getting Medieval*, pp. 100-82.

23. Thomas Laqueur, *Making Sex: Body and Gender from the Greeks to Freud* (Cambridge, MA: Harvard University Press, 1990), pp. 63-64.

24. See Joan Cadden, *Meanings of Sexual Difference in the Middle Ages: Medicine, Science and Culture* (Cambridge: Cambridge University Press, 1993), and 'Western Medicine and Natural Philosophy', in Bullough and Brundage (eds.), *Handbook of Medieval Sexuality*, pp. 51-80. See also Danielle Jascquart and Claude Thomasset, *Sexuality and Medicine in the Middle Ages* (trans. Matthew Adamson; Princeton: Princeton University Press, 1988).

25. Georges Duby, *Love and Marriage in the Middle Ages* (trans. Jane Dunnett; Cambridge: Polity Press, 1994), pp. 22-35.

26. See, for example, Bernard O'Donoghue, *The Courtly Love Tradition* (Manchester: Manchester University Press, 1982), Stephen C. Jaeger, *The Origins of Courtliness: Civilizing Trends and the Formation of Courtly Ideals, 939–1210* (Philadelphia, 1985) and Nathaniel B. Smith and Joseph T. Snow (eds.), *The Expansions and Transformations of Courtly Literature* (Athens, GA: University of Georgia Press, 1980).

27. See Mikhail Bakhtin, *Rabelais and his World* (trans. Hélene Iswolsky; Cambridge, MA: M.I.T. Press, 1968).

28. See Thomas Goddard Bergin, *Boccaccio* (New York: Viking Press, 1981); David Wallace, *Chaucer and the Early Writings of Boccaccio* (Woodbridge: D.S. Brewer, 1985); Donald R. Howard, *Chaucer and the Medieval World* (London: Weidenfeld & Nicolson, 1987) and Murray, 'Hiding behind the Universal Man', pp. 138-39.

29. For discussion of the interactions between elite and popular ideas of sex, biology, medicine and science see, for example, Paul Slack, 'Mirrors of Health and Treasures of Poor Men', in Charles Webster (ed.), *Health, Medicine and Mortality in the Sixteenth Century* (Cambridge: Cambridge University Press, 1979), pp. 237-73 and Herman W. Roodenburg, 'The Autobiography of Isabella de Moerloose: Sex, Childbearing and Popular

Belief in Seventeenth Century Holland', *Journal of Social History* 18 (1985), pp. 517-40.

30. See Cadden, 'Western Medicine and Natural Philosophy'.
31. James A. Brundage, 'The Problem of Impotence', in Vern L. Bullough and James A. Brundage, *Sexual Practices and the Medieval Church* (Buffalo: Prometheus Books, 1982), pp. 135-40.
32. Jean-Louis Flandrin, 'Sex in Married Life in the Early Middle Ages: The Church's Teaching and Behavioural Reality', in Philippe Aries and André Béjin (eds.), *Western Sexuality: Practice and Precept in Past and Present Times* (trans. Anthony Forster; Oxford: Basil Blackwell, 1985), pp. 114-16.
33. Laqueur, *Making Sex*, pp. 1-24.
34. Laqueur, *Making Sex*, pp. 70-98.
35. In addition to Laqueur see also Jascquart and Thomasset, *Sexuality and Medicine in the Middle Ages*, Londa Schiebinger, *The Mind Has No Sex? Women and the Origins of Modern Science* (Cambridge, MA: Harvard University Press, 1989), pp. 191-200, Katherine Park, *Doctors and Medicine in Early Renaissance Florence* (Princeton: Princeton University Press, 1985) and Carolyn Merchant, *The Death of Nature: Women, Ecology and the Scientific Revolution* (San Francisco: Harper & Row, 1980).
36. Laqueur, *Making Sex*, pp. 96-113.
37. Laqueur, *Making Sex*, pp. 1-27.
38. Laqueur, *Making Sex*, pp. 136-37.
39. Laqueur, *Making Sex*, pp. 122-34.
40. See James A. Brundage, 'Sexual Behaviour and Legal Norms in Medieval Europe', in Jacqueline Murray and Konrad Eisenbichler (eds.), *Desire and Discipline Sex and Sexuality in the Premodern West* (Toronto: Toronto University Press, 1996), pp. 23-41.
41. See Murray, 'Hiding behind the Universal Man', pp. 129-32.
42. See for example Kate Chedgzoy, Melanie Hansen and Suzanne Trill (eds.), *Voicing Women: Gender and Sexuality in Early Modern Writing* (Keele: Keele University Press, 1996) and Noel James Menuge (ed.), *Medieval Women and the Law* (Woodbridge: Boydell Press, 2000).
43. Joanne M. Ferraro, *Marriage Wars in Late Renaissance Venice* (Oxford: Oxford University Press, 2001).
44. Ruth Mazo Karras, *Common Women: Prostitution and Sexuality in Medieval England* (Oxford: Oxford University Press, 1996) and 'Prostitution and the Question of Sexual Identity in Medieval Europe', *Journal of Women's History* 11.2 (1999), pp. 159-77. See also Carla Freccero, 'Acts, Identities, and Sexuality's (Pre) Modern Regimes', *Journal of Women's History* 11.2 (1999), pp. 186-92 and David M. Halperin, 'The First Homosexuality?', in David M. Halperin, *How to Do the History of Homosexuality* (Chicago: University of Chicago Press, 2002), pp. 66-67.
45. Philippe Aries, 'The Indissoluble Union' in Aries and Bejin (eds.), *Western Sexuality*, pp. 140-57.
46. See Murray, 'Hiding behind the Universal Man', pp. 123-52 and Ruggerio, *The Boundaries of Eros*, pp. 16-108.

47. See, for example, Brooten, *Love between Women*, Jacqueline Murray, 'Twice Marginal and Twice Invisible: Lesbians in the Middle Ages', in Bullough and Brundage (eds.), *Handbook of Medieval Sexuality*, pp. 191-222 and Brown, *Immodest Acts*.

48. See Joseph Cady, 'Masculine Love, Renaissance Writing and the "New Invention" of Homosexuality', in Claude J. Summers (ed.), *Homosexuality in Renaissance and Enlightenment England: Literary Representations in Historical Context*, special issue *Journal of Homosexuality* 23.1-2 (1992), pp. 9-40, 'Renaissance Awareness and the Language for Heterosexuality "love" and "Feminine Love"', in Claude J. Summers and Ted-Larry Pebworth (eds.), *Renaissance Discourses of Desire* (Columbia, MI: University of Missouri Press, 1993), pp. 143-58 and Giovanni Dall'Orto, 'Socratic Love as a Disguise for Same-Sex Love in the Italian Renaissance', in Gerard and Hekma, *The Pursuit of Sodomy*, pp. 33-66.

49. John Boswell, *Christianity, Social Tolerance, and Homosexuality: Gay People in Western Europe from the Beginning of the Christian Era to the Fourteenth Century* (Chicago: Chicago University Press, 1980).

50. Boswell, *Christianity, Social Tolerance*, pp. 333-34.

51. Boswell, *Christianity, Social Tolerance*, pp. 243-66.

52. Ruggiero, *The Boundaries of Eros*, pp. 109-45, and Alan Bray, *Homosexuality in Renaissance England* (London: Gay Men's Press, 1982), pp. 81-114.

53. See B.R. Burg, *Sodomy and the Perception of Evil: English Sea Rovers in the Seventeenth-Century Caribbean* (New York: New York University Press, 1983).

54. Payer, *Sex and the Penitentials* and James A. Brundage, *Law, Sex and Christian Society in Medieval Europe* (Chicago: University of Chicago Press, 1987).

55. Michael Rocke, *Forbidden Friendships: Homosexuality and Male Culture in Renaissance Florence* (Oxford: Oxford University Press, 1996).

56. Rocke, *Forbidden Friendships*, pp. 10-15.

57. This resemblance is noted by some historians such as Ruggiero, *The Boundaries of Eros*, p. 116, but it is only a passing remark. The full implications of this resemblance have yet to be explored.

Chapter 5

1. See Lynn Hunt (ed.), *The Invention of Pornography: Obscenity and the Origins of Modernity 1500–1800* (New York: Zone Books, 1993), Robert Darnton, *The Literary Underground of the Old Regime* (Cambridge, MA: Harvard University Press, 1982) and *idem, The Corpus of Clandestine Literature in France 1769–1789* (New York: W.W. Norton, 1995).

2. Guido Ruggiero, *The Boundaries of Eros: Sex, Crime and Sexuality in Renaissance Venice* (Oxford: Oxford University Press, 1985), Alan Macfarlane, *Marriage and Love in England: Modes of Reproduction 1300–1840* (Oxford: Basil Blackwell, 1986) and *idem, The Origins of English Individualism: The Family, Property and Social Transition* (Oxford: Basil Blackwell, 1978).

3. Merry E. Wiesner-Hanks, *Christianity and Sexuality in the Early Modern World: Regulating Desire, Reforming Practice* (London: Routledge, 2000), pp. 60-93.

4. See, for example, Steven Ozment, *When Fathers Ruled: Family Life in Reformation Europe* (Cambridge, MA: Harvard University Press, 1983); Lorna Jane Abray, *The People's Reformation: Magistrates, Clergy, and Commons in Strasbourg 1500–1598* (Ithaca: Cornell University Press, 1985); Edmund Leites, *Puritan Conscience and Modern Sexuality* (New Haven: Yale University Press, 1986) and Martin Ingram, *Church Courts, Sex and Marriage in England, 1570–1640* (Cambridge: Cambridge University Press, 1987).

5. See Wiesner-Hanks, *Christianity and Sexuality in the Early Modern World*, pp. 60-62.

6. See Eamon Duffy, *The Stripping of the Altars: Traditional Religion in England, 1400–1580* (New Haven: Yale University Press, 1996) and *The Voices of Morebath: Reformation and Rebellion in an English Village* (New Haven: Yale University Press, 2001). See also Christopher Haigh, *English Reformations: Religion, Politics and Society under the Tudors* (Oxford: Clarendon Press, 1993).

7. See, for example, Warren Chernaik, *Sexual Freedom in Restoration Literature* (Cambridge: Cambridge University Press, 1995); Harold Weber, *The Restoration Rake Hero: Transformations in Sexual Understanding in Seventeenth Century England* (Madison: University of Wisconsin Press, 1986); James Turner, 'The Properties of Libertinism', in R.P. Maccubbin (ed.), *'Tis Nature's Fault: Unauthorized Sexuality during the Eighteenth Century in England* (Cambridge: Cambridge University Press, 1987), pp. 75-87; Stephanie Wood, 'Sexual Violation in the Conquest of the Americas' and Wayne Bodle, 'Soldiers in Love: Patrolling the Gendered Frontiers of the Early Republic', in Merril D. Smith (ed.), *Sex and Sexuality in Early America* (New York: New York University Press, 1998).

8. Edward Shorter, *The Making of the Modern Family* (London: Collins, 1976), pp. 255-68.

9. See, for example, Margaret Hunt, *The Middling Sort: Commerce, Gender and the Family in England, 1680–1780* (Berkeley, CA: University of California Press, 1996); Richard Rand, *Intimate Encounter: Love and Domesticity in Eighteenth Century France* (Princeton: Princeton University Press, 1997); Peter C. Hoffer (ed.), *Colonial Women and Domesticity: Selected Articles on Gender in Early America* (New York: Garland, 1988) and Cynthia A. Kierner, *Beyond the Household: Women's Place in the Early South, 1700–1835* (Ithaca: Cornell University Press, 1998).

10. Thomas Laqueur, *Making Sex: Body and Gender from the Greeks to Freud* (Cambridge, MA: Harvard University Press, 1990), pp. 149-92.

11. Randolph Trumbach, *Sex and the Gender Revolution*. I. *Heterosexuality and the Third Gender in Enlightenment London* (Chicago: Chicago University Press, 1998).

12. See Linda Gordon, *Woman's Body, Woman's Right: A Social History of Birth*

Control in America (New York: Grossman, 1976), pp. 47-49 and John Demos, 'Demography and Psychology in the Historical Study of Family Life: A Personal Report', in Peter Laslett and Richard Wall (eds.), *Household and Family in Past Times* (Cambridge: Cambridge University Press, 1979), p. 56.

13. For a good summary of some of this evidence see R.A. Houston, 'The Population History of Britain and Ireland 1500–1750', in Michael Anderson (ed.), *British Population History: From the Black Death to the Present Day* (Cambridge: Cambridge University Press, 1996), pp. 125-37.

14. Richard Godbeer, *Sexual Revolution in Early America* (Baltimore: The Johns Hopkins University Press, 2002), pp. 255-63.

15. Historians clearly dispute which was the most important factor. See Shorter, *The Making of the Modern Family*, pp. 255-68 for an emphasis on intercourse. Others who stress birth control include Gordon, *Woman's Body, Woman's Right*, pp. 3-71 and Judith Allen, *Sex and Secrets: Crimes Involving Australian Women since 1880* (Melbourne: Oxford University Press, 1990), pp. 67-72.

16. Mary Fissell, 'Gender and Generation: Representing Reproduction in Early Modern England', in Kim M. Phillips and Barry Reay (eds.), *Sexualities in History: A Reader* (New York: Routledge, 2002), pp. 105-26.

17. There is now an enormous literature on these developments. Some of the key texts are Peter Laslett, *The World We Have Lost* (London; Methuen, 1965); Peter Laslett, D.E.C. Eversley and E.A. Wrigley (eds.), *An Introduction to English Historical Demography from the Sixteenth to the Nineteenth Century* (London: Weidenfeld & Nicolson, 1966); E.A. Wrigley and R.S. Schofield, *The Population History of England 1541–1871: A Reconstruction* (London: Edward Arnold, 1981); Peter Laslett, Karla Oosterveen and Richard M. Smith (eds.), *Bastardy and its Comparative History: Studies in the History of Illegitimacy and Marital Nonconformism in Britain, France, Germany, Sweden, North America, Jamaica and Japan* (London: Edward Arnold, 1980) and Jean-Louis Flandrin, *Families in Former Times: Kinship, Household and Sexuality* (trans. Richard Southern; Cambridge: Cambridge University Press, 1979). For America see Gordon, *Woman's Body, Woman's Right*, pp. 47-71 and Daniel Scott Smith, 'The Demographic History of Colonial New England', in Michael Gordon (ed.), *The American Family in Social-Historical Perspective* (New York: St Martin's Press, 1973).

18. Edward Shorter, John Knodel and Etienne van de Walle, 'The Decline in Non-marital Fertility in Europe 1880–1940', *Population Studies* 25.3 (1971), pp. 375-93.

19. See Wrigley and Schofield, *The Population History of England 1541–1871*, and Laslett, *The World We Have Lost*.

20. Angus McLaren, *A History of Contraception: From Antiquity to the Present Day* (Oxford: Basil Blackwell, 1990), pp. 144-49.

21. David Levine, *Family Formation in an Age of Nascent Capitalism* (New York: Academic Press, 1977), p. 96.

22. Henry Abelove, 'Some Speculations on the History of Sexual Intercourse during the Long Eighteenth Century in England', *Genders* 6 (November 1989), pp. 125-30.

23. Peter Laslett, 'Introduction: Comparing Illegitimacy over Time and between Cultures', in Laslett, Oosterveen and Smith, *Bastardy and its Comparative History*, pp. 10-11 and Godbeer, *Sexual Revolution in Early America*, pp. 125-32.

24. The two founding texts in this debate are Shorter, *The Making of the Modern Family* and Lawrence Stone, *The Family, Sex and Marriage: England, 1500–1800* (London: Weidenfeld & Nicholson, 1977).

25. See Diana O'Hara, *Courtship and Constraint: Rethinking the Making of Marriage in Tudor England* (Manchester: Manchester University Press, 2000).

26. See, for example, Peter Laslett, *Family Life and Illicit Love in Earlier Generations: Essays in Historical Sociology* (Cambridge: Cambridge University Press, 1977), pp. 110-11. See also Shorter, *The Making of the Modern Family*, pp. 54-78.

27. Godbeer, *Sexual Revolution in Early America*, pp. 19-51 and Else L. Hambleton, 'The Regulation of Sex in Seventeenth-Century Massachusetts: The Quarterly Court of Essex County vs Priscilla Willson and Mr Samuel Appleton', in Smith (ed.), *Sex and Sexuality in Early America*, pp. 89-115.

28. See, for example, Vern L. Bullough, 'Prostitution and Reform in Eighteenth Century England', in Maccubbin, *'Tis Nature's Fault*, pp. 61-74, Randolph Trumbach, 'Sex, Gender, and Sexual Identity in Modern Culture: Male Sodomy and Female Prostitution in Enlightenment London', in John C. Fout (ed.), *Forbidden History: The State, Society, and the Regulation of Sexuality in Modern Europe* (Chicago: University of Chicago Press, 1992), pp. 89-106 and Godbeer, *Sexual Revolution in Early America*, pp. 305-28.

29. See Godbeer, *Sexual Revolution in Early America*, pp. 119-224.

30. For some interesting work on early modern same-sex relations see the contributions to Kent Gerard and Gert Hekma (eds.), *The Pursuit of Sodomy: Male Homosexuality in Renaissance and Enlightenment Europe* (New York: Harrington Park Press, 1989), Wiesner-Hanks, *Christianity and Sexuality in the Early Modern World*, pp. 87-89 and Richard Davenport-Hines, *Sex, Death and Punishment: Attitudes to Sex and Sexuality in Britain since the Renaissance* (London: Collins, 1990), pp. 55-104. For lesbianism see Emma Donoghue, *Passions between Women: British Lesbian Culture 1668–1801* (London: Scarlett Press, 1993).

31. See Flandrin, *Families in Former Times*, pp. 194-98.

32. See Marilyn Yalom, *A History of the Breast* (New York: Knopf, 1997), pp. 84-87 and Ruth Perry, 'Colonizing the Breast: Sexuality and Maternity in Eighteenth-Century England', in Fout (ed.), *Forbidden History*, pp. 107-37.

33. For the wider history of birth control and abortion see McLaren, *A History of Contraception*, pp. 148-69; Gordon, *Woman's Body, Woman's Right*,

pp. 26-46; René Leboutte, 'Offense against Family Order: Infanticide in Belgium from the Fifteenth through the Early Twentieth Centuries', in Fout (ed.), *Forbidden History*, pp. 29-56 and Wiesner-Hanks, *Christianity and Sexuality in the Early Modern World*, pp. 80-86.

34. Shorter, *The Making of the Modern Family*, pp. 98-108.

35. Godbeer, *Sexual Revolution in Early America*, pp. 246-55.

36. Tim Hitchcock, *English Sexualities, 1700–1800* (New York: St Martins Press, 1997), pp. 24-41.

37. John R. Gillis, *Youth and History: Tradition and Change in European Age Relations, 1770 to the Present* (New York: Academic Press, 1981), pp. 29-35.

38. See especially Wrigley and Schofield, *The Population History of England*, pp. 402-53. See also Michael Anderson, 'Population Change in Northwestern Europe 1750–1850', in Anderson (ed.), *British Population History*, pp. 197-272.

39. Shorter, *The Making of the Modern Family*, pp. 255-68.

40. See John R. Gillis, 'Married but not Churched: Plebeian Sexual Relations and Marital Nonconformity in Eighteenth-Century Britain' in Maccubbin (ed.), *'Tis Nature's Fault*, pp. 31-42.

41. For some of these criticisms of Shorter see Louise A. Tilly, Joan W. Scott and Miriam Cohen, 'Women's Work and European Fertility', *Journal of Interdisciplinary History* 6.3 (1976), pp. 447-76 and Cissie Fairchilds, 'Female Sexual Attitudes and the Rise of Illegitimacy: A Case Study', *Journal of Interdisciplinary History* 8.4 (1978), pp. 627-67.

42. Stone, *The Family, Sex and Marriage*, pp. 527-45.

43. Godbeer, *The Sexual Revolution in Early America*, pp. 227-98.

44. See also Robert Shephard, 'Sexual Rumours in English Politics: The Case of Elizabeth I and James I' and Joseph Cady, 'The "Masculine Love" of the "Princes of Sodom" "Practising the Art of Ganymede" at Henri III's Court: The Homosexuality of Henri III and his *Mignons* in Pierre de L'Estoile's *Mémoires-Journaux*', in Jacqueline Murray and Konrad Eisenbichler (eds.), *Desire and Discipline: Sex and Sexuality in the Premodern West* (Toronto: Toronto University Press, 1996), pp. 101-54.

45. Stone, *The Family, Sex and Marriage*, pp. 527-45. See also Weber, *The Restoration Rake Hero* and Michel Rey, 'Parisian Homosexuals Create a Lifestyle, 1700–1750', in Maccubbin (ed.), *'Tis Natures's Fault*, pp. 179-91 and Trumbach, *Sex and the Gender Revolution*, pp. 69-111.

46. As above. See also Lawrence Stone, 'Libertine Sexuality in Post-Restoration England: Group Sex and Flagellation among the Middling Sort in Norwich in 1706–07', *Journal of the History of Sexuality* 2.4 (1992), pp. 511-25

47. See Trumbach, *Sex and the Gender Revolution*, pp. 112-68, Roy Porter, 'Mixed Feelings: The Enlightenment and Sexuality in Eighteenth-Century Britain' in Paul-Gabriel Boucé (ed.), *Sexuality in Eighteenth-Century Britain* (Manchester: Manchester University Press, 1982), pp. 1-27, Kathryn Norberg,

'The Libertine Whore: Prostitution in French Pornography from Margot to Juliette' in Hunt (ed.), *The Invention of Pornography*, pp. 225-52.

48. Steven Marcus, *The Other Victorians: A Study of Sexuality and Pornography in Mid-Nineteenth Century England* (New York: Basic Books, 1966). See also Hunt (ed.), *The Invention of Pornography* and Darnton, *The Literary Underground of the Old Regime*.

49. Marcus, *The Other Victorians*, pp. 268-71.

50. For discussion of the life and work of de Sade see Jane Gallop, *Intersections: A Reading of Sade with Bataille, Blanchot and Klossowski* (Lincoln: University of Nebraska Press, 1981) and Thomas Moore, *Dark Eros: The Imagination of Sadism* (Dallas: Spring Publications, 1990).

51. See, for example, Rudolf Dekker and Lotte C. van de Pol, *The Tradition of Female Transvestism in Early Modern Europe* (London: MacMillan, 1989), Terry Castle, 'The Culture of Travesty: Sexuality and Masquerade in Eighteenth Century England' and Lynne Friedli, '"Passing Women": A Study of Gender Boundaries in the Eighteenth Century', in G.S. Rousseau and Roy Porter (eds.), *Sexual Underworlds of the Enlightenment* (Chapel Hill: University of North Carolina Press, 1980).

52. See Marjorie Garber, *Vested Interests: Cross-Dressing and Cultural Anxiety* (New York: Routledge, 1993), Vern L. Bullough and Bonnie Bullough, *Cross Dressing, Sex, and Gender* (Philadelphia: University of Pennsylvania Press, 1993) and Ruth Mazo Karras and David Lorenzo Boyd, 'Ut cum muliere: A Male Transvestite Prostitute in Fourteenth-Century London', in Phillips and Reay (eds.), *Sexualities in History*, pp. 90-104.

53. See, for example, Mikhail Bakhtin, *The Dialogic Imagination* (trans. Michael Holquist; Austin: University of Texas Press, 1981).

54. For a typical account which stresses the greater sexual egalitarianism of libertinism see G.S. Rousseau, 'Nymphomania, Bienville and the Rise of Erotic Sensibility', in Boucé (ed.), *Sexuality in Eighteenth-Century Britain*, pp. 74-94. For some of the critical historiography see Trumbach, *Sex and the Gender Revolution*, pp. 73-111, 'Erotic Fantasy and Male Libertinism in enlightenment England', in Hunt (ed.), *The Invention of Pornography*, pp. 253-82 and Carole Pateman, *The Sexual Contract* (Cambridge: Polity Press, 1988), pp. 217-34.

55. On the patriarchal family in colonial America see Steven Mintz and Susan Kellog, *Domestic Revolutions: A Social History of Family Life* (New York: Free Press, 1988), pp. 1-42 and Jane Kamensky, 'The Colonial Mosaic: 1600–1760', in Nancy F. Cott (ed.), *No Small Courage: A History of Women in the United States* (New York: Oxford University Press, 2000), pp. 63-75.

56. For romantic ideals of marriage see G.J. Barker-Benfield, *The Culture of Sensibility: Sex and Society in Eighteenth-Century Britain* (Chicago: University of Chicago Press, 1992), pp. 287-350. On the sentimental family in colonial America see Daniel Blake Smith, *Inside the Great House: Planter Family Life in Eighteenth-Century Chesapeake Society* (Ithaca: Cornell University Press, 1980).

57. Stone, *The Family, Sex and Marriage*, pp. 527-45.
58. Ralph Houlbrooke, *The English Family 1450–1700* (London; Longman, 1984), pp. 1-16.
59. See Barker-Benfield, *The Culture of Sensibility*.
60. Norbert Elias, *The History of Manners: The Civilizing Process* (trans. Edmund Jephcott; New York: Urizen Books, 1978), I, pp. 184-85.
61. See especially Randolph Trumbach, *The Rise of the Egalitarian Family: Aristocratic Kinship and Domestic Relations in Eighteenth Century England* (New York: Academic Press, 1978), pp. 119-64.
62. See Margaret Hunt, 'Wife Beating, Domesticity, and Women's Independence in Eighteenth-Century London', *Gender and History* 4 (1992), pp. 10-33, Roderick Phillips, *Putting Asunder: A History of Divorce in Western Society* (Cambridge: Cambridge University Press, 1988) and Trumbach, *Sex and the Gender Revolution*, pp. 325-61.
63. See, for example, Marylynn Salmon, 'The Limits of Independence: 1760–1800', in Cott (ed.), *No Small Courage*, pp. 116-31 and Laurel Thatcher Ulrich, *Good Wives: Image and Reality in the Lives of Women in Northern New England* (New York: Knopf, 1982).
64. Flandrin, *Families in Former Times*, pp. 223-34.
65. McLaren, *A History of Contraception*, pp. 166-69.
66. Laqueur, *Making Sex*, pp. 149-92.
67. See Londa Schiebinger, 'Skeletons in the Closet: The First Illustrations of the Female Skeleton in Eighteenth-Century Anatomy', in Catherine Gallagher and Thomas Laqueur (eds.), *The Making of the Modern Body: Sexuality and Society in the Nineteenth Century* (Berkeley: University of California Press, 1987), pp. 42-82.
68. Ludmilla Jordanova, *Sexual Visions: Images of Gender in Science and Medicine between the Eighteenth and the Twentieth Centuries* (Hemel Hempstead: Harvester Wheatsheaf, 1989), pp. 57-58.
69. Laqueur, *Making Sex*, pp. 152-54.
70. For further work on these developments in biology, anatomy, physiology and clinical medicine more generally see Jordanova, *Sexual Visions*, pp. 134-59 and Michel Foucault, *The Birth of the Clinic: An Archaeology of Medical Perception* (trans. A.M. Sheridan; London: Tavistock, 1973).
71. Laqueur, *Making Sex*, pp. 181-92.
72. See Keith Thomas, 'The Double Standard', *Journal of the History of Ideas* 20.2 (1959), pp. 195-216.
73. Thomas, 'The Double Standard', p. 152.
74. Pateman, *The Sexual Contract*, pp. 219-34.
75. Laqueur, *Making Sex*, pp. 151-54.
76. See Trumbach, *Sex and the Gender Revolution*, pp. 3-22 and 'Sex, Gender, and Sexual Identity in Modern Culture', pp. 89-106.
77. Hitchcock, *English Sexualities*, pp. 58-75.
78. Rictor Norton, *Mother Clap's Molly House: The Gay Subculture in England, 1700–1830* (London: Gay Men's Press, 1992).

79. Alan Bray, *Homosexuality in Renaissance England* (London: Gay Men's Press, 1982), pp. 81-114.
80. Trumbach, *Sex and the Gender Revolution*, p. 8.
81. See Donoghue, *Passions between Women* and Valerie Traub, *The Renaissance of Lesbianism in Early Modern England* (London: Scarlett Press, 2002).
82. Ruggerio, *The Boundaries of Eros*, pp. 109-45.
83. Amy Richlin, 'Not before Homosexuality: The Materiality of the *Cinaedus* and the Roman Law against Love between Men', *Journal of the History of Sexuality* 3.4 (1993), pp. 523-73.
84. David M. Halperin, *How to Do the History of Homosexuality* (Chicago: University of Chicago Press, 2002), pp. 104-37.

Chapter 6

1. See Steven Marcus, *The Other Victorians: A Study of Sexuality and Pornography in Mid-Nineteenth Century England* (New York: Basic Books, 1966), Ronald Pearsall, *The Worm in the Bud: The World of Victorian Sexuality* (London: Weidenfeld & Nicholson, 1969) and Eric Trudgill, *Madonnas and Magdalens: The Origins and Development of Victorian Sexual Attitudes* (London: Heinemann, 1976). See also Peter Cominos, 'Late Victorian Sexual Respectability and the Social System', *International Review of Social History* 8 (1963), pp. 18-48 and 216-50.
2. The useful concept of sexual liberalism comes from John D'Emilio and Estelle B. Freedman, *Intimate Matters: A History of Sexuality in America* (New York: Harper & Row, 1988), pp. xviii-xx.
3. Michel Foucault, *The History of Sexuality*. I. *An Introduction* (trans. Robert Hurley; New York: Random House, 1978), pp. 15-50.
4. A useful discussion of these issues is Thomas Laqueur, 'Sexual Desire and the Market Economy during the Industrial Revolution', in Domna C. Stanton (ed.), *Discourses of Sexuality: From Aristotle to AIDS* (Ann Arbor: University of Michigan Press, 1992), pp. 183-91.
5. Linda Gordon, *Woman's Body, Woman's Right: A Social History of Birth Control in America* (New York: Grossman, 1976), pp. 101-10, Daniel Scott Smith, 'Family Limitation, Sexual Control and Domestic Feminism in Victorian America', *Feminist Studies* 1.3-4 (1973), pp. 40-57 and F.B. Smith, 'Sexuality in Britain, 1800–1900: Some Suggested Revisions' in Martha Vicinus (ed.), *A Widening Sphere: Changing Roles of Victorian Women* (Bloomington: Indiana University Press, 1977), pp. 188-93.
6. Simon Szreter, *Fertility, Class and Gender in Britain, 1860–1940* (Cambridge: Cambridge University Press, 1996), pp. 367-400.
7. Angus McLaren, *A History of Contraception: From Antiquity to the Present Day* (Oxford: Basil Blackwell, 1990), pp. 188-89. See also R.P. Neuman, 'Working Class Birth Control in Wilhelmine Germany', *Comparative Studies in History and Society* 20 (1978), pp. 408-28 and Gordon, *Woman's Body, Woman's Right*, pp. 95-135.
8. Richard Godbeer, *Sexual Revolution in Early America* (Baltimore: The Johns Hopkins University Press, 2002), pp. 59-60.

9. See Carroll Smith-Rosenberg, *Disorderly Conduct: Visions of Gender in Victorian America* (New York: Oxford University Press, 1985), pp. 127-64.

10. See Barbara Welter, 'The Cult of True Womanhood', *American Quarterly* 18 (1966), pp. 151-74 and Catharine Hall, 'The Early Formation of Victorian Domestic Ideology', in Sandra Burman (ed.), *Fit Work for Women* (London: Croom Helm in association with Oxford University's Women's Studies Committee, 1979), pp. 15-32.

11. For some discussion of this ideal see Walter E. Houghton, *The Victorian Frame of Mind* (New Haven: Yale University Press, 1964), p. 348; Harold Perkin, *The Origins of Modern English Society, 1780–1880* (London: Routledge & Kegan Paul, 1969), pp. 158-59; Patricia Branca, *Silent Sisterhood: Middle Class Women in the Victorian Home* (London: Croom Helm, 1975), pp. 1-19; Martha Vicinus, 'Introduction: The Perfect Victorian Lady', in *idem* (ed.), *Suffer and Be Still: Women in the Victorian Age* (Bloomington: Indiana University Press, 1972), pp. vii-xv; Pat Jalland, *Women, Marriage and Politics, 1860–1914* (Oxford: Oxford University Press, 1988), pp. 7-20 and Mary Poovey, *Uneven Developments: The Ideological Work of Gender in Mid-Victorian England* (London: Virago, 1989), pp. 1-23.

12. See Leonore Davidoff and Catherine Hall, *Family Fortunes: Men and Women of the English Middle Classes 1780–1850* (London: Hutchinson, 1987).

13. Smith-Rosenberg, *Disorderly Conduct*, pp. 127-64.

14. Nancy Cott, *The Bonds of Womanhood: "Woman's Sphere" in New England, 1789–1835* (New Haven: Yale University Press, 1977), pp. 197-206.

15. On the restrictions of the Southern lady ideal see Julia Cherry Spruill, *Women's Life and Work in the Southern Colonies* (New York: Russell & Russell, 1969) and Catherine Clinton and Christine Lunardini, *The Columbia Guide to American Women in the Nineteenth Century* (New York: Columbia University Press, 2000), pp. 122-23.

16. Mary P. Ryan, *Cradle of the Middle Class: The Family in Oneida County, New York, 1790–1865* (Cambridge: Cambridge University Press, 1983), pp. 155-57.

17. Laqueur, 'Sexual Desire and Market Economy', pp. 201-15.

18. For some interesting discussions of these attempts see J.R. Poynter, *Society and Pauperism: English Ideas on Poor Relief 1795–1834* (Melbourne: Melbourne University Press, 1969) and Gertrude Himmelfarb, *The Idea of Poverty* (London: Faber, 1984), pp. 307-400.

19. Smith, 'Sexuality in Britain', pp. 188-93. See also D'Emilio and Freedman, *Intimate Matters*, pp. 59-60.

20. For a very good summary and analysis of these reform efforts, particularly in relation to sexual regulation see Jeffrey Weeks, *Sex, Politics and Society: The Regulation of Sexuality since 1800* (London: Longman, 2nd edn, 1989), pp. 57-95.

21. McLaren, *A History of Contraception*, pp. 182-83.

22. McLaren, *A History of Contraception*, p. 180.

23. Ryan, *Cradle of the Middle Class*, pp. 55-56.

24. McLaren, *A History of Contraception*, pp. 180-88.
25. McLaren, *A History of Contraception*, pp. 180-88; Gordon, *Woman's Body, Woman's Right*, pp. 72-91; Andrea Tone, *Devices and Desires: A History of Contraceptives in America* (New York: Hill & Wang, 2001) and Janet Farrell Brodie, *Contraception and Abortion in Nineteenth-Century America* (Ithaca: Cornell University Press, 1994).
26. McLaren, *A History of Contraception*, pp. 186-204.
27. Szreter, *Fertility, Class and Gender in Britain*, pp. 367-400. See also Smith, 'Sexuality in Britain', pp. 188-93.
28. See for example, Gordon, *Woman's Body, Woman's Right*, pp. 40-60; Diana Gittins, *Fair Sex: Family Size and Structure 1900–1939* (London: Hutchinson, 1982), pp. 160-64; Carl Degler, *At Odds: Women and the Family in America from the Revolution to the Present* (New York: Oxford University Press, 1980), pp. 227-48; McLaren, *A History of Contraception*, pp. 185-92 and Judith Allen, *Sex and Secrets: Crimes Involving Australian Women since 1880* (Melbourne: Oxford University Press, 1990), pp. 66-77.
29. McLaren, *A History of Contraception*, p. 191 and Allen, *Sex and Secrets*, pp. 66-77.
30. James Mohr, *Abortion in America: The Origins and Evolution of Public Policy* (New York: Oxford University Press, 1978), pp. 34-35.
31. McLaren, *A History of Contraception*, pp. 187-93.
32. See Leslie J. Reagan, *When Abortion was a Crime: Women, Medicine and Law in the United States 1867–1973* (Berkeley: University of California Press, 1997), pp. 70-79.
33. For excellent overviews of the political and social interests driving the nineteenth-century anti-abortion movements see Reagan, *When Abortion was a Crime*, pp. 80-112 and Gordon, *Woman's Body, Woman's Right*, pp. 47-71.
34. See McLaren, *A History of Contraception*, pp. 189-94; Reagan, *When Abortion was a Crime*, pp. 1-18; Gordon, *Woman's Body, Woman's Right*, pp. 49-71 and Helen Lefkowitz Horowitz, *Rereading Sex: Battles over Sexual Knowledge and Suppression in Nineteenth Century America* (New York: Knopf, 2002), pp. 194-209.
35. On the issue of enforcement and male interests see Allen, *Sex and Secrets*, pp. 66-77, Reagan, *When Abortion was a Crime*, pp. 108-11 and Horowitz, *Rereading Sex*, pp. 194-209.
36. See Pearsall, *The Worm in the Bud*, pp. 285-92.
37. Alex Comfort, *The Anxiety Makers* (London: Nelson, 1967).
38. See Roy Porter and Lesley Hall, *The Facts of Life: The Creation of Sexual Knowledge in Britain, 1650–1950* (New Haven: Yale University Press, 1995), pp. 91-105.
39. Edward Shorter, *The Making of the Modern Family* (Harmondsworth: Penguin Books, 1976), pp. 119 and Jean-Louis Flandrin, *Families in Former Times: Kinship, Household and Sexuality* (trans. Richard Southern; Cambridge: Cambridge University Press, 1979).
40. Tim Hitchcock, *English Sexualities 1700–1800* (New York: St Martins Press, 1997), pp. 24-41.

41. Some of these ideas are advanced in Laqueur, 'Sexual Desire and Market Economy', pp. 190-91. See also Paula Bennett and Vernon A. Rosario (eds.), *Solitary Pleasures: The Historical, Literary and Artistic Discourses of Autoeroticism* (New York: Routledge, 1995).

42. Quoted in Thomas Laqueur, *Making Sex: Body and Gender from the Greeks to Freud* (Cambridge, MA: Harvard University Press, 1990), p. 229.

43. See, for example, H. Tristram Engelhardt Jr, 'The Disease of Masturbation: Values and the Concept of Disease', *Bulletin of the History of Medicine* 48 (1974), pp. 234-48, Lesley Hall, 'Forbidden by God, Despised by Men: Masturbation, Medical Warnings, Moral Panic, and Manhood in Great Britain, 1850–1950', in John C. Fout (ed.), *Forbidden History: The State, Society, and the Regulation of Sexuality in Modern Europe* (Chicago: University of Chicago Press, 1992), pp. 293-316 and D'Emilio and Freedman, *Intimate Matters*, pp. 68-69.

44. See G.J. Barker-Benfield, *The Horrors of a Half-Known Life: Aspects of the Exploitation of Women by Men* (New York: Harper & Row, 1976).

45. See Comfort, *The Anxiety Makers*, pp. 69-113.

46. Nancy Cott, 'Passionlessness: An Interpretation of Victorian Sexual Ideology, 1790–1850', *Signs* 4.2 (1978), pp. 219-36.

47. See Hall, 'Forbidden by God, Despised by Men', pp. 299-304.

48. Hall, 'Forbidden by God, Despised by Men', pp. 294-99.

49. See M. Jeanne Peterson, 'Dr Acton's Enemy: Medicine, Sex and Society in Victorian England', *Victorian Studies* 29.4 (1986), pp. 569-90, Weeks, *Sex, Politics and Society*, pp. 40-44, Degler, *At Odds*, pp. 258-66, and Smith, 'Sexuality in Britain', pp. 184-90.

50. Smith, 'Sexuality in Britain', pp. 189-94 and D'Emilio and Freedman, *Intimate Matters*, pp. 59-60.

51. Smith 'Sexuality in Britain', pp.192-98.

52. Porter and Hall, *The Facts of Life*, pp. 132-54.

53. Horowitz, *Rereading Sex*, pp. 3-15.

54. Horowitz, *Rereading Sex*, pp. 65-154.

55. See, for example, Anne Digby, 'Women's Biological Straightjacket', in Susan Mendus and Jane Rendall (eds.), *Sexuality and Subordination: Interdisciplinary Studies of Gender in the Nineteenth Century* (London: Routledge, 1989), pp. 192-220.

56. Michael Mason, *The Making of Victorian Sexuality* (Oxford: Oxford University Press, 1994), pp. 175-215.

57. Quoted in Laqueur, *Making Sex*, p. 190.

58. American pamphleteer and Eliza Duffy both quoted in D'Emilio and Freedman, *Intimate Matters*, p. 70.

59. D'Emilio and Freedman, *Intimate Matters*, p. 179.

60. D'Emilio and Freedman, *Intimate Matters*, pp. 173-88, Weeks, *Sex, Politics and Society*, pp. 40-44, and Degler, *At Odds*, pp. 258-66.

61. See Laqueur, *Making Sex*, pp. 149-92.

62. Smith-Rosenberg, *Disorderly Conduct*, pp. 197-216 and Elaine Showalter,

The Female Malady: Women, Madness and English Culture, 1830–1980 (London: Virago, 1987), pp. 121-44.

63. Mary Poovey, 'Scenes of Indelicate Character: The Medical Treatment of Victorian Women', in Catherine Gallagher and Thomas Laqueur (eds.), *The Making of the Modern Body: Sexuality and Society in the Nineteenth Century* (Berkeley: University of California Press, 1987), pp. 137-68.

64. Alison Winter, *Mesmerized: Powers of the Mind in Victorian Britain* (Chicago: University of Chicago Press, 1998), pp. 101-104.

65. See Weeks, *Sex, Politics and Society*, pp. 84-93.

66. See Pearsall, *The Worm in the Bud*, pp. 285-92.

67. See Prince Morrow, *Social Diseases and Marriage* (New York: Lea Brothers, 1904).

68. See Degler, *At Odds*, pp. 254-55.

69. See Deborah Gorham, 'The Maiden Tribute to Modern Babylon Revisited', *Victorian Studies* (Spring 1976), pp. 353-79, Judith Walkowitz, *City of Dreadful Delight: Narratives of Sexual Danger in Late-Victorian London* (Chicago: Chicago University Press, 1992), pp. 81-120 and D'Emilio and Freedman, *Intimate Matters*, p. 208.

70. See Alain Corbin, 'Commercial Sexuality in Nineteenth Century France: A System of Images and Regulations', in Gallagher and Laqueur (eds.), *The Making of the Modern Body*, pp. 209-19.

71. See, for example, Mark T. Connelly, *The Response to Prostitution in the Progressive Era* (Chapel Hill: University of North Carolina Press, 1980), p. 6, Ruth Rosen, *The Lost Sisterhood: Prostitution in America, 1900–1930* (Baltimore: The Johns Hopkins Press, 1982), pp. 38-50 and Barbara Meil Hobson, *Uneasy Virtue: The Politics of Repression and the American Reform Tradition* (Chicago: University of Chicago Press, 1990), p. xiv.

72. David J. Pivar, *Purity and Hygiene: Women, Prostitution and the 'American Plan', 1900–1930* (Westport: Greenwood Press, 2002), pp. xii-xiii.

73. See Rosen, *The Lost Sisterhood*, pp. 69-85, Allen, *Sex and Secrets*, pp. 90-96 and Timothy J. Gilfoyle, *City of Eros: New York City, Prostitution and the Commercialization of Sex, 1790–1920* (New York: W.W. Norton, 1992).

74. See Judith Walkowitz, *Prostitution and Victorian Society: Women, Class and the State* (Cambridge: Cambridge University Press, 1980); Frances Finnegan, *Poverty and Prostitution: a study of Victorian prostitutes in York* (Cambridge: Cambridge University Press, 1979); Rosen, *The Lost Sisterhood*, Joanne Meyerowitz, *Women Adrift: Independent Wage Earners in Chicago, 1880–1930* (Chicago: Chicago University Press, 1988) and Gilfoyle, *City of Eros*, pp. 197-223.

75. Peter Gay, *Education of the Senses. I. The Bourgeois Experience: Victoria to Freud* (New York: Oxford University Press, 1984), pp. 71-89.

76. Gay, *Education of the Senses*, pp. 3-68.

77. D'Emilio and Freedman, *Intimate Matters*, pp. 175-78.

78. Walkowitz, *City of Dreadful Delight*, pp. 81-134, Gilfoyle, *City of Eros*, pp. 181-269 and Lefkowitz, *Rereading Sex*, pp. 19-44.

79. Mary E. Odem, *Delinquent Daughters: Protecting and Policing Adolescent Female Sexuality in the United States, 1885–1920* (Chapel Hill: University of North Carolina, 1995), Kathy Peiss, *Cheap Amusements: Working Women and Leisure in Turn-of-the-Century New York* (Philadelphia: Temple University Press, 1986) and Ruth M. Alexander, *The Girl Problem: Female Sexual Delinquency in New York 1900–1930* (Ithaca: Cornell University Press, 1995).

80. D'Emilio and Freedman, *Intimate Matters*, pp. 194-201.

81. Mason, *The Making of Victorian Sexuality*, pp. 105-74.

82. Davidoff and Hall, *Family Fortunes*, pp. 13-69.

83. For a useful comparison of working-class and middle-class family forms, ideologies and ethics see Leonore Davidoff, Megan Doolittle, Janet Fink and Katherine Holden, *The Family Story: Blood, Contract and Intimacy 1830–1960* (London: Longman, 1999), pp. 101-82.

84. Barbara Taylor, *Eve and the New Jerusalem: Socialism and Feminism in the Nineteenth Century* (London: Virago, 1983).

85. Davidoff and Hall, *Family Fortunes*, pp. 149-62.

86. John Tosh, *A Man's Place: Masculinity and the Middle Class Home in Victorian England* (New Haven: Yale University Press, 1999).

Chapter 7

1. Gordon Sayre, 'Native American Sexuality in the Eyes of the Beholders 1535–1710', in Merril D. Smith (ed.), *Sex and Sexuality in Early America* (New York: New York University Press, 1998), pp. 35-54.

2. Trevor Burnard, 'The Sexual Life of an Eighteenth-Century Jamaican Slave Overseer', in Smith (ed.), *Sex and Sexuality in Early America*, pp. 163-89.

3. Walter, *My Secret Life: Abridged but Unexpurgated* (introduction by G. Legman; New York: Grove Press, 1966), pp. 381-84.

4. John D'Emilio and Estelle B. Freedman, *Intimate Matters: A History of Sexuality in America* (New York: Harper & Row, 1988), p. 123.

5. Quoted in Leon Litwack, *Trouble in Mind: Black Southerners in the Age of Jim Crow* (New York, 1998), p. 213.

6. See Klaus Theweleit, *Male Fantasies*, I (trans. Stephen Conway; Minneapolis: University of Minnesota Press, 1987).

7. One of the few that does dispute the violence thesis is Keith Windschuttle, *The Fabrication of Aboriginal History* (Sydney: Macleay Press, 2002).

8. For an excellent overview of 'mestizo' culture see Gary B. Nash, 'The Hidden History of Mestizo America', in Martha Hodes (ed.), *Sex, Love, Race: Crossing Boundaries in North American History* (New York: New York University Press, 1999), pp. 10-32.

9. See, for example, Carol Vance (ed.), *Pleasure and Danger: Exploring Female Sexuality* (Boston: Routledge & Kegan Paul, 1984); Fred Botting and Scott Wilson (eds.), *Bataille: A Critical Reader* (Oxford: Basil Blackwell, 1998); Lynn Hunt (ed.), *Eroticism and the Body Politic* (Baltimore: The Johns

Hopkins University, 1991); Alex Hughes and Kate Ince (eds.), *French Erotic Fiction: Women's Desiring Writing 1880–1990* (Washington, DC: Berg, 1996) and Russ Castronovo, *Necro Citizenship: Death, Eroticism and the Public Sphere in the Nineteenth-Century United States* (Durham, NC: Duke University Press, 2001).

10. Thomas Laqueur, *Making Sex: Body and Gender from the Greeks to Freud* (Cambridge, MA: Harvard University Press, 1992), pp. 230-33. See also Mary Spongberg, *Feminizing Venereal Disease: The Body of the Prostitute in Nineteenth-Century Medical Discourse* (London: Macmillan, 1997) and Lynda Nead, *Myths of Sexuality: Representations of Women in Victorian Britain* (Oxford: Basil Blackwell, 1988), pp. 91-64.

11. Quoted in Timothy J. Gilfoyle, *City of Eros: New York City, Prostitution, and the Commercialization of Sex, 1790–1920* (New York: W.W. Norton, 1992), p. 56.

12. See, for example, David J. Pivar, *Purity Crusade, Sexual Morality and Social Control, 1868–1900* (Westport: Greenwood Press, 1973).

13. For discussions of social investigation, fallen women and the emergence of ideas of female delinquency see Mary E. Odem, *Delinquent Daughters: Protecting and Policing Adolescent Female Sexuality in the United States, 1885–1920* (Chapel Hill: University of North Carolina, 1995); Regina G. Kunzel, *Fallen Women, Problem Girls: Unmarried Mothers and the Professionalization of Social Work, 1890–1945* (New Haven: Yale University Press, 1993); Robert H. Bremner, *From the Depths: The Discovery of Poverty in the United States* (New York: New York University Press, 1964) and Kathleen Woodroofe, *From Charity to Social Work in England and the United States* (London: Routledge & Kegan Paul, 1962).

14. See Nancy Cott, 'Passionlessness: An Interpretation of Victorian Sexuality Ideology, 1790–1850', *Signs* 4.2 (1978), pp. 219-36.

15. See D'Emilio and Freedman, *Intimate Matters*, pp. 73-84.

16. Helen Horowitz Lefkowitz, *Rereading Sex: Battles over Sexual Knowledge and Suppression in Nineteenth-Century America* (New York: Knopf, 2002), pp. 32-44.

17. See Steven Marcus, *The Other Victorians: A Study of Sexuality and Pornography in Mid-Nineteenth Century England* (New York: Basic Books, 1966), chapters 3-4.

18. Leonore Davidoff, 'Class and Gender in Victorian England', in Judith L. Newton, Mary P. Ryan and Judith R. Walkowitz (eds.), *Sex and Class in Women's History* (London: Routledge & Keegan Paul, 1983), pp. 17-71.

19. See Anne McClintock, *Imperial Leather: Race, Gender and Sexuality in the Colonial Contest* (London: Routledge, 1995), 132-60 and Liz Stanley, 'Introduction', *The Diaries of Hannah Cullwick: Victorian Maidservant* (New Brunswick, NJ; London: Rutgers University Press, 1984), p. 1.

20. McClintock, *Imperial Leather*, pp. 132-60.

21. See Edward Said, *Culture and Imperialism* (London: Chatto & Windus, 1993), Mary Louise Pratt, *Imperial Eyes: Travel Writing and Transculturation*

(London: Routledge, 1992) and Thomas Richards, *The Imperial Archive: Knowledge and the Fantasy of Empire* (London: Verso, 1993).

22. Edward Said, *Orientalism* (New York: Routledge & Kegan Paul, 1978).

23. Said, *Orientalism*, pp. 6, 207.

24. For a useful review of this issue see Ann Laura Stoler and Frederick Cooper, 'Between Metropole and Colony: Rethinking a Research Agenda', in Frederick Cooper and Ann Laura Stoler (eds.), *Tensions of Empire: Colonial Cultures in a Bourgeois World* (Berkeley: University of California Press, 1997), pp. 1-40. See also Homi Bhabha, *The Location of Culture* (London: Routledge, 1994), pp. 66-84.

25. See McClintock, *Imperial Leather*, p. 14.

26. McClintock, *Imperial Leather*. See also Eve Kosofsky Sedgwick, *Between Men: English Literature and Male Homosocial Desire* (New York: Columbia University Press, 1985).

27. Mrinalini Sinha, *Colonial Masculinity: The 'Manly Englishman' and the 'Effeminate Bengali'* (Manchester: Manchester University Press, 1995).

28. See Billie Melman, *Women's Orients: English Women and the Middle East, 1718–1918: Sexuality, Religion and Work* (Ann Arbor: University of Michigan Press, 1992), Reina Lewis, *Gendering Orientalism: Race, Femininity and Representation* (London: Routledge, 1996) and Sara Mills, *Discourses of Difference: An Analysis of Women's Travel Writing and Colonialism* (London: Routledge, 1991).

29. McClintock, *Imperial Leather*, pp. 21-31.

30. See Lenore Manderson, 'Colonial Desires Sexuality, Race and Gender in British Malaya', *Journal of the History of Sexuality* 7.3 (1997), p. 388 and Megan Vaughan, *Curing their Ills: Colonial Power and African Illness* (Cambridge: Polity Press, 1991).

31. Joanna de Groot, 'Sex and Race: The Construction of Language and Image in the Nineteenth Century', in Susan Mendus and Jane Rendall (eds.), *Sexuality and Subordination: Interdisciplinary Studies of Gender in the Nineteenth Century* (London: Routledge, 1989), pp. 89-130. See also Jill Beaulieu and Mary Roberts (eds.), *Orientalism's Interlocutors: Painting, Architecture, Photography* (Durham, NC: Duke University Press, 2002).

32. Sander L. Gilman, 'Black Bodies, White Bodies: Toward an Iconography of Female Sexuality in Late Nineteenth-Century Art, Medicine, and Literature', in Henry Louis Gates Jr (ed.), *'Race', Writing, and Difference* (Chicago: University of Chicago Press, 1986), pp. 223-61.

33. On violence and coercion see Stephanie Wood, 'Sexual Violation in the Conquest of the Americas' in Smith (ed.), *Sex and Sexuality in Early America*, pp. 9-35; Thelma Jennings, 'Us Colored Women Had to Go Through a Plenty: Sexual Exploitation of African American Slave Women', *Journal of Women's History* 1 (1990), pp. 45-74; Patricia Scully, 'Rape, Race, and Colonial Culture: The Sexual Politics of Identity in the Nineteenth Century Cape Colony, South Africa', *American Historical Review* 100 (1995), pp. 335-59 and Sharon Block, 'Lines of Color, Sex, and Service:

Comparative Sexual Coercion in Early America', in Hodes (ed.), *Sex, Love, Race*, pp. 141-63.

34. Richard Godbeer, *The Sexual Revolution in Early America* (Baltimore: The Johns Hopkins University Press, 2002), p. 222.

35. Godbeer, *Sexual Revolution*, pp. 190-94.

36. See Kirsten Fischer, 'False, Feigned, and Scandalous Words: Sexual Slander and Racial Ideology among Whites in Colonial North Carolina', in Catherine Clinton and Michele Gillespie (eds.), *The Devils' Lane: Sex and Race in the Early South* (New York: Oxford University Press, 1997), pp. 139-53 and Godbeer, *Sexual Revolution*, pp. 190-224.

37. See, for example, Peter Wallenstein, 'Indian Foremothers: Race, Sex, Slavery, and Freedom in Early Virginia', in Clinton and Gillespie (eds.), *The Devil's Lane*, pp. 57-73, Daniel R. Mandell, 'The Saga of Sarah Muckamugg: Indian and African American Intermarriage in Colonial New England', in Hodes (ed.), *Sex, Love, Race*, pp. 60-71 and Martin Bauml Duberman, 'Writhing Bedfellows in Antebellum South Carolina: Historical Interpretation and the Politics of Evidence', in Martin Bauml Duberman, Martha Vicinus and George Chauncey Jr (eds.), *Hidden from History: Reclaiming the Gay and Lesbian Past* (New York: North American Library, 1989), pp. 153-68.

38. See Catherine Clinton and Michele Gillespie, 'Introduction: Reflections on Sex, Race, and Region', in Clinton and Gillespie (eds.), *The Devil's Lane*, pp. xiii-xx; Peter W. Bardaglio, 'Shameful Matches: The Regulation of Interracial Sex and Marriage in the South before 1900', in Hodes (ed.), *Sex, Love, Race*, pp. 112-38; George M. Fredrickson, *White Supremacy: A Comparative Study in American and South African History* (New York: Oxford University Press, 1981) and Andrew Markus, *Australian Race Relations, 1788–1993* (St Leonards: Allen & Unwin, 1994).

39. See, for example, Susan Thorne, 'The Conversion of Englishmen and the Conversion of the World Inseparable: Missionary Imperialism and the Language of Class in Early Industrial Britain', in Cooper and Stoler, *Tensions of Empire*, pp. 238-62 and Clare Midgley, 'Anti-Slavery and the Roots of Imperial Feminism', in *idem* (ed.), *Gender and Imperialism* (Manchester: Manchester University Press, 1998), pp. 161-99.

40. Clinton and Gillespie, 'Introduction: Reflections on Sex, Race, and Region', pp. xiii-xx.

41. See George M. Fredrickson, *Racism: A Short History* (Princeton: Princeton University Press, 2002).

42. See Leslie K. Dunlap, 'The Reform of Rape Law and the Problem of White Men: Age of Consent Campaigns in the South, 1885–1910', in Hodes (ed.), *Sex, Love, Race*, pp. 352-72; Jocquelyn Dowd Hall, 'The Mind that Burns in Each Body: Women, Rape and Racial Violence', in Ann Snitow, Christine Stansell and Sharon Thompson (eds.), *Powers of Desire: The Politics of Sexuality* (New York: Monthly Review Press, 1983), pp. 328-49; Gail Bederman, *Manliness and Civilization: A Cultural History*

of Gender and Race in the United States, 1880–1917 (Chicago: University of Chicago Press, 1995).

43. Grace Elizabeth Hale, *Making Whiteness: The Culture of Segregation in the South, 1890–1940* (New York: Pantheon Books, 1998).

44. Godbeer, *Sexual Revolution*, pp. 202-203.

45. Martha Hodes, *White Women, Black Men: Illicit Sex in the Nineteenth-Century South* (New Haven: Yale University Press, 1997).

46. Glenda Elizabeth Gilmore, *Gender and Jim Crow: Women and the Politics of White Supremacy in North Carolina 1896–1920* (Chapel Hill: University of North Carolina Press, 1996).

47. Ronald Hyam, *Empire and Sexuality: The British Experience* (Manchester: Manchester University Press, 1990).

48. See T.G.P. Spear, *The Nabobs: A Study of the Social Life of the English in Eighteenth Century India* (London: Oxford University Press, 1963).

49. For a critique of Hyam see Ann Laura Stoler, *Race and the Education of Desire: Foucault's History of Sexuality and the Colonial Order of Things* (Durham, NC: Duke University Press, 1995), pp. 175-76.

50. John Tosh, *A Man's Place: Masculinity and the Middle Class Home in Victorian England* (New Haven: Yale University Press, 1999).

51. Graham Dawson, *Soldier Heroes: British Adventure, Empire and the Imagining of Masculinities* (London: Routledge, 1994). See also Martin Green, *Dreams of Adventure, Deeds of Empire* (New York: Basic Books, 1979) and Kelly Boyd, 'Knowing your Place: The Tensions of Manliness in Boys' Story Papers, 1918–39', in Michael Roper and John Tosh (eds.), *Manful Assertions: Masculinities in Britain since 1800* (London: Routledge, 1991), pp. 145-67.

52. See Gayatri Chakravorty Spivak, 'More on Power/Knowledge', in Donna Landry and Gerald MacLean (eds.), *The Spivak Reader* (London: Routledge, 1996), pp. 141-74 and *A Critique of Postcolonial Reason: Toward a History of the Vanishing Present* (Cambridge, MA: Harvard University Press, 1999).

53. See Himani Bannerji, 'Age of Consent and Hegemonic Social Reform', in Midgley, *Gender and Imperialism*, pp. 21-44; Ann Laura Stoler, 'Sexual Affronts and Racial Frontier: European Identities and the Cultural Politics of Exclusion in Colonial Southeast Asia', in Cooper and Stoler, *Tensions of Empire*, pp. 198-237; James F. Warren, *Ah-Ku and Karayuki-san: Prostitution in Singapore, 1870–1940* (Singapore: Oxford University Press, 1993) and McClintock, *Imperial Leather*, pp. 254-55.

54. Manderson, 'Colonial Desires: Sexuality, Race and Gender in British Malaya', pp. 372-88.

55. For the broader history of cross dressing and its association with the histories of homosexuality and gender transgression see Marjorie Garber, *Vested Interests: Cross-Dressing and Cultural Authority* (New York: Routlege, 1992); Vern L. Bullough and Bonnie Bullough, *Cross Dressing, Sex and Gender* (Philadelphia: University of Pennsylvania Press, 1993); Lynne Friedli, 'Passing women – A Study of Gender Boundaries in the Eighteenth Century', in

G.S. Rousseau and Roy Porter (eds.), *Sexual Underworlds of the Enlightenment* (Chapel Hill: University of North Carolina Press), pp. 234-60 and San Francisco Lesbian and Gay History Project, 'She Even Chewed Tobacco: A Pictorial Narrative of Passing Women', in Duberman, Vicinus and Chauncey Jr (eds.), *Hidden From History*, pp. 183-94.

56. Dawson, *Soldier Heroes*, pp. 198-200.

57. See McClintock, *Imperial Leather*, pp. 65-71.

58. See Homi Bhabha, 'Of Mimicry and Man: The Ambivalence of Colonial Discourse', *October* 28 (1984), pp. 126-30 and Frantz Fanon, *Black Skin, White Masks* (trans. Charles Lam Markman; New York: Grove Press, 1967).

59. Dipesh Chakrabarty, 'Postcoloniality and the Artifice of History: Who speaks for "Indian" Pasts', *Representations* 37 (1992), pp. 1-26.

60. Leela Gandhi, *Postcolonial Theory: A Critical Introduction* (Sydney: Allen & Unwin, 1998), p. 4.

61. See Bhabha, 'Of Mimicry and Man', pp. 126-30.

62. Bhabha, 'Of Mimicry and Man', pp. 126-30.

63. Ranajit Guha, 'On Some Aspects of the Historiography of Colonial India', in Ranajit Guha (ed.), *Subaltern Studies* (Delhi: Oxford University Press, 1982), I, pp. 1-8.

64. Gayatri Chakravorty Spivak, 'Can the Subaltern Speak?', in Cary Nelson and Lawrence Grossberg (eds.), *Marxism and the Interpretation of Culture* (Urbana: University of Illinois Press, 1988), pp. 271-313.

65. McClintock, *Imperial Leather*, pp. 352-70.

66. See Padma Anagol, 'Indian Christian Women and Indigenous Feminism, c1850-1920', in Midgley, *Gender and Imperialism*, pp. 79-103.

67. Pamela Pattynama, 'Secrets and Danger: Interracial Sexuality in Louis Couperus' *The Hidden Force* and Dutch Colonial Culture around 1900', in Julia Clancy-Smith and Frances Gouda (eds.), *Domesticating the Empire: Race, Gender, and Family Life in French and Dutch Colonialism* (Charlottesville: London University Press), pp. 84-107.

68. Foucault, *The History of Sexuality*, I, pp. 57-71.

69. See, for example, Xiaoming Xiong Zhu, *Zhongguo tong xing ai shi lu* (*History of Homosexuality in China*) (Xianggang: Fen hong san jiao chu ban she, 1984), Edward Conze, *Buddhism: Its Essence and Development*, (Oxford: Bruno Cassirer, 1974) and Robert Han van Gulik, *Sexual Life in Ancient China* (Leiden: Brill, 1961).

70. Bret Hinsch, *Passions of the Cut Sleeve: The Male Homosexual Tradition in China* (Berkeley: University of California Press, 1990).

71. For an interesting discussion of the globalization of gay and lesbian culture see Denis Altman, *Global Sex* (St Leonards: Allen & Unwin, 2001), pp. 86-105.

72. For a sample of some of this work see Chou Wah-shan, *Tongzhi: Politics of Same-Sex Eroticism in Chinese Societies* (New York: Haworth Press, 2000) and Gerard Sullivan and Peter A. Jackson (eds.), *Gay and Lesbian Asia: Culture, Identity, Community* (New York: Haworth Press, 2001).

73. Benedict Anderson, *Imagined Communities: Reflections on the Origin and Spread of Nationalism* (London: Verso, 1983).

74. Ernest Gellner, *Nations and Nationalism* (Oxford: Basil Blackwell, 1983).

75. Peter Gay, *The Cultivation of Hatred* (New York: Oxford University Press, 1993).

76. George L. Mosse, *Nationalism and Sexuality: Respectability and Abnormal Sexuality in Modern Europe* (New York: H. Fertig, 1985).

77. Klaus Theweleit, *Male Fantasies:* I and II (trans. Stephen Conway; Minneapolis: University of Minnesota Press, 1987).

Chapter 8

1. Josephine Butler, 'An Appeal to the People of England on the Recognition and Superintendence of Prostitution by Governments' in Sheila Jeffreys (ed.), *The Sexuality Debates* (London: Routledge & Kegan Paul, 1987), pp. 111-46.

2. David J. Pivar, *Purity and Hygiene: Women, Prostitution and the "American Plan" 1900–1930* (Westport: Greenwood Press, 2002). See also Timothy J. Gilfoyle, *City of Eros: New York City, Prostitution and the Commercialization of Sex, 1790–1920* (New York: W.W. Norton, 1992), pp. 181-96.

3. Helen Lefkowitz Horowitz, *Rereading Sex: Battles over Sexual Knowledge in Nineteenth Century America* (New York: Knopf, 2002), pp. 19-44.

4. See Roy Porter and Lesley Hall, *The Facts of Life: The Creation of Sexual Knowledge in Britain, 1650–1950* (New Haven: Yale University Press, 1995), pp. 141-44.

5. See David J. Pivar, *Purity Crusade: Sexual Morality and Social Control, 1868–1900* (Westport: Greenwood Press, 1973); Edward J. Bristow, *Vice and Vigilance: Purity Movements in Britain since 1700* (Dublin: Gill & Macmillan, 1977), pp. 1-3; Rachel Harrison and Frank Mort, 'Patriarchal Aspects of Nineteenth-Century State Formation: Property Relations, Marriage, Divorce and Sexuality', in Philip Corrigan (ed.), *Capitalism, State Formation and Marxist Theory: Historical Investigations* (London: Quartet Books, 1980), pp. 79-109 and Jeffrey Weeks, *Sex, Politics and Society: The Regulation of Sexuality since 1800* (London: Longman, 2nd edn, 1989), pp. 81-84.

6. See Linda Gordon and Ellen DuBois, 'Seeking Ecstasy on the Battlefield: Danger and Pleasure in Nineteenth Century Feminist Thought', *Feminist Review* 13 (1983).

7. For a good summary of these debates and characterizations see Judith Allen, *Rose Scott: Vision and Revision in Feminism* (Melbourne: Oxford University Press, 1994), pp. 5-16.

8. See, for example, Shulamith Firestone, *The Dialectic of Sex* (London: Paladin, 1972), pp. 26-31; Sheila Rowbotham, *Woman, Resistance and Revolution* (Harmondsworth: Penguin, 1974), pp. 245-47; Ellen DuBois, *Feminism and Suffrage: The Emergence of an Independent Women's Movement in America, 1848–1869* (Ithaca: Cornell University Press, 1978), p. 20; Marianna Valverde, *The Age of Light and Soap and Water* (Toronto: McClelland &

Stewart, 1991), pp. 58-76 and Ann Summers, *Damned Whores and God's Police: The Colonization of Women in Australia* (Ringwood, Victoria: Penguin Books, 1975), pp. 469-70.

9. Nancy Cott, *The Grounding of Modern Feminism* (New Haven: Yale University Press, 1987), pp. 4-5.

10. See Barbara Caine, *Victorian Feminists* (London: Oxford University Press, 1992), pp. 6-7, Karen Offen, 'Defining Feminism: A Comparative Historical Approach', *Signs* 14.1 (1988), pp. 119-57 and Allen, *Rose Scott*, pp. 5-16.

11. Christine Stansell, *American Moderns: Bohemian New York and the Creation of a New Century* (New York: Metropolitan Books, 2000), pp. 225-72.

12. Quoted in Carroll Smith-Rosenberg, 'The Female World of Love and Ritual: The Relations between Women in Nineteenth-Century America', *Signs* 1.1 (1975), pp. 1-29.

13. Lillian Faderman, *Odd Girls and Twilight Lovers: A History of Lesbian Life in Twentieth-Century America* (New York: Columbia University Press, 1991), pp. 11-36.

14. Faderman, *Odd Girls and Twilight Lovers*, pp. 11-36. See also Lillian Faderman, *Surpassing the Love of Men: Romantic Friendships and Love between Women from the Renaissance to the Present* (New York: Morrow, 1981).

15. Lillian Faderman, *Scotch Verdict: Miss Pirie and Miss Woods v. Dame Cumming Gordon* (New York: Morrow, 1983).

16. Martha Vicinus, 'One Life to Stand behind Me: Emotional Conflicts in First Generation College Women in England', *Feminist Studies* 8.3 (1982), pp. 610-11.

17. Elizabeth Mavor, *The Ladies of Llangollen* (London: Michael Joseph, 1972).

18. See, for example, Margaret Gibson, 'Clitoral Corruption: Body Metaphors and American Doctors' Constructions of Female Homosexuality, 1870–1900', in Vernon A. Rosario (ed.), *Science and Homosexualities* (New York: Routledge, 1997), pp. 108-32.

19. See also Lillian Faderman, 'The Morbidification of Love between Women by Nineteenth Century Sexologists', *Journal of Homosexuality* 4 (1978), pp. 73-90 and *Odd Girls and Twilight Lovers*, pp. 11-36.

20. Helena Whitbread (ed.), *The Diaries of Ann Lister, 1791–1840* (London: Virago, 1988).

21. Quoted in Liz Stanley, 'Romantic Friendship? Some Issues in Researching Lesbian History and Biography', *Women's History Review* 1.2 (1992), pp. 193-216.

22. See Vern L. Bullough and Bonnie Bullough, *Cross Dressing, Sex, and Gender* (Philadelphia: University of Pennsylvania Press, 1993), pp. 145-73.

23. Stanley, 'Romantic Friendship? Some Issues in Researching Lesbian History and Biography', pp. 196-98.

24. Quoted in Martha Vicinus, 'They Wonder to Which Sex I Belong: The Historical Roots of Modern Lesbian Identity', *Feminist Studies* 18.3 (1992), p. 471.

25. Sheila Jeffreys, *The Spinster and her Enemies* (London: Pandora Press, 1985), pp. 102-27.
26. Stanley, 'Romantic Friendship? Some Issues Researching Lesbian History and Biography', pp. 195-97.
27. Vicinus, 'They Wonder to Which Sex I Belong', pp. 467-97.
28. John Tosh, 'Domesticity and Manliness in the Victorian Middle Class: The Family of Edward White Benson', in Michael Roper and John Tosh (eds.), *Manful Assertions: Masculinities in Britain since 1800* (London: Routledge, 1991), pp. 44-73.
29. Ray Strachey, *The Cause: A Short History of the Women's Movement in Great Britain* (London: G. Bell, 1928).
30. See Barbara Caine, *English Feminism, 1780–1980* (Oxford: Oxford University Press, 1997), pp. 11-52.
31. Carol Pateman, *The Sexual Contract* (Oxford: Polity Press, 1988), pp. 77-115. See also Olwyn Hufton, *Women and the Limits of Citizenship in the French Revolution* (Toronto: University of Toronto Press, 1992), Joan Landes, *Women and the Public Sphere in the Age of the French Revolution* (Ithaca: Cornell University Press, 1988) and Joan W. Scott, *Only Paradoxes to Offer: French Feminists and the Rights of Man* (Cambridge, MA: Harvard University Press, 1996).
32. See, for example, Caine, *English Feminism*, pp. 53-130; Phillippa Levine, *Victorian Feminism, 1850–1900* (London: Hutchinson, 1987), pp. 11-24; DuBois, *Feminism and Suffrage* and Eleanor Flexner, *Century of Struggle: The Woman's Rights Movement in the United States* (New York: Atheneum, 1970).
33. See Brian Harrison, *Separate Spheres: The Opposition to Women's Suffrage in Britain* (London: Croom Helm, 1978) and Karen Offen, *European Feminisms, 1700–1950* (Stanford: Stanford University Press, 2000), pp. 188-200.
34. Barbara Taylor, *Eve and the New Jerusalem: Socialism and Feminism in the Nineteenth Century* (London: Virago, 1983) and Offen, *European Feminisms*, pp. 200-12.
35. See Gordon and DuBois, 'Seeking Ecstasy on the Battlefield', Firestone, *The Dialectic of Sex*, pp. 26-31 and Rowbotham, *Woman, Resistance and Revolution*, pp. 245-47.
36. See, for example, Mark T. Connelly, *The Response to Prostitution in the Progressive Era* (Chapel Hill: University of North Carolina Press, 1980).
37. See, for example, John D'Emilio and Estelle B. Freedman, *Intimate Matters: A History of Sexuality in America* (New York: Harper & Row, 1988), pp. 150-56, Horowitz, *Rereading Sex*, pp. 251-70 and Pivar, *Purity Crusade*, pp. 78-130.
38. In addition to texts cited already see Frank Mort, *Dangerous Sexualities: Medico-Moral Politics in England since 1830* (London: Routledge & Kegan Paul, 1987), pp. 63-150.
39. D'Emilio and Freedman, *Intimate Matters*, pp. 202-21.

40. Margaret Jackson, *The Real Facts of Life: Feminism and the Politics of Sexuality c1850–1940* (London: Taylor & Francis, 1994), pp. 26-28.

41. See also Jeffreys, *The Spinster and her Enemies*, pp. 6-26 and Lucy Bland, 'Purifying the Public World: Feminist Vigilantes in Late Victorian England', *Women's History Review* 1.3 (1992), pp. 397-412.

42. Horowitz, *Rereading Sex*, pp. 256-70.

43. D'Emilio and Freedman, *Intimate Matters*, pp. 150-56.

44. Offen, *European Feminisms*, pp. 150-64.

45. Judith Walkowitz, *City of Dreadful Delight: Narratives of Sexual Danger in Late-Victorian London* (Chicago: Chicago University Press, 1992), pp. 81-120.

46. Jeffreys, *The Spinster and her Enemies*, p. 7.

47. See Pivar, *Purity and Hygiene*, pp. 119-238. See also D'Emilio and Freedman, *Intimate Matters*, pp. 150-56, Ellen Fitzpatrick, *Endless Crusade: Women, Social Scientists and Progressive Reform* (New York: Oxford University Press, 1990) and Janet Beer and Katherine Joslyn, 'Diseases of the Body Politic: White Slavery in Jane Addams' "A New Conscience and an Ancient Evil" and Selected Short Stories by Charlotte Perkins Gilman', *Journal of American Studies* 33 (April 1999).

48. Butler, 'An Appeal to the People of England'. For an insightful analysis of Butler see Caine, *Victorian Feminists*, pp. 150-95.

49. D'Emilio and Freedman, *Intimate Matters*, p. 153.

50. Jackson, *The Real Facts of Life*, pp. 28-29.

51. See Caine, *Victorian Feminists*, pp. 103-49; Levine, *Victorian Feminism*, pp. 128-55; Offen, *European Feminisms*, pp. 170-80 and Jackson, *The Real Facts of Life*, pp. 8-14.

52. Jeffreys, *The Spinster and her Enemies*, pp. 1-5.

53. For some general overviews of sexology and its impact see Weeks, *Sex, Politics and Society*, pp. 141-59, Elaine Showalter, *The English Malady: Women, Madness and English Culture, 1830–1980* (London: Virago, 1987), pp. 121-64 and Sheila Rowbotham and Jeffrey Weeks, *Socialism and the New Life: The Personal and Sexual Politics of Edward Carpenter and Havelock Ellis* (London: Pluto Press, 1977).

54. See Carroll Smith-Rosenberg, 'Discourses of Sexuality and Subjectivity: The New Woman, 1870-1939', in Martin Bauml Duberman, Martha Vicinus and George Chauncey Jr (eds.), *Hidden from History: Reclaiming the Gay and Lesbian Past* (New York: New American Library, 1989), pp. 264-80.

55. See Barbara Caine and Glenda Sluga, *Gendering European History, 1760–1920* (London: Leicester University Press, 2000), pp. 130-36.

56. See Caine, *English Feminism*, pp. 131-72; Jackson, *The Facts of Life*, pp. 80-105; Lucy Bland, 'Marriage Laid Bare: Middle-Class Women and Marital Sex, 1880s–1914', in Jane Lewis (ed.), *Labour and Love: Women's Experience of Home and Family, 1850–1940* (Oxford; Basil Blackwell, 1986), pp. 123-46 and D'Emilio and Freedman, *Intimate Matters*, pp. 229-35.

57. Bram Dijkstra, *Idols of Perversity: Fantasies of Feminine Evil at the Fin de Siecle* (Oxford: Oxford University Press, 1986). See also Caine and Sluga, *Gendering European History*, pp. 130-36.

58. Caine and Sluga, *Gendering European History*, pp. 134-36.

59. Cott, *The Grounding of Modern Feminism*, pp. 59-62.

60. See Stansell, *American Moderns*, pp. 225-72 and June Sochen, *The New Woman: Feminism in Greenwich Village 1910–1920* (New York: Quadrangle Books, 1972).

61. See Caine, *English Feminism*, pp. 131-72; Ellen Kay Trimberger, 'Feminism, Men, and Modern Love: Greenwich Village, 1900–1925', in Ann Snitow, Christine Stansell and Sharon Thompson (eds.), *Desire: The Politics of Sexuality* (New York: Monthly Review Press, 1984), pp. 169-89; Cott, *Grounding of Modern Feminism*, pp. 13-50; Rowbotham and Weeks, *Socialism and the New Life*, pp. 25-128 and D'Emilio and Freedman, *Intimate Matters*, pp. 229-35.

62. See Caine, *English Feminism*, pp. 173-221; Carol Dyhouse, *Feminism and the Family in England, 1880–1930* (Oxford: Basil Blackwell, 1989); Martin Pugh, *Women and the Women's Movement in Britain, 1914–1959* (London: Macmillan, 1992); Kevin White, *The First Sexual Revolution: The Emergence of Male Heterosexuality in Modern America* (New York: New York University Press, 1993); Cott, *Grounding of Modern Feminism*, pp. 145-74 and Ellen Holtzman, 'The Pursuit of Married Love: Women's Attitudes Toward Sexuality and Marriage in Great Britain, 1918–1939', *Journal of Social History* 16.2 (1982), pp. 39-52.

63. Weeks, *Sex, Politics and Society*, pp. 122-98.

64. See Edward Shorter, *A History of Women's Bodies* (Harmondsworth: Penguin, 1984), pp. 294-96; Sidney Ditzion, *Marriage Morals and Sex in America* (New York: Norton, 2nd edn, 1969); Henry May, *The End of American Innocence* (Chicago: Quadrangle Books, 1964) and Lawrence Stone, *The Family, Sex and Marriage in England, 1500–1800* (London: Weidenfeld and Nicholson, 1977). For a critical overview of this historiography see Christina Simmons, 'Modern Sexuality and the Myth of Victorian Repression', in Kathy Peiss and Christina Simmons (eds.), *Passion and Power: Sexuality in History* (Philadelphia: Temple University Press, 1989), pp. 157-77.

65. D'Emilio and Freedman, *Intimate Matters*, pp. 239-55.

66. Jeffreys, *The Spinster and her Enemies*, pp. 128-85 and 'Sex Reform and Anti-Feminism in the 1920s', in London Feminist History Group (ed.), *The Sexual Dynamics of History: Men's Power, Women's Resistance* (London: Pluto Press, 1983), pp. 177-202. See also Jackson, *The Real Facts of Life*, pp. 106-58.

67. Caine, *English Feminism*, pp. 173-221 and Cott, *The Grounding of Modern Feminism*, pp. 86-99.

68. See Lesley Hall, 'Impotent Ghosts from No Man's Land, Flappers' Boyfriends, or Cryptopatriarchs? Men, Sex and Social Change in 1920s Britain', *Social History* 21.1 (1996), pp. 54-70, and Lucy Bland, 'Middle Class Marriage Laid Bare'.

69. Lesley Hall, 'Feminist Reconfigurations of Heterosexuality in the 1920s', in Lucy Bland and Laura Doan (eds.), *Sexology in Culture: Labelling Bodies and Desires* (Chicago: University of Chicago Press, 1998), pp. 135-49.

70. See Joseph Bristow, 'Symond's History, Ellis's Heredity: Sexual Inversion', in Bland and Doan, *Sexology in Culture*, pp. 79-99, Rowbotham and Weeks, *Socialism and the New Life* and George Chauncey Jr, 'From Sexual Inversion to Homosexuality: The Changing Medical Conceptualisation of Female "Deviance"', in Peiss and Simmons, *Passion and Power*, pp. 87-117.

71. See Beverley Brown, 'A Disgusting Book When Properly Read: The Obscenity Trial', *Hecate* 10.2 (1984) and Esther Newton, 'The Mythic Mannish Lesbian: Radclyffe Hall and the New Woman', in Duberman, Vicinus and Chauncey Jr (eds.), *Hidden from History*, pp. 281-93.

Chapter 9

1. Richard von Krafft-Ebing, *Psychopathia Sexualis* (trans. F.J. Rebman; ed. and intro. Brian King; Burbank: Bloat, 1999), pp. ix-x.

2. Figures quoted in Andreas Hill, 'May the Doctor Advise Extramarital Intercourse?: Medical Debates on Sexual Abstinence in Germany, c.1900', in Roy Porter and Mikulas Teich (eds.), *Sexual Knowledge, Sexual Science: The History of Attitudes to Sexuality* (Cambridge: Cambridge University Press, 1994), p. 286 and Jeffrey Weeks, 'Movements of Affirmation: Sexual Meanings and Homosexual Identities', in Kathy Peiss and Christina Simmons (eds.), *Passion and Power: Sexuality in History* (Philadelphia: Temple University Press, 1989), p. 73.

3. Steven Marcus, *The Other Victorians: A Study of Sexuality and Pornography in Mid-Nineteenth Century England* (New York: Basic Books, 1966). See also Phyllis Grosskurth, *Havelock Ellis: A Biography* (New York: Knopf, 1980) and Marthe Roberts, *The Psychoanalytic Revolution: Sigmund Freud's Life and Achievement* (trans. Kenneth Morgan; London: Allen & Unwin, 1966).

4. John D'Emilio and Estelle B. Freedman, *Intimate Matters: A History of Sexuality in America* (New York: Harper & Row, 1988), pp. 171-235.

5. Frank Sulloway, *Freud: Biologist of the Mind* (London: Burnett Books in association with André Deutsch, 1979).

6. See, for example, Foucault's essays and interviews 'Truth and Power' and 'The Confession of the Flesh', in Colin Gordon (ed.), *Power/Knowledge: Selected Interviews and other Writings 1972–75 by Michel Foucault* (New York: Harvester Wheatsheaf, 1980), pp. 109-33 and 194-228.

7. Michel Foucault, *The History of Sexuality*. I. *An Introduction* (trans. Robert Hurley; New York: Random House, 1978).

8. See David M. Halperin, 'How to Do the History of Male Homosexuality', in *How to Do the History of Homosexuality* (Chicago: University of Chicago Press, 2002), pp. 104-37; Arnold I. Davidson, *The Emergence of Sexuality: Historical Epistemology and the Formation of Concepts* (Cambridge MA: Harvard University Press, 2001); Jennifer Terry, *An American Obsession: Science, Medicine, and Homosexuality in Modern Society* (Chicago: Chicago University

Press, 1999) and Vernon A. Rosario (ed.), *Science and Homosexualities* (New York: Routledge, 1997).

9. Jonathan Ned Katz, *The Invention of Heterosexuality* (New York: Dutton, 1995).

10. See, for example, Foucault's essays 'Power and Strategies', 'The Eye of Power' and 'The Politics of Health in the Eighteenth Century', in Gordon (ed.), *Power/Knowledge*, pp. 134-82.

11. See, for example, Roy Porter, *Health for Sale: Quackery in England, 1660–1850* (New York: St Martin's Press, 1989); Alex Comfort, *The Anxiety Makers* (London: Nelson, 1967); W.F. Bynum and Roy Porter (eds.), *Medical Fringe and Medical Orthodoxy, 1750–1850* (London: Croom Helm, 1987) and Michael Mason, *The Making of Victorian Sexuality* (Oxford: Oxford University Press, 1994).

12. For good studies of these developments see Mason, *The Making of Victorian Sexuality*, pp. 175-215, G.J. Barker-Benfield, *The Horrors of a Half-Known Life: Aspects of the Exploitation of Women by Men* (New York: Harper & Row, 1976) and Harry Oosterhuis, 'Richard von Krafft-Ebing's "Step-Children of Nature": Psychiatry and the Making of Homosexual Identity', in Rosario (ed.), *Science and Homosexualities*, pp. 67-88.

13. See Andrew Scull, *The Most Solitary of Afflictions: Madness and Society in Britain, 1700–1900* (New Haven: Yale University Press, 1993), David J. Rothman, *The Discovery of the Asylum: Social Order and Disorder in the New Republic* (Boston: Little, Brown, 1971) and Klaus Doerner, *Madmen and the Bourgeoisie: A Social History of Insanity and Psychiatry* (Oxford: Basil Blackwell, 1981).

14. See Elaine Showalter, *The Female Malady: Women, Madness and English Culture, 1830–1980* (London: Virago, 1987), pp. 146-56.

15. See Michael Ignatieff, *A Just Measure of Pain: The Penitentiary in the Industrial Revolution, 1750–1850* (London: Macmillan, 1978); Patricia O'Brien, *The Promise of Punishment: Prisons in Nineteenth-Century France* (Princeton: Princeton University Press, 1982); Sean McConville, *A History of English Prison Administration* (London: Routledge & Kegan Paul, 1981); Susan B. Carrafiello, *The Tombs of the Living: Prisons and Prison Reform in Liberal Italy* (New York: P. Lang, 1998) and David Garland, *Punishment and Welfare: A History of Penal Strategies* (Aldershot: Gower, c.1985).

16. See Roger Smith, *Trial by Medicine: Insanity and Responsibility in Victorian Trials* (Edinburgh: Edinburgh University Press, 1981).

17. See, for example, Angus McLaren, *Prescription for Murder: The Victorian Serial Killings of Dr Thomas Neill Cream* (Chicago: University of Chicago Press, 1993).

18. See Randolph Trumbach, *Sex and the Gender Revolution. I. Heterosexuality and the Third Gender in Enlightenment London* (Chicago: Chicago University Press, 1998); Roy Porter, *London: A Social History* (Cambridge, MA: Harvard University Press, 1995), pp. 160-84; Roy Porter and Marie Mulvey Roberts (eds.), *Pleasure in the Eighteenth Century* (Basingstoke: Macmillan

Press, 1996) and Alan Bray, *Homosexuality in Renaissance England* (London: Gay Men's Press, 1982).

19. George Chauncey Jr, *Gay New York: Gender, Urban Culture, and the Making of the Gay Male World, 1890–1940* (New York: Basic Books, 1994). See also Timothy J. Gilfoyle, *City of Eros: New York City, Prostitution, and the Commercialization of Sex, 1790–1920* (New York: W.W. Norton, 1992), pp. 228-30.

20. See George Mosse, 'Masculinity and Decadence', in Porter and Teich, *Sexual Knowledge, Sexual Science*, pp. 251-66, Renate Hauser, 'Krafft-Ebing's Psychological Understanding of Sexual Behaviour', in Porter and Teich, *Sexual Knowledge, Sexual Science*, pp. 210-27 and Vernon A. Rosario, 'Inversion's Histories/History's Inversions: Novelizing fin-de-siecle Homosexuality', in Rosario (ed.), *Science and Homosexualities*, pp. 89-107.

21. See, for example, Peter Gay, *Freud: A Life for our Time* (New York: W.W. Norton, 1988), pp. 103-49 and Foucault, 'The Confession of the Flesh', in Gordon (ed.), *Power/Knowledge*, pp. 194-228.

22. See Merl Storr, 'Transformations: Subjects, Categories and Cures in Krafft-Ebing's Sexology', in Lucy Bland and Laura Doan (eds.), *Sexology in Culture: Labelling Bodies and Desires* (Chicago: University of Chicago Press, 1998), pp. 11-26 and Oosterhuis, 'Richard von Krafft-Ebing's "Step-Children of Nature": Psychiatry and the Making of Homosexual Identity', pp. 67-88.

23. See, for example, James D. Steakley, 'Per scientiam ad justitiam: Magnus Hirschfeld and the Sexual Politics of Innate Homosexuality', in Rosario (ed.), *Science and Homosexualities*, pp. 133-54; Lawrence Birken, *Consuming Desire: Sexual Science and the Emergence of a Culture of Abundance, 1870–1914* (Ithaca: Cornell University Press, 1988), pp. 72-91; Gay, *Freud: A Life for our Time*, pp. 153-305; Grosskurth, *Havelock Ellis: A Biography*, pp. 165-234; Terry, *An American Obsession*, pp. 74-119 and Elizabeth Lunbeck, *The Psychiatric Persuasion: Knowledge, Gender, and Power in Modern America* (Princeton; Princeton University Press, 1994).

24. See Roy Porter and Lesley Hall, *The Facts of Life: The Creation of Sexual Knowledge in Britain, 1650–1950* (New Haven: Yale University Press, 1995), pp. 155-77, Jeffrey Weeks, *Sex, Politics and Society: The Regulation of Sexuality since 1800* (London: Longman, 2nd edn, 1989), pp. 184-87 and Nathan G. Hale Jr, *The Rise and Crisis of Psychoanalysis in the United States: Freud and the Americans, 1917–1985* (New York: Oxford University Press, 1995), pp. 25-73.

25. For some overviews of some of these tensions see Eugene Weber, *France: Fin de Siecle* (Cambridge, MA: Belknap Press, 1986), p. 2, Elaine Showalter, *Sexual Anarchy: Gender and Culture at the Fin de Siecle* (London: Bloomsbury, 1991) and E.J. Hobsbawm, *The Age of Empire, 1870–1914* (London: Weidenfeld & Nicolson, 1987).

26. See Daniel Pick, *Faces of Degeneration: A European Disorder, c.1848–c.1918* (Cambridge: Cambridge University Press, 1989); Weeks, *Sex, Politics and*

Society, pp. 96-159; Judy Greenway, 'Its What You Do With It That Counts: Interpretations of Otto Weininger', in Bland and Doan, *Sexology in Culture*, pp. 27-43 and Daniel J. Kelves, *In the Name of Eugenics: Genetics and the Uses of Human Heredity* (New York: Knopf, 1985), pp. 3-84.

27. See, for example, G.R. Searle, *Eugenics and Politics in Britain, 1900–1914* (Leyden: Noordhoff, 1976), M.H. Haller, *Eugenics: Hereditarian Attitudes in American Thought* (New Jersey: Rutgers University Press, 1963) and Richard Hofstadter, *Social Darwinism in American Thought* (Boston: Beacon Press, 2nd edn, 1955).

28. Kurt Danziger, *Constructing the Subject: Historical Origins of Psychological Research* (Cambridge: Cambridge University Press, 1990), pp. 13-14.

29. John Bristow, 'Symond's History, Ellis's Heredity: Sexual Inversion', in Bland and Doan, *Sexology in Culture*, pp. 79-99.

30. See Sulloway, *Freud: Biologist of the Mind*, pp. 70-100, Diane J. Paul, *Controlling Human Heredity 1865 to the Present* (Atlantic Highlands: Humanities Press, 1995) and G.R. Searle, *The Quest for National Efficiency, 1899–1914* (Oxford: Basil Blackwell, 1971).

31. See, for example, Terry, *American Obsession*, pp. 27-119, Frank Tallis, *Changing Minds: The History of Psychotherapy as an Answer to Human Suffering* (London: Cassell, 1998) and Stanley W. Jackson, *Care of the Psyche: A History of Psychological Healing* (New Haven: Yale University Press, 1999).

32. Renate Hauser, 'Krafft-Ebing's Psychological Understanding of Sexual Behaviour', in Porter and Teich, *Sexual Knowledge, Sexual Science*, pp. 210-27.

33. Sulloway, *Freud: Biologist of the Mind*, pp. 135-418.

34. See Gay, *Freud: A Life for our Times*, pp. 55-102.

35. See Weeks, *Sex, Politics and Society*, pp. 152-56.

36. See Nathan G. Hale Jr, *The Beginnings of Psychoanalysis in the United States, 1876–1917* (New York: Oxford University Press, 1971), pp. 462-86.

37. Lydston is quoted in Angus McLaren, *Twentieth-Century Sexuality: A History* (Oxford: Basil Blackwell, 1999), p. 93.

38. See Matthew Thomson, *The Problem of Mental Deficiency: Eugenics, Democracy and Social Policy in Britain, c1870–1950* (Oxford: Oxford University Press, 1998).

39. See Lunbeck, *The Psychiatric Persuasion*, pp. 229-55.

40. Patrick Geddes and J. Arthur Thompson, *The Evolution of Sex* (London: W. Scott, 1889).

41. Hauser, 'Krafft-Ebing's Psychological Understandings of Sexual Behaviour', pp. 210-21.

42. Porter and Hall, *The Facts of Life*, pp. 155-73, Sheila Rowbotham and Jeffrey Weeks, *Socialism and the New Life: The Personal and Sexual Politics of Edward Carpenter and Havelock Ellis* (London: Pluto Press, 1977), pp. 141-85 and Bristow, 'Symond's History, Ellis's Heredity', pp. 79-99.

43. See Steakley, 'Magnus Hirschfeld and the Sexual Politics of Innate Homosexuality', pp. 133-40.

44. See Rowbotham and Weeks, *Socialism and the New Life*, pp. 141-85.
45. In addition to historians already cited see Vernon A. Rosario, *The Erotic Imagination: French Histories of Perversity* (New York: Oxford University Press, 1997).
46. Halperin, 'How to do the History of Male Homosexuality', pp. 104-37.
47. See also George Chauncey Jr, 'From Sexual Inversion to Homosexuality: The Changing Medical Conceptualisation of Female "Deviance"', in Peiss and Simmons (eds.), *Passion and Power*, pp. 87-117; Jay Prosser, 'Transsexuals and the Transexologists: Inversion and the Emergence of Transsexual Subjectivity', in Bland and Doan, *Sexology in Culture*, pp. 116-31; Chris Waters, 'Havelock Ellis, Sigmund Freud and the State: Discourses of Homosexual Identity in Interwar Britain', in Bland and Doan, *Sexology in Culture*, pp. 165-79 and Porter and Hall, *The Facts of Life*, pp. 193-94.
48. Waters, 'Havelock Ellis, Sigmund Freud and the State: Discourses of Homosexual Identity in Interwar Britain', in Bland and Doan, *Sexology in Culture*, pp. 165-79.
49. Lillian Faderman, *Odd Girls and Twilight Lovers: A History of Lesbian Life in Twentieth-Century America* (New York: Columbia University Press, 1991), pp. 37-61.
50. See George Chauncey Jr, 'From Sexual Inversion to Homosexuality', pp. 87-117, Terry, *An American Obsession*, pp. 40-73 and Leila J. Rupp, *A Desired Past: A Short History of Same-Sex Love* (Chicago: University of Chicago Press, 1999), pp. 73-100.
51. Terry, *An American Obsession*, pp. 353-77.
52. Faderman, *Odd Girls and Twilight Lovers*, pp. 37-61.
53. Rupp, *A Desired Past*, 73-100 and Chauncey Jr, 'From Sexual Inversion to Homosexuality', pp. 87-117.
54. Sheila Jeffreys, 'Sex Reform and Anti-Feminism in the 1920s', in London Feminist History Group (ed.), *The Sexual Dynamics of History: Men's Power, Women's Resistance* (London: Pluto Press, 1983), pp. 177-202 and Margaret Jackson, *The Real Facts of Life: Feminism and the Politics of Sexuality c1850–1940* (London: Taylor & Francis, 1994), pp. 106-28.
55. Greenway, 'Its What You Do With It That Counts: Interpretations of Otto Weininger', pp. 27-43.
56. Lesley Hall, 'Feminist Reconfigurations of Heterosexuality in the 1920s', in Bland and Doan, *Sexology in Culture*, pp. 135-49 and *Hidden Anxieties: Male Sexuality 1900–1950* (Cambridge: Polity Press, 1991).
57. See, for example, Steven Selden, *Inheriting Shame: The Story of Eugenics and Racism in America* (New York: Teachers College Press, 1999).
58. Sander Gilman, 'Sigmund Freud and the Sexologists: A Second Reading', in Porter and Teich, *Sexual Knowledge, Sexual Science*, pp. 323-49.
59. See, for example, Estelle B. Freedman, *Their Sisters' Keepers: Women's Prison Reform in America, 1830–1930* (Ann Arbor: University of Michigan Press, 1981), Nicole Hahn Rafter, *Creating Born Criminals* (Urbana: University of Illinois Press, 1997) and Lunbeck, *The Psychiatric Persuasion*, pp. 229-53.

60. Estelle B. Freeman, 'Uncontrolled Desires: The Response to the Sexual Psychopath, 1920–1960', *Journal of American History* 74.1 (June 1987), pp. 83-106.

61. Stephen Robertson, 'Separating the Men from the Boys: Masculinity, Psycho-Sexual Development, and Sex Crime in the United States, 1930s–1960s', *Journal of the History of Medicine and Allied Sciences* 56.1 (2001), pp. 3-35.

62. See Frederick C. Crews (ed.), *Unauthorized Freud: Doubters Confront the Legend* (New York: Viking, 1998).

63. See Gilles Deleuze and Felix Guattari, *Anti-Oedipus: Capitalism and Schizophrenia* (trans. Robert Hurley, Mark Seem and Helen R. Lane; New York: Viking, 1977). For a critical appreciation of psychoanalysis and an overview of feminist criticism of Freudianism, particularly the work of Lacan, see Elizabeth Grosz, *Jacques Lacan: A Feminist Introduction* (London: Routledge, 1990).

64. For example one influential feminist assessment of Freud is Juliet Mitchell, *Psychoanalysis and Feminism* (London: Allen Lane, 1974).

65. Marcus, *The Other Victorians*, pp. 282-86.

66. Weeks, *Sex, Politics and Society*, pp. 152-54.

67. Showalter, *The Female Malady*, pp. 155-62.

68. McLaren, *Twentieth-Century Sexuality*, pp. 110-15.

69. Foucault, *The History of Sexuality*, I, pp. 53-73.

Chapter 10

1. Vern L. Bullough, 'The Development of Sexology in the USA in the Twentieth Century', in Roy Porter and Mikulas Teich (eds.), *Sexual Knowledge, Sexual Science: The History of Attitudes to Sexuality* (Cambridge: Cambridge University Press, 1994), pp. 303-22.

2. See Jennifer Terry, *An American Obsession: Science, Medicine, and Homosexuality in Modern Society* (Chicago: Chicago University Press, 1999), pp. 178-219.

3. For a fascinating cultural history of transsexuality see Joanne Meyerowitz, *How Sex Changed: A History of Transsexuality in the United States* (Cambridge, MA: Harvard University Press, 2002).

4. For a general overview of some of these developments see Angus McLaren, *Twentieth-Century Sexuality: A History* (Oxford: Basil Blackwell, 1999), pp. 23-109.

5. McLaren, *Twentieth-Century Sexuality*, pp. 110-23 and Jeffrey Weeks, *Sex, Politics and Society: The Regulation of Sexuality since 1800* (London: Longman, 2nd edn, 1989), pp. 141-98.

6. See Frank Mort, *Dangerous Sexualities: Medico-Moral Politics in England since 1830* (London: Routledge & Kegan Paul, 1987), pp. 189-207; Vern L. Bullough, *Science in the Bedroom: A History of Sex Research* (New York: Basic Books, 1994), pp. 136-47; Ruth Hall, *Passionate Crusader: Marie Stopes, A Biography* (London: Deutsch, 1977), pp. 128-241; June Rose, *Marie Stopes and the Sexual Revolution* (London: Faber, 1992), pp. 105-75;

Ellen Chesler, *Woman of Valor: Margaret Sanger and the Birth Control Movement in America* (New York: Simon & Schuster, 1992), pp. 179-286 and Madeline Gay, *Margaret Sanger: A Biography of the Champion of Birth Control* (New York: R. Marek, 1979), pp. 121-81.

7. Kevin White, *Sexual Liberation or Sexual License? The American Revolt against Victorianism* (Chicago: Ivan R. Dee, 2000).

8. See Steven Seidman, *Romantic Longings: Love in America, 1830–1980* (New York: Routledge, 1991), pp. 65-91. See also, Weeks, *Sex, Politics and Society*, pp. 199-213, John D'Emilio and Estelle B. Freedman, *Intimate Matters: A History of Sexuality in America* (New York: Harper & Row, 1988), pp. 239-300 and Kathy Peiss, *Cheap Amusements: Working Women and Leisure in Turn-of-the-Century New York* (Philadelphia: Temple University Press, 1986).

9. Seidman, *Romantic Longings*, pp. 61-95.

10. See David J. Pivar, *Purity and Hygiene: Women, Prostitution and the "American Plan", 1900–1930* (Westport: Greenwood Press, 2002); D'Emilio and Freedman, *Intimate Matters*, pp. 202-15; Weeks, *Sex, Politics and Society*, pp. 122-40; Matthew Thomson, *The Problem of Mental Deficiency: Eugenics, Democracy and Social Policy in Britain c1870–1950* (Oxford: Oxford University Press, 1998); M.H. Haller, *Eugenics: Hereditarian Attitudes in American Thought* (New Jersey: Rutgers University Press, 1963) and Daniel J. Kevles, *In the Name of Eugenics: Genetics and the Uses of Human Heredity* (Cambridge, MA: Harvard University Press, 1995), pp. 96-112.

11. Beth Bailey, *Sex in the Heartland* (Cambridge, MA: Harvard University Press, 1999).

12. For the new woman of the 1890s see Barbara Caine and Glenda Sluga, *Gendering European History, 1780–1920* (London: Leicester University Press, 2000), pp. 125-40 and Carroll Smith-Rosenberg, *Disorderly Conduct: Visions of Gender in Victorian America* (New York: Oxford University Press, 1985), pp. 245-96.

13. Christine Stansell, *American Moderns: Bohemian New York and the Creation of a New Century* (New York: Metropolitan Books, 2000).

14. D'Emilio and Freedman, *Intimate Matters*, pp. 239-99.

15. See Paul Robinson, *The Modernization of Sex: Havelock Ellis, Alfred Kinsey, William Masters and Virginia Johnson* (New York: Harper & Row, 1976).

16. For example David Allyn, *Make Love Not War: An Unfettered History of the Sexual Revolution* (Boston: Little, Brown, 2000).

17. See, for example, Alison Oram, 'Sex is an Accident: Feminism, Science and the Radical Sexual Theory of Urania, 1915–40', in Lucy Bland and Laura Doan (eds.), *Sexology in Culture: Labelling Bodies and Desires* (Chicago: University of Chicago Press, 1998), pp. 214-30, Lucy Bland, *Banishing the Beast: English Feminism and Sexual Morality 1885–1914* (Harmondsworth: Penguin, 1995), Sheila Rowbotham and Jeffrey Weeks, *Socialism and the New Life: The Personal and Sexual Politics of Edward Carpenter and Havelock Ellis* (London: Pluto Press, 1977) and White, *Sexual Liberation or Sexual License*, pp. 27-81.

18. For example Weeks, *Sex, Politics and Society*, pp. 141-98, McLaren, *Twentieth-Century Sexuality*, pp. 64-142 and Molly Ladd-Taylor, 'Saving Babies and Sterilizing Mothers: Eugenics and Welfare Politics in the Interwar United States', *Social Politics* 4 (Spring 1997), pp. 137-53.

19. Smith-Rosenberg, *Disorderly Conduct*, pp. 245-96

20. See Terry, *An American Obsession*, pp. 159-77 and McLaren, *Twentieth-Century Sexuality*, pp. 110-23.

21. Terry, *An American Obsession*, pp. 168-75.

22. See Bullough, *Science in the Bedroom*, pp. 92-136.

23. For studies of the mental hygiene movement see Norman Dain, *Clifford W. Beers: Advocate for the Insane* (Pittsburgh: University of Pittsburg Press, 1980) and Gerald N. Grob, *Mental Illness and American Society, 1875–1940* (New Jersey: Princeton University Press, 1983), pp. 144-78.

24. D'Emilio and Freedman, *Intimate Matters*, pp. 231-35.

25. See Hall, *Passionate Crusader*, pp. 128-241.

26. McLaren, *Twentieth-Century Sexuality*, pp. 110-23.

27. Thomas Laqueur, *Making Sex: Body and Gender from the Greeks to Freud* (Cambridge, MA: Harvard University Press, 1990), pp. 236-37.

28. Sheila Jeffreys, *The Spinster and her Enemies: Feminism and Sexuality 1880–1930* (London: Pandora Press, 1985), pp. 165-85, Lillian Faderman, *Odd Girls and Twilight Lovers: A History of Lesbian Life in Twentieth-Century America* (New York: Columbia University Press, 1991), pp. 37-61 and Margaret Jackson, *The Real Facts of Life: Feminism and the Politics of Sexuality c1850–1940* (London: Taylor & Francis, 1994), pp. 159-81.

29. See, for example, Ruth Hall, *Dear Dr Stopes: Sex in the 1920s* (London: Deutsch, 1978).

30. Norman Haire *et al.*, *The Encyclopaedia of Sex Practice* (London: Encyclopaedic Press, 2nd edn, 1951 [1938]).

31. See Mark Haller, *Eugenics: Hereditarian Attitudes in American Thought* (New Brunswick: Rutgers University Press, 1984), Kevles, *In the Name of Eugenics*, pp. 3-84 and Geoffrey R. Searle, *Eugenics and Politics in Britain, 1900–1914* (Leyden: Noordhoff, 1976).

32. Mary Ellen Richmond, *Social Diagnosis* (New York: Russell Sage Foundation, 1917). For the wider context see Regina G. Kunzel, *Fallen Women, Problem Girls: Unmarried Mothers and the Professionalisation of Social Work, 1890–1945* (New Haven: Yale University Press, 1993); Robert M. Mennel, *Thorns and Thistles: Juvenile Delinquents in the United States, 1825–1940* (Hanover: University Press of New England, 1973); Kathleen Woodroofe, *From Charity to Social Work in England and the United States* (London: Routledge & Kegan Paul, 1962) and John H. Ehrenreich, *The Altruistic Imagination: A History of Social Work and Social Policy in the United States* (Ithaca: Cornell University Press, 1985).

33. See Kathleen W. Jones, *Taming the Troublesome Child: American Families, Child Guidance and the Limits of Psychiatric Authority* (Cambridge, MA: Harvard University Press, 1999), Elizabeth Lunbeck, *The Psychiatric Persuasion:*

Knowledge, Gender, and Power in Modern America (Princeton: Princeton University Press, 1994), pp. 81-181 and Estelle B. Freedman, *Their Sister's Keepers: Women's Prison Reform in America, 1830–1930* (Ann Arbor: University of Michigan Press, 1981), pp. 109-57.

34. Bedford Hills Reformatory for Women, Laboratory of Social Hygiene Case Files, New York State Archives, 14610-77B–C415/3.

35. Ruth M. Alexander, *The 'Girl Problem': Female Sexual Delinquency in New York, 1900–1930* (Ithaca: Cornell University Press, 1995), Peiss, *Cheap Amusements: Working Women and Leisure in Turn-of-the-Century New York*, and Mary E. Odem, *Delinquent Daughters: Protecting and Policing Adolescent Female Sexuality in the United States, 1885–1920* (Chapel Hill: University of North Carolina Press, 1995).

36. Lunbeck, *The Psychiatric Persuasion*, p. 228.

37. Alexander, *The 'Girl Problem'*, pp. 149-53.

38. See Terry, *An American Obsession*, pp. 178-219.

39. Carl Degler, *At Odds: Women and the Family in America from the Revolution to the Present* (New York: Oxford University Press, 1980), pp. 262-66.

40. Seidman, *Romantic Longings*, pp. 94-96.

41. See Bullough, *Science in the Bedroom*, pp. 106-19.

42. Bullough, *Science in the Bedroom*, pp. 106-19.

43. Bullough, *Science in the Bedroom*, pp. 162-67.

44. See Weeks, *Sex, Politics and Society*, pp. 199-201.

45. Liz Stanley, *Sex Surveyed, 1949–1994: From Mass Observation's 'Little Kinsey' to the National Survey and the Hite Reports* (London: Taylor & Francis, 1995), pp. 28-35.

46. Stanley, *Sex Surveyed*, pp. 28-35 and see also Liz Stanley, 'Mass Observation's "Little Kinsey" and the British Sex Survey Tradition', in Jeffrey Weeks and Janet Holland (eds.), *Sexual Cultures: Communities, Values, and Intimacy* (Basingstoke: Palgrave, 1996), pp. 97-114.

47. Quoted in Regina Markell Morantz, 'The Scientist as Sex Crusader: Alfred C. Kinsey and American Culture', *American Quarterly* 29.5 (1977), p. 563.

48. For the critical response to the Kinsey Reports see Morantz, 'The Scientist as Sex Crusader', pp. 575-79, Bullough, *Science in the Bedroom*, pp. 180-83 and Robinson, *The Modernization of Sex*, pp. 42-43.

49. Quoted in Morantz, 'The Scientist as Sex Crusader', p. 563.

50. Bullough, *Science in the Bedroom*, pp. 172-73.

51. Robinson, *The Modernization of Sex*, p. 119; Morantz, 'Scientist as Sex Crusader', pp. 563-89; Carolyn Dean, *Sexuality and Western Culture* (New York: Twayne, 1996), p. 51 and Edward M. Brecher, *The Sex Researchers* (Boston: Little, Brown, 1969).

52. Judith A. Reisman and Edward W. Eichel, *Kinsey, Sex and Fraud* (Louisiana: Huntington House, 1990) and Judith A. Reisman, *Kinsey: Crimes and Consequences* (Arlington: Institute for Media Education, 1998).

53. James H. Jones, *Alfred C. Kinsey: A Public/Private Life* (New York: W.W. Norton, 1997).

54. Jonathan Gathorne-Hardy, *Sex the Measure of All Things: A Life of Alfred C. Kinsey* (Bloomington: Indiana University Press, 1998).

55. Robinson, *The Modernization of Sex*, p. 43.

56. See Morantz, 'The Scientists as Sex Crusader', pp. 568-75 and Robinson, *The Modernization of Sex*, pp. 58-75.

57. Robinson, *The Modernization of Sex*, pp. 43-49.

58. Alfred C. Kinsey, Wardell B. Pomeroy, Clyde E. Martin, *Sexual Behavior in the Human Male* (Philadelphia: W.B. Saunders, 1948).

59. Alfred C. Kinsey, Wardell B. Pomeroy, Clyde E. Martin and Paul H. Gebhard, *Sexual Behavior in the Human Female* (Philadelphia: W.B. Saunders, 1953).

60. See D'Emilio and Freedman, *Intimate Matters*, pp. 265-88, Robinson, *The Modernization of Sex*, pp. 115-19, and Bullough, *Science in the Bedroom*, pp. 168-85.

61. Weeks, *Sex, Politics and Society*, p. 242.

62. McLaren, *Twentieth-Century Sexuality*, pp. 164-65.

63. Robinson, *The Modernization of Sex*, pp. 95-99.

64. McLaren, *Twentieth-Century Sexuality*, p. 165.

65. Lynne Segal, *Straight Sex: The Politics of Pleasure* (London: Virago, 1994), pp. 88-92.

66. Janice Irvine, *Disorders of Desire: Sex and Gender in Modern American Sexology* (Philadelphia: Temple University Press, 1990), pp. 56-59.

67. McLaren, *Twentieth-Century Sexuality*, pp. 177-78 and Irvine, *Disorders of Desire*, pp. 187-227.

68. Shere Hite, *The Hite Report: A Nationwide Survey of Female Sexuality* (New York: Macmillan, 1976).

69. Segal, *Straight Sex*, pp. 102-16.

Chapter 11

1. Quoted in John D'Emilio and Estelle B. Freedman, *Intimate Matters: A History of Sexuality in America* (New York: Harper & Row, 1988), pp. 302-304.

2. See David Allyn, *Make Love Not War: The Sexual Revolution an Unfettered History* (Boston: Little, Brown, 2000).

3. Shulamith Firestone, *The Dialectic of Sex: The Case for Feminist Revolution* (London: Cape, 1971), pp. 232-74.

4. Denis Altman, *Homosexual: Oppression and Liberation* (New York: Outerbridge & Dienstfrey, 1971), p. xii.

5. Guy Hocquenghem, *Homosexual Desire* (trans. Daniella Dangoor; London: Allison & Busby, 1978), pp. 119-24.

6. Robert Nye (ed.), *Sexuality* (Oxford: Oxford University Press, 1999), p. 307.

7. Angus McLaren, *Twentieth-Century Sexuality: A History* (Oxford: Basil Blackwell, 1999), pp. 166-67.

8. Allyn, *Make Love Not War*, pp. 3-9.

9. See Lawrence Stone, *The Family, Sex and Marriage in England, 1500–1800* (London: Weidenfeld & Nicholson, 1977), p. 658, D'Emilio and Freedman, *Intimate Matters*, pp. 239-300 and Linda Gordon, *Woman's Body, Woman's Right: A Social History of Birth Control in America* (New York: Grossman, 1976), p. 194.

10. Richard Godbeer, *Sexual Revolution in Early America* (Baltimore: The Johns Hopkins University Press, 2002).

11. Pamela Hagg, *Consent: Sexual Rights and the Transformation of American Liberalism* (Ithaca: Cornell University Press, 1999).

12. See Paul Robinson, *The Modernization of Sex: Havelock Ellis, Alfred Kinsey, William Masters and Virginia Johnson* (New York: Harper & Row, 1976), pp. 102-104 and Regina Markell Morantz, 'The Scientist as Sex Crusader: Alfred C. Kinsey and American Culture', *American Quarterly* 29.5 (1977), pp. 574-75.

13. Jeffrey Weeks, *Sex, Politics and Society: The Regulation of Sexuality since 1800* (London: Longman, 2nd edn, 1989), pp. 208-14.

14. Weeks, *Sex, Politics and Society*, pp. 199-24 and D'Emilio and Freedman, *Intimate Matters*, pp. 256-65.

15. See D'Emilio and Freedman, *Intimate Matters*, pp. 256-65; Ruth M. Alexander, *The 'Girl Problem': Female Sexual Delinquency in New York 1900–1930* (Ithaca: Cornell University Press, 1995); Lewis Erenberg, *Steppin' Out: New York Nightlife and the Transformation of American Culture, 1890–1930* (Westport: Greenwood Press, 1981) and Kathy Peiss, *Cheap Amusements: Working Women and Leisure in Turn-of-the-Century New York* (Philadelphia: Temple University Press, 1986).

16. See Peter Bailey (ed.), *Music Hall: The Business of Pleasure* (Milton Keynes: Open University Press, 1986) and Judith R. Walkowitz, *City of Dreadful Delight: Narratives of Sexual Danger in Late Victorian London* (Chicago: Chicago University Press, 1992), pp. 41-46.

17. See Christine Stansell, *American Moderns: Bohemian New York and the Creation of a New Century* (New York: Metropolitan Books, 1992); Weeks, *Sex, Politics and Society*, pp. 199-231; Carroll Smith-Rosenberg, *Disorderly Conduct: Visions of Gender in Victorian America* (New York: Oxford University Press, 1985), pp. 245-96 and McLaren, *Twentieth-Century Sexuality*, pp. 46-63.

18. D'Emilio and Freedman, *Intimate Matters*, pp. 256-65.

19. See Beth Bailey, *Sex in the Heartland* (Cambridge, MA, Harvard University Press: 1999) and Sharon Ullman, *Sex Seen: The Emergence of Modern Sexuality in America* (Berkeley: University of California Press, 1997).

20. John D'Emilio, *Sexual Politics, Sexual Communities: The Making of the Homosexual Minority in the United States, 1940–1970* (Chicago: University of Chicago Press, 2nd edn, 1998), pp. 23-39.

21. See John D'Emilio, 'The Homosexual Menace: The Politics of Sexuality in Cold War America', in Kathy Peiss and Christina Simmons (eds.), *Passion and Power: Sexuality in History* (Philadelphia: Temple University Press,

1989), pp. 226-40, Allan Bérubé, *Coming Out Under Fire: The History of Gay Men and Women in World War II* (New York: Plume, 1990) and Lillian Faderman, *Odd Girls and Twilight Lovers: A History of Lesbian Life in Twentieth Century America* (New York: Columbia University Press, 1991), pp. 139-58.

22. Jeffrey Weeks, *Coming Out: Homosexual Politics in Britain, from the Nineteenth Century to the Present* (London: Quartet Books, 1977), pp. 9-44, Greenberg, *The Construction of Homosexuality*, pp. 397-433 and Katz, *The Invention of Heterosexuality*, pp. 83-112.

23. George Chauncey, *Gay New York: Gender, Urban Culture and the Making of the Gay Male world, 1890–1940* (New York: Basic Books, 1994), p. 9.

24. Chauncey, *Gay New York*, pp. 1-23 and Leila Rupp, *A Desired Past: A Short History of Same-Sex Love in America* (Chicago: University of Chicago Press, 1999), pp. 73-129.

25. Chauncey, *Gay New York*, pp. 33-130.

26. See Chauncey, *Gay New York*, pp. 33-130, Weeks, *Sex, Politics and Society*, pp. 108-17.

27. See Randolph Trumbach, *Sex and the Gender Revolution. I. Heterosexuality and the Third Gender in Enlightenment London* (Chicago: Chicago University Press, 1998) and David M. Halperin, *One Hundred Years of Homosexuality and Other Essays on Greek Love* (New York: Routledge, 1990).

28. Chauncey, *Gay New York*, pp. 33-130.

29. Chauncey, *Gay New York*, pp. 23-29 and 'Christian Brotherhood or Sexual Perversion? Homosexual Identities and the Construction of Sexual Boundaries in the World War I Era', *Journal of Social History* 19 (Winter 1985), pp. 189-211, and Rupp, *A Desired Past*, pp. 101-29.

30. John Howard, *Men Like That: A Southern Queer History* (Chicago: Chicago University Press, 1999).

31. McLaren, *Twentieth-Century Sexuality*, pp. 166-67.

32. See Barbara Caine and Glenda Sluga, *Gendering European History, 1780–1920* (London: Leicester University Press, 2000), pp. 143-69; Stansell, *American Moderns*, pp. 225-72; June Rose, *Marie Stopes and the Sexual Revolution* (London: Faber, 1992), pp. 105-75; Ellen Chesler, *Woman of Valor: Margaret Sanger and the Birth Control Movement in America* (New York: Simon & Schuster, 1992), pp. 179-286 and Lesley Hall, 'Feminist Reconfigurations of Heterosexuality in the 1920s', in Lucy Bland and Laura Doan (eds.), *Sexology in Culture: Labelling Bodies and Desires* (Chicago: University of Chicago Press, 1998), pp. 135-49.

33. See Martin Pugh, *Women and the Women's Movement in Britain, 1914–59* (London; Macmillan, 1992), p. 284 and Cynthia Harrison, *On Account of Sex: The Politics of Women's Issues* (Berkeley: University of California Press, 1988).

34. See, for example, Zillah Eisenstein, *The Radical Future of Liberal Feminism* (New York: Longman, 1981). For an alternative view see Dale Spender, *There's Always Been a Women's Movement This Century* (London: Pandora Press, 1983).

35. See, for example, Robin Morgan (ed.), *Sisterhood Is Powerful: An Anthology of Writings from the Women's Liberation Movement* (New York: Random House, 1970), Kate Millett, *Sexual Politics* (New York: Doubleday, 1970) and Germaine Greer, *The Female Eunuch* (London: MacGibbon & Kee, 1970).

36. See Barbara Caine, *English Feminism, 1780–1980* (Oxford: Oxford University Press, 1997), pp. 222-54 and Harrison, *On Account of Sex*.

37. See Weeks, *Sex, Politics and Society*, pp. 96-121 and George Chauncey Jr, 'From Sexual Inversion to Homosexuality: The Changing Medical Conceptualization of Female "Deviance"', in Kathy Peiss and Christina Simmons (eds.), *Passion and Power: Sexuality in History* (Philadelphia: Temple University Press, 1989), pp. 87-117.

38. See Greenberg, *The Construction of Homosexuality*, pp. 397-433.

39. Chauncey, *Gay New York*, pp. 281-82.

40. Teresa de Lauretis, *The Practice of Love: Lesbian Sexuality and Perverse Desire* (Bloomington: Indiana University Press, 1994), p. xix.

41. See Weeks, *Coming Out*, pp. 115-82; D'Emilio, *Sexual Politics, Sexual Communities*, pp. 57-128; John Lauritsen and David Thorstad, *The Early Homosexual Rights Movement* (New York: Times Change Press, 1974) and James D. Steakley, *The Homosexual Emancipation Movement in Germany* (New York: Arno Press, 1975).

42. See Steakley, *The Homosexual Emancipation Movement in Germany*, pp. 103-19 and Weeks, *Sex, Politics and Society*, pp. 96-117

43. For American developments see Rupp, *A Desired Past*, pp. 130-69, Jonathan Katz, *Gay American History* (New York: Crowell, 1976) and John D'Emilio, *Sexual Politics, Sexual Communities: The Making of a Homosexual Minority in the United States, 1940–1970* (Chicago: University of Chicago Press, 2nd edn, 1998).

44. D'Emilio, *Sexual Politics, Sexual Communities*, pp. 240-49 and Weeks, *Coming Out*, pp. 115-82.

45. See Paul A. Robinson, *Sexual Radicals: Wilhelm Reich, Geza Roheim, Herbert Marcuse* (London: Maurice Temple Smith, 1970), Richard King, *The Party of Eros: Radical Social Thought and the Realm of Freedom* (Chapel Hill: University of North Carolina Press, 1973) and Weeks, *Sex, Politics and Society*, pp. 249-52.

46. See Allyn, *Make Love Not War*, pp. 196-205.

47. For an interesting critical overview of activism in this period see Terry Anderson, *The Movement and the Sixties* (New York: Oxford University Press, 1996).

48. Allyn, *Make Love Not War*, p. 8.

49. See, for example, D'Emilio and Freedman, *Intimate Matters*, pp. 301-25; McLaren, *Twentieth-Century Sexuality*, pp. 166-92; R.W. Connell, 'Sexual Revolution', in Lynne Segal (ed.), *New Sexual Agendas* (London: Macmillan, 1997), pp. 60-76 and Rickie Solinger, 'The Population Bomb and the Sexual Revolution: Toward Choice', in Elizabeth Reis (ed.), *American Sexual Histories* (Oxford: Basil Blackwell, 2001), pp. 343-64.

50. Allyn, *Make Love Not War*, p. 7.

51. See D'Emilio and Freedman, pp. 250-51 and 301-308, and McLaren, *Twentieth-Century Sexuality*, pp. 166-79.

52. See, for example, Elizabeth Nelson, *The British Counter-Culture, 1966–73: A Study of the Underground Press* (Basingstoke: Macmillan, 1989).

53. Richard Neville, *Playpower* (London: Paladin, 1971), pp. 72-92 and Theodore Roszak, *The Making of a Counter Culture: Reflections on the Technocratic Society and its Youthful Opposition* (New York: Doubleday, 1969).

54. See Linda Grant, *Sexing the Millennium: A Political History of the Sexual Revolution* (London: Harper Collins, 1994); Nelson, *The British Counter-Culture*; Arthur Marwick, *The Sixties: Cultural Revolution in Britain, France, Italy and the United States, c1958–c1974* (Oxford: Oxford University Press, 1998) and Peter Clecak, *Radical Paradoxes: Dilemmas of the American Left, 1945–1970* (New York: Harper & Row, 1973).

55. Neville, *Playpower*, pp. 72-92. For an incisive critique of some of the failings of the 'sexual revolution', see Jeffrey Weeks, *Sexuality and its Discontents: Meanings, Myths and Modern Sexualities* (London: Routledge & Kegan Paul, 1985), pp. 15-32.

56. Two useful compendiums of late 1960s and early 1970s feminist approaches to a wide variety of topics are Morgan (ed.), *Sisterhood is Powerful* and Anne Koedt, Ellen Devine and Anita Rapone (eds.), *Radical Feminism* (New York; Quadrangle Books, 1973).

57. Sheila Rowbotham, *Hidden from History* (London: Pluto Press, 1973), Ellen DuBois, *Feminism and Suffrage: The Emergence of an Independent Women's Movement in America 1848–1869* (Ithaca: Cornell University Press, 1978) and Juliet Mitchell, *Women's Estate* (Harmondsworth: Penguin, 1971).

58. Nancy Cott, *The Grounding of Modern Feminism* (New Haven: Yale University Press, 1987).

59. See Barbara Caine, *English Feminism, 1780–1980* (Oxford: Oxford University Press, 1997), Susan Kent, *Sex and Suffrage in Britain, 1860–1914* (Princeton: Princeton University Press, 1987) and Judith Allen, *Rose Scott: Vision and Revision in Feminism* (Melbourne: Oxford University Press, 1994).

60. Adrienne Rich, 'Compulsory Heterosexuality and Lesbian Existence', in Ann Snitow, Christine Stansell and Sharon Thompson (eds.), *Powers of Desire: The Politics of Sexuality* (London: Virago, 1983), pp. 212-41.

61. Sheila Jeffreys, *The Spinster and her Enemies: Feminism and Sexuality, 1880–1930* (London: Pandora Press, 1985).

62. See Lynne Segal, 'Feminist Sexual Politics and the Heterosexual Predicament', in Segal, *New Sexual Agendas*, pp. 77-89; Caine, *English Feminism*, pp. 255-71; Cott, *The Grounding of Modern Feminism*; Amanda Sebestyen, *Feminist Practices* (London, 1980) and Sheila Rowbotham, *The Past is Before Us: Feminism in Action since the 1960s* (London: Pandora, 1989).

63. See D'Emilio and Freedman, *Intimate Matters*, pp. 318-25 and McLaren, *Twentieth-Century Sexuality*, pp. 187-92.

64. See Altman, *Homosexual: Oppression and Liberation*, pp. 1-29. See also Hocquenghem, *Homosexual Desire*, pp. 119-33 and Carl Wittman, *A Gay Manifesto* (San Francisco: Agitprop, 1970).

65. D'Emilio and Freedman, *Intimate Matters*, pp. 318-25.

66. Weeks, *Coming Out*, pp. 185-206.

67. Rupp, *A Desired Past*, pp. 170-99.

68. See D'Emilio and Freedman, *Intimate Matters*, pp. 301-25 and McLaren, *Twentieth-Century Sexuality*, pp. 166-92.

69. For discussions of 'backlash' see Allyn, *Make Love Not War*, pp. 270-94 and McLaren, *Twentieth-Century Sexuality*, pp. 193-218.

70. Suzanna Walters, *All the Rage: The Story of Gay Visibility in America* (Chicago: Chicago University Press, 2001).

SELECT BIBLIOGRAPHY

Abelove, Henry, 'Some Speculations on the History of Sexual Intercourse during the Long Eighteenth Century in England', *Genders* 6 (November 1989), pp. 125-30.

Alexander, Ruth M., *The 'Girl Problem': Female Sexual Delinquency in New York 1900-1930* (Ithaca: Cornell University Press, 1995).

Allen, Judith, *Sex and Secrets: Crimes Involving Australian Women since 1880* (Melbourne: Oxford University Press, 1990).

Allyn, David, *Make Love Not War: The Sexual Revolution an Unfettered History* (Boston: Little, Brown, 2000).

Altman, Denis, *Homosexual: Oppression and Liberation* (New York: Outerbridge & Dienstfrey, 1971).

—*Global Sex* (St Leonards: Allen & Unwin, 2001).

Anderson, Terry T., *The Movement and the Sixties* (New York: Oxford University Press, 1996).

Aries, Philippe, and André Béjin (eds.), *Western Sexuality: Practice and Precept in Past and Present Times* (trans. Anthony Forster; Oxford: Basil Blackwell, 1985), pp. 114-16.

Bailey, Beth, *Sex in the Heartland* (Cambridge, MA: Harvard University Press, 1999).

Baldwin, John, *The Language of Sex: Five Voices from Northern France around 1200* (Chicago: Chicago University Press, 1994).

Barker-Benfield, G.J., *The Horrors of a Half-Known Life: Aspects of the Exploitation of Women by Men* (New York: Harper & Row, 1976).

—*The Culture of Sensibility: Sex and Society in Eighteenth-Century Britain* (Chicago: University of Chicago Press, 1992).

Bederman, Gail, *Manliness and Civilization: A Cultural History of Gender and Race in the United States, 1880–1917* (Chicago: University of Chicago Press, 1995).

Beer, Janet, and Katherine Joslyn, 'Diseases of the Body Politic: White Slavery in Jane Addams' "A New Conscience and an Ancient Evil", and Selected Short Stories by Charlotte Perkins Gilman', *Journal of American Studies* 33 (April 1999).

Bérubé, Allan, *Coming Out under Fire: The History of Gay Men and Women in World War II* (New York: Plume, 1990).

Birken, Lawrence, *Consuming Desire: Sexual Science and the Emergence of a Culture of Abundance, 1870–1914* (Ithaca: Cornell University Press, 1988).

Bland, Lucy, 'Marriage Laid Bare: Middle-Class Women and Marital Sex, 1880s–1914', in Jane Lewis (ed.), *Labour and Love: Women's Experience of Home and Family, 1850–1940* (Oxford: Basil Blackwell, 1986), pp. 123-46.

—'Purifying the Public World: Feminist Vigilantes in Late Victorian England', *Women's History Review* 1.3 (1992), pp. 397-412.

—*Banishing the Beast: English Feminism and Sexual Morality 1885–1914* (London: Penguin Books, 1995).

Bland, Lucy, and Laura Doan (eds.), *Sexology in Culture: Labelling Bodies and Desires* (Chicago: University of Chicago Press, 1998).

Boswell, John, *Christianity, Social Tolerance and Homosexuality: Gay People in Western Europe from the Beginning of the Christian Era to the Fourteenth Century* (Chicago: Chicago University Press, 1980).

—'Revolutions, Universals and Sexual Categories', *Salmagundi* 58-59 (Fall 1982–Winter 1983), pp. 89-113.

—*Same-Sex Unions in Pre-Modern Europe* (New York: Villard Books, 1994).

Boucé, Paul-Gabriel (ed.), *Sexuality in Eighteenth-Century Britain* (Manchester: Manchester University Press, 1982).

Bray, Alan, *Homosexuality in Renaissance England* (London: Gay Men's Press, 1982).

Brecher, Edward M., *The Sex Researchers* (Boston: Little, Brown, 1969).

Bristow, Edward J., *Vice and Vigilance: Purity Movements in Britain since 1700* (Dublin: Gill & Macmillan, 1977).

Brodie, Janet Farrell, *Contraception and Abortion in Nineteenth-Century America* (Ithaca: Cornell University Press, 1994).

Brooton, Bernadette J., *Love between Women: Early Christian Responses to Female Homoeroticism* (Chicago: Chicago University Press, 1996).

Brown, Judith, *Immodest Acts: The Life of a Lesbian Nun in Renaissance Italy* (New York: Oxford University Press, 1986).

Brown, Peter, *Religion and Society in the Age of Saint Augustine* (New York: Harper & Row, 1972).

—*The Body and Society: Men, Women and Sexual Renunciation in Early Christianity* (New York: Columbia University Press, 1988).

Bruker, Eloise A., 'Hidden Desires and Missing Persons: A Feminist Deconstruction of Foucault', *Western Political Quarterly* 43.4 (1990), pp. 811-32.

Brundage, James A., *Law, Sex and Christian Society in Medieval Europe* (Chicago: University of Chicago Press, 1987).

—*Sex, Law and Marriage in the Middle Ages* (Brookfield: Variorum, 1993).

Bullough, Vern L., 'Heresy, Witchcraft and Sexuality', *Journal of Homosexuality* 1.2 (1974), pp. 183-202.

—*Science in the Bedroom: A History of Sex Research* (New York: Basic Books, 1994), pp. 136-47.

Bullough, Vern L., and Bonnie Bullough, *Cross Dressing, Sex, and Gender* (Philadelphia: University of Pennsylvania Press, 1993).

Bullough, Vern L., and James A. Brundage, *Sexual Practices and the Medieval Church* (Buffalo: Prometheus Books, 1982).

Bullough, Vern L., and James A. Brundage (eds.), *Handbook of Medieval Sexuality* (New York: Garland, 1996).

Burg, B.R., *Sodomy and the Perception of Evil: English Sea Rovers in the Seventeenth-Century Caribbean* (New York: New York University Press, 1983).

Butler, Judith, *Gender Trouble: Feminism and the Subversion of Identity* (New York: Routledge, 1990).

—*Bodies That Matter: On the Discursive Limits of 'Sex'* (New York: Routledge, 1993).

Bynum, Caroline Walker, *Fragmentation and Redemption: Essays on Gender and the Human Body in Medieval Religion* (Cambridge, MA: Harvard University Press, 1992).

Cadden, Joan, *Meanings of Sexual Difference in the Middle Ages: Medicine, Science and Culture* (Cambridge: Cambridge University Press, 1993).

Caine, Barbara, and Glenda Sluga, *Gendering European History, 1760–1920* (London: Leicester University Press, 2000).

Cameron, Averil, and Amelie Kuhrt (eds.), *Images of Women in Antiquity* (London: Croom Helm, 1983).

Cantarella, Eva, *Pandora's Daughters: The Role and Status of Women in Greek and Roman Antiquity* (Baltimore: The Johns Hopkins University Press, 1987).

—*Bisexuality in the Ancient World* (trans. Cormac O. Cuilleanain; New Haven: Yale University Press, 2nd edn, 2002).

Chauncey Jr, George, 'Christian Brotherhood or Sexual Perversion? Homosexual Identities and the Construction of Sexual Boundaries in the World War I Era', *Journal of Social History* 19 (1985), pp. 189-211.

—'From Sexual Inversion to Homosexuality: The Changing Medical Conceptualization of Female "Deviance"', in Kathy Peiss and Christina Simmons (eds.), *Passion and Power: Sexuality in History* (Philadelphia: Temple University Press, 1989), pp. 87-117.

—*Gay New York: Gender, Urban Culture, and the Making of the Gay Male World, 1890–1940* (New York: Basic Books, 1994).

Chauncey Jr, George, Martin Duberman and Martha Vicinus (eds.), *Hidden from History: Reclaiming the Gay and Lesbian Past* (New York: New American Library, 1989).

Chedgzoy, Kate, Melanie Hansen and Suzanne Trill (eds.), *Voicing Women: Gender and Sexuality in Early Modern Writing* (Keele: Keele University Press, 1996).

Chernaik, Warren, *Sexual Freedom in Restoration Literature* (Cambridge: Cambridge University Press, 1995).

Clark, Elizabeth A., *Ascetic Piety and Women's Faith: Essays on Late Ancient Christianity* (Lewiston: E. Mellen Press, 1986).

Clinton, Catherine, and Michele Gillespie (eds.), *The Devils' Lane: Sex and Race in the Early South* (New York: Oxford University Press, 1997).

Cohen, David, *Law, Sexuality and Society: The Enforcement of Morals in Classical Athens* (Cambridge: Cambridge University Press, 1991).

—*Law, Violence and Community in Classical Athens* (Cambridge: Cambridge University Press, 1995).

Cohen, David, and Richard Saller, 'Foucault on Sexuality in Greco-Roman Antiquity', in Jan Goldstein (ed.), *Foucault and the Writing of History* (Oxford: Basil Blackwell, 1994), pp. 35-59.

Cole, Susan G., 'Greek Sanctions against Sexual Assault', *Classical Philology* 79 (1984), pp. 111-13.

Comfort, Alex, *The Anxiety Makers* (London: Nelson, 1967).

Cominos, Peter, 'Late Victorian Sexual Respectability and the Social System', *International Review of Social History* 8 (1963), pp. 18-48 and 216-50.

Connelly, Mark T., *The Response to Prostitution in the Progressive Era* (Chapel Hill: University of North Carolina Press, 1980).

Cott, Nancy, *The Bonds of Womanhood: "Woman's Sphere" in New England, 1789–1835* (New Haven: Yale University Press, 1977).

—'Passionlessness: An Interpretation of Victorian Sexual Ideology', *Signs* 4.2 (1978), pp. 219-36.

—*The Grounding of Modern Feminism* (New Haven: Yale University Press, 1987).

Davenport-Hines, Richard, *Sex, Death and Punishment: Attitudes to Sex and Sexuality in Britain since the Renaissance* (London: Collins, 1990).

Davidson, Arnold I., *The Emergence of Sexuality: Historical Epistemology and the Formation of Concepts* (Cambridge, MA: Harvard University Press, 2001).

Dean, Carolyn J., 'The Productive Hypothesis: Foucault, Gender and the History of Sexuality', *History and Theory* 33.3 (1994), pp. 271-96.

— *Sexuality and Modern Western Culture* (New York: Twayne, 1996).

—*The Frail Social Body: Pornography, Homosexuality and Other Fantasies in Interwar France* (Berkeley: University of California Press, 2000).

Dean-Jones, Lesley, *Women's Bodies in Classical Greek Science* (Oxford: Clarendon Press, 1994).

Degler, Carl, *At Odds: Women and the Family in America from the Revolution to the Present* (New York: Oxford University Press, 1980).

Dekker, Rudolf, and Lotte C. van de Pol, *The Tradition of Female Transvestism in Early Modern Europe* (London: Macmillan, 1989).

de Lauretis, Teresa, *The Practice of Love: Lesbian Sexuality and Perverse Desire* (Bloomington: Indiana University Press, 1994).

D'Emilio, John, *Sexual Politics, Sexual Communities: The Making of the Homosexual Minority in the United States, 1940–1970* (Chicago: University of Chicago Press, 2nd edn, 1998), pp. 23-39.

D'Emilio, John, and Estelle B. Freedman, *Intimate Matters: A History of Sexuality in America* (New York: Harper & Row, 1988).

Dinshaw, Carolyn, *Getting Medieval: Sexualities and Communities, Pre and Post-modern* (Durham: Duke University Press, 1999).

Ditzion, Sidney, *Marriage Morals and Sex in America: A History of Ideas* (New York: Norton, 2nd edn, 1978).

Donoghue, Emma, *Passions between Women: British Lesbian Culture 1668–1801* (London: Scarlett Press, 1993).

Dover, K.J., *Greek Homosexuality* (London: Duckworth, 1978).

Duby, Georges, *The Knight, the Lady and the Priest: The Making of Modern Marriage in Medieval France* (trans. Barbara Bray; Harmondsworth: Penguin, 1984).

—*Love and Marriage in the Middle Ages* (trans. Jane Dunnett; Cambridge: Polity Press, 1994).

Dyhouse, Carol, *Feminism and the Family in England, 1880–1930* (Oxford: Basil Blackwell, 1989).

Eglinton, J.Z., *Greek Love* (New York: O. Layton Press, 1964).

Elliott, Dyan, *Spiritual Marriage: Sexual Abstinence in Medieval Wedlock* (Princeton: Princeton University Press, 1993).

—*Fallen Bodies: Pollution, Sexuality and Demonology in the Middle Ages* (Philadelphia: University of Pennsylvania Press, 1999).

Elm, Susanna, *'Virgins of God': The Making of Asceticism in Late Antiquity* (Oxford: Oxford University Press, 1996).

Engelhardt Jr, H. Tristram, 'The Disease of Masturbation: Values and the Concept of Disease', *Bulletin of the History of Medicine* 48 (1974), pp. 234-48.

Epstein, Steven, 'Gay Politics, Ethnic Identity: The Limits of Social Constructionism', *Socialist Review* 93-94 (May-August 1987), pp. 9-54.

Erenberg, Lewis, *Steppin' Out: New York Nightlife and the Transformation of American Culture, 1890–1930* (Westport: Greenwood Press, 1981).

Faderman, Lillian, *Surpassing the Love of Men: Romantic Friendship and Love between Women from the Renaissance to the Present* (New York: Morrow, 1981).

—*Odd Girls and Twilight Lovers: A History of Lesbian Life in Twentieth-Century America* (New York: Columbia University Press, 1991).

Fairchilds, Cissie, 'Female Sexual Attitudes and the Rise of Illegitimacy: A Case Study', *Journal of Interdisciplinary History* 8.4 (1978), pp. 627-67.

Farr, James R., *Authority and Sexuality in Early Modern Burgundy 1550–1730* (Oxford: Oxford University Press, 1995).

Ferraro, Joanne M., *Marriage Wars in Late Renaissance Venice* (Oxford: Oxford University Press, 2001).

Finnegan, Frances, *Poverty and Prostitution: A Study of Victorian Prostitutes in York* (Cambridge: Cambridge University Press, 1979).

Flandrin, Jean-Louis, *Families in Former Times: Kinship, Household and Sexuality* (trans. Richard Southern; Cambridge: Cambridge University Press, 1979).

Foley, Helene P. (ed.), *Reflections of Women in Antiquity* (New York: Gordon and Breach, 1981).

Foucault, Michel, *The Birth of the Clinic: An Archaeology of Medical Perception* (trans. A.M. Sheridan; London: Tavistock, 1973).

—*The History of Sexuality*. I. *An Introduction* (trans. Robert Hurley; New York: Random House, 1978).

—'Afterword: The Subject and Power', in Hubert L. Dreyfus and Paul Rabinow, *Michel Foucault: Beyond Structuralism and Hermeneutics* (Brighton: Harvester, 1982), pp. 208-26.

—*The Use of Pleasure: The History of Sexuality*, II (trans. Robert Hurley; New York: Random House, 1985).

—*The Care of the Self: The History of Sexuality*, III (trans. Robert Hurley; New York: Random House, 1986).

Fout, John C. (ed.), *Forbidden History: The State, Society, and the Regulation of Sexuality in Modern Europe* (Chicago: University of Chicago Press, 1992).

Freccero, Carla, 'Acts, Identities, and Sexuality's (Pre) Modern Regimes', *Journal of Women's History* 11.2 (1999), pp. 186-92.

Freedman, Estelle B., 'Uncontrolled Desires: The Response to the Sexual Psychopath, 1920–1960', *Journal of American History* 74 (June 1987), pp. 83-106.

Gallagher, Catherine, and Thomas Laqueur (eds.), *The Making of the Modern Body: Sexuality and Society in the Nineteenth Century* (Berkeley: University of California Press, 1987).

Garber, Marjorie, *Vested Interests: Cross-Dressing and Cultural Authority* (New York: Routledge, 1992).

Garrison, Daniel A., *Sexual Culture in Ancient Greece* (Norman: University of Oklahoma Press, 2000).

Gay, Peter, *Education of the Senses*. I. *The Bourgeois Experience: Victoria to Freud* (New York: Oxford University Press, 1984).

—*The Cultivation of Hatred* (New York: Oxford University Press, 1993).

Gerard, Kent, and Gert Hekma (eds.), *The Pursuit of Sodomy: Male Homosexuality in Renaissance and Enlightenment Europe* (New York: Harrington Park Press, 1989).

Gilfoyle, Timothy J., *City of Eros: New York City, Prostitution and the Commercialization of Sex, 1790–1920* (New York: W.W. Norton, 1992).

Gilman, Sander L., 'Black Bodies, White Bodies: Toward an Iconography of Female Sexuality in Late Nineteenth-Century Art, Medicine, and Literature', in Henry Louis Gates Jr (ed.), *'Race', Writing, and Difference* (Chicago: University of Chicago Press, 1986), pp. 223-61.

Gittins, Diana, *Fair Sex: Family Size and Structure 1900–1939* (London: Hutchinson, 1982).

Gleason, Maud W., *Making Men: Sophists and Self-Presentation in Ancient Rome* (Princeton: Princeton University Press, 1995).

Godbeer, Richard, *Sexual Revolution in Early America* (Baltimore: The Johns Hopkins University Press, 2002).

Gordon, Linda, *Woman's Body, Woman's Right: A Social History of Birth Control in America* (New York: Grossman, 1976).

Gordon, Linda, and Ellen DuBois, 'Seeking Ecstacy on the Battlefield: Danger and Pleasure in Nineteenth Century Feminist Thought', *Feminist Review* 13 (1983).

Grant, Linda, *Sexing the Millennium: A Political History of the Sexual Revolution* (London: HarperCollins, 1994).

Greenberg, David F., *The Construction of Homosexuality* (Chicago: University of Chicago Press, 1988).

Grosz, E.A., *Volatile Bodies: Toward a Corporeal Feminism* (Bloomington: Indiana University Press, 1994).

Hagg, Pamela, *Consent: Sexual Rights and the Transformation of American Liberalism* (Ithaca: Cornell University Press, 1999).

Haliczer, Stephen, *Sexuality in the Confessional: A Sacrament Profaned* (New York: Oxford University Press, 1996).

Hall, Lesley, *Hidden Anxieties: Male Sexuality 1900–1950* (Cambridge, Polity Press, 1991).

—'Impotent Ghosts from No Man's Land, Flappers' Boyfriends, or Cryptopatriarchs? Men, Sex and Social Change in 1920s Britain', *Social History* 21.1 (1996), pp. 54-70.

Hallett, Judith P., 'Perjusinae Glandes and the Changing Image of Augustus', *American Journal of Ancient History* 2 (1977), pp. 151-71.

Hallett, Judith P., and Martin B. Skinner (eds.), *Roman Sexualities* (Princeton: Princeton University Press, 1997).

Halperin, David M., *One Hundred Years of Homosexuality and Other Essays on Greek Love* (New York: Routledge, 1990).

—*Saint Foucault: Towards a Gay Hagiography* (New York: Oxford University Press, 1995).

—'Forgetting Foucault: Acts, Identities, and the History of Sexuality', *Representations* 63 (Spring 1998), pp. 93-120.

—*How to Do the History of Homosexuality* (Chicago: University of Chicago Press, 2002).

Halperin, David M., John J. Winkler and Froma I. Zeitlin (eds.), *Before Sexuality: The Construction of Erotic Experience in the Ancient Greek World* (Princeton: Princeton University Press, 1990).

Harrison, Cynthia, *On Account of Sex: The Politics of Women's Issues* (Berkeley: University of California Press, 1988).

Harrison, Rachel, and Frank Mort, 'Patriarchal Aspects of Nineteenth-Century State Formation: Property Relations, Marriage, Divorce and Sexuality', in Philip Corrigan (ed.), *Capitalism, State Formation and Marxist Theory: Historical Investigations* (London: Quartet, 1980), pp. 79-109.

Hinsch, Bret, *Passions of the Cut Sleeve: The Male Homosexual Tradition in China* (Berkeley: University of California Press, 1990).

Hitchcock, Tim, *English Sexualities, 1700–1800* (New York: St Martin's Press, 1997).

Hobson, Barbara Meil, *Uneasy Virtue: The Politics of Repression and the American Reform Tradition* (New York: Basic Books, 1987).

Hocquenghem, Guy, *Homosexual Desire* (trans. Daniella Dangoor; London: Allison and Busby, 1978).

Hodes, Martha, *White Women, Black Men: Illicit Sex in the Nineteenth-Century South* (New Haven: Yale University Press, 1997).

Hoffer, Peter Charles (ed.), *Colonial Women and Domesticity: Selected Articles on Gender in Early America* (New York: Garland, 1988).

Holtzman, Ellen, 'The Pursuit of Married Love: Women's Attitudes toward Sexuality and Marriage in Great Britain, 1918–1939', *Journal of Social History* 16.2 (1982), pp. 39-52.

Horowitz Helen Lefkowitz, *Rereading Sex: Battles over Sexual Knowledge and Suppression in Nineteenth Century America* (New York: Knopf, 2002).

Howard, John, *Men Like That: A Southern Queer History* (Chicago: University of Chicago Press, 1999).

Hughes, Alex, and Kate Ince (eds.), *French Erotic Fiction: Women's Desiring Writing 1880–1990* (Washington, DC: Berg, 1996).

Hunt, Lynn (ed.), *Eroticism and the Body Politic* (Baltimore: The Johns Hopkins University Press, 1991).

—*The Invention of Pornography: Obscenity and the Origins of Modernity 1500–1800* (New York: Zone Books, 1993).

Hunt, Margaret, 'Wife Beating, Domesticity, and Women's Independence in Eighteenth-Century London', *Gender and History* 4 (1992), pp. 10-33.

—*The Middling Sort: Commerce, Gender and the Family in England, 1680–1780* (Berkeley: University of California Press, 1996).

Hyam, Ronald, *Empire and Sexuality: The British Experience* (Manchester: Manchester University Press, 1990).

Ingram, Martin, *Church Courts, Sex and Marriage in England, 1570–1640* (Cambridge: Cambridge University Press, 1987).

Irvine, Janice, *Disorders of Desire: Sex and Gender in Modern American Sexology* (Philadelphia: Temple University Press, 1990).

Jackson, Margaret, *The Real Facts of Life: Feminism and the Politics of Sexuality c1850–1940* (London: Taylor & Francis, 1994).

Jascquart, Danielle, and Claude Thomasset, *Sexuality and Medicine in the Middle Ages* (trans. Matthew Adamson; Princeton: Princeton University Press, 1988).

Jeffreys, Sheila, *The Spinster and her Enemies: Feminism and Sexuality 1880–1930* (London: Pandora Press, 1985).

Jeffreys, Sheila (ed.), *The Sexuality Debates* (London: Routledge and Kegan Paul, 1987).

Jennings, Thelma, 'Us Colored Women Had to Go Through a Plenty: Sexual Exploitation of African American Slave Women', *Journal of Women's History* 1 (1990), pp. 45-74.

Jordan, Mark D., *The Invention of Sodomy in Christian Theology* (Chicago: Chicago University Press, 1997).

Jordanova, Ludmilla, *Sexual Visions: Images of Gender in Science and Medicine between the Eighteenth and the Twentieth Centuries* (Hemel Hampstead: Harvester Wheatsheaf, 1989).

Karras, Ruth Mazo, *Common Women: Prostitution and Sexuality in Medieval England* (Oxford: Oxford University Press, 1996).
—'Prostitution and the Question of Sexual Identity in Medieval Europe', *Journal of Women's History* 11.2 (1999), pp. 159-77.
Katz, Jonathan, *Gay American History: Lesbians and Gay Men in the USA* (New York: Crowell, 1976).
Katz, Jonathan Ned, *The Invention of Heterosexuality* (New York: Dutton, 1995).
Kent, Susan, *Sex and Suffrage in Britain, 1860–1914* (Princeton: Princeton University Press, 1987).
King, Helen, *Hippocrates' Women: Reading the Female Body in Ancient Greece* (London: Routledge, 1998).
King, M.H., *The Desert Mothers* (Toronto: Toronto University Press, 2nd edn, 1989).
King, Richard, *The Party of Eros: Radical Social Thought and the Realm of Freedom* (Chapel Hill: University of North Carolina Press, 1973).
Knight, Patricia, 'Women and Abortion in Victorian and Edwardian England', *History Workshop* 4 (1977), pp. 57-69.
Kunzel, Regina G., *Fallen Women, Problem Girls: Unmarried Mothers and the Professionalization of Social Work, 1890–1945* (New Haven: Yale University Press, 1993).
Ladd-Taylor, Molly, 'Saving Babies and Sterilizing Mothers: Eugenics and Welfare Politics in the Interwar United States', *Social Politics* 4 (Spring 1997), pp. 137-53.
Laqueur, Thomas, *Making Sex: Body and Gender from the Greeks to Freud* (Cambridge, MA: Harvard University Press, 1990).
Larmour, David H.J., Paul Allen Miller and Charles Platter (eds.), *Rethinking Sexuality* (Princeton: Princeton University Press, 1998).
Laslett, Peter, *Family Life and Illicit Love in Earlier Generations: Essays in Historical Sociology* (Cambridge: Cambridge University Press, 1977).
Laslett, Peter, and Richard Wall (eds.), *Household and Family in Past Times: Comparative Studies in the Size and Structure of the Domestic Group over the Last Three Centuries in England, France, Serbia, Japan and Colonial North America, with Further Materials from Western Europe* (Cambridge: Cambridge University Press, 1972).
Laslett, Peter, Karla Oosterveen and Richard M. Smith (eds.), *Bastardy and its Comparative History: Studies in the History of Illegitimacy and Marital Nonconformism in Britain, France, Germany, Sweden, North America, Jamaica and Japan* (London: Edward Arnold, 1980).
Lauritsen, John, and David Thorstad, *The Early Homosexual Rights Movement* (New York: Times Change Press, 1974).
Lefkowitz, Mary, *Women in Greek Myth* (Baltimore: The Johns Hopkins University Press, 1986).
Leites, Edmund, *Puritan Conscience and Modern Sexuality* (New Haven: Yale University Press, 1986).
Levine, David, *Family Formation in an Age of Nascent Capitalism* (New York: Academic Press, 1977).

Levine, Phillippa, *Victorian Feminism, 1850–1900* (London: Hutchinson, 1987).

Licht, Hans, *Sexual Life in Ancient Greece* (trans. J.H. Freese; London: Routledge, 1932).

London Feminist History Group (ed.), *The Sexual Dynamics of History: Men's Power, Women's Resistance* (London: Pluto Press, 1983).

Maccubbin, R.P. (ed.), *'Tis Nature's Fault; Unauthorized Sexuality during the Eighteenth Century in England* (Cambridge: Cambridge University Press, 1987).

Macfarlane, Alan, *Marriage and Love in England: Modes of Reproduction 1300–1840* (Oxford: Basil Blackwell, 1986).

Makowski, Elizabeth, *Canon Law and Cloistered Women: Periculoso and its Commentators, 1298–1545* (Washington, DC: Catholic University Press, 1997).

Manderson, Lenore, 'Colonial Desires: Sexuality, Race and Gender in British Malaya', *Journal of the History of Sexuality* 7.3 (1997).

Marcus, Steven, *The Other Victorians: A Study of Sexuality and Pornography in Mid-Nineteenth Century England* (New York: Basic Books, 1966).

Markell Morantz, Regina, 'The Scientist as Sex Crusader: Alfred C. Kinsey and American Culture', *American Quarterly* 29.5 (1977), pp. 574-75.

Marwick, Arthur, *The Sixties: Cultural Revolution in Britain, France, Italy and the United States, c1958–c1974* (Oxford: Oxford University Press, 1998).

Mason, Michael, *The Making of Victorian Sexuality* (Oxford: Oxford University Press, 1994).

McClintock, Anne, *Imperial Leather: Race, Gender and Sexuality in the Colonial Contest* (London: Routledge, 1995).

McIntosh, Mary, 'The Homosexual Role', *Social Problems* 16 (Fall 1968), pp. 182-92.

McLaren, Angus, *A History of Contraception: From Antiquity to the Present Day* (Oxford: Basil Blackwell, 1990).

—*Twentieth-Century Sexuality: A History* (Oxford: Basil Blackwell, 1999).

Melman, Billie, *Women's Orients: English Women and the Middle East, 1718–1918: Sexuality, Religion and Work* (Ann Arbor: University of Michigan Press, 1992).

Mendus, Susan, and Jane Rendall (eds.), *Sexuality and Subordination: Interdisciplinary Studies of Gender in the Nineteenth Century* (London: Routledge, 1989).

Meyerowitz, Joanne, *Women Adrift: Independent Wage Earners in Chicago, 1880–1930* (Chicago: Chicago University Press, 1988).

—*How Sex Changed: A History of Transsexuality in the United States* (Cambridge, MA: Harvard University Press, 2002).

Midgley, Clare (ed.), *Gender and Imperialism* (Manchester: Manchester University Press, 1998).

Mohr, James, *Abortion in America: The Origins and Evolution of Public Policy* (New York: Oxford University Press, 1978).

Montserrat, Dominic, *Sex and Society in Graeco-Roman Egypt* (London: Kegan Paul, 1996).

Moore, R.I., *The Formation of a Persecuting Society: Power and Deviance in Western Europe, 950–1250* (Oxford: Basil Blackwell, 1987).

Mort, Frank, *Dangerous Sexualities: Medico-Moral Politics in England since 1830* (London: Routledge & Kegan Paul, 1987).

Mosse, George L., *Nationalism and Sexuality: Respectability and Abnormal Sexuality in Modern Europe* (New York: H. Fertig, 1985).

Moxnes, Halvor (ed.), *Constructing Early Christian Families* (London: Routledge, 1997).

Murray, Jacqueline, and Konrad Eisenbichler (eds.), *Desire and Discipline: Sex and Sexuality in the Premodern West* (Toronto: Toronto University Press, 1996).

Nead, Lynda, *Myths of Sexuality: Representations of Women in Victorian Britain* (Oxford: Basil Blackwell, 1988).

Nelson, Elizabeth, *The British Counter-Culture, 1966–1973: A Study of the Underground Press* (Basingstoke: Macmillan, 1989).

Neuman, R.P., 'Working Class Birth Control in Wilhelmine Germany', *Comparative Studies in History and Society* 20 (1978), pp. 408-28.

Newton, Judith L., Mary P. Ryan and Judith R. Walkowitz (eds.), *Sex and Class in Women's History* (London: Routledge & Kegan Paul, 1983).

Norton, Rictor, *Mother Clap's Molly House: The Gay Subculture in England, 1700–1830* (London: Gay Men's Press, 1992).

—*The Myth of the Modern Homosexual: Queer History and the Search for Cultural Unity* (London: Cassell, 1997).

Nussbaum, Martha C., and Juha Sihvola (eds.), *The Sleep of Reason: Erotic Experience and Sexual Ethics in Ancient Greece and Rome* (Chicago: Chicago University Press, 2002).

Nye, Robert (ed.), *Sexuality* (Oxford: Oxford University Press, 1999).

O'Donoghue, Bernard, *The Courtly Love Tradition* (Manchester: Manchester University Press, 1982).

O'Hara, Diana, *Courtship and Constraint: Rethinking the Making of Marriage in Tudor England* (Manchester: Manchester University Press, 2000).

O'Higgins, James, 'Sexual Choice, Sexual Act: An Interview with Michel Foucault', *Salmagundi* 58-59 (Fall 1982–Winter 1983), pp. 10-12.

Odem, Mary E., *Delinquent Daughters: Protecting and Policing Adolescent Female Sexuality in the United States, 1885–1920* (Chapel Hill: University of North Carolina Press, 1995).

Offen, Karen, 'Defining Feminism: A Comparative Historical Approach', *Signs* 14.1 (1988), pp. 119-57.

—*European Feminisms, 1700–1950: A Political History* (Stanford: Stanford University Press, 2000).

Ozment, Steven, *When Fathers Ruled: Family Life in Reformation Europe* (Cambridge, MA: Harvard University Press, 1983).

Pagels, Elaine, *Adam, Eve and the Serpent* (New York: Random House, 1988).

Pateman, Carole, *The Sexual Contract* (Cambridge: Polity Press, 1988).

Pattynama, Pamela, 'Secrets and Danger: Interracial Sexuality in Louis Couperus's *The Hidden Force* and Dutch Colonial Culture around 1900', in

Julia Clancy-Smith and Frances Gouda (eds.), *Domesticating the Empire: Race, Gender, and Family Life in French and Dutch Colonialism* (Charlottesville: University Press of Virginia, 1998), pp. 84-107.

Payer, Pierre, *Sex and the Penitentials* (Toronto: University of Toronto Press, 1984).

Pearsall, Ronald, *The Worm in the Bud: The World of Victorian Sexuality* (London: Weidenfeld & Nicholson, 1969).

Pearson, Michael, *The Age of Consent: Victorian Prostitution and its Enemies* (Newton Abbot: David & Charles, 1972).

Peiss, Kathy, *Cheap Amusements: Working Women and Leisure in Turn-of-the-Century New York* (Philadelphia: Temple University Press, 1986).

Peiss, Kathy, and Christina Simmons (eds.), *Passion and Power: Sexuality in History* (Philadelphia: Temple University Press, 1989).

Peterson, M. Jeanne, 'Dr Acton's Enemy: Medicine, Sex and Society in Victorian England', *Victorian Studies* 29.1 (1986), pp. 569-90.

Phillips, Kim M., and Barry Reay (eds.), *Sexualities in History: A Reader* (New York: Routledge, 2002).

Phillips, Roderick, *Putting Asunder: A History of Divorce in Western Society* (Cambridge: Cambridge University Press, 1988).

Pivar, David J., *Purity Crusade: Sexual Morality and Social Control 1868–1900* (Westport: Greenwood Press, 1973).

—*Purity and Hygiene: Women, Prostitution and the "American Plan", 1900–1930* (Westport: Greenwood Press, 2002).

Plummer, Kenneth, *Sexual Stigma: An Interactionist Account* (London: Routledge & Kegan Paul, 1975).

—*Telling Sexual Stories: Power, Change and Social Worlds* (London: Routledge, 1995).

Plummer, Kenneth (ed.), *The Making of the Modern Homosexual* (London: Hutchinson, 1981).

Poovey, Mary, *Uneven Developments: The Ideological Work of Gender in Mid-Victorian England* (London: Virago, 1989).

Porter, Roy, and Lesley Hall, *The Facts of Life: The Creation of Sexual Knowledge in Britain, 1650–1950* (New Haven: Yale University Press, 1995).

Porter, Roy, and Mikulas Teich (eds.), *Sexual Knowledge, Sexual Science: The History of Attitudes to Sexuality* (Cambridge: Cambridge University Press, 1994).

Power, Kim, *Veiled Desire: Augustine's Writing on Women* (London: Darton, Longman & Todd, 1995).

Rand, Richard, *Intimate Encounter: Love and Domesticity in Eighteenth Century France* (Princeton: Princeton University Press, 1997).

Ranke-Heinemann, Uta, *Eunuchs for Heaven: The Catholic Church and Sexuality* (trans. John Brownjohn; London: Deutsch, 1990).

Reagan, Leslie J., *When Abortion Was a Crime: Women, Medicine and Law in the United States 1867–1973* (Berkeley: University of California Press, 1997).

Reis, Elizabeth (ed.), *American Sexual Histories* (Oxford: Basil Blackwell, 2001).

Rich, B. Ruby, 'Feminism and Sexuality in the 1980s', *Feminist Studies* 12 (1986), pp. 525-61.

Richards, Jeffrey, *Sex, Dissidence and Damnation: Minority Groups in the Middle Ages* (London: Routledge, 1991).

Richlin, Amy, *Pornography and Representation in Greece and Rome* (New York: Oxford University Press, 1992).

—*The Garden of Priapus: Sexuality and Aggression in Roman Humor* (New York: Oxford University Press, 2nd edn, 1992).

—'Not before Homosexuality: The Materiality of *Cinaedus* and the Roman Law against Love between Men', *Journal of the History of Sexuality* 3.4 (1993), pp. 523-73.

Riley, Patrick D.G., *Civilising Sex: On Chastity and the Common Good* (Edinburgh: T. & T. Clark, 2000).

Robertson, Stephen, 'Separating the Men from the Boys: Masculinity, Psycho-Sexual Development, and Sex Crime in the United States, 1930s–1960s', *Journal of the History of Medicine and Allied Sciences* 56.1 (2001), pp. 3-35.

Robinson, Paul A., *Sexual Radicals: Wilhelm Reich, Geza Roheim, Herbert Marcuse* (New York: Harper & Row, 1969).

—*The Modernization of Sex: Havelock Ellis, Alfred Kinsey, William Masters and Virginia Johnson* (New York: Harper & Row, 1976).

Rocke, Michael, *Forbidden Friendships: Homosexuality and Male Culture in Renaissance Florence* (Oxford: Oxford University Press, 1996).

Roodenburg, Herman W., 'The Autobiography of Isabella de Moerloose: Sex, Childbearing and Popular Belief in Seventeenth Century Holland', *Journal of Social History* 18 (1985), pp. 517-40.

Roper, Lyndal, *Oedipus and the Devil: Witchcraft, Sexuality and Religion in Early Modern Europe* (London: Routledge, 1994).

Roper, Michael, and John Tosh (eds.), *Manful Assertions: Masculinities in Britain since 1800* (London: Routledge, 1991).

Rosario, Vernon A., *The Erotic Imagination: French Histories of Perversity* (New York: Oxford University Press, 1997).

Rosario, Vernon A. (ed.), *Science and Homosexualities* (New York: Routledge, 1997).

Rosen, Ruth, *The Lost Sisterhood: Prostitution in America, 1900–1930* (Baltimore: The Johns Hopkins University Press, 1982).

Rousseau, G.S., and Roy Porter (eds.), *Sexual Underworlds of the Enlightenment* (Chapel Hill: University of North Carolina Press).

Rousselle, Aline, *Porneia: On Desire and the Body in Antiquity* (trans. Felicia Pheasant; Oxford: Basil Blackwell, 1988).

Rowbotham, Sheila, and Jeffrey Weeks, *Socialism and the New Life: The Personal and Sexual Politics of Edward Carpenter and Havelock Ellis* (London: Pluto Press, 1977).

Ruggiero, Guido, 'Sexual Criminality in Early Renaissance Venice 1338-1358', *Journal of Social History* 8.4 (1974).

—*The Boundaries of Eros: Sex, Crime and Sexuality in Renaissance Venice* (Oxford: Oxford University Press, 1985).

Rupp, Leila J., *A Desired Past: A Short History of Same-Sex Love* (Chicago: University of Chicago Press, 1999).

Ryan, Mary P., *Cradle of the Middle Class: The Family in Oneida County, New York, 1790–1865* (Cambridge: Cambridge University Press, 1983).

Saller, Richard, 'Men's Age at Marriage and its Consequences for the Roman Family', *Classical Philology* 82 (1987), pp. 21-34.

Sawyer, Erin, 'Celibate Pleasures: Masculinity, Desire, and Asceticism in Augustine', *Journal of the History of Sexuality* 6.1 (1995), pp. 1-29.

Schiebinger, Londa, *The Mind Has No Sex? Women and the Origins of Modern Science* (Cambridge, MA: Harvard University Press, 1989).

Schulenburg, Jane, *Forgetful of their Sex: Female Sanctity and Society ca. 500–1100* (Chicago: University of Chicago Press, 1998).

Scully, Patricia, 'Rape, Race, and Colonial Culture: The Sexual Politics of Identity in the Nineteenth Century Cape Colony, South Africa', *American Historical Review* 100 (1995), pp. 335-59.

Sedgwick, Eve Kosofsky, *Between Men: English Literature and Male Homosocial Desire* (New York: Columbia University Press, 1985).

—*Epistemology of the Closet* (Berkeley: University of California Press, 1990).

Segal, Lynne, *Straight Sex: The Politics of Pleasure* (London: Virago, 1994).

Segal, Lynne (ed.), *New Sexual Agendas* (Basingstoke: Macmillan, 1997), pp. 60-76.

Seidman, Steven, *Romantic Longings: Love in America, 1830–1980* (New York: Routledge, 1991).

Sennett, Richard, *Flesh and Stone: The Body and the City in Western Civilization* (London: Faber, 1994).

Shorter, Edward, *The Making of the Modern Family* (London: Collins, 1976).

—*A History of Women's Bodies* (Harmondsworth: Penguin, 1984).

Shorter, Edward, John Knodel and Etienne van de Walle, 'The Decline in Non-marital Fertility in Europe 1880–1940', *Population Studies* 25.3 (1971), pp. 375-93.

Showalter, Elaine, *Sexual Anarchy: Gender and Culture at the Fin de Siecle* (London: Bloomsbury, 1991).

Sinha, Mrinalini, *Colonial Masculinity: The 'Manly Englishman' and the 'Effeminate Bengali'* (Manchester: Manchester University Press, 1995).

Smith, Merril D. (ed.), *Sex and Sexuality in Early America* (New York: New York University Press, 1998).

Smith-Rosenberg, Carroll, 'The Female World of Love and Ritual: The Relations between Women in Nineteenth-Century America', *Signs* 1.1 (1975), pp. 1-29.

—*Disorderly Conduct: Visions of Gender in Victorian America* (New York: Oxford University Press, 1985).

Snitow, Ann, Christine Stansell and Sharon Thompson (eds.), *Powers of Desire: The Politics of Sexuality* (New York: Monthly Review Press, 1983).

Sochen, June, *The New Woman: Feminism in Greenwich Village 1910–1920* (New York: Quadrangle Books, 1972).

Spongberg, Mary, *Feminizing Venereal Disease: The Body of the Prostitute in Nineteenth-Century Medical Discourse* (Basingstoke: Macmillan, 1997).

Stanley, Liz, 'Romantic Friendship? Some Issues in Researching Lesbian History and Biography', *Women's History Review* 1.2 (1992), pp. 193-216.

—*Sex Surveyed, 1949–1994: From Mass Observation's 'Little Kinsey' to the National Survey and the Hite Reports* (London: Taylor & Francis, 1995).

Stanley, Liz (ed.), *The Diaries of Hannah Cullwick: Victorian Maidservant* (London: Virago, 1984).

Stansell, Christine, *American Moderns: Bohemian New York and the Creation of a New Century* (New York: Metropolitan Books, 2000).

Stanton, Domna C. (ed.), *Discourses of Sexuality: From Aristotle to AIDS* (Ann Arbor: University of Michigan Press, 1992).

Steakley, James D., *The Homosexual Emancipation Movement in Germany* (New York: Arno Press, 1975).

Stein, Edward (ed.), *Forms of Desire: Sexual Orientation and the Social Constructionist Controversy* (New York: Routledge, 1992).

Stoler, Ann Laura, *Race and the Education of Desire: Foucault's History of Sexuality and the Colonial Order of Things* (Durham: Duke University Press, 1995).

Stone, Lawrence, *The Family, Sex and Marriage in England, 1500–1800* (London: Weidenfeld & Nicholson, 1977).

—'Libertine Sexuality in Post-Restoration England: Group Sex and Flagellation among the Middling Sort in Norwich in 1706–07', *Journal of the History of Sexuality* 2.4 (1992), pp. 511-25.

Sullivan, Gerard, and Peter A. Jackson (eds.), *Gay and Lesbian Asia: Culture, Identity, Community* (New York: Haworth Press, 2001).

Summers, Claude J. (ed.), *Homosexuality in Renaissance and Enlightenment England: Literary Representations in Historical Context*, special issue, *Journal of Homosexuality* 23.1-2 (1992).

Summers, Claude J., and Ted-Larry Pebworth (eds.), *Renaissance Discourses of Desire* (Columbia: University of Missouri Press, 1993).

Szreter, Simon, *Fertility, Class and Gender in Britain, 1860–1940* (Cambridge: Cambridge University Press, 1996).

Taylor, Gordon Rattray, *Sex in History* (London: Thames & Hudson, 1953).

Taylor, Rabun, 'Two Pathic Subcultures in Ancient Rome', *Journal of the History of Sexuality* 7.3 (1997), pp. 319-71.

Tentler, Thomas N., *Sin and Confession on the Eve of the Reformation* (Princeton: Princeton University Press, 1977).

Terry, Jennifer, *An American Obsession: Science, Medicine, and Homosexuality in Modern Society* (Chicago: Chicago University Press, 1999).

Theweleit, Klaus, *Male Fantasies*, I and II (trans. Stephen Conway; Minneapolis: University of Minnesota Press, 1987).

Thomas, Keith, 'The Double Standard', *Journal of the History of Ideas* 20.2 (1959), pp. 195-216.

Thorp, John, 'The Social Construction of Homosexuality', *Phoenix* 46 (1992), pp. 54-61.

Tilly, Louise A., Joan W. Scott and Miriam Cohen, 'Women's Work and European Fertility', *Journal of Interdisciplinary History* 6.3 (1976), pp. 447-76.

Tone, Andrea, *Devices and Desires: A History of Contraceptives in America* (New York: Hill & Wang, 2001).

Torjesen, Karen Jo, *When Women Were Priests: Women's Leadership in the Early Church and the Scandal of their Subordination in the Rise of Christianity* (New York: Harper & Row, 1995).

Tosh, John, *A Man's Place: Masculinity and the Middle Class Home in Victorian England* (New Haven: Yale University Press, 1999).

Traub, Valerie, *The Renaissance of Lesbianism in Early Modern England* (Cambridge: Cambridge University Press, 2002).

Treggiari, Susan, *Roman Marriage: Iusti Coniuges from the Time of Cicero to the Time of Ulpian* (Oxford: Claredon Press, 1991).

Trudgill, Eric, *Madonnas and Magdalens: The Origins and Development of Victorian Sexual Attitudes* (London: Heinemann, 1976).

Trumbach, Randolph, *The Rise of the Egalitarian Family: Aristocratic Kinship and Domestic Relations in Eighteenth Century England* (New York: Academic Press, 1978).

—'Sex, Gender, and Sexual Identity in Modern Culture: Male Sodomy and Female Prostitution in Enlightenment London', *Journal of the History of Sexuality* 2.2 (1991), pp. 186-203.

—*Sex and the Gender Revolution*. I. *Heterosexuality and the Third Gender in Enlightenment London* (Chicago: Chicago University Press, 1998).

Ullman, Sharon, *Sex Seen: The Emergence of Modern Sexuality in America* (Berkeley: University of California Press, 1997).

Ulrich, Laurel Thatcher, *Good Wives: Image and Reality in the Lives of Women in Northern New England* (New York: Knopf, 1982).

Vance, Carol (ed.), *Pleasure and Danger: Exploring Female Sexuality* (Boston: Routledge & Kegan Paul, 1984).

Vicinus, Martha, 'Sexuality and Power: A Review of Current Work in the History of Sexuality', *Feminist Studies* 8.1 (1982), pp. 134-56.

—'One Life to Stand behind Me: Emotional Conflicts in First Generation College Women in England', *Feminist Studies* 8.3 (1982), pp. 610-11.

—'They Wonder to Which Sex I Belong: The Historical Roots of Modern Lesbian Identity', *Feminist Studies* 18.3 (1992).

Vicinus, Martha (ed.), *Suffer and Be Still: Women in the Victorian Age* (Bloomington: Indiana University Press, 1972).

—*A Widening Sphere: Changing Roles of Victorian Women* (Bloomington: Indiana University Press, 1977).

Wah-shan, Chou, *Tongzhi: Politics of Same-Sex Eroticism in Chinese Societies* (New York: Haworth Press, 2000).

Walkowitz, Judith, *Prostitution and Victorian Society: Women, Class and the State* (Cambridge: Cambridge University Press, 1980).

—*City of Dreadful Delight: Narratives of Sexual Danger in Late-Victorian London* (Chicago: Chicago University Press, 1992).

Walters, Suzanna, *All the Rage: The Story of Gay Visibility in America* (Chicago: Chicago University Press, 2001).

Warren, James F., *Ah-Ku and Karayuki-san: Prostitution in Singapore, 1870–1940* (Singapore: Oxford University Press, 1993).

Weber, Harold, *The Restoration Rake Hero: Transformations in Sexual Understanding in Seventeenth Century England* (Madison: University of Wisconsin Press, 1986).

Weeks, Jeffrey, *Coming Out: Homosexual Politics in Britain, from the Nineteenth Century to the Present* (London: Quartet Books, 1977).

—'Foucault for Historians', *History Workshop Journal* 14 (Autumn 1982).

—*Sexuality and its Discontents: Meanings, Myths and Modern Sexualities* (London: Routledge & Kegan Paul, 1985).

—*Sex, Politics and Society: The Regulation of Sexuality since 1800* (London: Longman, 2nd edn, 1989).

—*Coming Out: Homosexual Politics in Britain Since the Nineteenth Century* (London: Quartet Books, 1990).

—*Against Nature: Essays on History, Sexuality and Identity* (London: Rivers Oram Press, 1991).

—*Making Sexual History* (Cambridge: Polity Press, 2000).

Weeks, Jeffrey, and Janet Holland (eds.), *Sexual Cultures: Communities, Values, and Intimacy* (Basingstoke: Palgrave, 1996).

White, Carolinne, *Christian Friendship in the Fourth Century* (Cambridge: Cambridge University Press, 1992).

White, Kevin, *The First Sexual Revolution: The Emergence of Male Heterosexuality in Modern America* (New York: New York University Press, 1993).

—*Sexual Liberation or Sexual License? The American Revolt against Victorianism* (Chicago: Ivan R. Dee, 2000).

Wiener, Carol Z., 'Sex Roles and Crime in Late Elizabethan Hertfordshire', *Journal of Social History* 8.4 (1974), pp. 38-60.

Wiesner-Hanks, Merry E., *Christianity and Sexuality in the Early Modern World: Regulating Desire, Reforming Practice* (London: Routledge, 2000).

Williams, Craig A., *Roman Homosexuality: Ideologies of Masculinity in Classical Antiquity* (New York: Oxford University Press, 1999).

Winkler, John J., *The Constraints of Desire: The Anthropology of Sex and Gender in Ancient Greece* (New York: Routledge, 1990).

Wolf, Charlotte, 'Sex Roles as Portrayed in Marriage and the Family Textbooks: Contributions to the Status Quo', *Women's Studies* 3.1 (1975), pp. 45-60.

Wrigley, E.A., and R.S. Schofield, *The Population History of England 1541–1871: A Reconstruction* (London: Edward Arnold, 1981).

Wrigley, E.A., D.E.C. Eversley and Peter Laslett (eds.), *An Introduction to English Historical Demography from the Sixteenth to the Nineteenth Century* (London: Weidenfeld & Nicolson, 1966).

INDEX